"*Speaking in the Public Sphere* is a unique way to engage students in public speaking by putting a focus on social responsibility and civic engagement."

—Jeffrey W. Fox, *Northern Kentucky University*

"An excellent new speech textbook . . . a must have for our public speaking courses!"

—Mark Frank, *Coffeyville Community College*

"This text offers a nice change of pace from other public speaking textbooks while still covering all of the basics of public communication."

—Armeda Celestine Reitzel, *Humboldt State University*

PENGUIN ACADEMICS

Speaking in the Public Sphere

STEVE SCHWARZE
University of Montana

PEARSON

Boston   Columbus   Indianapolis   New York   San Francisco   Upper Saddle River   Amsterdam
Cape Town   Dubai   London   Madrid   Milan   Munich   Paris   Montreal   Toronto   Delhi   Mexico City
São Paulo   Sydney   Hong Kong   Seoul   Singapore   Taipei   Tokyo

Editor in Chief, Communication: Karon Bowers
Director of Development: Eileen Calabro
Senior Development Editor: Carol Alper
Marketing Manager: Blair Zoe Tuckman
Associate Development Editor: Angela Mallowes
Editorial Assistant: Megan Sweeney
Senior Digital Editor: Paul DeLuca
Digital Editor: Lisa Dotson
Project Manager: Anne Ricigliano
Project Coordination, Text Design, and Electronic Page Makeup: Nesbitt Graphics, Inc.
Cover Design Manager: Nancy Danahy
Cover Photo: © Jeff Greenberg /Alamy
Manufacturing Buyer: Mary Ann Gloriande
Printer/Binder: R.R. Donnelley/ Crawfordsville
Cover Printer: Lehigh-Phoenix Color/ Hagerstown

For more information about the Penguin Academics series, please contact us by mail at Pearson Education, attn. Marketing Department, 51 Madison Avenue, 28th Floor, New York, NY 10010, or visit us online at www.pearsonhighered.com/communication

Credits and acknowledgments borrowed from other sources and reproduced, with permission, in this textbook appear on page 438.

Library of Congress Control Number: 2011034088

10 9 8 7 6 5 4 3 2 1—DOC—14 13 12 11

PEARSON

www.pearsonhighered.com

ISBN 10: 0-205-56708-8
ISBN 13: 978-0-205-56708-9

Brief Contents

Detailed Contents

6 Researching Public Problems 139

7 Criticizing and Crafting Public Discourse: The Power of Language 169

15   Developing Your Ceremonial Speech   386

Preface

"The last thing the world needs is another public speaking textbook." That line kept nagging me when I first considered writing this book. Public speaking has a broad range of excellent textbook options, each with its own distinctive approach. What could I add? Yet I often found myself agreeing with my students' criticisms of textbooks: Many are too long and too simplistic. Students want a book that is readable and that gives them something more than just common sense advice.

In response, I wrote *Speaking in the Public Sphere* to offer students and instructors a sophisticated yet concise treatment of public speaking—one that teaches the fundamentals of public speaking in the context of encouraging students to engage significant public issues. Informed by traditional rhetorical principles as well as contemporary approaches to public discourse, the book highlights the canon of invention in the process of developing the rhetorical skills necessary for effective citizenship. Throughout the book, students are urged to think carefully and creatively about how their own public speaking can make a real contribution to the public sphere. Ultimately, *Speaking in the Public Sphere* seeks to enhance students' capacity for meaningful participation in democratic decision making through effective and ethical public speaking.

Rather than a watered-down approach that tries to be all things to all people or an advanced approach that works only for a small niche of students, *Speaking in the Public Sphere* engages students where they are and shows them how public speaking can connect them to the public sphere.

The Public Sphere as a Learning Opportunity

Pedagogically, *Speaking in the Public Sphere* puts research skills and audience analysis in the foreground as important precursors to effective public speaking. Starting with the first chapter on public speaking and the public sphere, students are encouraged to see how the quality of their own public speaking will improve as they attend to the voices of other people in the public sphere. Through much greater attention to topic development and research than other books provide, the approach found here will enhance the quality of student speeches in the classroom and improve students' ability to effectively engage in public issues outside the classroom.

The guiding principles of *Speaking in the Public Sphere* have emerged from nearly twenty years of teaching public speaking and its variants. Whether at a large research university or a small liberal arts college, I have found that students benefit most when a public speaking course focuses on a handful of central themes and reinforces those themes across contexts. In turn, *Speaking in the Public Sphere* develops key areas of focus that lend themselves to a rigorous and energetic approach to public speaking.

- **A focus on the "public" in public speaking.** Chapter 1 introduces students to the idea of the *public sphere* and offers models of the public speaking process that show how instances of public speaking are situated in the broader flow of public discourse. Coverage of standard topics in public speaking, such as listening, topic development, audience analysis, research, and speech organization, highlight *public significance* as a key consideration for students during the production of their speeches. *Speaking in the Public Sphere* shows how making strategic choices in stating the central idea, organizing the speech, and adapting to audience beliefs and attitudes can lead to speeches that enhance the quality of public deliberation and decision making.

- **A focus on invention.** Unique to introductory public speaking books, *Speaking in the Public Sphere* gives significant attention to the classical canon of invention. The book expands on the usual range of informative and persuasive purposes to give students more specific guidance in inventing speeches that address typical audience concerns in the public sphere. In addition, the book builds simple systems of invention across chapters to give students concrete and increasingly in-depth guidance for using topic research and audience research to develop ideas for speeches. The book gives special attention in early chapters to inventing topics of public significance.

- **A focus on research.** Because of the sheer quantity and divergent quality of source material available to students today, this book provides extensive coverage of the research process. Rather than merely giving students an overview of existing resources, the research chapter is grounded in the theme of building a research plan, which speaks directly to the challenges and obstacles students face in locating and evaluating credible sources. This approach is intended to help students think strategically about research so that they will feel less overwhelmed by the process, more efficient in their work, and more confident in their performances. In addition to standard coverage of conducting research, using sources effectively and ethically, and avoiding plagiarism, the book gives extra attention to the challenges of discerning the quality of sources in an online environment, selecting source material for use in speeches, and citing and explaining source material thoroughly.

- **A focus on language.** Expanding the emphasis on research skills, a chapter and an appendix offer students multiple ways of understanding the importance of language in public speaking and the public sphere more broadly. Intended to help students understand how public issues are rhetorically constructed, this coverage of language is distinctive in placing a discussion of language earlier than is done in other textbooks and connecting the rhetorical construction of public issues to one's own language choices as a public speaker. Students who are interested in more advanced ideas about rhetorical strategies in political discourse will find a unique discussion in the Understanding Public Discourse appendix.

- **A focus on the connections between informative and persuasive speaking.** While the book follows a traditional format of taking up informative and persuasive speaking in separate chapters, it treats both modes of speaking as a process of engagement with audience obstacles and opportunities, and it contextualizes both in terms of their contribution to public deliberation and decision making. In addition to these theoretical linkages, students are encouraged to explore the linkages in practice. Examples throughout the latter half of the book show how students might begin with an informative speech on a topic of interest and then expand on that topic, using persuasive strategies in their later speeches. The book demonstrates how such an approach can enhance students' credibility as speakers and improve the quality and efficiency of their research.

- **A focus on ethics.** *Speaking in the Public Sphere* treats ethical action not only in terms of a speaker's personal choices, but also as a public achievement made possible through shared commitments to democratic participation, social justice, and sustainable natural and social systems. The "Ethical Dimension" boxes raise some of the most persistent ethical issues in public speaking and use rhetorical scholarship to help students think through those issues.

Features of *Speaking in the Public Sphere*

Important special features of this book can be used to enhance and enrich student learning while building on the guiding principles noted above.

CASE CONCLUSION

Sara's Speech: Developing a Topic

To develop her topic, Sara first thought about her rhetorical situation. She knew that her exigence needed to be defined so that it was directly connected to her listeners' everyday lives. She also knew that most of her acquaintances believed in fairness, so that was a constraint that she could turn into an opportunity; they might be open to a speech that illustrated some sort of global inequality. But she wasn't quite sure how her audience might see themselves as empowered to influence or change inequality.

Then one day on campus, Sara observed a group that had been demonstrating and distributing information about sweatshop labor. After browsing through some magazines and websites, she found out that sweatshop labor was a big issue on college campuses. She guessed that most of her classmates probably owned clothes that were made by companies targeted for sweatshop labor, so she thought that might be a good topic.

Here is her initial topic:

Sara's topic: Sweatshop labor in the clothing industry

After talking with several of her classmates, Sara came to the conclusion that her audience was mostly neutral about sweatshop labor. Other than a couple of people who were adamantly opposed to sweatshops, most of Sara's classmates did not know whether their own clothing was made in sweatshops. Nor did they seem ready to take action related to sweatshops. They had never really thought about whether they could influence the practice of sweatshop labor.

After assessing the rhetorical situation, identifying her topic, and thinking about her audience's disposition toward sweatshops, Sara generated the following purpose statements for possible speeches for her class:

Topic: Sweatshop labor in the clothing industry
General purpose: To inform
Specific purpose: To inform my audience how major U.S. clothing companies use sweatshop labor
General purpose: To persuade
Specific purpose: To persuade my audience to support a ban on the importation of sweatshop clothing in the United States.

Questions

1. What are the bases for the attitudes among Sara's audience?

2. If Sara had a choice, would you encourage her to give an informative speech or a persuasive speech to this audience? Why?

3. For an informative speech, how else might Sara adapt the specific purpose to her neutral audience?

4. If Sara were trying to persuade an oppositional audience—one that did not perceive a problem with sweatshop labor in the clothing industry—what might be an appropriate specific purpose statement?

5. What would be appropriate central ideas for speeches based on the specific purposes that Sara generated?

Case Studies

Each chapter provides a student speech scenario, posing a common challenge or opportunity that students typically face in a public speaking class. Then the chapter ends with a case conclusion describing how the student met the challenge using concepts and skills from the chapter. For some of these cases, you can see a student's outline as well as a video version of the speech.

CASE SCENARIO

Sara's Speech: Developing a Topic

Sara racked her brain trying to come up with a speech topic. Her own experiences traveling around the world led her to be interested in global issues. Human trafficking, the drug trade, and pandemics were just a few of the topics that fascinated her. She hoped to work or volunteer internationally after she finished college, too, so she looked for every possible opportunity to explore these topics.

But she also knew that most of her classmates had not been outside the United States and would not be interested in topics that did not have a direct impact on themselves. As a result, she struggled to identify a good topic. Should she pursue something that she thinks is important, regardless of what her audience cares about, or should she focus on things that her classmates talk about, even if those topics do not interest her or seem very significant?

Public Spotlight

Each chapter includes a box that spotlights how speakers have made an impact on the world through public speaking. Topics range from examples of college students working on publicly significant issues to prominent political leaders, authors, and activists. In addition, icons in these boxes spotlight social media outlets such as Facebook and YouTube that are providing new means for circulating information, mobilizing citizens, and organizing action.

The Ethical Dimension

Each chapter contains an Ethical Dimension box that poses a key ethical issue related to that chapter for anyone involved in public speaking. Traditional issues such as pandering, omitting premises in arguments, and "preaching to the choir" are covered in these boxes. In addition, several boxes ask students to explore contemporary cases of apparent ethical violations of norms of propriety related to public speaking. Each Ethical Dimension box concludes with discussion questions that can serve as springboards to class discussion, role-playing activities, or individual essays.

Content-Related Features

Several unique, content-related features provide helpful information to help students invent and deliver effective speeches.

- **Early attention to confidence and delivery.** While *Speaking in the Public Sphere* emphasizes the aspects of constructing a speech, it also discusses delivery issues earlier than many introductory textbooks. Chapter 2 devotes fully half of its coverage to these issues as students prepare for their first formal speech. It gives special attention to how students can make the most of rehearsal sessions to build confidence and improve specific aspects of delivery before their actual speech performance in class.

- **Distinctive coverage of feedback.** Chapter 3 on listening and feedback not only provides standard coverage of obstacles to and strategies for attentive, comprehensive, and critical listening, it also shows students

---

PUBLIC SPOTLIGHT
Michael J. Fox

Michael J. Fox has been a prominent public advocate for research on Parkinson's disease. As someone who has the disease, Fox has used the power of public speaking to raise awareness and influence the broader public discussion about the disease and potential treatments. In 1998, Fox famously testified before Congress without taking medication, which gave public visibility to the physical symptoms of the disease. Since then, Fox has been especially active in writing about his life and in advocacy for stem cell research that could lead to cures for the disease (Fox, *Always Looking Up*).

Fox has become a prominent voice on this issue not only because of his personal situation, but also because of his ongoing research on the disease. As he learns about the disease from doctors and about potential cures from scientists, he brings that information into his speeches and books. Fox also has gained insight from others who are afflicted with Parkinson's disease. As he says in his memoir *Lucky Man*, "My greatest teachers now came from within the P.D. community itself. My coming out had an impact on their lives, as it turned out, but even before that, their stories, gleaned from what I read on P.D. web sites suddenly lit up with conversation, had at least as profound an impact on mine" (230).

 Social Networking Spotlight

The Michael J. Fox Foundation for Parkinson's Research focuses on funding the scientific research

Michael J. Fox incorporates both research and firsthand experience in his public advocacy about Parkinson's disease.

that has the greatest potential for treating and curing Parkinson's disease. One way in which the foundation communicates with supporters and donors is through a monthly *FoxFlash* e-newsletter, which can be found along with other organization publications at http://www.michaeljfox.org/about_publications.cfm

Another organization, the Parkinson's Disease Foundation, takes advantage of Facebook to circulate educational information about the disease, promote fundraising activity, and engage in advocacy and activism: http://www.facebook.com/parkinsonsdiseasefoundation

---

THE ETHICAL DIMENSION
Listening as an Ethical Practice

The practices of listening and then giving feedback are rooted in broad ethical principles about the process of communication. In a 1994 speech, communication scholar Lana Rakow identified three ethical principles or ground rules for communication that show how even the acts of listening and feedback have ethical dimensions. These principles are inclusiveness, participation, and reciprocity.

Inclusiveness refers to an openness to diverse viewpoints and a willingness to listen to others regardless of their race, gender, socioeconomic status, religion, age, or sexual orientation. **Participation** refers to a right of all people to have the opportunity to voice their opinions, to be heard by others, and "to have their opinions count in public decision making." Consequently, the principle of **reciprocity** is grounded in a sense of equality among participants, indicating everyone has the opportunity to speak and to listen in a particular communication situation.

These principles provide an ethical justification for why you should engage in the listening and feedback practices described in this chapter. Inclusiveness requires attentive listening to all speakers regardless of their point of view or the preconceptions that you might have about a particular speaker. Even if you disagree with a speaker's viewpoint on an issue, it is imperative to include that speaker's viewpoint in public discussion and that you as an audience member are at least willing to listen to what the speaker has to say. After all, if you were speaking, you would want your audience to listen attentively so that you would feel included in the community. The principle of inclusiveness, then, implies reciprocity or taking turns. Including and listening to all viewpoints require that we take turns in the role of speaker and listener. And by taking turns, we serve the overall purpose of promoting participation in the public sphere.

These principles help to explain why the practices of descriptive feedback are so important. Speaking only for yourself allows others to express their own

A well-functioning public sphere allows listeners to take their turn as speakers.

opinions in the discussion. Likewise, focusing on the speech rather than the speaker keeps feedback from getting personal or suggesting that the speaker as a person should not be involved in the discussion. Even if a speaker advances a questionable idea or a troubling position, that person still has a right to be included. Thus, inclusiveness and reciprocity reinforce the principle of participation.

WHAT DO YOU THINK?

1. What can you do in your public speaking class to ensure reciprocity?

2. Is it ever ethical to "heckle," or interrupt, a speaker?

3. Examine the following YouTube clip from a town hall meeting about health care reform during the summer of 2009:

   http://www.youtube.com/watch?v=J-Bpshk5nX0&feature=fvw

   Which principles apply to this situation? How would you evaluate the different kinds of listening and feedback by this audience?

how to promote effective public speaking by giving useful responses to other speakers. Rooted in the concept of *descriptive feedback*, this part of Chapter 3 facilitates student learning by providing simple guidelines for effective feedback and plenty of examples so that students can apply these ideas directly in the classroom.

- **Strategic approach to audience analysis.** Chapter 5's traditional coverage of audience demographics and opinions extends into a more strategic discussion of how to glean relevant information for invention of informative and persuasive speeches. In addition to showing how to construct good interview and survey questions, Chapter 5 devotes an entire section to how audience analysis can be used to refine one's purpose and constitute an audience.

- **Distinctive coverage of informative speaking.** Chapter 8 provides a more rhetorical treatment of informative speaking, as it emphasizes the audience obstacles to understanding information as a key consideration for invention. In turn, it offers audience-oriented and topic-oriented systems for invention that are relevant for all types of speaking. Chapter 9 includes explanations of comparative and key issues organizational patterns that are especially useful for certain kinds of informative speaking on public issues.

- **Thorough discussion of visual aids and visual rhetoric.** Chapter 12 clarifies similarities and differences between the use of traditional visual aids in public speaking and the emergence of predominantly visual forms of rhetoric that can influence the basic steps of inventing and organizing a speech. The chapter gives a thorough treatment of traditional principles of visual aid preparation and presentation while also applying those principles to the development of PowerPoint™ presentations. As a result, the chapter provides a wealth of concrete guidance no matter what kind of visuals students choose to use for their speeches.

- **Straightforward models of reasoning**. Chapter 14 displays several simple patterns of reasoning using Stephen Toulmin's well-known visual model as an alternative to formal patterns of logic. The chapter uses the model to help speakers understand specific patterns of reasoning, identify potential areas of audience disagreement, and avoid the typical problems of argument construction that lead to fallacies.

Pedagogical Tools

Each chapter contains a variety of learning tools to help students engage and grasp the key ideas in the chapter. The beginning of each chapter lists a set of learning objectives that help students to focus on the important issues they will encounter in that chapter. A summary, organized by major chapter headings, provides a brief review of the core principles and topics covered. Key terms, which appear in boldface in the text as well as in a list at the end of the chapter, help students to understand essential information. For convenience, definitions for these terms also appear in a glossary at the end of the book. Comprehension questions can be used as an effective way to ensure that students have learned the key content. Application activities provide a venue for practicing the skills that are taught in the chapter.

This chapter is intended to help you:

- Understand some of the basic units of public discourse
- Use language that is concrete, familiar, and active in your speeches
- Incorporate figurative and rhythmic language in your speeches

---

Summary

UNDERSTANDING PUBLIC DISCOURSE

- Effective public speakers need to be able to critically analyze the language that other people use to discuss public issues.
- Ideographs, myths, and characterizations are some of the key units of public discourse that shape perception of public issues.

USING EFFECTIVE LANGUAGE IN YOUR SPEECHES

- Effective style in public speaking requires adaptation of language to an oral context.
- Concrete, familiar, active, and figurative language can enhance effective style.

USING APPROPRIATE LANGUAGE IN YOUR SPEECHES

- Speeches should use wording and style that reflect contemporary usage patterns for naming groups and that are sensitive to situational differences.

Key Terms

ideograph, p. 170	clutter, p. 177
myth, p. 172	active language (or active voice), p. 177
characterization, p. 173	nominalization, p. 00
connotative meaning, p. 174	figurative language, p. 179
denotative meaning, p. 174	metaphor, p. 179
style, p. 174	simile, p. 180
concrete language, p. 175	euphemism, p. 182
abstract language, p. 175	rhythmic language, p. 182
boilerplate language, p. 176	alliteration, p. 182
jargon, p. 176	anaphora, p. 183
pretentious language, p. 177	antithesis, p. 183

Comprehension

1. What are some contemporary examples of ideographs?
2. Is a myth a false story? Why or why not?
3. What is the difference between connotative meaning and denotative meaning?
4. What is the difference between active voice and passive voice?
5. How does nominalization affect style? How should speakers change nominalization?
6. What is euphemism?

Application

1. Examine the website of your senator or representative or another prominent national political candidate. On what ideographs does this person rely to explain his or her positions on issues?
2. Examine a recent State of the Union address or speech of response from the opposing party. What myths are used in these speeches? How do they attempt to alter perception of issues?
3. Develop a one-minute speech that exhibits the characteristics of effective language described in the chapter. Your speech should attempt to describe one of the following:

   A college football game

   Your college's student center

   A night at your favorite restaurant

   Your favorite season of the year

Resources in Print and Online

Name of Supplement	Available	Instructor or Student Supplement	Description
Instructor's Manual and Test Bank (ISBN: 0205217524)	Online	Instructor Supplement	Prepared by Kristopher Willis, University of Florida, the **Instructor's Manual** offers a chapter-by-chapter guide to teaching *Speaking in the Public Sphere*, including chapter summaries, learning objectives, lecture outlines, discussion questions, and activities. The **Test Bank**, also prepared by Kristopher Willis, contains multiple choice, true/false, completion, and essay questions. Each question has a correct answer and is referenced by page and topic. Available for download on Pearson's Instructor's Resource Center at www.pearsonhighered.com/irc (access code required).
MyTest (ISBN: 0205217508)	Online	Instructor Supplement	This flexible, online test-generating software includes all questions found in the Test Bank allowing instructors to create their own personalized exams. Instructors can also edit any of the existing test questions and even add new questions. Other special features of this program include random generation of test questions, creation of alternative versions of the same test, scrambling of question sequence, and test preview before printing. Available at www.pearsonmytest.com (access code required).
PowerPoint™ Presentation Package (ISBN: 0205217494)	Online	Instructor Supplement	Prepared by Kristopher Willis, University of Florida this text-specific package provides a basis for your lecture with PowerPoint™ slides for each chapter of the book. These slides provide key concepts and selected art, along with some instructor notes. Available for download at www.pearsonhighered.com/irc (access code required).
Pearson's ClassPrep	Online	Instructor Supplement	ClassPrep makes lecture preparation simpler and less time-consuming. It collects the very best class presentation resources—art and figures from our texts, videos, lecture activities, audio clips, classroom activities, and much more—in one convenient online destination. You may search through ClassPrep's extensive database of tools by content topic (arranged by standard topics within the public speaking curriculum) or by content type (video, audio, activities, etc.). You will find ClassPrep in the Instructor's section of MySpeechLab (access code required).
Pearson's Contemporary Classic Speeches DVD (ISBN: 0205405525)	DVD	Instructor Supplement	This exciting supplement includes over 120 minutes of video footage in an easy-to-use DVD format. Each speech is accompanied by a biographical and historical summary that helps students understand the context and motivation behind each speech. Speakers featured include Martin Luther King, Jr.; John F. Kennedy; Barbara Jordan; the Dalai Lama; and Christopher Reeve. Please contact your Pearson representative for details; some restrictions apply.
Pearson's Public Speaking Video Library	DVD/VHS	Instructor Supplement	This series of videos contains a range of different types of speeches delivered on a multitude of different topics, allowing you to choose the speeches that are best suited for your students. Please contact your Pearson representative for details and a complete list of videos and their contents to choose which would be most useful in your class. Samples from most of our public speaking videos are available on www.mycoursetoolbox.com. Some restrictions apply.
A *Guide for New Public Speaking Teachers*, Fifth Edition (ISBN: 0205828108)	In Print Online	Instructor Supplement	Prepared by Calvin L. Troup, Duquesne University, with a new chapter on using MySpeechLab by Jennifer Fairchild, Eastern Kentucky University, this guide helps new teachers prepare for and teach the introductory public speaking course effectively. It covers such topics as preparing for the term, planning and structuring your course, evaluating speeches, utilizing the textbook, integrating technology into the classroom, and much more. Available for download at www.pearsonhighered.com/irc (access code required).

Name of Supplement	Available	Instructor or Student Supplement	Description
Public Speaking in the Multicultural Environment, Second Edition (ISBN: 0205265111)	In Print	Student Supplement	Prepared by Devorah A. Lieberman, Portland State University, this booklet helps students learn to analyze cultural diversity within their audiences and adapt their presentations accordingly (available for purchase).
The Speech Outline (ISBN: 032108702X)	In Print	Student Supplement	Prepared by Reeze L. Hanson and Sharon Condon of Haskell Indian Nations University, this workbook includes activities, exercises, and answers to help students develop and master the critical skill of outlining (available for purchase).
Multicultural Activities Workbook (ISBN: 0205546528)	In Print	Student Supplement	By Marlene C. Cohen and Susan L. Richardson of Prince George's Community College, this workbook is filled with hands-on activities that help broaden the content of speech classes to reflect the diverse cultural backgrounds. The checklists, surveys, and writing assignments all help students succeed in speech communication by offering experiences that address a variety of learning styles (available for purchase).
Speech Preparation Workbook (ISBN: 013559569X)	In Print	Student Supplement	Prepared by Jennifer Dreyer and Gregory H. Patton of San Diego State University, this workbook takes students through the stages of speech creation—from audience analysis to writing the speech—and includes guidelines, tips, and easy-to-fill-in pages (available for purchase).
Study Card for Public Speaking (ISBN: 0205441262)	In Print	Student Supplement	Colorful, affordable, and packed with useful information, Pearson Study Cards make studying easier, more efficient, and more enjoyable. Course information is distilled down to the basics, helping students quickly master the fundamentals, review a subject for understanding, or prepare for an exam. Because they are laminated for durability, the cards can be kept for years to come and can be pulled out whenever students need a quick review (available for purchase).
Pearson's Public Speaking Study Site	Online	Student Supplement	This open-access student web resource features practice tests, learning objectives, and web links organized around the major topics that are typically covered in the Introduction to Public Speaking course and correlated to the table of contents for your book (available at www.pearsonpublicspeaking.com).
VideoLab CD-ROM (ISBN: 0205561616)	In Print	Student Supplement	This interactive study tool for students can be used independently or in class. It provides digital video of student speeches that can be viewed in conjunction with corresponding outlines, manuscripts, note cards, and instructor critiques. Following each speech, a series of drills helps students analyze content and delivery (available for purchase).
MySpeechLab	Online	Instructor and Student Supplement	MySpeechLab is a state-of-the-art interactive and instructive solution for public speaking courses. Designed to be used as a supplement to a traditional lecture course or to completely administer an online course, MySpeechLab combines a Pearson eText, MySearchLab™ Pearson's MediaShare, multimedia, video clips, activities, research support, and tests and quizzes to completely engage students. MySpeechLab can be packaged with your text and is available for purchase at www.myspeechlab.com (access code required). See next page for more details.

Save time and improve results with **myspeechlab**

Designed to amplify a traditional course in numerous ways or to administer a course online, **MySpeechLab®** combines pedagogy and assessment with an array of multimedia activities—videos, speech preparation tools, assessments, research support, multiple newsfeeds—to make learning more effective for all types of students. Now featuring more resources, including a video upload tool, this new release of **MySpeechLab®** is visually richer and even more interactive than the previous version—a leap forward in design with more tools and features to enrich learning and aid students in achieving classroom success.

Teaching and Learning Tools

▶ **Pearson eText:** Identical in content and design to the printed text, a Pearson eText provides students access to their text whenever and wherever they need it. In addition to contextually placed multimedia features in every chapter, the Pearson eText allows students to take notes and highlight, just like a traditional book.

▶ **Videos and Video Quizzes:** Interactive videos provide students with the opportunity to watch and evaluate sample speeches, both student and professional. Selected videos are annotated with instructor feedback or include short, assignable quizzes that report to the instructor's grade book. Professional speeches include classic and contemporary speeches as well as video segments from communication experts.

▶ **MyOutline:** MyOutline offers step-by-step guidance for writing an effective outline, along with tips and explanations to help students better understand the elements of an outline and how all the pieces fit together. Outlines that students create can be downloaded to their computer, emailed as an attachment, or saved in the tool for future editing. Instructors can select from several templates based on our texts, or they can create their own outline structure for students to use.

▶ **Topic Selector:** This interactive tool helps students get started generating ideas and then narrowing down topics. Our Topic Selector is question based, rather than drill-down, to help students really learn the process of selecting their topic. Once they have determined their topic, students are directed to credible online sources for guidance in the research process.

▶ **Self-Assessments:** Online self-assessments, including the PRCA-24 and the PRPSA, provide students with opportunities to assess and confirm their comfort level with speaking publicly. Instructors can use these tools to show learning over the duration of the course via MyPersonalityProfile, Pearson's online self-assessment library and analysis tool. MyPersonalityProfile enables instructors to assign self-assessments, such as the PRPSA, at the beginning and end of the course so that students can compare their results and see where they have improved.

▶ **Study Plan:** Pre-Tests and Post-Tests for each chapter test students on their knowledge of the material in the course. The tests generate a customized study plan for further assessment and focus students on areas in which they need to improve.

Speech Evaluation Tools

Instructors have access to a host of Speech Evaluation Tools to use in the classroom. An additional assortment of evaluation forms and guides for students and instructors offers further options and ideas for assessing presentations.

Building Speaking Confidence Center

In this special section of **MySpeechLab®**, students will find self-assessments, strategies, video, audio, and activities that provide additional guidance and tips for overcoming their speech apprehension—all in one convenient location.

Cutting-Edge Technology

▶ MediaShare: With Pearson's video upload tool, students are able to upload their speeches for their instructor and classmates to watch (whether face to face or online) and provide online feedback and comments, at time-stamped intervals, including the option to include an evaluation rubric for instructors and/or students to fill out. Instructors can also opt to include a final grade when reviewing a student's video. Grades can be exported from MediaShare to a SCORM-compliant .csv spreadsheet that can be imported into most learning management systems. Structured much like a social networking site, MediaShare can help to promote a sense of community among students.

▶ AmericanRhetoric.com partnership: Through an exclusive partnership with AmericanRhetoric.com, **MySpeechLab®** incorporates many great speeches of our time (without linking out to another site and without advertisements or commercials!). Many speeches are accompanied by assessment questions that ask students to evaluate specific elements of those speeches.

▶ Audio Chapter Summaries: Every chapter includes an audio chapter summary for online streaming use, perfect for students to use in reviewing material before a test or for instructors to use in reviewing material before class.

Online Administration

No matter what course management system you use—or if you do not use one at all but still wish to easily capture your students' grade and track their performance—Pearson has a **MySpeechLab®** option to suit your needs. Contact one of Pearson's Technology Specialists for more information and assistance.

A **MySpeechLab®** access code is provided at no additional cost when packaged with selected Pearson Communication texts. To get started, contact your local Pearson Publisher's Representative at **www.pearsonhighered.com/replocator.**

Acknowledgments

Bringing this book to fruition was a humbling experience—not only because of the amount of work that I put into it as author, but also because so many other people have invested their own time and effort to bring this work to the pages you are reading now. I must begin with the team at Pearson, whose patience and encouragement know no bounds. First on the list is Carol Alper, development editor; her steady guidance and eye for options and alternatives kept this project going through all of its ups and downs. Karon Bowers, editor-in-chief, has been tremendously supportive throughout the entire process and has done a terrific job of navigating the book through a changing environment while allowing us to stay committed to its core philosophy. Thank you to the following team members at Pearson who helped to make this book possible: Blair Tuckman, marketing manager; Angela Mallowes, associate editor; Megan Sweeney, editorial assistant; Paul DeLuca, Senior Digital Editor, Lisa Dotson, Digital Editor, and Anne Ricigliano, production manager.

Students and instructors too numerous to mention have provided countless direct and indirect contributions to this book. Generous colleagues in the Communication Studies departments at the University of Iowa, Augustana College, and the University of Montana have shared advice and teaching materials that have become part of the great general fund of resources that flows through academia. In my role as course director for the Introduction to Public Speaking course at the University of Montana, I also have had the good fortune of generous and energetic graduate students who have been willing to teach many of the ideas and glean some of the examples found in this book.

I wish to acknowledge the many focus group participants and reviewers who helped to shape the final manuscript:

Allison Ainsworth, Gainesville State College

Richard Bello, Sam Houston State University

Sally Blomstrom, Embry-Riddle Aeronautical University

Edward C. Brewer, Murray State University

Sheena Carey, Marquette University

Nick Carty, Dalton State College

Kathleen Clark, University of Akron

Cindi Clarke, Belmont Technical College

Ellen R. Cohn, University of Pittsburgh

Elaine Davies, University of Missouri–Columbia

Terri Easley, Johnson County Community College

Alycia Ehlert, Darton College

Jeffrey W. Fox, Northern Kentucky University

Mark Frank, Coffeyville Community College

Lyn J. Freymiller, Pennsylvania State University

Todd S. Frobish, Fayette State University

Terilyn J. Goins, Christopher Newport University

Kathleen Golden, Edinboro University of Pennsylvania

Donna Goodwin, Tulsa Community College

Carla Harrell, Old Dominion University

M'Liss Hindman, Tyler Junior College

Kristen Hoerl, Auburn University

Pamela A. Kaylor, Ohio University, Lancaster

Thomas M. Lessl, University of Georgia

John Levine, University of California, Berkeley

Stacey Mann, Mississippi State University

Donna Munde, Mercer County Community College

Tami McCray Olds, Northern Virginia Community College

Doug Parry, University of Alaska, Anchorage

C. Thomas Preston, Jr., Gainesville State College

Susan Rabideau, University of Wisconsin, Fox Valley

Armeda C. Reitzel, Humboldt State University

Alena Amato Ruggerio, Southern Oregon University

Tom Sabetta, Jefferson Community and Technical College

Kristi Schaller, University of Georgia

Paul Schliefer, Southern Wesleyan University

David Schneider, Saginaw Valley State University

Cynthia Marie Stover, Metropolitan Community College

Helen Tate, Columbia College

Jerry D. Thomas, Lindsey Wilson College

Jeffrey Tyus, Sinclair Community College

Janice Vierk, Metropolitan Community College

Sara Chudnovsky Weintraub, Regis College

Jessica W. Weisel, Collin County Community College

Ryan Wyckoff, Danville Area Community College

I also want to acknowledge the teachers and mentors who provided the foundation, motivation, and inspiration for much of what appears in this book. Joanne Biederwolf and Sharon Iverson, my middle and high school speech coaches, set me on this path with their support many years ago. They are among the unsung public school teachers whose dedication has yielded untold riches in the lives of their students. In their unique ways, Bill Lewis, Jon Ericson, and Bob Hariman at Drake University each shaped how I thought of public speaking, its importance in a liberal arts education, and its role as a force in the public sphere. My many mentors at the University of Iowa—John Lyne, Michael Calvin McGee, Kathleen Farrell, Ralph Cintron, and Takis Poulakos—each reminded me of the ongoing interplay between pedagogy, rhetorical scholarship, and public life.

With equal joy, I want to acknowledge the wonderful personal support of my friends and family. My peers and colleagues have provided the intellectual camaraderie and friendship that have buoyed me along the way. There are many more, but I especially want to acknowledge Anthony Hurst, Norm Clark, Deb Hauser, Meg Garvin, Pete Simonson, John Delicath, Barb Willard, Marilyn DeLaure, Chris Kamrath, Sharon Varallo, Janet Novak, Heidi Hamilton, Jason Jarvis, Shiv Ganesh, Phaedra Pezzullo, Jen Peeples, Pete Bsumek, Jen Schneider, Lisa Swallow, and my colleagues in Communication Studies at the University of Montana. My parents, Jim and Shirley Schwarze, always impressed on me the value of education and made so many opportunities available for me to develop my talents. Finally, my wife Caryn and my son Charlie deserve the greatest acknowledgement possible. I owe much to both of them and can only hope to recover much of what we have deferred these past few years. They experienced all the successes and tribulations that are part of a project like this, and they managed to keep going through our toughest challenges and in spite of our many sacrifices. They surely are as thrilled as I am to see this book in print!

About the Author

STEVE SCHWARZE is an Associate Professor and Chair of the Department of Communication Studies at the University of Montana in Missoula, Montana. Steve's success in competitive speech while growing up in Minnesota sparked a lifelong interest in public speaking. He earned a B.A. in Speech Communication at Drake University in Des Moines, Iowa, before earning his Ph.D. in Communication Studies at the University of Iowa in Iowa City, Iowa. At Iowa, he gained valuable experience teaching public speaking in a variety of contexts and courses, from the first-year required rhetoric course to courses in business and professional speaking and argumentation. He then taught public speaking and oral advocacy courses at Augustana College in Rock Island, Illinois, before moving to Montana.

At the University of Montana, Steve directs the Introduction to Public Speaking course that serves more than 1,300 students each year. He also teaches courses in Persuasive Speaking and Criticism; Rhetorical Theory; Environmental Rhetoric; and Communication, Consumption and Climate. Steve's research focuses on the rhetorical construction of environmental issues, and he is increasingly interested in the public discourse surrounding climate change and sustainable consumption. He believes that it is vital for all students to get involved in these issues and includes several examples pertaining to sustainability throughout *Speaking in the Public Sphere*. You can contact Steve at steven.schwarze@umontana.edu.

Public Speaking and the Public Sphere

This chapter is intended to help you:

- See how public speaking benefits you in many areas of life
- Understand the public dimensions of public speaking
- Learn how public speaking is part of a communication process
- Identify how public speaking is connected to democracy
- Recognize the ethical challenges and opportunities of public speaking

Colleges and universities today are encouraging students to engage with public issues in a variety of ways. Inside the classroom, you may find yourself exploring daunting topics such as terrorism, globalization, climate change, and health care. Outside the classroom, students are engaging in diverse forms of service in their local communities and around the world. Traditional political activity has seen resurgence, too—through voter registration drives, face-to-face campaigning, and lobbying by and for students. Even getting involved with clubs, student government, or your residence hall are ways in which you can engage with issues that affect your campus community.

CASE SCENARIO

Carlos Serves His Community through Public Speaking

Carlos is in his last semester of college and is thinking about his future, but he is also thinking about how he got to this point in his life. In high school, his guidance counselor did not give Carlos much help in identifying colleges or careers that might suit him. His parents had not attended college and were unfamiliar with the details of the admissions process. Somehow, he managed to figure it out on his own, and he is now about to graduate with a degree in engineering. He just wished it could have been a little easier.

One day on campus, Carlos saw a flyer for a group called MEChA, or Movimiento Estudiantil Chicano de Aztlán. He read that the group was planning its annual youth conference, which brought Latino high school students to campus to inform them about their options after graduation, including college. Carlos thought this would be a great opportunity. He thought he could help out by reserving rooms or making the lunch arrangements. But by the end of the first planning meeting, he found himself on the list of potential speakers; he would be speaking about the rights of students from immigrant families. He was a little nervous but also excited by the prospect of contributing something to his community. ■

Indeed, the stereotypes of lazy or self-absorbed students no longer fit. No matter what their background, students are active participants in public life. Some of you may come with experience in such activities—volunteering for a soup kitchen or a political campaign, for example—while others of you may have little familiarity with or interest in them (CIRCLE, 2006). Ideally, during the course of your college career, each of you will find some opportunity for engagement. No matter when or where that happens, you can be more confident and more effective if you have training and practice in public speaking.

This book can give you guidance for becoming a better public speaker. Like other books on public speaking, it will help you to understand the basic principles of effective speaking and will provide you with many techniques for crafting and delivering speeches. It also will show you how the principles and skills of public speaking are applicable to public life, as well as to your college classes, your job, and your personal life. Skill in public speaking can help you to thrive in all areas of your life.

This first chapter is intended to orient you to a concept of public speaking that fits our times. After illustrating why a course in public speaking is such an important course for you to take, this chapter will define public speaking and illustrate three models for thinking about the process of public speaking. This part of the chapter introduces the idea of the public sphere that will be a guiding theme of this book. The next section of the chapter elaborates on this idea, showing how public speaking is related to democracy and public life. The chapter concludes by introducing you to some of the key ethical considerations of public speaking. ■

Why Study Public Speaking?

For many of you, your public speaking course fulfills some sort of requirement. At some schools, public speaking is a required course for all students.
At others, public speaking is required for certain majors. It is not only students
majoring in the liberal arts or in communication who find it on their list of
required courses. Professional programs in areas such as business, education,
engineering, natural resources, and pharmacy often require public speaking
for their students. Why is public speaking so often a required course?

*Public speaking is a common requirement because it is a fundamental skill
that has direct personal and social benefits.* These benefits make public speaking
a vitally important course for every college student. No matter how students
feel about public speaking, by the end of the course, they consistently recognize and appreciate these benefits. Comments like these are typical on course
evaluation forms:

> I wasn't looking forward to taking this course, but now I feel like I really im-
> proved during the semester.
>
> I have always been nervous about public speaking. Now I am a lot more confi-
> dent. I might even take another speech course so I can keep practicing!
>
> This course really helped me figure out how to organize my thoughts and sup-
> port my ideas. It has already helped me at my job—I persuaded my boss to
> give me a raise!
>
> I never used to feel comfortable expressing my opinions or taking a position on
> issues. But the skills we learned in class have helped me get over that. Thanks!

Indeed, the tangible benefits that come from public speaking are obvious to
students as well as to the faculty members and administrators who make curriculum decisions at colleges. They see that public speaking courses teach foundational
skills that help students to lead fulfilling and successful lives and contribute to
their community. From a student's perspective, a public speaking course can enhance
your development in three areas of life: achievement in the classroom, success in
your job and personal life, and empowerment in public life.

Achievement in the Classroom

> Jeremy's sociology class had a group project at the end of the semester. His
> grade hinged on how well he and his group could pull the project off. He had
> confidence in his groupmates Sookoun and Kayla; all of them were doing well
> in the class. But the group presentation made him a little nervous. Fortunately,
> Sookoun was taking a public speaking class and had some great ideas about
> how to organize their presentation. Sookoun also encouraged the group to
> rehearse their presentation and offered Kayla and Jeremy some helpful tips for
> how to improve their delivery. This helped them to feel more confident about
> their presentation, and their instructor said that it was one of the clearest she
> had seen.

The most immediate payoff for taking this course is that public speaking can help you to do better in your other classes (Morreale, Osborn, and Pearson 7–9). No matter what your major, you will need to make oral presentations. If you are in the sciences, you need to be able to present data effectively and put it into context for your audience. If you are in the humanities, you need to offer clear interpretations that you can support with historical and textual evidence. In every discipline, group projects are common assignments that require presentations. The public speaking practice that you gain in this class can be directly and immediately transferred to improve your performance in other classes.

Public speaking courses also develop knowledge and skills beyond giving presentations. Knowing the principles of communication that are covered later in this chapter, as well as the skills of listening and giving feedback that are discussed in chapter 3, can help you to be a better participant in classroom discussions. The research skills that are discussed in chapter 6 provide a solid foundation for doing research in a variety of disciplines. The ability to develop a compelling central idea, organize those ideas coherently, and support your ideas applies to writing papers as well as to speaking. In many ways, public speaking is an all-purpose course that focuses on many of the core skills that faculty members say college students need to succeed (Diamond).

Finally, public speaking can help you to build the confidence you need to thrive in college. Even if you feel somewhat nervous about public speaking right now, by the end of this course, you are likely to feel far more confident about yourself and in your speaking skills. The guidance that is provided in this book, the feedback and support from your instructor and classmates, and the extensive speaking practice you will get will all contribute to enhancing your confidence. You will likely find it easier to participate in class discussion, engage your instructors, and tackle challenging assignments.

Success in Your Job and Personal Life

Maria never thought of herself as a "people person." Ever since she was a little girl, she liked being outdoors and was fascinated by animals of all kinds. In college, she discovered the field of wildlife biology and knew that it was the right career path for her. Her courses took her out in the field and prepared her well for a job with her state's Department of Natural Resources. When she interviewed for the job, the interviewer was impressed by the fact that Maria had taken several classes in communication and public speaking. "A big part of this job is interacting with the public and giving interpretive talks at state parks," he said. Maria mentioned several of the skills she learned in these classes, but it was her performance in the interview—her confidence and ability to explain ideas clearly and concisely—that ultimately won her the job.

For many students, the big question about any college class is: Will it help me get a job? When it comes to public speaking, the answer is an absolute "Yes!"

Surveys of employers and scholarly research studies consistently show that communication skills in general—and oral communication skills in particular—are among the most desired competencies for workers (Pittenger, Miller, and Mot). The ability to interview effectively, deliver oral reports, and participate in meetings is crucial for success in your job and career. The renowned business-man Warren Buffett, when asked his opinion of the most valuable skill for college students entering the job market, said unequivocally: public speaking ("Buffett and Gates").

You might be surprised to learn that even technical fields or jobs that "crunch numbers" involve public speaking. One study of business students, for example, found that their expectations about the frequency of oral presentations and meetings are far too low (McPherson). Meetings and presentations are a basic part of virtually every career, even if public speaking is not a primary part of your day-to-day work. It will be to your advantage to develop your public speaking skills now.

Public speaking skills also can help you to lead a fulfilling personal and social life. Everyone wants to be able to give a good toast at the wedding of a friend or family member. Similarly, giving a speech that praises a friend or co-worker, participating in a club meeting, and celebrating a group accomplishment are among the many situations in which you can put your public

VIDEOCONFERENCING
Not even the explosion of electronic forms of communication will replace the need for public speaking in the workplace.

speaking skills to good use. Speaking at rituals like these can go much more smoothly when thinking about your audience and purpose becomes second nature to you.

Empowerment in Public Life

Public speaking also prepares you for participation in public life. For instance, if you are concerned about parking on your campus, you might decide to speak to administrators or present your concerns to your student government. If you want to start a program to help teens who are at risk for suicide, you might need to enlist the help of your friends and discuss the idea with high school counselors or public health professionals. If you want to help out a political candidate, you might be asked to go door to door and answer questions about your candidate. Skill in public speaking can help you in all of these activities.

For some of you, participation in public life might seem distant or unrealistic. How can one college student have a real impact? The answer, as the examples above suggest, is that you can participate in public life in many different ways. This perspective on participation in public life emerges from a large study, the National Youth Civic Engagement Project Index, which recently examined citizen engagement in the United States and gave special attention to people under 40 years old (Zukin et al.). On the basis of data collected from focus groups, telephone and web-based surveys, and expert panels, researchers revealed four broad ways in which people in the United States participate in public life:

- *Civic engagement.* **Civic engagement** is hands-on work with others that seeks to achieve a public good. Addressing an important issue or concern in your community—for example, improving access to buildings for disabled people or raising awareness of public transportation—is at the heart of civic engagement. Volunteering for a community group or service organization is a common form of civic engagement.

- *Political engagement.* **Political engagement** focuses on government, and your participation aims to influence policy or the election of public officials. Voting, persuading others to support a candidate or legislation, and participating in a political organization fall into this category.

- *Cognitive engagement.* Simply paying attention to politics and public issues is another type of participation in public life. Following the news and discussing issues with other people are examples of **cognitive engagement**.

- *Public voice.* When you express your opinion or viewpoint on an issue that is important to you and others, you are exercising your **public voice**. Contacting public officials, signing petitions, publicizing your viewpoint in a letter to the editor or through social media, and raising awareness of issues via a rally or protest are some of the ways of using your public voice.

Public speaking skills certainly help you to exercise your public voice, but they also can help you in other forms of engagement. As the researchers point out, there is definitely some overlap between the categories: "Notably, the expression of public voice is characteristic of *both* political and civic activists" (Zukin et al. 54). Furthermore, people who are involved in both civic and political engagement are typically more vocal than other citizens are.

No matter how much or how little you are engaged in public life right now, the point is that developing your public speaking skills can empower you as well as your audience. Public speaking has long been associated with encouraging people to stand up for their own interests, make a difference in their society, and participate in the exercise of political power. As a result, public speaking is a crucial skill for everyone in a democracy, not just members of the elite or elected officials. As one scholar puts it, "The power of speech is not the power to command obedience by replacing argument with silence. It is the power to challenge silent obedience by opening arguments" (Billig 48). This connection between public speaking and empowerment is perhaps the most crucial reason to study public speaking. Skill in public speaking helps you to have a sense of power over the direction of your life.

What Is Public Speaking?

What comes to your mind when you think of public speaking? Do you think of yourself standing in front of a room full of people? Maybe you recall attending a meeting of a community organization at which a member of the group informed others about the group's activities? Perhaps you think of an activist inspiring a crowd on your campus, or you might envision the President giving the State of the Union address. Each of these events reveals some of the basic characteristics of public speaking and shows the diversity of situations that call for public speaking. To understand what public speaking is all about, let's take a closer look at both words in that phrase.

The "Speaking" in Public Speaking

Courses in public speaking are concerned not just with the physical act of speaking. Instead, speaking is understood as a type of **communication**: interaction that creates meaning through symbols. You may be taking this course within a department called "Communication Studies" or "Speech Communication," where scholars study and teach about different types of communication. When a speaker gives a speech to an audience, symbols such as words, voice changes, and gestures help the speaker and audience to create meaning.

To help you understand the unique aspects of public speaking, then, it can be useful to compare it to other forms of communication, such as interpersonal communication, group communication, and mass communication.

INTERPERSONAL COMMUNICATION
Compared to an interpersonal conversation, public speaking should be somewhat more formal and structured.

Interpersonal Communication Chatting with your roommate, having a heart-to-heart talk with a family member, and socializing with your co-workers are all examples of **interpersonal communication**: one-on-one conversations that are primarily about negotiating relationships. Like interpersonal communication, public speaking involves negotiating relationships with your listeners; but in public speaking, you are communicating with many listeners—an audience—not just one person. An important part of public speaking is learning how to adapt to audiences composed of a diverse range of people.

In addition, interpersonal communication is typically casual and unstructured. A conversation with your friends over dinner is probably informal and may cover a wide range of different topics in no particular order. You probably do not prepare notes or an outline for these conversations. In contrast, public speaking is almost always more formal than conversation. Although it is common advice for public speakers to have a "conversational" tone, be careful of taking this too far. Your language and your body should convey confidence, intelligence, and preparation in order to make a good impression on your audience. Effective public speaking also is more structured than a free-flowing conversation. Good speeches logically follow a set of points and are focused by a specific purpose.

Group Communication Classroom discussions, committee meetings, and work projects all involve **group communication**: interaction among multiple people for purposes such as mutual understanding, exploration of ideas, or coordination of action.

Like group communication, public speaking may try to achieve these purposes. You certainly want your audience to understand you. Some types of public speaking, such as informative speaking, may explore ideas, while persuasive speaking may encourage collective action among audience members.

The key difference between group communication and public speaking is where responsibility for communication lies. Even in groups that have a definite leader, people expect that most if not all group members should contribute to the discussion. The point of most group meetings is to encourage communication and involvement among members. In other words, each group member has an equal responsibility to participate.

But in public speaking, the primary responsibility for communication lies with the speaker. It is the speaker's job to take the lead: He or she must consider the audience, prepare material, and organize and deliver a speech. For example, imagine that you were excited to attend a speech by someone who had climbed Mount Everest. You probably would be disappointed if the speaker, someone with a wealth of knowledge and firsthand experience, didn't prepare a thing and simply said, "So, what do you want to talk about?" A group conversation might be nice, but you likely would learn much more if the speaker had fulfilled the responsibility of preparing in advance.

Mass Communication　Television programs, radio shows, Internet sites, podcasts, and newspapers are just a few examples of **mass communication**: interaction between a source and large, impersonal audiences via mediated messages. Both mass communication and public speaking circulate messages to audience composed of many people. In that way, both types of communication involve the challenge of adapting a message so that it is compelling to a diverse range of people. What makes public speaking different from some forms of mass communication—such as television and newspapers—is the capacity for the audience to talk back to the speaker immediately and directly. Other forms of mass communication, however, have more interactive capabilities. Email, social media, and even radio can be used in ways that are nearly as interactive as face-to-face communication (see Figure 1.1).

Mass communication and public speaking also overlap when mass media transmit or circulate speeches. The speeches of Adolf Hitler and the fireside chats of Franklin Delano Roosevelt are two classic examples of how radio was used to create large audiences for public speaking. These days, television and YouTube allow both leaders and ordinary citizens to circulate the verbal and visual messages of public speaking. For speakers, this means that the audience for a public speech may be much bigger than just the people who are physically present. This makes audience adaptation all the more challenging.

The "Public" in Public Speaking

Think back to the examples at the beginning of this section. Whether you are speaking in front of a room full of people, listening to a speaker at a meeting of a campus or community organization, or watching a televised speech about important political issues, you are part of an event that is public in some way.

FIGURE 1.1 Comparing Public Speaking to Other Forms of Speech Communication

	How Public Speaking Is Similar	**How Public Speaking Is Different**
Interpersonal Communication	Both involve developing and maintaining relationships between participants.	Public speakers must adapt to multiple audience members, while interpersonal communication is between just two people.
	Both involve negotiating meaning and taking into account the beliefs, values, and attitudes of one another.	Public speakers typically speak with more formality and structure, while interpersonal communication is informal and conversations are rarely structured.
Group Communication	Both involve interaction among multiple people.	One public speaker has primary responsibility for communication. In a group, the responsibility is shared.
	Both occur in settings that usually have a clear purpose.	Public speakers usually give a predetermined speech and then take feedback. Group communication involves spontaneous dialogue and ongoing feedback.
Mass Communication	Both involve interaction among multiple people.	Audiences typically have the ability to interact directly and immediately with a public speaker.
	Both assume a model of one person communicating to many, some of whom may be strangers.	Most mass communication involves barriers between speaker and audience.

Using the word "public" to describe these varied speaking events suggests that speaking can be public for many different reasons.

On the most basic level, public speaking *addresses an audience.* As mentioned above, public speaking is not simply the physical act of using your voice. It involves using your voice to communicate with others. To do so effectively, you need to learn about your audience and adapt your message accordingly. You also need to practice speaking in front of audiences. Through practice, you can reduce your nervousness and become more comfortable in future speaking situations. A class in public speaking helps you with all of these things as it encourages you to think not only about speaking, but primarily about speaking to particular audiences.

Another way in which speaking can be public is if it *addresses common interests* (Hauser). Even if you are talking about a personal experience, reporting to a group about work you have done, or describing a private concern, effective public speaking connects those ideas to the interests of your audience. For example, a report at your job should show how your contribution helps the group to complete their project. In other situations, you might describe personal concerns in terms of broader public issues. If you had difficulty registering for classes, you might frame that personal experience as an instance of why many students are concerned about basic services on your campus. Making this connection between personal and common interests is a crucial aspect of public speaking.

Finally, speaking has a public dimension when it *addresses the exercise of power* (Habermas, Hove). In democratic societies, this is the key role that public speaking plays. In the United States, the First Amendment protects freedom of speech and assembly so that citizens can come together and freely discuss matters that affect their lives, especially matters of power and self-governance. Formally elected bodies, such as your student senate or city council, provide a space for this kind of public speaking, but civic associations, neighborhood groups, and clubs also give people opportunities to speak to others about things that matter in their community. Participating in these organizations helps you to have a say in the direction of your campus, your community, and your society.

These "public" dimensions reinforce how public speaking can be empowering. Public speaking connects you with others so that you can make a difference in your community. It helps you to contribute to civic life by influencing the interests and issues that should matter to everyone. And as the rest of this book will encourage you to do, public speaking can help you to engage in issues of public significance, ones that are important for civic life and political decision making.

Three Models of Public Speaking

Visual models can further represent how public speaking works. One model, often called the transmission model, reflects many common beliefs about how communication works. Because this is such an easy way to think about communication, the first part of this section will look at this model and explain some of its shortcomings. Then we will turn to two better models: a speech communication model and a public sphere model.

The Transmission Model

The model of communication that is frequently used to visualize the public speaking process is not based on public speaking at all. Instead, engineers working on telephone systems generated this model to study how messages were

FIGURE 1.2 The Transmission Model of Communication

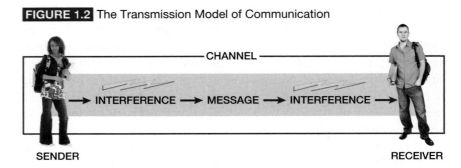

SENDER   RECEIVER

transmitted and where various problems could emerge (Shannon). It is commonly called the **transmission model** of communication because, for these researchers, effective communication meant the clear transmission of sound via the telephone. This model's elements are based on the idea that effective communication involves a *sender* who transmits a *message* through a *channel* to a *receiver* (see Figure 1.2). In addition, effective communication must minimize the amount of *interference* that might disrupt the transmission of the message.

This model translates easily to represent a public speaking situation:

- The sender is equivalent to the speaker.

- The message is the speech.

- The receiver is an audience member.

- The channel is the medium that carries the message. For the telephone researchers, the channel was the physical equipment—the handsets and wires that transmitted the message. In public speaking, the channels may be technologies such as television, radio, or the Internet. Speakers themselves have two main channels: the auditory channel, which carries the sound of words and voice changes, and the visual channel, which carries the appearance of the speaker, body movements, gestures, and visual aids.

- Interference is anything that disrupts the transmission of the message. On telephones, interference might be static or a bad connection. In public speaking, interference means the physical and psychological barriers that prevent an audience from hearing the message.

Take a few moments to think about this model. Does it accurately reflect how public speaking works? Are there significant differences between public speaking and communicating via telephone?

The limitations of the transmission model become apparent when you consider that the model encourages you to think about communication as if you were playing catch. The message is a ball. The sender throws the ball, and as long as there is no interference, it is up to the receiver to catch the ball. Either she catches it or she doesn't. (Our everyday language about public speaking often reflects the transmission model; we talk about "getting the message across" or "passing along information" to the audience.)

But why might this not be an adequate model for public speaking?

First, *the transmission model shows whether listeners receive a message but does not show how they understand and interpret that message.* While a telephone researcher merely wants receivers to hear the words, public speakers want audiences to *understand* words—what their meaning is, how they support an idea, and why they are relevant to the overall purpose of the speech. Because audience members bring their own beliefs, attitudes, opinions, and experiences to a public speaking situation, they are likely to interpret the message in ways that are different than the speaker intended.

In other words, the transmission model depicts listeners as passive recipients of messages. For example, consider the slogan "We must take back America!" It is not clear who is part of the "we" in that slogan and what specifically should be taken back. Those words probably would mean one thing to a group of immigration activists and something else to a group of Native Americans. A model based on simply hearing a message suggests little about how audiences understand and interpret messages.

Second, *the transmission model downplays the situation of the speech.* In the transmission model the speaker appears to convey a message to an audience member without any connection to time or place. But the situation is crucial to determining the meaning and effectiveness of a speech. For example, during the 2008 presidential campaign, Barack Obama gave a prominent speech about race shortly after some commentators raised concerns about remarks made by Rev. Jeremiah Wright, pastor of Obama's church. Although Obama had spoken about racial issues before, this speech took on added meaning in relation to the concerns about Rev. Wright's statements.

Third, the transmission model does not include feedback. The verbal and nonverbal responses that audience members give to speakers are a crucial part of the communication process. They show that communication is not really a one-way process of speakers sending messages to receivers, but rather a two-way process involving messages going back and forth between speakers and audiences. Think again about the metaphor of playing catch: What does it mean if your partner returns your throw with a fastball aimed at your head? A better understanding of communication process comes from examining the entire interaction and not just a single "transmission."

Taken together, these problems with the transmission model point to a clear conclusion: The transmission model provides little insight about *meaning*. Because the model depicts communication as simply transmitting information from the sender to a passive receiver without reference to particular situations, the model downplays the complex process of negotiating meaning. Other models are more useful in showing the factors you need to consider for effective public speaking.

The Speech Communication Model

The **speech communication model** displays a more dynamic view of the public speaking process. While the transmission model focused on the one-way action of sending a message, the speech communication model emphasizes the ongoing transaction between speaker and audience (see Figure 1.3). There are two important ways in which this dynamic model can help you to think more carefully about effective public speaking.

Most important, this model shows that *audiences are active participants in the communication process.* This is a central idea in contemporary communication theory (Ceccarelli, Fiske). Rather than being passive "receivers" or "targets," audience members bring their own beliefs, attitudes, opinions, and experiences into public speaking situations. Therefore, this model reminds speakers that their job is not one of "hitting the target" with their own viewpoints and lots of information. Rather, speakers should think of their audience as equal participants whose ideas must be examined during speech preparation if speakers want to be effective. Indeed, the audience will be participating even before the speaker begins to speak.

Audiences also participate by giving feedback. During a speech, audience members may nod, look puzzled, start reading the campus newspaper, or stare out the window. Rather than thinking of these as distractions, the speaker

FIGURE 1.3 The Speech Communication Model of Public Speaking

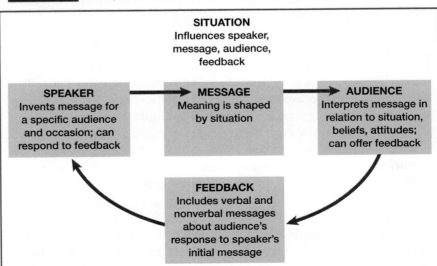

should think of them as messages. With practice and experience, speakers can pick up on this kind of feedback and adapt messages accordingly. By adding feedback into the mix, this model reminds speakers to attend to the messages that others are sending in addition to their own.

The speech communication model also shows that *the situation influences the entire communication process*. Chapter 4 will examine this issue in more detail; for now, think of situation as the setting or occasion for the speech. Like differences among audience members, differences between situations can greatly influence the meanings of a speech. One relevant aspect of the situation is the physical setting; for example, the President may give a speech in the Oval Office, in the White House Rose Garden, or at Camp David. These different backgrounds shape the message and can influence how audiences perceive the speech's meaning. Situation also includes the history or past events that led up to a speech. For example, in the workplace, even a simple factual announcement such as "Everyone gets a $1,000 bonus this year" means something different depending on how bonuses have been distributed in the past. It might not mean much if that is the standard bonus, but it will mean something different if the usual bonus is $3,000 or if only a few people have received the bonus in the past.

The Public Sphere Model

While the speech communication model focuses on the immediate speaking situation, the **public sphere model** (Figure 1.4) focuses on the role of public speaking in a democratic society. This model draws on recent scholarship about the public sphere in communication studies and other disciplines (Asen and Brouwer, Hauser, Loehwing and Motter). The public sphere model is not meant to replace the speech communication model. Instead, it adds another layer to our understanding of public speaking and shows how public speaking is connected to political and civic engagement—think of it as helping you see the "big picture."

You can begin to see the big picture by observing how a specific public speaking situation is part of the broader flow of messages in society:

> Scott had been hearing a lot about climate change. One day, he read an editorial that was discussing the connection between climate change and national security; another day, he was encouraged to become a Facebook "fan" of a climate action group that was forming on campus; the following day, he came across a flyer in a store touting the benefits of compact fluorescent light bulbs. As he got more interested in the issue, he gave speeches about it in his class and eventually joined the student group. Because of his speaking skills, other members of the group encouraged him to speak about climate change at a rally on campus.
>
> Scott's speech went over really well with the audience. The group gained some new members, and several signed a petition for the campus

FIGURE 1.4 The Public Sphere Model of Public Speaking

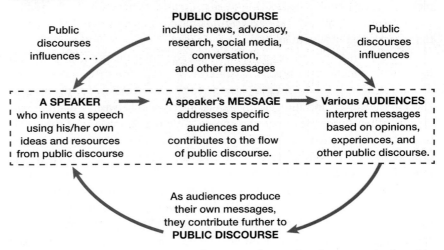

The constant flow of messages among diverse speakers and audiences can be thought of as CIRCULATION.

to become "carbon-neutral." One of new members mentioned that he had heard about the rally from a friend who was in Scott's public speaking class. The group also posted a video of Scott's speech on YouTube. He could hardly believe that it had over 500 views in just a couple of weeks! He later found out that similar organizations at other campuses had posted it on their websites, too.

Like those of most public speakers, Scott's ideas and interest in the topic did not come out of nowhere. Instead, messages that were available in his everyday experience helped to shape Scott's thinking and speaking. And in speaking, he was not only addressing his immediate audience; he also reached others who were not immediately present but had an interest in the topic. This constant and unpredictable flow of messages among diverse speakers and audiences—what scholars call **circulation**—is a defining feature of the contemporary public sphere (Warner). Circulation provides another metaphor for thinking about public speaking that is different from the ideas of transmission and communication in the previous two models.

The idea of circulation is crucial for understanding how your own speaking is connected to the public sphere. First, *a speaker's message is influenced by other messages that circulate in the public sphere*. As Scott's example suggests, speakers do not come up with ideas entirely on their own. Rather, the ideas of both speakers and audiences are shaped by the messages that are already circulating in the public sphere—what we will call **public discourse**, including conversations, news reports, and public advocacy. For public speaking, the research process that will be explored in chapter 6 is essentially a strategy for helping you to manage that flow of messages. After thinking critically about those messages, you are better prepared to create your own message for a particular audience.

Second, *a speaker's message contributes to the circulation of messages in the public sphere.* While communication is a useful concept for thinking about the goal with your immediate audience, circulation indicates how a message may reach beyond your immediate audience. In some instances, circulation is intentional; you might agree to have your speech recorded or transcribed so that others can have access to it. But in many cases, circulation happens unintentionally or indirectly. A classmate might talk about your speech with one of her friends. If you are speaking in a public meeting, a journalist might quote some of your words when reporting about the meeting. These words can then reach all kinds of people who may respond very differently from your immediate audience.

Finally, *the circulation of messages helps to create publics.* For our purpose, a **public** can be thought of as a group of people who are engaged in addressing issues of common interest. For example, the public that is involved in addressing climate change is not limited to Scott's audience but includes everyone who engages with the issue: ordinary citizens reading magazine articles about it, activists campaigning about it, church members discussing it, government officials debating it. Many of these people will never hear Scott's message, but they are still connected by other messages about the issue. This public is constantly changing as new messages circulate and different people pay attention to those messages (Warner).

What does all this have to do with your own public speaking? The public sphere model and the idea of circulation have at least two very concrete, practical implications for effective public speaking. *First, public speakers need to pay close attention to messages that are already circulating in the public sphere.* Because your audience may be familiar with some of these messages, you need to be familiar with them, too. This will enhance your credibility and help you to adapt how you explain your ideas to the beliefs and values that your audience holds.

Second, *public speakers need to encourage their audience members to see themselves as part of a public.* Your audience is not necessarily part of a public; publics emerge and develop only when messages get people's interest and attention. In the public sphere, your basic task as a speaker is to help your audience members engage with issues on a civic or political level. Chapters 4 and 5 will offer you concrete ways to help your audience see themselves as part of a public.

Public Speaking and Democracy

The art of public speaking traditionally has been closely connected to effective citizenship and political decision making. But the public dimension of public speaking has not always had this focus. Both the theory and the practice of public speaking, in fact, have changed in relation to historical and political circumstances. In this section, we take a brief look at how the focus of public speaking has changed through history. Then we explore some of the distinctive features of contemporary public speaking.

Traditions of Public Speaking

The earliest teachings about public speaking in the Western world were very concerned with public impact and political engagement. The Sophists, the first teachers of rhetoric in ancient Greece, recognized that effective participation in political institutions, such as the courts and the Assembly, required skill in public speaking. Therefore, they trained aspiring leaders in public speaking techniques that could help them to gain power in the political arena (Herrick).

However, some people questioned the ethical basis of the Sophists' teachings. For example, Plato claimed that the Sophists and their students were more concerned with achieving success than with telling the truth. As a result, many later theorists of rhetoric, such as the Greek teacher Isocrates and the Roman orator Cicero, emphasized that ethical public speaking requires both eloquence and wisdom. The Roman educator Quintillian even defined the perfect orator as the "good man, speaking well."

Other historical eras further show how the public dimension of public speaking has changed over time. During the Middle Ages, the rise of the Christian church shifted the focus of public speaking away from preparation for debating in political institutions. Instead, public speaking was oriented toward preaching, defending the Scriptures, and using poetic language. During the Enlightenment period, theorists of rhetoric and public speaking tended to emphasize matters of style, language, and delivery more than the invention of arguments. Some people saw public speaking as "a path to personal refinement and an avenue into polite social circles," focusing on the possibilities for social advancement (Herrick).

In the United States, early theorists of rhetoric and public speaking advanced both of these traditions. The importance of freedom of religion during the colonial period meant that much public speaking training was concerned with preaching. At the same time, ideas of the Enlightenment influenced the conception of public speaking as a means for cultural refinement among elites. But theorists also incorporated the idea of speaking for the public good. For example, John Quincy Adams—who was not only the second President of the United States but also the first professor of rhetoric at Harvard University—revived the Ciceronian ideal of public speaking as the unity of eloquence and wisdom embodied in the political orator, whose main role was to unite the community. However, Adams suggested that civic elites, not ordinary citizens, were the ones who could play this role (Potkay).

As you can see, ideas about public speaking in previous eras have some similarities with the vision of public speaking that has been emphasized in this book so far. As in the ancient world, contemporary public speaking has a connection with effective citizenship and political decision making. People also remain concerned about the ethics of public speaking. And public speaking has long been viewed as a means of personal advancement in one's society. But other ideas about public speaking have changed, especially in relation to the practice of democracy. Recognizing these differences can help you to become a more effective speaker in the contemporary public sphere.

Contemporary Public Speaking and Diversity

The differences that are most important for speaking in the public sphere today can be summed up in a single word: diversity. While attention to diversity on college campuses often involves celebrating cultural differences, our reason for focusing on diversity is to help you see how cultural differences raise both challenges and opportunities for effective speaking and listening in the public sphere.

Diversity of Speakers As you have seen, even in democratic societies, the public sphere has not always been welcoming or open to everyone. But people have long struggled to gain access to the public sphere and have used public speaking to persuade others to move toward a more democratic and inclusive society. In the United States, nineteenth-century speakers such as Frederick Douglass, Sojourner Truth, and Elizabeth Cady Stanton paved the way for African-Americans and women to be recognized as equal participants whose voices deserved to be heard.

As a result, public speaking is no longer a skill that is reserved for elites. The emergence of the public sphere as a space for participation by everyone means that public speaking is important for everyone. Even if you do not aspire to being active in traditional politics, public speaking is a crucial skill that helps you to participate in your society.

Diversity of Speaking Styles The wide range of speakers in the contemporary public sphere leads to a diversity of speaking styles. Traditionally, training in public speaking has reinforced the norms of "manly speech" that were attributed to men from elite backgrounds (Jamieson). Speech that was factual, analytical, and impersonal was presumed to be an inherently superior style of speech.

But the practice of public speaking has increasingly involved people from diverse backgrounds whose speaking styles have often diverged from those norms. For example, many women speakers in the nineteenth and twentieth centuries adopted a "feminine style" of speaking that placed greater emphasis on concrete examples, audience participation, domestic concerns, and personal experience (Campbell). In African-American cultural traditions, public speaking has often involved a form of interaction between speaker and audience known as call and response. And many Native American tribes share a cultural perception of time that differs from the dominant perception of time in the United States that affects both Native and Euro-American public speech (Lake).

Awareness of diversity in speaking styles is extremely important for both speakers and audiences. For example, the dominant culture's expectations about appropriate speaking style can cause other speaking styles to be judged as inadequate or inferior. As many speakers know from experience, there is no clear answer about how one should negotiate these tensions between cultural expectations and one's preferred speaking style. In turn, audiences need to be attentive to how their assumptions about the "best" form of speech may prevent them from appreciating different speaking styles.

Diversity of Issues   Although public speaking has historically been connected with decision making in government institutions, the public sphere involves a much wider range of issues (Asen and Brouwer). It provides a space

AUDIENCE DIVERSITY
Diverse backgrounds and experiences among audience members often leads to different interpretations of a speaker's message.

for ordinary citizens to discuss what matters to them. These discussions may address issues of power, social needs, and common interests. But these issues do not necessarily intersect with official government action. In other words, speaking in the public sphere is not limited to speaking about traditional politics. For example, speaking in your community about ways to reduce your carbon footprint might focus on personal habits or neighborhood initiatives.

Similarly, an apparently private or personal matter can be an appropriate topic for speaking in the public sphere. For example, abuse within marriage was once considered a strictly private matter; now domestic violence is an important public issue. Likewise, some troubles at work are not merely personal; concerns about equal pay and working conditions affect others and therefore have a public dimension, too.

The lack of a clear dividing line between private and public issues presents a wonderful opportunity for you as a public speaker. The concerns of elected officials and the interests of dominant groups in society are not the only legitimate subjects for discussion. The sheer number of magazines, websites, blogs, and social media outlets that circulate messages about issues and interests means that virtually no issue is off limits for discussion. Through effective public speaking, you can bring to light the issues that matter to you.

Diversity of Publics Perhaps the most important impact of public speaking is that it enables free people to engage one another in discussion about the direction of their society. But because there are so many issues and concerns that merit discussion, the public sphere allows for many publics that may overlap, intersect, or collide with one another. Indeed, it would be impossible to make a list of publics, since they are not the same as formal organizations.

The diversity of publics is important for public speakers because it pushes speakers to think carefully about the audience they are trying to reach. For most public speakers, it is rarely useful to think about the audience as a single, monolithic group called "the public" or "the general public." Even if you are trying to reach a diverse group of people, think less about speaking to "the public" and more about inspiring listeners to actively engage with a particular issue. The real power of public speaking lies in its capacity to create groups of engaged people who were not engaged before.

Ethical Dimensions of Public Speaking

As you have already seen, ethical concerns have been a persistent part of the theory and practice of public speaking. And for good reason: public speaking is like any other type of human conduct. It can be performed appropriately or inappropriately. Lying, promoting violence, and manipulating emotions are some of the most egregious ethical violations in public speaking, but there are other tactics that raise ethical issues. In the remaining chapters in this book, you will learn about several ethical issues related to public speaking in a feature called "The Ethical Dimension."

There are many different traditions or ways of thinking about ethics. Some traditions conceive of ethics as a set of virtues that one aspires to follow, while others frame ethics as applying absolute principles to specific situations and yet others focus on the consequences of one's actions. Classes in philosophy and ethics can teach you about these different traditions. For the purposes of introductory public speaking, however, the differences between ethical traditions are less important than the overarching idea that **ethics** are guides for personal conduct in relation to one's community.

In this view, ethical public speaking has both personal and social dimensions. It involves making sound personal choices while constructing speeches *and* supporting broadly shared commitments in your society. Democratic participation, social justice, and sustainable natural and social systems are some of the shared commitments that orient this book's approach to the ethics of public speaking. Because communities are strengthened through these commitments and because each of us is dependent on the communities that surround us, ethical public speaking requires attention to both personal and social concerns.

Ethics and the Speaker

On the personal level, you can observe some of the most important ethical issues in public speaking by thinking about the three broad ways in which individual speakers appeal to audiences. The ancient Greek theorist Aristotle identified these appeals as follows:

- **Ethos**, the character and credibility of the speaker
- **Pathos**, the emotions that can be evoked in the audience
- **Logos**, the reasoning that is offered in the speech

Each of these appeals can be used to speak ethically. But each can also be deformed or used inappropriately by speakers. Understanding the basic pitfalls of each of these appeals can help you to identify some of the fundamental challenges of ethical public speaking. (Chapter 14 examines these three appeals in more detail.)

Your ethos as a speaker is a complex mix of factors as perceived by your audience. Your *knowledge or expertise* on the topic, your *honesty and trustworthiness*, and your appearance of *goodwill toward others* all play a part in shaping the audience's perception of you as a speaker. In turn, each of these factors raises ethical issues and principles:

- *Knowledge.* Have you become adequately knowledgeable about your topic? To what extent are you truthful in describing your expertise rather than exaggerating or misrepresenting it?

- *Honesty.* To what extent are you honest with the audience about your motives and purpose for speaking? Can they trust that you have researched your topic adequately? To what extent have you ignored or misrepresented competing ideas?

- *Goodwill.* How respectful are you of other points of view? Why should the audience trust that you have their best interests in mind as you speak?

At its core, the ethical use of appeals to ethos requires two things of you simultaneously. It involves both being a good person and appearing to be a good person. Being ethical and being effective, then, are not opposed to one another; in fact, being ethical can enhance your effectiveness.

The appeal of pathos always raises ethical concerns, in part because this appeal is misunderstood. Emotion is often viewed as being opposed to reason and therefore as an unethical influence on an audience's judgment. But emotions are better understood as judgments—as responses to a situation that may or may not be appropriate depending on the circumstances and our values. For example, if racial slurs have been painted on the door of a fellow student's dorm room, it would be appropriate to feel sympathy for the student and to feel angry about racism. Conversely, it would be inappropriate to appeal to joy if you were advocating for punishment for the student who painted the slurs.

Ethical public speaking, then, does not mean eliminating emotional appeals. Instead, your goal should be to use emotional appeals in a way that promotes fair judgment in relation to your topic, the situation, and shared values. Ask yourself: *Will my audience recognize these emotional appeals as fair judgments about my topic?* Also ask yourself about consistency: *Are my emotional appeals consistent with reasonable arguments, or do they undermine reasonable thinking?* For example, imagine a speech that tells a sad story about victims of a natural disaster and then blames the federal government for not providing enough support for those victims. Such an emotional appeal is ethically questionable. Although the story may be appropriate for generating sympathy for victims, it would be inappropriate for generating anger at the federal government if the speech does not include evidence about what the government has done or what it should reasonably be expected to do. The ethical concern is that the emotional appeal substitutes for supporting material and sound reasoning.

Finally, appeals to logos might not seem to harbor any ethical concerns. Most of us would appreciate appeals to reason in a speech. But both the supporting material in a speech and the patterns of reasoning in a speech are susceptible to being used in unethical ways. One crucial ethical question about supporting material asks: *Has the supporting material been accurately and fairly represented?*

For example, it is generally considered unethical to take a quotation or statistic out of context and make it mean something that the original author did not intend. Unfortunately, many political speakers violate this rule when they quote one part of an opponent's statement and leave out other parts that would make that opponent's position appear more reasonable or more complex.

Some appeals to logos might appear to be reasonable, but critical inspection could show that these are **fallacies**, or faulty patterns of reasoning. Fallacies will be discussed in depth in chapter 14 on persuasive speaking. For now, be aware that one of the fundamental ethical questions related to reasoning and fallacies is: *Does this reasoning cut off a fair examination of alternatives?* It is easy to make it appear as if you are giving your audience choices and then using reason to identify the best choice. But if your speech presents a distorted or extreme picture of one alternative or suggests that there are two and only two choices, then your speech is prematurely cutting off discussion of alternatives. This fails to empower your audience to make sound decisions.

Ethics and Society

While ethical public speaking concerns the personal choices you make as a speaker, it also involves how your speech relates to the rest of your society. Because each of us is a member of various communities of interdependent parts, each of us has an obligation to support and sustain those communities. Thus, ethical public speaking should be shaped by the values and commitments of the communities that surround us. Fortunately, this does not mean that everyone must have exactly the same beliefs; we can disagree about the meaning of these values and the best ways to put those commitments into practice. But acknowledging these values and commitments gives us a common ground for speaking to one another. Consider the following three values.

Democratic Participation No matter what our differences, we must acknowledge that in a democratic society, all people should be able to participate freely in public discussion, community problem solving, and decision making. Consequently, public speakers have an obligation to avoid speech that degrades individuals or groups, that intimidates or coerces others, or that attempts to stifle disagreement or dissent. The principles of freedom of speech and freedom of association, enshrined in the First Amendment to the U.S. Constitution, is central to the commitment to democratic participation.

Many individuals and groups work to improve and ensure democratic participation specifically among college students. For example, the organization Rock the Vote has been active in getting young people to register and vote in elections. A key part of their efforts has involved assisting students who are challenged when trying to vote where they attend college. Another organization, Campus Compact, has helped more than 20 million college students engage in service opportunities such as tutoring, building homes, and volunteering at nonprofit agencies, and it has helped students to articulate the connection between community service and politics as a new form of civic engagement known as "service politics" (Long).

Social Justice While differences and inequalities persist in all societies, most nations and religious traditions also acknowledge the existence of basic human rights and the principle of social justice. Fair treatment, equal opportunity, and equal access to the benefits of living in the society are fundamental commitments in societies that are concerned about human rights and social justice. In turn, ethical public speakers need to be mindful of how their positions may promote or undermine these commitments.

For example, for more than ten years, college students have partnered with immigrant tomato pickers in the Student/Farmworker Alliance. Since 2009, their "Dine with Dignity" campaign has pressured campus food service providers such as Aramark and Sodexo to improve pay and working conditions as well as to give workers a greater voice in the company (Student/Farmworker Alliance). Speaking out on these issues has included raising awareness among students and soliciting more than 80,000 signatures on a petition. Dominique Aulisio, a student leader at the University of Central Florida, told her campus newspaper that students should consider the issue as a topic for their speech classes (Fortis).

Sustainable Natural and Social Systems As an ethical guide, the idea of sustainability encourages human activity that "meets the needs of the present without compromising the ability of future generations to meet their own needs" (World Commission on Environment and Development 43). Under this ethic, current decisions need to take into account long-term impacts on the environment as well as on society and human institutions. For public speakers, the ethic of sustainability entails an obligation to consider how our messages are constructive or destructive in relation to future generations, not just our own.

Many college students are actively involved in speaking out about issues of sustainability. For example, a group of thirty students met with elected officials in Washington, D.C., to share the Evangelical Youth Climate Initiative, a declaration signed by more than 1,500 Christian college students. Their declaration emphasized the need to address climate change in relation to the long-term needs of natural and social systems: "We seek a secure nation that is economically and environmentally sound for generations to come" (Evangelical Youth Climate Initiative). Ben Lowe, a student at Wheaton College who was part of the delegation to Washington, also appealed to the ethic of stewardship in explaining his support for the Initiative: "Making the world safer for our generation, and for their grandchildren, is not exclusively Republican or Democratic; it is a moral issue, and the faithful expression of God's people" ("Cooling Our Future").

CASE CONCLUSION

Carlos Serves His Community through Public Speaking

As the speaking event approached, Carlos thought about what he was going to try to accomplish in his speech. He decided that the central theme would be to help his listeners understand how their immigration status might affect college admission, financial aid, and other opportunities.

Carlos found connections with issues surrounding immigration on many levels of communication. The more he focused on the issue, the more he found himself in interpersonal conversations with friends outside of class. He also was regularly engaged in group communication at his MEChA meetings. And it seemed that every time he picked up a newspaper or turned on the television, immigration issues immediately grabbed his attention through those forms of mass communication.

It was not surprising that immigration was a prominent topic in the news, since it has important public dimensions. Especially in his state of California, speakers were addressing audiences about immigration all the time—during electoral campaigns, rallies for ballot initiatives, and even on campus. In addition, all the personal stories involving legal and illegal immigrants could easily be connected to broader public concerns about social services, taxes, and race relations. And since much of the discussion about immigration was directly related to official action—legislation, law enforcement, university policies—the exercise of power was always involved in those discussions.

Carlos had to think carefully about how best to communicate with his audience. He recognized that his own interests in immigration issues and the things that were important to him about college probably would not intersect with the interests and needs of most members of his audience. So he contacted his college's admissions office to find out what kinds of information prospective students might be interested in hearing. Carlos also learned about the questions that these students and their parents usually asked so that he could anticipate how they would be active listeners to his speech.

He also started reading newspaper and magazine articles about immigration and got materials about his school's admissions and financial aid process. Not only did this give him a sense of what might be on his audience's mind, it also gave him the knowledge he needed to assemble an effective speech.

Carlos's speech went well. His audience seemed to have a great deal of respect for him, not only because he was well-informed about his topic but also because he displayed true concern for his audience and their success. He shared his own story about struggling to get to college and how he wanted to give something back to his community. And rather than using the event to generate anger that would do little to help these students, he inspired them with his own success story and the experiences of successful Latino alumni. In the end, Carlos was not only empowering these students; he was helping to make his society more democratic and more just.

Summary

WHY STUDY PUBLIC SPEAKING?

- Public speaking can strengthen your performance in other classes.
- Public speaking can help you to achieve success at work.
- Public speaking can enhance important moments in your personal life.
- Public speaking empowers you as a citizen, allowing you to effectively engage with your community and address political issues.

WHAT IS PUBLIC SPEAKING?

- Public speaking involves developing and maintaining positive relationships and negotiating meaning with others.
- Public speaking is typically more formal and structured than interpersonal communication, more speaker-centered than group communication, and more interactive than mass communication.
- Public speaking gains its public character as it addresses audiences, common interests, and the exercise of power.

THREE MODELS OF PUBLIC SPEAKING

- The transmission model depicts public speaking as a form of one-way communication from the speaker to the audience.
- The speech communication model emphasizes the ongoing transaction between speaker and audience; audiences are active participants in the communication process.
- The public sphere model contributes to the ongoing circulation of discourse in the public sphere and helps to create publics around issues of common interest.

PUBLIC SPEAKING AND DEMOCRACY

- While public speaking traditionally has been connected to political decision making, the theories and the practices of effective public speaking have constantly shifted between an elite focus and a more democratic focus.
- The contemporary public sphere exhibits increasing diversity in speakers, speaking styles, issues, and publics.

ETHICAL DIMENSIONS OF PUBLIC SPEAKING

- Ethical speaking focuses on your character and credibility as a speaker by relying on sound knowledge, being honest about your evidence and your motives, and keeping the audience's interests at the forefront of your thinking.
- Be attentive to whether your emotional appeals represent fair judgments and are consistent with reasonable arguments.
- Use supporting materials accurately and fairly, and avoid patterns of reasoning that undermine your audience's ability to make rational choices among alternatives.
- Ethical public speaking should be consistent with fundamental social commitments, such as democratic participation, social justice, and sustainable natural and social systems.

Key Terms

civic engagement, p. 6
political engagement, p. 6
cognitive engagement, p. 6
public voice, p. 6
communication, p. 7
interpersonal communication, p. 8
group communication, p. 8
mass communication, p. 9
transmission model, p. 12
speech communication model, p. 14

public sphere model, p. 15
circulation, p. 16
public discourse, p. 17
public, p. 17
ethics, p. 22
ethos, p. 22
pathos, p. 22
logos, p. 22
fallacies, p. 28

Comprehension

1. Identify three ways in which public speaking can help you in other classes.

2. What is the difference between political and civic engagement?

3. How does public speaking differ from group communication?

4. What are three ways in which public speaking can have a public dimension?

5. What are the problems with the transmission model of communication?

6. What practical implications can public speakers draw from the public sphere model and the idea of circulation?

7. In what ways is diversity exhibited in the contemporary public sphere?

8. What are the three basic appeals that are used in public speaking?

9. Are emotional appeals inherently unethical? Why or why not?

Application

1. Ask your instructor or alumni office to get you into contact with some alumni of your school. Interview them about the importance of public speaking and communication skills in their work, their personal life, and their public life. Share your results with your class.

2. Using a copy of your local or campus newspaper, identify articles that have the clearest "public" dimensions and those that are the least publicly relevant. Discuss your conclusions with your classmates.

3. Identify a prominent speech by an elected official or spokesperson for an organization. Working with your classmates, see whether you

can produce a public sphere model of messages circulating around that speech. Identify some prior public messages that may have influenced the speech and subsequent messages that were influenced by the speech.

4. Examine a list of your state's legislators and/or the issues they addressed during their last session. Discuss the extent to which these speakers and issues exhibit diversity.

5. Go to a public speech on your campus or in your community. Identify all the ways in which the speaker appeals to his or her ethos. Also, see whether there are other messages—newspaper articles, flyers, or the introduction of the speaker—that contribute to the speakers' ethos.

2

Developing and Delivering Your First Speech

This chapter is intended to help you:

- Follow a process for developing your first speech
- Organize your speech with a clear introduction, body, and conclusion
- Manage your nervousness
- Identify the main areas for enhancing your delivery

Your first speech is an opportunity to build a foundational set of skills for public speaking. This chapter introduces four broad skills that you will develop throughout this course. The first two, inventing your speech and organizing your speech, focus on speech content. **Invention** refers to the generation of ideas, strategies, and appeals for a speech. This is the creative process of topic development, audience analysis, and research to build the content of your speech. After you have generated these ideas, you can turn to **arrangement**, the process of organizing your ideas and appeals strategically to help you accomplish your purpose. This chapter will address general principles of speech organization; later chapters will offer detailed strategies for specific purposes.

CASE SCENARIO

Faye's First Speech

Faye was excited about her first speech in her public speaking class. She was excited because she was passionate about the idea of human rights and looked forward to any opportunity she might have to talk about it. The assignment for her first speech was to raise awareness about a public issue connected to her life, and she had a few ideas for what she would say in her speech.

On the other hand, Faye was a little anxious. She had recently come to the United States from Malaysia and was not sure what her audience knew about life in Malaysia. In addition, she often got nervous among people she did not know very well, and in the past, her voice had trembled when she spoke in front of a group. Fayed hoped that her public speaking class would give her some techniques for dealing with her nervousness.

The second half of this chapter focuses on speech performance, starting with a section on building your confidence. Nervousness is inevitable for public speakers, no matter how experienced they are, so it is important to learn techniques that can help you to manage those feelings and build your confidence. This added confidence can help you to improve your delivery skills. The final section of the chapter offers concrete advice for how to work on your delivery skills while you rehearse your speech. ■

Inventing Your Speech

Inventing your speech is the first major step in public speaking. Whether you are in the classroom or in other public settings, you will typically have some guidance about the overall purpose of the speech at the beginning of the invention process. For example, your first speech assignment might take one of these forms:

- *Speech of introduction.* You are assigned to introduce yourself or a classmate to the rest of the class.

- *One-point speech.* You are assigned to identify a single idea and support it with several reasons or pieces of evidence.

- *Personal belief speech.* You are assigned to explain why you have come to hold some belief or opinion.

- *Campus or community issue speech.* You are assigned to raise awareness of an important issue that affects you and your classmates.

Each assignment gives some boundaries to the invention process. But no matter what your assignment or speaking situation, the invention process involves four basic tasks: thinking about your topic, thinking about your audience and occasion, determining your purpose and central idea, and providing support for your central idea. This section provides guidelines and questions for each of those tasks.

Thinking about Your Topic

Even if your speech assignment gives you clear directions about the purpose of the speech, you may have flexibility in selecting the specific topic. That does not necessarily make your job as a speaker easier! You might feel as if you have nothing interesting to say; alternatively, you might feel completely overwhelmed by all the things you would like to discuss. No matter what, get started early to give yourself time to think about potential topics rather than picking one randomly or quickly.

Two common techniques for generating topic ideas are brainstorming and taking a personal inventory. **Brainstorming**, or generating many ideas rapidly without criticizing, analyzing, or discarding any of them, is a terrific way to jump-start your thinking about speech topics. Write down these ideas or record them, or have a friend jot them down as you produce the ideas. Later, you can use the list to identify ideas that might work for your speech.

Taking a personal inventory offers a more structured way to generate potential topics. This technique uses a set of categories to guide thinking about your own experiences, knowledge, and interests. Even if you think your experiences and concerns are boring or mundane, they can be good choices for a first classroom speech. Those topics can resonate with audience members, who might think, "Yes, a similar thing happened to me" or "That matters to me, too," and help you to build connections with your classmates. Both your commonalities and your unique qualities can lead you to an interesting speech (see Figure 2.1).

After you have identified several topics, begin to narrow your down your list. To help you home in on good topics, consider a few general guidelines:

- *Speak on a topic that is familiar to you.* This is especially important for your first speech to help you minimize speech anxiety. You will have a much easier time speaking about something that you are already comfortable discussing rather than struggling with a topic that is new, unfamiliar, or complicated.

- *Make your topic concrete rather than abstract.* **Concrete words** and topics refer to specific, tangible things, while **abstract words** and topics direct our attention to ideas or concepts. For a first speech, it will be easier and more interesting if you talk about something concrete. Instead of talking about the abstract idea of "freedom" with vague generalities and clichés, talk about specific situations related to freedom. Can students demonstrate freely on your campus? What challenges do international students face in entering or leaving the country?

FIGURE 2.1

TAKING A PERSONAL INVENTORY

Use the categories below to stimulate your thinking about speech topics. After you have generated some ideas, you can think about which ideas might work best for your specific speech assignment. The descriptions below, for example, reflect on how personal experiences might connect with public issues.

Places you have lived. Your experiences are largely shaped by your surroundings. I grew up on a farm in rural Minnesota, so my childhood experiences are very different from my wife's, who grew up in Seattle. I vividly recall playing in the woods and working in the corn fields, while she fondly remembers the great cultural diversity among her friends and in her community. Each of these memories could be recalled through a specific story and could be connected to a public issue—for example, the decline in family farms or the benefits of cultural diversity.

Even ordinary places can be a rich source for speech ideas about public issues. Try a Google search for "Walmart controversy" and see what you discover.

Jobs you have had. Your work experience can be a rich source of ideas. Many people love telling or hearing stories about a "worst job." While these can be entertaining, they also can lead to important public issues. But just about any job can do. For example, I detasseled corn on a hybrid corn farm when I was 14. That experience could lead to a speech about child labor, genetically modified organisms, farm subsidies, or the role of corn in the U.S. food system.

Trips you have taken. Just like places you have lived, trips you have taken can suggest interesting topics. For example, a backcountry trip might lead to a speech about wildlife or national parks. Think not only about the destination, but also about your preparation for the trip, how you got there, and things you saw and people you met along the way.

Hobbies you have pursued. While hobbies may seem to be purely matters of individual interest, they often connect to interesting public issues. Your experiences playing guitar, for example, might intersect with issues about the music industry. Or, your experiences with computers and online activity may lead to reflection about issues of privacy.

Groups you have joined. Every organization has some purpose or mission it is trying to fulfill, which gives it the potential for public significance. Your work with a service organization, an advocacy group, a religious community, or a political party can give you first-hand knowledge about these issues.

Challenges you have faced. Stories about overcoming adversity strike a chord with many audience members. They can be inspiring to others, and they often indicate larger public problems. Speaking about the challenges of aiding an ill family member can point to a whole host of issues related to health care.

- *Limit the scope of your topic.* Your topic needs to be limited enough that you can speak about it adequately in the time available. For example, a speech that is shorter than five minutes probably cannot cover the history of your college. However, you might be able to inform your audience about the history of a particular tradition on your campus.

Thinking about Your Audience and the Occasion

Deciding on your topic also requires you to consider your particular audience and the specific occasion of the speech. You already know this from your own experiences; you probably talk differently about your classes with your friends than you do with your parents. The occasion matters, too; speaking at a wedding in a place of religious worship is a different occasion from making a toast at the reception afterward. Your choice of topic needs to account for these differences in audience and occasion.

Later chapters will address adaptation in more detail. For now, keep in mind these basic questions as you develop your topic and compose your speech:

- *How can you make this topic relevant to your audience?* In college classrooms, topics such as graduation requirements or parking availability have direct relevance. Other topics might require you to make the connection explicit so that your audience can perceive the relevance to their lives. For example, if you are talking about your upbringing in a mixed-race family, you might connect this to the challenges and joys of family life in general or to current public issues about race in society.

- *What is the knowledge level of your audience?* Because you are addressing your audience for the first time, you might know little about them and probably cannot expect them to have in-depth knowledge on any particular topic. The importance of saving money for retirement might be an accessible topic, but a speech detailing the financial problems of a federal pension insurance program will probably be too technical and appear irrelevant as well.

- *What style of speaking is appropriate for the occasion?* Class presentations, business reports, and religious ceremonies are just a few examples of occasions at which audiences usually expect a more formal style of speaking. If you are too informal, your audience might not take you seriously or might think that you do not respect them. Conversely, excessive formality in a casual setting can hurt a speaker's connection with an audience. Speaking in a very formal style and wearing a business suit probably would not be appropriate when speaking to your residence hall meeting.

- *What purpose does the audience expect on this occasion?* The occasion also shapes an audience's expectations about appropriate rhetorical purposes.

THE ETHICAL DIMENSION

Adapting to the Occasion

The importance of adapting to the occasion can be seen in speeches at funeral services. In August 2009, the private memorial service for Senator Ted Kennedy involved "music, laughter and plenty of anecdotes about Edward Kennedy's ferocious sense of humor and kindnesses shown to strangers who soon became friends" ("Family, Political Luminaries"). One report of the event stated that speakers steered away from discussing current political events at the service because of what had happened at a 2002 memorial service for another Senator, Paul Wellstone.

Wellstone's death occurred near the end of his reelection campaign, throwing the election into uncertainty as to who might fill Wellstone's spot on the ballot. The memorial generated significant public attention, in part because of how some speakers responded to the occasion. Rick Kahn, a longtime friend of Wellstone and treasurer for his campaigns, gave a passionate speech that attempted to rally support for the Democratic candidate who would replace Wellstone on the ballot. "We are begging you all to help us win the Senate election for Paul Wellstone. We need to win this election for Paul Wellstone," said Kahn at one point in his speech (McCallum). Wellstone's son Mark and U.S. Senator Tom Harkin followed with energetic speeches that urged listeners to continue Wellstone's legacy with support in the remaining days of the campaign. Afterward, Wellstone's political opponents and some media reports criticized the speakers for turning the memorial into a political rally. Governor Jesse Ventura had even walked out in the middle of the event. Other people viewed the overall tone of the event as consistent with Wellstone's life as a fierce

Mark Wellstone's speech at his father's memorial service urged political action. Was this ethically appropriate?

political advocate and an understandable reaction to a tragic and unusual occasion.

WHAT DO YOU THINK?

1. How would you define the occasion of this speech?
2. What style of speaking do you think is appropriate for speaking on this occasion about this person?
3. Listen to some of the eulogies for Wellstone at the following website:

   http://news.minnesota.publicradio.org/features/200210/25_khoom_wellstoneobit/memorialservice.shtml

   How would you judge their appropriateness?

Is it appropriate for a commencement speaker at a public high school to testify about his or her religious faith? What is appropriate to say at a memorial ceremony for a political figure? (See The Ethical Dimension for an example.) In most instances, speakers try to follow cultural norms and fulfill audience expectations; sometimes, though, speakers may violate these expectations to shock the audience or to call attention to the situation itself.

Determining Your Purpose and Central Idea

After thinking about potential topics, your audience, and the occasion, you should generate a few key statements that will help you to clarify the focus of your speech. First, determine the general purpose of your speech. Then create a specific purpose that is tailored to your particular audience, and on the basis of your specific purpose, craft the central idea of your speech.

The **general purpose** of your speech is its overall goal or the desired effect of your speech. This book focuses on the general purposes of informing, persuading, and commemorating. (For this first assignment, be sure to clarify the general purpose of your speech assignment with your instructor.) Your **specific purpose** identifies your desired effect on this particular audience with this particular topic. In other words, it helps you to connect your general purpose to the particular speaking event.

For example, suppose that you started with the topic "bicycling in your community" and then narrowed that topic to "bike lanes in our city." For this topic, a general and a specific purpose might look like this:

General purpose: To inform

Specific purpose: To inform my audience about changes in bicycle lanes on city streets

Or you might attempt to persuade your audience that the bicycle lane situation is a problem or that it should be changed. Some examples might be as follows:

General purpose: To persuade

Specific purpose: To persuade my audience that our city is not providing adequate support for alternative modes of transportation

or

General purpose: To persuade

Specific purpose: To persuade my audience that bike lanes should be established near campus

Even a commemorative speech could be rooted in a speech about bicycling. As with the other examples, the specific purpose situates the general purpose within a particular topic.

General purpose: To commemorate

Specific purpose: To celebrate with my audience the joys of bicycling

The **central idea** of your speech is the one-sentence statement that you want your audience to accept by the end of the speech. This statement expands on the specific purpose and is what you will actually say in your speech.

For example, for the specific purposes described above, these would be appropriate central ideas:

> Largeville is decreasing the number of bicycle lanes on city streets.
>
> Maxtown's support for carpooling and bicycling is inadequate.
>
> Littleville and our college should cooperate to establish bicycle lanes within a mile of our campus.

The phrase *central idea* is synonymous with concepts that you may have heard or read about in other courses, such as *main claim* or *thesis statement*. Whether in speaking or in writing, the ability to craft a clear and concise central idea is a fundamental skill that is necessary for success in the classroom and beyond.

Providing Support for Your Central Idea

In a good conversation, people often respond to provocative ideas with questions that elicit more information: *Why do you think that? Could you say more about this? What's your proof for that?* In public speaking, listeners have the same questions, so speakers need to provide support to answer those questions.

The types of supporting material for your first speech may be dictated by your specific assignment. You may be asked to focus on **personal experience**, or events that have happened to you, by telling a story about an incident in your life. Your experience of studying in a foreign country, for example, might have proved to you why second language instruction is necessary for all high school students. Or you may be asked to introduce a classmate using a general theme, such as "Barry is an accomplished athlete." In this case, you would use several **examples**, or specific instances of Barry's athletic successes, to support the general theme.

If you are encouraged to do some research for your speech, you might try to find **testimony**, or the words of others, that back up your central idea. Speaking about tuition on your campus could be more effective if you included a quote from someone who is affected by an increase or from an administrator who works on your college's budget. Similarly, outside research can lead you to **statistics**, numbers that summarize specific instances or express relationships. If you claim that your city does not provide adequate support for alternative transportation, your audience probably would like to see some figures compared over time.

These types of supporting material, along with their strengths and limitations, will be discussed in more detail later in this book. For a first classroom speech, expectations for supporting material are usually modest. No matter how much supporting material you use in any speech, though, you must meet a few important ethical criteria:

- *Supporting material must be accurate.* Personal experiences and examples must be true. Testimony must reflect the person's exact words and not be taken out of context to distort his or her meaning. Statistics must be gathered through sound methods and not biased to advance a particular point of view.

- *Supporting material from outside sources must be acknowledged.* **Plagiarism,** the use of another person's words or ideas without citing the source, is a significant violation of academic ethics. It might seem like extra work to acknowledge your sources, but doing so can enhance your credibility as a speaker (Reynolds and Reynolds).

To avoid plagiarism, plan to cite the source of any words or ideas that are not your own. As you will learn throughout this book, a good citation includes three pieces of information: author, date, and publication. In other words, tell your audience *who* said it, *when* they said it, and *the source* where the words or ideas can be found. For example:

> In the April 28, 2008, edition of *Time Magazine,* obstetrician William Callaghan is quoted as saying, "We put a lot of emotional, psychological, and spiritual value around birthing."

Check with your instructor to clarify citation expectations for your first speech.

Organizing Your Speech

Once you have invented the central idea and generated the primary content of your speech, you can move on to organize your speech. For your first speech, a very simple, three-part organizational pattern should serve you well: introduction, body, conclusion. This section of the chapter will start with tips on the introduction, then move to tips on the body and tips on the conclusion. As you organize your speech, however, plan the body first. After you are satisfied with the body, it will be easier to compose the introduction and conclusion.

Tips on the Introduction

An **introduction**, the opening sentences of a speech, serves many functions. For a short speech, focus on two functions in particular: *arousing the audience's attention* and *preparing them for the rest of the speech.*

Arousing the Audience's Attention   To arouse the audience's attention, try to create a virtual experience for your audience that leads directly to your central idea. For example, you might use adjectives and active verbs to vividly describe an experience or an example that illustrates your central idea. Consider how the following two sentences use very different language to describe the same situation:

> Darcy ran to the finish line and won.
>
> Darcy sprinted fiercely, lunging through the yellow tape for a victory.

Creative language choices are one way to arouse the audience's attention in an introduction. Another common tactic is to begin with a shocking statistic or a provocative quotation. A speech about a campus problem such as sexual assault or binge drinking can be illustrated through a surprising statistic or the words of someone who has firsthand experience with the issue.

No matter what tactic you use, an effective introduction in a classroom speech often moves the audience from the classroom to another part of the world. By doing so, you not only encourage your audience to actively imagine that world but also set the stage for the possibility of civic or political engagement.

Preparing the Audience for the Rest of the Speech For most speeches, preparing the audience for the rest of your speech involves stating your central idea in the introduction. Stating your central idea lets your audience know the focus of your speech and suggests where the rest of the speech is likely to go. Just like taking a walk or a drive, it helps to know your destination ahead of time.

In addition, many introductions include a **preview**, a statement that tells your audience how you will proceed through your speech. This statement usually comes after the statement of your central idea. It might briefly mention your main points or state the main sections of your speech so that your audience understands your organizational strategy. If the central idea is your destination, the preview is the road map.

Once you have finished your introduction, use voice and body changes to signal a change in the direction of your speech. For example, at the end of your introduction, you can use a brief pause to set that part of the speech apart from the body that will follow. Also, consider taking a few steps or directing eye contact to the other side of the room. These shifts reinforce the movement in the speech itself.

Tips on the Body

The **body** is the middle and largest portion of the speech and is the heart of the speech; it is where you present your information or persuasive argument. You will learn several organizational patterns in chapters 9 and 13, but two patterns are often useful for many first speech assignments: chronological order and topical order.

Chronological Order With **chronological order**, you present ideas and events in the order in which they actually happened. For example, a speech of introduction might discuss important moments in your life by starting with your childhood and ending with the most recent events. Or a speech to inform your audience about a proposal on your campus or community might explain how that proposal got started and changed over time.

PUBLIC SPOTLIGHT

Les Skramstad

Speaking on a topic that was familiar to him, Les Skramstad was able to bring attention to a serious public health problem in his community. Les lived in Libby, Montana, where the Zonolite and W.R. Grace companies operated a vermiculite mine for many years. The vermiculite was contaminated with asbestos, a mineral that can lead to lung diseases and cancer. Les worked at the mine in the late 1950s and later developed asbestosis and mesothelioma, a severe form of cancer.

Les used concrete words, personal experiences, and specific examples to inform his audience about working conditions at the mine:

"We backed the truck up to a huge pile of stuff and loaded it with our hands. It was pure asbestos. . . . I remember the boss came over to us and said, 'We have so much asbestos up here we have to find a market for it. If we do, we'll be in business forever.' I only worked at that mine for two and a half years. But they had us down on our hands and knees sorting through the asbestos. They wanted the asbestos to be pure. They were trying to see if they could manufacture a product out of it. . . . By the time we were done, we'd go home covered with asbestos dust. The kids would hug me and get it all over themselves. Norita would wash my clothes and she'd get contaminated. We had no idea it was lethal. No one at the mine ever said a word" (Bowker 8-9).

Eventually, Les's wife Norita and several of his children developed lung diseases. Using chronological order, Les often told his story by first describing working conditions at the mine and then talking about the effects that working at the mine had on his family:

"Never in my wildest dreams did I ever think that I was doing anything to hurt my family. That's what makes me the maddest. They gave me a job that had fatal consequences and knowingly let me take that death home to my wife and kids. You tell me, what kind of people could do that?" Les told his stories in a gentle, mild-mannered way,

but the meaning of his experience came through loud and clear (Bowker 9).

By telling his story in chronological order, Les ended on a strong point, driving home the injustice and immorality of the situation to his audiences.

Les told his story to anyone who would listen: elected leaders, government officials, journalists, scholars, and filmmakers. By telling his story in a way that generated sympathy and identification, he helped to persuade the state and federal governments to clean up asbestos contamination in Libby and to dedicate resources to health care in the community. Les died in January 2007, but the power of his story remains strong in the public discourse about asbestos exposure in Libby.

 Social Networking Spotlights

In the contemporary public sphere, social networking sites are an increasingly important means for circulating discourse about important public issues. In addition to looking at individual speakers, then, the Public Spotlight features throughout this book will also highlight related social networking sites.

- Nonprofit research foundations are using social networking platforms for fund-raising and advocacy. On its Facebook page, the Mesothelioma Applied Research Foundation has urged interested citizens to lobby Congress for a Mesothelioma Awareness Day: http://www.facebook.com/note.php?note_id=131224857784#!/meso

- Facebook also provides a sense of community for victims of diseases and their families. If you were planning a presentation on the personal toll of mesothelioma, this Facebook page would be a source of anecdotes and quotes for you to use (for more on proper attribution of such anecdotes and quotes, see chapter 12): http://www.facebook.com/note.php?note_id=131224857784#!/meso

Topical Order Using **topical order**, you simply divide your material into a series of topics or main points. Some subjects have natural divisions. A speech about a local service organization, for example, could be organized topically with main points about each part of its mission. Speeches that are persuasive or that explain why you hold some belief or opinion may use topical order to organize a series of reasons that support the central idea.

Organizational Markers In addition to using organizational patterns to structure your speech, you can include **organizational markers**, which are phrases and sentences that connect your main points and signal organizational shifts in your speech. For instance, you can use sentences to signal a connection between a specific piece of supporting material and a broader theme:

> My difficulties in biking to campus that day have led me to become concerned about bicycle lanes in our city.
>
> In light of these experiences while volunteering at the Sexual Assault Center, I'm convinced that rape is a prevalent problem on our campus.

Similarly, you can use a transitional phrase to emphasize the connection between supporting material and your central idea. For example, you might lead into your central idea with a statement such as the following:

> This experience reinforced my belief that . . .
>
> As a result, I have come to the conclusion that . . .

Perhaps the easiest organizational marker to use is a **signpost**, a simple word used at the beginning of a sentence to mark a series of related points. For example, if you have several reasons for your position, mark them by saying "First," "Second," and "Third" as you introduce each reason. These markers make it much easier for your audience to understand where you are in your speech.

Tips on the Conclusion

Your **conclusion** should reinforce your central idea and indicate the end of your speech. Initially, signal your conclusion with a pause and an organizational marker that separates the body of the speech from the conclusion. Especially in the classroom, some markers of conclusion are overused; people soon grow tired of hearing every speech end with "In conclusion, ..." So try something a little different:

> As I have shown in this speech, . . .
>
> To recap, . . .

For a speech that begins with a personal experience, an especially satisfying conclusion will come back to your introductory story and provide an update or a resolution to that story. In this case, your organizational marker is simply a statement that refers to material from the introduction.

> Think back to Les Skramstad and his family.

> Remember the difficulties with the university I described at the beginning of my speech? Things now appear to be changing for the better.

The content of your conclusion should remind the audience of your central idea. Restate your central exactly as you stated it earlier in your speech. In addition, try to leave your audience with a memorable quotation, dramatic statement, or call to action that you want your audience to associate with your speech. Finally, use your voice and body to clearly signal that you have finished speaking. In the rest of this chapter, we will further discuss voice and body techniques that will help you reinforce your verbal message.

Building Your Confidence

Almost everyone has some degree of anxiety about speaking in public. For some people, that fear can be intense. One survey in the United States found that the number of people who reported **speech anxiety**—the unpleasant physical and psychological responses to public speaking situations—ranked second only to the number who reported a fear of snakes (Gallup)! If you are feeling anxiety about your speech, your classmates and other audiences surely sympathize with you. But this might not give you much comfort. Just because they may feel similar about public speaking does not change the fact that you feel nervous and are the one who has to give the speech. What can you do?

Understanding Your Nervousness

Understanding the symptoms, causes, and timing of speech anxiety are an important first step toward speaking with confidence. Armed with this general knowledge, you can observe your own unique patterns of speech anxiety and then figure out the best ways to deal with it.

Our definition of speech anxiety indicates two main types of symptoms:

- *Physical symptoms*, such as an increased heart rate, noticeable sweating, the sense of butterflies in your stomach, trembling hands, a dry mouth
- *Psychological symptoms*, such as worry, fear, denial, or irritability

Physical symptoms are mostly involuntary responses to situations that are perceived to be threatening or uncertain. Remember how you felt on your first day of college, when interviewing for a job, or when approaching someone for a date. These kinds of situations can trigger the flow of adrenaline, signaling to your body that something important is about to happen.

As you recognize these physical symptoms and start thinking about your situation, psychological symptoms emerge. You might start worrying about your performance or turn your attention to something else. But these feelings are not inevitable. They are shaped by the beliefs and concerns that influence your perception of the situation. If those beliefs are incorrect or if the concerns are exaggerated, they can lead you to be far more anxious about speaking than you need to be. Consider how the following beliefs and concerns might heighten anxiety about public speaking:

- *"I don't know what's going to happen."* Uncertainty is a source of nervousness for virtually all public speakers. If you have had little experience with public speaking, the entire process can be discomforting. But uncertainty can be pegged to more specific sources, too. You might feel uncertainty about how to prepare, about the setting in which you will speak, or about how the question and answer period will go. Your audience can be a major source of uncertainty. In the classroom, your first speech may involve listeners whom you do not know very well. More generally, you might think that listeners will pounce on every possible mistake. Some uncertainty cannot be avoided, but you can learn how to reduce some sources of uncertainty and think differently about other sources.

- *"I'm going to look weird, sound funny, and screw up."* Concerns about your *performance* are normal. It is common for public speakers to be worried about trembling or shaking, having their mind go blank, being unable to speak, doing something embarrassing, or making no sense (Stein, Walker, and Forde). The physical symptoms, if they occur, feed into these worries. But many of these occurrences are rare, and when they do happen, listeners are not necessarily bothered by them. Listeners might not even notice that your hand is trembling or that you forgot a sentence. So while these concerns are normal and real, be wary of exaggerating their effect on the real focus of your speech: your audience.

- *"This speech will make or break me."* Another understandable concern among speakers is the *consequences* that a particular speech might have. In the classroom, an obvious consequence of speaking is one's grade. In the workplace, the consequence might be securing a deal to get a bonus or defending your performance to save your job. In the political arena, a speech might be seen as the crucial factor for advancing a program. Although we like to think that speeches have such direct effects, in most areas of life there are other contributing factors. Even in the classroom, your grade will usually be determined by several factors (such as the quality of your outline and your research), not just your performance. The paradox is that worrying excessively about your performance can distract you from doing the very things that lead to effective communication in the first place (MacIntyre, Thivierge, and MacDonald).

From what you have learned so far, you can probably make some educated guesses about when speakers tend to feel high levels of anxiety. Much speech anxiety is really a matter of **anticipatory anxiety**, or anxiety that is felt before speech performance. Research among college students shows that the typical student feels most nervous during the minute immediately before the speech (Behnke and Sawyer). As the adrenaline rush occurs and speakers become acutely aware that they will be on display, it is not surprising that this moment is typically one of high anxiety. Another moment of anxiety occurs during the instructor's explanation of the assignment. Uncertainty is generally high at that point, and attention to evaluation and grading of the assignment heightens awareness of the speech's consequences.

Now that you know a bit more about the dynamics of nervousness, how do you deal with it? The next two sections provide concrete tips for building confidence during the preparation of your speech and handling nervousness during the presentation itself. Since anticipatory anxiety is such a major factor in speech anxiety, extra attention will be given to preperformance tips.

Gaining Confidence during Preparation

The best thing you can do to minimize nervousness and enhance the quality of your presentation is to prepare your speech well ahead of your performance. This might seem obvious, but there are several aspects of speech preparation that can help you to minimize, if not eliminate, some subtle sources of anxiety. Advance preparation allows you to do the following:

- *Select your topic and purpose wisely.* Picking something at the last minute will heighten your uncertainty about the speech. In contrast, you will have confidence about topics that you are familiar with and that interest both you and your audience.

- *Increase your familiarity with the content and organization of your speech.* The more time you devote to researching and learning about your topic, the more confident you will feel. Similarly, you will feel less worried about making mistakes or losing your place if you have developed a well-organized speech.

- *Learn about your audience.* In the rush to finish their speeches, students who delay often ignore audience analysis and adaptation. This makes it all the more difficult to gauge the likely consequences of your speech.

- *Focus attention on your introduction.* The better you know your introduction, the better you will feel during that minute before your speech.

These tips will not make anxiety disappear, but they can help you to enter a speaking situation with confidence that you have assembled a solid speech.

Advance preparation also gives you the time to *develop an effective outline or set of note cards* and to *rehearse your speech multiple times.* Later in this chapter, you will learn how to create note cards and how to focus your rehearsals. But in terms of anxiety, hasty production of speaking notes increases your chance of making mistakes and can leave you feeling uncertain during your performance. Taking time to prepare note cards gives you a chance to think through all the elements of your speech. Likewise, when you have the opportunity to rehearse your speech, you can correct potential problems and work on your strengths outside the public spotlight.

Finally, *get to know your audience on a personal level.* Especially in the classroom, you will find that most of your classmates are as nervous about speaking as you are. This is helpful to remember when you see everyone looking at you when you speak. And as you develop relationships with your classmates, many of those eyes will become sources of comfort rather than anxiety. Contributing to a positive environment among your classmates pays off in many ways, not the least of which is less anxiety for everyone on speech days.

Managing Nervousness on the Day of Your Speech

Because symptoms of anxiety are both physical and psychological, you will want to have some ideas for dealing with both of those dimensions. On the day of your speech—and in some instance, even before that—the following techniques can help you to manage your nervousness:

- *Take care of your needs for rest and food.* Get a good night's sleep before your speech; a late night on the town will keep you from performing at your best and is often easier to spot than any problems with the content of your speech. Also, eat normal and healthy meals to keep your body in balance.

- *Use relaxation techniques.* Consciously attending to your breathing is a time-honored relaxation technique for body and mind. As you are waiting to speak, take several slow, deep breaths. This helps to slow your heart rate and consequently can minimize the other physical symptoms associated with speech anxiety. In addition, try consciously relaxing your parts of your body, starting with your feet and moving upward

- *Use positive self-talk.* This is sometimes called **cognitive restructuring**, or mentally reframing your thoughts and perceptions. When negative thoughts come up, transform them into positive affirmations. For example, negative thoughts could develop like this: "I am going to make a mistake. My speech will be ruined. I will get really embarrassed and look really stupid." These thoughts can be changed to "If I lose my place in my speech or make a mistake, it's not the end of the world. My friends in the audience will get a mental break while I look at my notes and move on to the next point." Consider writing out your personal fears and converting them into positive statements.

- *Redirect your nervous energy.* Cognitive restructuring also can shift your perception of the physical symptoms of anxiety. Since the nervous energy surrounding public speaking is normal, you need not think about that energy as fear or worry. Instead, think of it as *positive energy* waiting to be unleashed as part of your speech.

- *Visualize and embody success.* Envision your speech exactly as you want it to happen, from walking into class, to starting your speech, to the round of applause you receive at the end. Imagine your presentation occurring just as you would like it to happen. Make your visualizations a reality by carrying yourself with confidence. Your posture, facial expressions, and responsiveness to supportive audience members can enhance your confidence during the performance.

Delivering Your Speech

After all of the hard work of developing your speech, the time will finally come to deliver the speech. For a first classroom speech, try not to think in terms of perfection; neither your instructor nor your classmates are expecting that anyone is going to give a perfectly polished speech. Instead, use the first speech as an opportunity to identify your areas of strengths as well as areas for improvement. One of the most satisfying aspects of a public speaking class is seeing your improvement as you get more comfortable, more experienced, and more skilled at public speaking.

In most introductory public speaking courses, you will focus **extemporaneous speaking**, a delivery style that involves advance preparation and rehearsal of a speech that is neither fully written nor memorized. For this type of delivery, speakers develop note cards or an outline but do not write out their speech as if it were an essay. In chapter 12, you will learn about other delivery styles that are appropriate for certain occasions; but for your first speech, work on extemporaneous delivery.

Constructing Your Delivery Notes

For your first speech, a short outline or a set of note cards should be sufficient for rehearsing your speech. (For longer speeches, it is useful to prepare two outlines: a preparation outline and a speaking outline. Chapter 11 discusses these types of outlines.) Whether you use an outline or a set of notes is largely a matter of personal preference. A short outline can be placed on a lectern or held in your hand, eliminating the need to shuffle through a series of cards and avoiding the risk of dropping cards. However, some people find note cards easier to use. Because only a few notes can fit on one card, it can be easier to keep track of your place in the speech with cards than with an outline. Ask your instructor before your first speech whether he or she has preferences or specific requirements.

Whether you use an outline or note cards, keep in mind these basic guidelines for preparing delivery notes (see Figure 2.2):

FIGURE 2.2 Constructing Note Cards

These cards illustrate the basic guidelines for preparing delivery notes.

Less Effective:

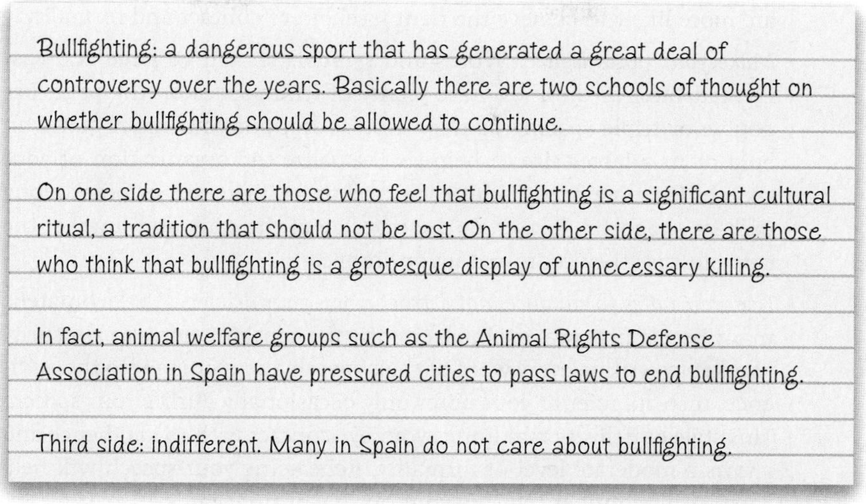

> Bullfighting: a dangerous sport that has generated a great deal of controversy over the years. Basically there are two schools of thought on whether bullfighting should be allowed to continue.
>
> On one side there are those who feel that bullfighting is a significant cultural ritual, a tradition that should not be lost. On the other side, there are those who think that bullfighting is a grotesque display of unnecessary killing.
>
> In fact, animal welfare groups such as the Animal Rights Defense Association in Spain have pressured cities to pass laws to end bullfighting.
>
> Third side: indifferent. Many in Spain do not care about bullfighting.

This card is essentially a word-for-word manuscript. With its small writing and lack of cues for key words and ideas, this card will do little to promote the actual delivery of the speech.

More Effective:

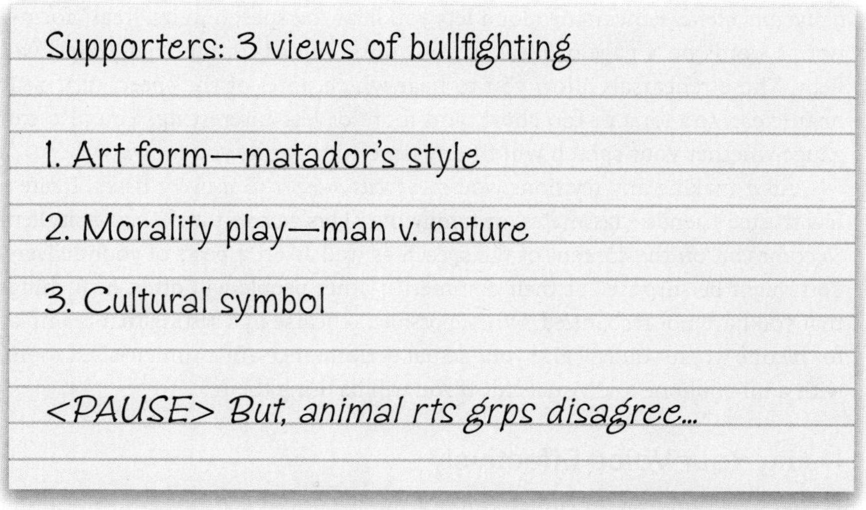

> Supporters: 3 views of bullfighting
>
> 1. Art form—matador's style
>
> 2. Morality play—man v. nature
>
> 3. Cultural symbol
>
> <PAUSE> But, animal rts grps disagree...

In contrast, this note card uses larger type, fewer words, abbreviations, plenty of white space, and delivery cues. With some practice, the speaker using these notes is far more likely to have good eye contact and a better overall delivery.

- *Be brief.* Use short phrases or single words or symbols that will remind you of what you want to say. The exception would be something that needs to be stated in precise terms: a main point, an important piece of evidence, or a quotation. By keeping your outline and notes brief, you are more likely to achieve the right level of eye contact and formality.

- *Make your notes legible.* Words and symbols should be large and easily readable. For outlines, have plenty of white space on the page; use double or triple spacing between lines. Also, put your main points in bold or in a larger size to help you visualize the organization of your speech. For note cards, limit each card to a single idea or point along with its supporting material. Use one side of the card, and number the cards in case they get mixed up or dropped.

- *Use your notes to enhance, not detract from, your delivery.* Unfortunately, many beginning speakers inadvertently use speaking notes as a security blanket by writing every word of their speech and reading it to the audience. Instead, refer to your notes only occasionally during your speech. This style of delivery maximizes your eye contact with the audience and allows a moderate level of formality. Rehearsing your speech will help you to gain confidence using your outline or note cards.

Rehearsing Your Speech

Once you have put your notes into an outline or onto a set of note cards, you are ready to begin rehearsing your speech. *For the first few times, try rehearsing aloud and alone.* Rehearsing aloud lets you hear the speech in its "real" form—not as words on a page or ideas in your mind but as sounds that people will hear. These rehearsals allow you to hear which parts of the speech are clear or unclear, too long or too short, and more or less interesting. You also can gauge whether your speech will fit any time constraints you may have.

After making any revisions, you can *focus on specific delivery issues.* Invite a few trusted friends, classmates, or family members as a test audience. Ask them to comment on the content of the speech as well as on aspects of your delivery. You might be surprised at their comments; other people will often hear things that you have not recognized. When possible, rehearse in a setting that is similar to the one where you will give your actual performance—in a similar-sized room, with a microphone and visual aids if you will be using them.

Using Your Voice Effectively

Perhaps the most significant speech of the twentieth century, Martin Luther King's "I Have a Dream" reflects the importance of voice in effective public speaking. Not only did the ideas and artistry of Dr. King's speech make it memorable; the vocal dynamics of his delivery also stirred the passion and excitement of his audience. The speech would not have had the same effect if King did not have such amazing vocal skills: powerful volume, variety in pitch, gradually increasing rate, and strategic use of pauses. While Dr. King was an extraordinary speaker, even beginning public speakers can benefit from giving attention to these aspects of delivery.

Volume Your speech must be heard to have any effect. Consequently, **volume**— the relative loudness of the speaker's voice—should be your first consideration. When you rehearse, try to create the conditions under which you will speak. Then, on the day you speak, get to the room early and pay attention to any external noises that could interfere with listening. Fans, heaters, air conditioners, students in the hallway, or things outside the building—lawn mowers, construction equipment, even the weather—all can interfere with your volume. You want to speak loudly enough to overcome those other noises.

The best gauge of appropriate volume is your audience. Watch for signs from them. If they are leaning forward or putting their hands behind their ears, they might be having trouble hearing you. Conversely, pained facial expressions from those in the front of the room or listeners pushing away from you could be a sign that your volume is overwhelming. To get your volume right, focus on listeners at the back of the room during the beginning of your speech. If they appear to be unable to hear you, adjust your volume accordingly. Then attend to the listeners who are closer to you, so that you do not overwhelm them.

Beyond the classroom, be prepared for a much broader range of speaking conditions. During conferences or public meetings, you might find yourself in a large auditorium with different volume needs. In some instances, you might be able to use a microphone at the front of the room. Do what you can to assess the room, the audience, and any distractions so that you can adapt your volume accordingly.

Rate Rate is one of the biggest challenges for many introductory public speaking students. That is because speaking **rate**—the speed at which a person speaks—can be affected by the anxiety you feel in a situation (Christenfeld and Creager). Think again about other stressful situations: Did you find yourself speaking rapidly and going on and on? Or were you hesitant to speak, stammering through sentences and speaking slowly? As you prepare your speech, you might need to adjust your rate to compensate for your anxiety.

Rehearsal provides many opportunities for working on your speaking rate. Record your speech and listen to it, or have your rehearsal listeners give you feedback. Then you can decide whether you need to consciously adjust your rate during your speech. If you are worried about exceeding time constraints, you can cut portions of the speech so that you will not feel rushed. This has the added benefit of helping to reduce your anxiety, which may help you to maintain a moderate rate. Finally, you can identify specific rate changes that can contribute to the mood of a speech or enhance your message. For example, if you are revealing a startling statistic, you might consider slowing down during that portion of the speech to emphasize the seriousness of the issue.

Pitch   **Pitch** designates where a sound lies on the musical spectrum. On one end are high-pitched sounds that come out the treble or tweeter speakers on a stereo. On the other end are low-pitched sounds that come out of the woofer or bass speaker. If you have ever listened to just one of the speakers on a stereo, you know that it can be unpleasant if you listen for a long period of time. Consequently, your speaking pitch generally should be aimed toward the middle of the spectrum.

Some inflection, or variability in pitch, is good as long as it is not overly dramatic. A voice that lacks variation in pitch, such as the teacher's voice in *Ferris Bueller's Day Off,* is referred to as a monotone and should be avoided. Conversely, some beginning speakers end all of their sentences with rising pitch—every sentence sounds like a question. While unintentional, this pattern of inflection leaves the impression that the speaker is uncertain about his or her comments. This can hurt your credibility, so be aware of this pattern.

Pauses   Among the ways to use your voice to create an effect, perhaps none is more powerful than *not* using your voice. A **pause**, or brief period of silence in a speech, interrupt the flow of words. Like written punctuation marks, pauses can add structure and meaning to your actual words. They can be used to signal a change of idea, to create rhythm or suspense, or to let the audience dwell on an important point in your speech.

For example, read the following sentences aloud twice, the first time as you would normally read them and the second time with a definite pause between the sentences:

> Homeschooling clearly creates a better social environment for students. Another strength of homeschooling is the greater capacity for individualized instruction.

Note how in the first reading, the two sentences sound like a series of short items in a list. Adding the pause, however, sets off the second sentence more distinctly as a separate, unique idea.

During preparation, note places in your speech where pause would be appropriate, and mark them on your outline or note cards by writing PAUSE. Then during rehearsal, ask your listeners whether they can reiterate your main points. If they have difficulty, you might want to include pauses (as well as transitional markers, described in chapter 11) to make the main portions of your speech more apparent to your audience. Also, ask your rehearsal audience what was the most surprising or fascinating thing they heard in your speech, and consider using a pause to emphasize that point. For example, a powerful quotation can be delivered at a slow rate followed by a pause to maximize its impact on the audience.

Finally, be aware of vocalized pauses, meaningless sounds such as "uh" or "umm" that fill moments that would be appropriate for a pause. These are usually unintentional and occur because silence can feel unnerving. Even short words can function as a vocalized pause, such as using "like" excessively or stretching out the vowel sound on words such as "Sooooo" or "Aaaand." Listen to yourself on tape to determine whether vocalized pauses become a distraction. During rehearsal with listeners, have them signal when you use a vocalized pause.

Articulation and Pronunciation　Effective delivery also requires attention to **pronunciation,** or how you speak individual words and syllables. Personal, regional, and cultural differences will affect what an audience perceives as the accepted way to say a word. You should aim to speak in a way that sounds right to your audience, but be wary of adopting an accent that makes you sound phony. Rehearsing with a listener who comes from a different region or cultural background can help you to pinpoint awkward pronunciations. Dictionaries also can give you acceptable pronunciations.

In addition, be mindful of commonly mispronounced words. Some of these so-called mispronunciations have become increasingly acceptable. For example, the first "d" in candidate is often left out when speakers say that word aloud, resulting in the pronunciation "can-i-date." In contrast, other words stick out when they are overpronounced. Some words seem to invite extra syllables and sounds, resulting in ath-uh-lete and sal-mon instead of ath-lete and sam-on.

Articulation, or the clear utterance of syllables, is another important characteristic of delivery. When syllables or short words are run together or spoken so rapidly that it becomes difficult to understand those words, there is an articulation problem. For example, consider how a fast rate can lead to an awkward articulation of this standard speech line:

"I'm going to talk about three main ideas"

turns into

"I'm gonna talk 'bout three men-uh-dees."

Even little words such as "and," "for," and "to" become "an," "fer," and "tuh."

As with pronunciation, your goal is to articulate words in a way that is acceptable to your audience. Sloppy articulation can be difficult to understand, but overarticulation can make your delivery stilted. Use your rehearsal time to identify any recurring articulation issues that you have with specific words.

Vocal Variety Although this section has directed your attention to several distinct aspects of effective vocal quality, vocal variety should be your over-arching goal as you work on using your voice effectively. Even if you speak with an adequate volume or a moderate rate, you can improve your speaking by varying the volume or rate to fit the content of the speech and keep the audience's attention. For example, during a persuasive speech on stem cell research, you might speak slowly if you are trying to clarify the technical differences between different types of research and more quickly when you are trying to convey the sense of accomplishment that could come from the outcomes of that research.

Using Your Body Effectively

Your physical appearance and movement can be used strategically for positive effect in public speaking. Even your body itself can be a resource for information and persuasion. Contemporary speakers in the public sphere have displayed their bodies to show the physical effects of AIDS and exposure to environmental toxins (DeLuca; Pezzullo). Not every speech needs to include such bold uses of one's body. But these examples show that public speaking is not just about words. The bodily dimension—including physical appearance, eye contact, gestures, and movement—is an inescapable part of public speaking (Hawhee).

Physical Appearance You likely formed some impressions of your instructor and your classmates on the first day of class before you ever talked with them. Did you notice whether the woman sitting next to you was wearing a dress, a business suit, or a sweatshirt and jeans? Did your instructor carry an athletic bag, a backpack with a peace emblem, or a computer case? Although making snap judgments based on these characteristics is not necessarily fair, it is a common occurrence that speakers must consider as they approach a public speaking situation.

Your physical appearance should enhance the audience's sense that you are prepared and competent and should not distract attention from your overall message. Consider the following example:

> Erik shuffled into class a minute late on the day of his speech. He was wearing flip-flops, athletic shorts, and a sweatshirt that looked as though it had a few pizza sauce stains on it. He was scheduled to speak first, so he went to the front of the room, plopped down his backpack, and starting digging through it to find his outline. He rubbed the paper flat against a desk a few times so that it wouldn't be crumpled. As he started his speech, his audience wasn't quite sure what to make of this guy, who said that he was going to "provide information on how recent changes to the Foreign Intelligence Surveillance Act affect your civil rights."

Generally, you would do well to attend to your appearance and dress somewhat more formally than your listeners do. At some schools, it is not uncommon for students to roll out of bed shortly before class in attire like Erik's. At other schools, fashionable dress or professional attire is the norm. Plan to dress appropriately, given your audience, without looking too casual or appearing out of place with attire that is too formal.

When speaking in the broader public sphere, be attentive to how situations and audiences may differ from the classroom setting. For example, dressing like a "typical college student" may reinforce stereotypes and hurt your credibility if you are speaking to a group of business leaders in your city. Also, you will encounter a wider range of situations than the ones that you encounter in the classroom. Formal attire might be the best choice for arguing a traffic ticket in front of a judge, whereas a local club might be less concerned if your dress and appearance emphasize your individuality.

Eye Contact Making and sustaining eye contact distinguish public speaking from the mere reading of an outline or manuscript. Effective eye contact helps you to receive feedback, an idea that you learned in chapter 1. It allows you to see whether your audience is on the edge of their seats or falling asleep. It also can create a positive bond between you and your audience. Most of all, eye contact conveys confidence. It shows that you are familiar with your speech and are comfortable talking about your topic. These skills take time to develop, but for now, try to work on the following basic principles of effective eye contact:

- *Establish eye contact immediately.* Since one of the purposes of an introduction is to capture the audience's attention, you should know the first few lines of your introduction well enough—perhaps even memorize them—that you do not need to look at your notes.

- *Make eye contact directly.* As in conversation, look people in the eye. This can be intimidating for beginning speakers, but remember that you are speaking to people—not to the tops of their heads, the empty spaces between them, or the corner or back wall of the room.

- *Distribute eye contact evenly.* You might not make eye contact with every single person in your audience, but make sure that each section of your audience feels involved in the speech. Some student speakers will inadvertently focus on one side of the room, on their friends, or on the instructor. Instead, split the audience into three sections—left, center, right—and make eye contact with people in each section.

Developing eye contact skills makes it imperative that you rehearse with an audience. When you rehearse, even if you have only two or three listeners, ask them to sit apart. Having a small number will make it awkward for you to avoid eye contact, and having them sit apart will accustom you to distributing eye contact when you move to a larger room and audience.

Movement   It is impossible—and undesirable—to remain completely still during a speech. A speaker who does not move will appear nervous and stiff to an audience. At the other extreme, a speaker who constantly taps the lectern, races from one side of the room to the other, or shuffles his or her feet also is likely to distract the audience from the message. The main principle for effective body movement, then, is to appear natural and minimize distractions.

Focus first on avoiding movements and mannerisms that create distractions. You can reduce these by having a comfortable, relaxed body position. If you are standing, bend your knees slightly, and consciously put your weight on your big toes. This can keep you from swaying, leaning on the sides of your feet, or moving your feet unintentionally. If you are worried about fidgeting with your hands or making distracting arm movements, rest your hands on the lectern or keep them at your sides. If you

HOW MOVEMENT CAN ENHANCE YOUR SPEECH
Moving closer to your audience can help them to feel more connected to you and your ideas.

have an outline or note cards, hold them in one hand and keep the other hand at your side, moving it to turn a page or for gestures. Try to avoid a tight grip on the lectern ("driving" or "steering" the lectern), leaning on or over the lectern, and constantly shifting your notes from one hand to the other.

For beginning speakers, perhaps the most important movements are ones that establish credibility at the beginning of the speech and closure at its conclusion. (Think back to Erik's entrance into the classroom and his actions before his speech. Did he project credibility and confidence?) As you move into position before the speech, move with quiet confidence to enhance your initial credibility with the audience before you speak a single word. This is especially important in public settings where you may be unknown to many of your audience members.

At the end of your speech, use multiple delivery elements to signal your conclusion. Bring your inflection and rate down; after the last word, hold eye contact for a few seconds and intentionally stop your movement while you are silent. Say, "Thank you," collect your notes, and move away from the podium or microphone. The right time to move is often triggered by the audience's applause. Not only does their applause recognize you for a job well done, it also signals that they recognize that you have reached the end of your speech.

As you become more comfortable with public speaking, you might want to incorporate a few intentional movements. Public speaking instructors have different attitudes about planned movements and gestures, so discuss this with your instructor before your first speech.

Gestures As with other body movements, gestures should appear natural and avoid creating a distraction. It can be difficult to strike the right balance. A planned gesture may seem mechanical or robotic, while gestures that occur without any thought may be repetitive or distracting. The challenge, then, is to consciously include a few gestures in your speech and minimize the number of unintentional arm and hand movements that might become a distraction to your audience.

Theoretically, there is an infinite number of gestures one might use, but many speakers rely on a few basic gestures that signal common ideas and work in conjunction with body movements. For example, to show unity among people or ideas, some speakers will bring their hands together or clasp them. In some religious rituals, participants will lift their hands up as they sing or talk about a higher power. Contrasts may be accompanied by moving one hand to introduce one idea and then the other hand to signal the contrasting idea. Like body movement in general, hand gestures can imitate the action described by a speaker.

Do not dwell excessively on gestures. Many beginning speakers err on the side of excess and gesture during every sentence because they feel awkward leaving their hands at their sides. Again, with time and practice, this feeling will subside. Over time, your conscious use of gestures may start to shape your repertoire of "natural" gestures so that you will not need to spend a lot of time working on gestures during your rehearsals.

CASE CONCLUSION

Faye's First Speech

Faye knew that she wanted to talk about the topic of human rights, but she quickly recognized that this topic would not be workable for a short speech. She narrowed the topic to the oppression of women in developing countries. But how would that topic connect with her mostly white and mostly U.S. audience? Rather than focusing on facts and figures, she decided to focus on the struggles of young women close in age to her audience.

Faye crafted her purposes like this:

General purpose: To inform
Specific purpose: To inform my audience how young women continue to face oppression in developing countries.

To organize her speech, Faye used topical order. Because she wanted to inform her audience of the various ways in which women face oppression in developing countries, it made sense to structure her speech by country. Each country formed a main point, and she provided an example from that country to fill out that point. Her introduction had a clear preview of this speech structure, and her conclusion reminded her audience of her central idea.

As Faye prepared for her speech, she kept thinking about previous speeches she had given for other classes. "I hate that my voice starts shaking as soon as I get up to give a speech. It's going to happen again, I can just feel it. But I really want to make a good first impression on my instructor and my classmates." Fortunately, Faye didn't let that stop her from preparing for her speech. She asked a couple of classmates who lived in her residence hall if they were interested in practicing their speeches a few days before the due date. "We had a great time. I was so relieved to find out that they liked my topic."

FAYE'S FIRST SPEECH

A video of Faye's first speech is available at MySpeechLab.com.

Women's Rights in Developing Countries

Here in the United States, we often take human rights for granted. The Constitution has a Bill of Rights that establishes freedom of speech and freedom of religion. Women have the right to vote and have made great strides in achieving political equality. But that is not the case around the world. As I will show you in the next few minutes, women are still being denied basic human rights, especially in less developed countries. I will tell you some stories that show the injustices that women face.

But the first story is my own. Both my boyfriend and I are from Malaysia, a country where, like the United States, many religions are practiced. I am Christian and he is Muslim. Currently, Malaysian law has strict rules about interfaith marriages involving Muslims. If I were to marry my boyfriend, the Islamic law in Malaysia states that I would have to give up my religion and convert to Islam. If I refuse to convert, my boyfriend would be legally charged and sent to jail. Later in my marriage, if I were to leave him, I would have no legal rights to our children or to inherit property. But I am fortunate, because I have the education and support to fight this injustice to women. In other countries, women are being silenced to death.

Sarnia Sawar, a 29-year-old mother in Pakistan, faced a huge problem. Her husband was abusing her, and she decided that she was not going to take it any-more. She left her husband to stay with her family. But instead of offering love and understanding, they threatened to kill her if she ever tried to get a divorce. She defied them and ran away to a shelter that was run by the Legal Aid Cell. She filed a divorce while hiding from her parents. After some time had passed, she decided to meet her mother to talk things over. Unfortunately, the mother brought her a present. Her killer. Sarnia was shot in the head and was killed instantly for her family's "honor."

Not very far away in a small village in Nepal, twenty men came to the house of Reena Rasailli. They questioned her family and searched the house only to find noth-ing. They were convinced that this family was involved with the Communist Party of Nepal. Angry that their search proved to be fruitless, they took Reena to the cow-shed. The next morning, her family found her dead with blood on her clothes and underwear. She was only 18.

These are only a few examples of injustices that are happening now as we sit in our classes. Women in less developed countries are still being denied basic human rights: Rights that we take for granted. Rights that we were born with. What makes us any better to have these rights while they have to die?

Other examples show how political and religious leaders participate in the denial of human rights. Last month in Malaysia, the Parliament passed an Islamic Family Law. It contains provisions that now give men more power to divorce their wives and contract polygamous marriages. As if that was not bad enough, there is a postscript to this law. It also allows the men to freeze the assets of the first wife if she does not allow the suffering husband to have a second wife. The few women in Parliament did not take this law sitting down. However, the female senators were told that if they did not vote for this bill, they would be kicked out. No more female representation. It scares me to know that this is coming from one of the fastest-growing and developing countries in Asia, a country that is consid-ers itself modern and civilized.

In Pakistan, women face discrimination by religious leaders who consistently put obstacles in front of them, preventing them from working, getting an education and playing any part in social development. These are basic things that we grew up knowing that we could have. Women are also considered to be useless in the court of law. Two women witnesses are equivalent to one man. And women have inadequate health care, which causes hundreds of thousands to die each year from childbirth and other diseases.

I feel sad knowing that many girls out there would never experience the kind of life that I take for granted. They will never know what it is like to have a father treat you as equal to your brothers or tell you that you are special. They will never know the joy of going to school. Some may never even know what being 21 is like, since they might not live that long. I want to be able to do something to make that change, and even though right now I might not have all the answers, I do know that by sharing these stories of women's oppression in developing countries with all of you today, I have been able to make a start towards making a difference in their lives.

Questions

1. What are Faye's purpose and central idea? Does she provide appropriate support for her central idea?

2. Evaluate Faye's introduction, body, and conclusion. What changes would you recommend?

3. Log into MySpeechLab, and watch the video of this speech. Identify what you see as Faye's main delivery strengths and the main areas for improvement.

Summary

INVENTING YOUR SPEECH

- The process of invention generates the content of your speech.

- Inventing your speech involves thinking about your topic, thinking about your audience and the speaking occasion, determining your topic and central idea, and providing supporting material.

ORGANIZING YOUR SPEECH

- Even the most complicated organizational strategy typically follows the pattern of introduction-body-conclusion.

- The introduction should arouse the audience's attention and prepare them for the rest of the speech.

- The body should have an organizational pattern that has distinct main points. Organizational markers such as signposts can help you indicate relationships between your main points.

- The conclusion reinforces the central idea and signals that the speech is coming to an end.

BUILDING YOUR CONFIDENCE

- Speech anxiety has both physical and psychological symptoms of speech anxiety. Recognizing these symptoms and understanding their causes can help you reduce anxiety and speak with confidence.

- Advance preparation, a good set of note cards, and familiarity with your audience can help you to gain confidence in the days prior to your speech.

- On the day of your speech, attending to both your physical and psychological needs is critical. Rest, healthy meals, deliberate relaxation, and cognitive restructuring all can work to minimize symptoms of nervousness.

DELIVERING YOUR SPEECH

- Enhancing your delivery starts by constructing an effective outline or a set of simple, readable note cards that promote an extemporaneous speaking style.

- Rehearsing aloud and alone and then with a small audience gives you opportunities to make adjustments to your content as well as your delivery. During these rehearsals, pay attention to voice issues such as volume, rate, pitch, pause, articulation, pronunciation, and overall vocal variety.

- Pay attention to other physical aspects of delivery, such as appearance, eye contact, movement, and gestures.

Key Terms

invention, p. 30
arrangement, p. 30
brainstorming, p. 32
concrete words, p. 32
abstract words, p. 32
general purpose, p. 36
specific purpose, p. 36
central idea, p. 36
personal experience, p. 37
examples, p. 37
testimony, p. 37
statistics, p. 37
plagiarism, p. 38
introduction, p. 38
preview, p. 39

body, p. 39
chronological order, p. 39
topical order, p. 39
organizational markers, p. 41
signpost, p. 41
conclusion, p. 41
speech anxiety, p. 42
anticipatory anxiety, p. 44
cognitive restructuring, p. 45
volume, p. 49
rate, p. 49
pitch, p. 50
pause, p. 50
pronunciation, p. 51
articulation, p. 51

Comprehension

1. After deciding on a topic, you should adapt your topic in relation to what two things?

2. What is the difference between your specific purpose and your central idea?

3. Name four types of supporting material.

4. What is the term for failing to cite the source of words or ideas that are not your own?

5. What are two important functions of an introduction?

6. Give three examples of physical symptoms of speech anxiety.

7. In what ways can advance preparation help you to reduce anticipatory speech anxiety?

8. Why is vocal variety important for effective delivery?

9. What are three principles for effective eye contact?

Application

1. To practice brainstorming, engage in free association with a few of your classmates. Have one person say a word or phrase, and then have the next person say the first thing that comes to his or her mind.

2. Generate three possible specific purpose statements for your topic. Then discuss with a friend or a classmate how you might adapt these statements for your audience and occasion.

3. Copy or print one of the speeches from MySpeechLab, and cut up the speech by paragraphs. Then try to identify paragraphs according to whether they are part of the introduction, body, or conclusion.

4. Write down negative thoughts about your performance that occur during preparation for your speech. Circulate your list, and have other people transform these statements using the principle of cognitive restructuring.

5. Make a checklist of things you can do to help reduce anxiety during the twenty-four hours before your speech.

Listening and Feedback

This chapter is intended to help you:

- Recognize and overcome distractions when listening to speeches
- Enhance your ability to comprehend a speech and critically evaluate its ideas
- Give descriptive feedback to other speakers
- Ask useful questions and offer constructive suggestions to other speakers

Listening skills are some of the most practical skills you can develop in a public speaking class. These skills help you to better understand and evaluate speeches by your classmates, and they also can improve your learning in other classes. Beyond the classroom, listening skills are essential for success in all areas of life. In interpersonal and family contexts, careful listening is an important part of developing positive, nurturing relationships. At work, listening is crucial for interviewing successfully, understanding directions and shared goals, and participating effectively in groups and teams. Finally, listening is especially important for effective political and civic engagement. You can come to understand the

Kelly Evaluates Her Classmates' Speeches

Kelly is in the midst of the first round of speeches in her public speaking class, and she is discovering that listening to them is more challenging than she thought it would be. At first, she figured that it would be a lot easier to listen to a few short speeches than to one long lecture as she does in some of her other classes. But some of the speeches have been a little boring, and she often finds herself daydreaming or thinking about her next class. Other speeches, such as Nathan's speech about life in Shanghai, China, have kept her on the edge of her seat, but she was surprised afterward when a few of her other classmates were critical of his evidence. Kelly was excited to hear Maya's speech about oil development in African countries but found it impossible to keep up with all the statistics and details and had to talk to Maya after class to figure out the "bottom line" of her speech. To top it all off, Kelly's instructor is asking her to communicate her reactions to her classmates' speeches. It is clear that the process of giving feedback—providing verbal and nonverbal response to a speaker—is a skill that she must learn and practice to be effective.

beliefs, experiences, and opinions of others in your community by listening to what they have to say. In turn, you can make better decisions after listening to a range of viewpoints and considering the arguments and concerns of others.

A related skill, but one that is often overlooked, is the skill of giving feedback. While you listen to a speech, you will inevitably provide feedback through nonverbal means such as body language and eye contact, and in some situations, it can be appropriate to respond verbally during a speech. In the classroom, speeches are often followed by a short feedback period during which other students and the instructor may ask questions or comment on the speech. Because this immediate feedback is so important for speakers, the last part of this chapter focuses on how to give the best kinds of feedback to other speakers. ■

The Challenge of Attentive Listening

Scholars of listening identify many different types of listening, such as appreciative, empathic, discriminative, comprehensive, and critical listening (Wolvin and Coakley). These types are not absolutely distinct, though; you can listen deliberately for several different reasons or purposes. For example, high points of political speaking in the United States are the acceptance addresses by presidential nominees during political party conventions. When listening to speeches like these, you might engage in **comprehensive listening** by attempting to understand the speaker's primary messages; in this case, you would listen to learn which issues the candidate will emphasize during the general campaign. In addition, you might engage in **critical listening** for the purpose of evaluating the speaker's arguments and appeals. You might also engage in **discriminative listening**, paying attention to aspects of delivery that shape the speaker's intended meaning. You might even try **appreciative listening**, simply enjoying the candidate's speaking abilities and his or her participation in the dynamic world of politics. It would be difficult to engage in **empathic listening** during mass-mediated speeches like these, since empathic listening involves providing emotional support for the speaker.

You could listen to the same speech, then, for several different purposes or reasons. But to do any of this, you must be able to engage in attentive listening. This mode of listening is what makes listening different from mere hearing, and it is a foundation for other types of listening (Clark).

Attentive listening is listening that focuses attention and minimizes distractions. If you are unable to attend to a speaker's message, it will be impossible to critically evaluate the speech. Likewise, if you get distracted easily, it will be much more difficult to be a supportive, empathic listener. Your main listening challenge, then, is to keep these distractions at bay so that you can stay focused on the speech.

To meet this challenge, it helps to be aware of two basic categories of distractions: internal distractions and external distractions. **Internal distractions** are obstacles to listening that emerge primarily from the listener; **external distractions** are obstacles that are outside the listener's control. This distinction is a little fuzzy; an external distraction does not have to be a hindrance to your listening if you internally choose to ignore it. But that is precisely the point: By anticipating distractions, you are better able to consciously resist them and remain an attentive listener. One of the premiere scholars of listening put it this way: "Learning through listening is an inside job—inside action on the part of the listener" (Nichols).

Internal Distractions

Many internal distractions stem from what can be called the **processing gap**, which is the difference between a normal speaking rate and the rate at which listeners process words. Although speakers talk at an average rate of 120 to 150 words per minute, most listeners can process information at a rate two to three times higher than that without a loss in comprehension (Ritzhaupt, Gomes, and Barron). Because of the processing gap, it is easy for our minds to start churning on something else, no matter how dynamic a speaker might be. The processing gap provides mental space for other concerns to occupy your thinking.

You can reflect on your own patterns of distraction by taking note of the things you think about during the processing gap. During a class, jot down your thoughts that are unrelated to the class, and see whether they fall into any of the following categories:

- *Physical problems* inevitably arise, since we are not simply brains processing information but bodies living in the world. Your most basic physical sensations—hunger, thirst, pain, or feeling hot or cold—can keep you from giving full attention to speakers.

- *Social and personal concerns* can easily crowd out immediate messages. Financial challenges, romantic breakups, family squabbles, or excitement about an upcoming concert or your spring break plans can deflect your attention.

- *Free associations* can happen even if you are listening attentively to a speech. It is easy for active listeners to start reflecting on just a few words from a speech and suddenly find themselves thinking about something entirely unrelated.

Taylor was looking forward to Ayana's speech about the separation of church and state. As Ayana began to speak about the experiences she had had while attending a religious high school, Taylor wondered how those experiences might have differed from his own public school experiences. He remembered having friends who attended a Catholic high school in his hometown, and he thought about the big football rivalry between the two schools. It was a big deal; the entire week before the game was exciting and full of school spirit. It was a heart-wrenching game his senior year when his best friend suffered a season-ending leg injury. "As you can see," Ayana said, "supporters have several strong arguments on their side." *Supporters of what?*, thought Taylor? *What were those arguments?*

Taylor's example shows that even a brief lapse in listening can set the mind reeling in unexpected directions. Although public speaking is always a negotiation of meaning between speakers and audiences, free association among listeners cuts the speaker off from that negotiation.

Premature conclusions are another way of mentally cutting off the speaker. If you assume that you know what the speaker is going to say or you reject or ignore the speaker's ideas before the message has been fully stated, then you have made a premature conclusion about the speech. Jumping to conclusions is not only unfair to the speaker; it also prevents you from gathering new ideas and insights.

External Distractions

External distractions also can hinder your ability to listen attentively. If you have ever tried to carry on a conversation with someone who is texting or listening to music, you can understand that those sources truly do compete for your attention. External distractions can fall into a few common categories.

Aural distractions, or noises, present a problem for listeners just as they do for speakers. Even if equipment in a room or a commotion outside a room is not very loud, it still can be annoying and start your mind on another chain reaction of thoughts unrelated to the speech. College campuses, in particular, are filled with the sounds of lawnmowers, heating and air conditioning units, hallway chatter, and construction and renovation activity.

Visual distractions are strong competitors for attention. Classroom windows invite daydreaming; bulletin boards may have flyers announcing campus events, posters advertising a band that is coming to town, or public service messages encouraging students to limit their alcohol consumption. Many of these are explicitly designed to cut through the communication saturation of the contemporary world and grab your attention. Whether intentionally or not, all of these visual elements compete for listeners' attention.

Scent distractions, or smells, might be rare, but they can be powerful. Strong perfume or cologne can overwhelm some people or provoke allergies; the smells of various foods can be off-putting or simply distracting. As a listener, try to respect your fellow audience members by refraining from introducing powerful scents, especially in confined settings.

Personal media in the form of cell phones, MP3 players, iPods, or other electronic devices add another layer of potential distractions to the classroom. There is a growing area of cultural discussion and scholarly research on the extent to which these media affect our habits of mind and the ability to concentrate (Carr; Jackson). But in the context of public speaking, digital devices can create immediate aural distractions for you and other listeners (and even for the speaker).

People are probably the most interesting and potentially distracting things in any public speaking situation. A friend might want to talk to you about plans for meeting after class. Someone else might have mentioned something at the beginning of class that seems much more interesting than the speech that is being delivered. And more than a few romantic relationships have emerged from attraction between two people in a college classroom. Although people are certainly more than mere distractions, it is important to recognize that giving attention to some people can distract your attention from speakers who rightfully expect it.

Tips for Attentive Listening

With some conscious effort, you can keep these distractions from interrupting your attention to speakers. To improve your concentration, consider the following techniques:

- *Explore the room ahead of time for external distractions.* Consider all five of your senses, and be mindful of what you need to tune out. If something attracts your attention, deal with it before the time when you need to be listening.

- *Block off the event as separate time and space.* Allow yourself to put your other concerns aside for a bit, and turn off your cell phone and computer. Even though you will be listening to speeches that address issues beyond the

DISTRACTIONS
Text messages are just one of the many kinds of messages that compete for our attention. As a speaker, how would you feel about audience members who are texting during your speech?

classroom, let this particular room and these unique speakers have the focus of your attention.

- *Fill the processing gap by summarizing the speaker's main points.* Try a few times during the speech to mentally paraphrase what the speaker has said. Summarizing keeps you focused on what the speaker actually says rather than on tangents related to the topic or your own views on the issue.

- *Fill the processing gap by taking notes.* Not only does this help you to attend to the speech, it also develops your outlining skills. Keep your notes brief, using symbols, abbreviations, and short phrases so that your note taking does not become a distraction in itself. The next section will discuss note taking in more detail.

- *Fill the processing gap by formulating questions.* Generating questions pushes you to listen carefully to the rest of the speech to see if the speaker ultimately answers those questions. Also, questions can aid the critical dimension of your listening by getting you to consider what the speaker has ignored or might be leaving out of his or her speech.

Comprehensive and Critical Listening

The better you are able to listen attentively to a speech, the better you are able to listen comprehensively and critically. Comprehensive listening is needed as you try to understand the full scope of what a speaker has to say, especially as he or she attempts to describe the complexity of an issue, the range of competing viewpoints, the barriers to effective action, and the consequences that actions may have. By using what you learn through comprehensive listening, critical listening helps you to evaluate the strengths and weaknesses of a speaker's position. Because these two types of listening are so closely related, this section discusses techniques for strengthening both comprehensive listening and critical listening.

Comprehensive Listening

For the purpose of public speaking, comprehensive listening does not mean trying to capture every single detail of a speech. That approach to listening is aptly described by the phrase "missing the forest for the trees." If you focus too narrowly on specific details, it can be more difficult to grasp the overall point of a speech and the connections that the speaker is trying to make. This is a common experience among students who try to remember every example mentioned during an instructor's lecture but struggle days later to recall the broader themes of that lecture and to understand how the lecture fits into the course as a whole. As you learned in chapter 1, the transmission of information is not the same as the creation of meaning.

Instead, think of comprehensive listening as trying to understand the speaker's main ideas. In this context, comprehensive does not mean remembering everything but rather understanding the important things. So as you listen to speeches, try to focus on the following components and their relationship to one another:

1. The central idea
2. The major points or reasons that support the central idea
3. The evidence and other materials that support the major points

This list is roughly in order of importance. For example, you need to understand the central idea of a speech before you can fairly evaluate the evidence in the speech. Your knowledge of how to construct a speech should pay off here, since you know that in most speeches, the central idea usually emerges after an attention-grabbing introduction and before a preview of the main points of the body of the speech. As a result, you can anticipate when key components of the speech are likely to be stated.

After identifying the central idea, listen for the major points that support the main claim. Usually, these points are previewed at the end of the introduction, before the body of the speech. By listening for these points, you can sketch a rough skeleton of the speech and get a sense for the kinds of evidence the speaker will need to support those points.

For practice, have a roommate or friend read aloud to you the following speech introduction. Pay attention for words that signal the main idea and the major points of the speech.

> Homeschooling has become a household word in the United States. According to the National Center for Education Statistics, approximately 1.5 million K through 12 students were homeschooled in 2007. Although that represents just over 3% of the entire student population, homeschooling is clearly on the rise. A study by the National Home Education Research Institute estimated 2 million homeschooled students just three years later. The rapid growth in homeschooling is happening for several reasons, and today I want to share with you some of those reasons. In my speech, I will inform you of the many significant benefits to homeschooling. These include a better social environment for students, more individually tailored academic instruction, and greater opportunity for moral and religious education. My speech will cover each of these benefits in detail with statistics and testimony as well as personal experiences from homeschooling students and parents.

It would be easy to dwell on the attention-grabbing statistics at the beginning of the speech. But your first priority should be to identify the central idea: that there are many significant benefits to homeschooling. An attentive listener would then ask: What are those benefits? Fortunately, this speaker identifies those benefits immediately.

Finally, listen for the pieces of evidence and other supporting materials that the speaker uses to strengthen the major points. For the purpose of comprehensive listening, it is sufficient to note the materials on which the speaker is relying to support his or her major points. A speech on changes in weather patterns, for example, might rely on evidence about temperature and precipitation changes to support the major points. As you shift into a more critical mode of listening, you will begin to ask questions about the quality of these supporting materials.

PUBLIC SPOTLIGHT

Tony Blair

Tony Blair, former Prime Minister of the United Kingdom, is widely recognized as an effective leader and an accomplished public speaker. But his ability to address challenging public issues also stems from another important communication skill: listening.

Blair's listening skills were especially important in negotiating peace in Northern Ireland. For much of the twentieth century, Northern Ireland was shaped by violent conflict between unionists, who supported the region's being part of the United Kingdom, and nationalists, who sought to reclaim the region as part of the Republic of Ireland. As a major participant in negotiating the 1998 Good Friday Agreements that were pivotal in the peace process, Blair needed both speaking and listening skills to broker an effective and long-lasting agreement.

Many prominent figures praised Blair's role in the agreements. At the tenth anniversary of the agreements, Irish singer and activist Bono said, "It's rare for politicians to be great listeners and I think Tony Blair is a great listener" (Daly). The Irish prime minister, Bertie Ahern, also complimented Blair, who "had given tirelessly of himself to bring to an end decades of suffering and bloodshed" (Daly). And the *Financial Times,* a leading British newspaper, editorialized that "Northern Ireland saw Mr Blair at his best—the patience, the

resilience and the genius for persuasion" (Stephens). Clearly, Blair's contribution to resolving a lengthy and deep-seated conflict is a testament to the power—and necessity—of both speaking and listening when engaging difficult public issues.

 Social Networking Spotlights

- In spite of the great strides toward peace in Northern Ireland, violence continues. Some observers claim that recruiting and riots by paramilitary groups are facilitated through social networking sites such as Bebo. This January 2010 article from the BBC describes such activity: http://www.bbc.co.uk/newsbeat/10005113

  Meanwhile, organizations such as the Integrated Education Fund are working to promote better relations among Protestants and Catholics in Northern Ireland: http://www.facebook.com/sections/default.asp?secid=22#!/IntegratedEducationFund?v=info

- The National Coalition Building Institute is active on more than sixty college campuses with efforts to reduce prejudice and intergroup conflict: http://www.ncbi.org/campuses/

Critical Listening

The point of critical listening is not to immediately identify or criticize all the faults of a speech. For example, even if you have doubts about homeschooling, you do a disservice to yourself and the speaker if you immediately start to generate a list of all the drawbacks of homeschooling. This is a type of premature conclusion that hurts your listening in several ways:

- It prevents *attentive* listening, since it creates a significant internal distraction.

- It prevents *comprehensive* listening, since it diverts you from fully understanding the speaker's ideas and reasons.

- Although it might seem like critical listening, in fact it prevents you from fairly evaluating the speaker's message.

After all, if your comprehension of that message has been limited, you might end up criticizing a position that the speaker didn't actually state. Or you might challenge the speaker on something that he or she addressed while you were busy thinking up objections. Ethically, it is unfair to reject a position before the speaker has had a chance to explain himself or herself and provide support for the position.

Instead, think of critical listening as an ongoing process of testing the arguments and appeals in a speech. Simply raising objections to a speaker's message is not necessarily the most effective way to test ideas. Rather, approach the speech with an open mind while also identifying areas that need to be tested. Two important techniques can promote this kind of critical listening.

First, try to *suspend judgment*. Withhold your own opinions until the speaker has had a chance to fully explain his or her ideas and opinions. Even if you disagree with a point, give the speaker an opportunity to develop his or her viewpoint in full. The speaker might bring up new information or insights that you would miss if you made a premature judgment.

Second, *formulate questions* to guide your critical listening (Browne and Keeley). Not only does asking questions help you to fill the processing gap and improve your attention, but it also helps you to figure out the strengths and weaknesses of the speaker's message. As you listen to the rest of the speech, proceed through the following questions:

- *Does the speech omit any major points?* Ask this question immediately after noting the main claim and major points. It encourages you to think about the "big picture" of the speech before you get into the details. For example, if a speech lists three major points, consider whether there might be an obvious fourth point. Or if a speech is advocating one point of view, ask whether it acknowledges objections or other points of view. This is not the same as generating a complete list of *what* those objections might be, which would be extremely distracting. Instead, you are simply noting *that* there may be objections and that an informed and ethical speaker on the topic should recognize them.

- *How accurate and credible is the supporting material?* Ask this question as the speaker introduces various pieces of evidence. The point of this question is simply to consider whether the evidence itself is a reliable description of what is actually happening in the world. Compare the speech with other things that you have read or heard, and determine their recency. Also, consider who the sources are and whether they have expertise on the topic. Later chapters will give you additional guidance on how to evaluate evidence.

- *How well does the evidence support the major points?* Ask this question at the end of each major section of a speech. Again, rather than agreeing or disagreeing with a major point right off the bat, wait until the speaker has presented the evidence before deciding whether you accept or reject that point. Be aware that the strongest speeches typically rely on several different types of evidence to support a larger point. In addition, you might reflect on whether there is any evidence that undermines support for the major point.

- *How well do the major points support the central idea?* Ask this question near the conclusion of the speech. By this time, you should have a sense of the strongest major points. Also, speakers often conclude a speech by showing how all the points support the central idea. You can now begin to test your own evaluation of the major points against the speaker's views. Be open to the possibility that the major points might provide different levels of support for the central idea. Your ultimate reaction to the speech does not have to be a simple "You're absolutely right!" or "I completely disagree!" A critical listener will consider each of the main points on its own merits to determine the overall strength of the central idea.

- *What voices are left out?* Communication ethics scholar Paula Tompkins encourages **rhetorical listening** as a type of listening that pays attention to the rhetorical forms and language patterns that shape our perception of a situation. The goal of this type of listening is to "recognize others who have an interest in an issue or problem, but are absent from communication about that issue or problem" (Tompkins). This aspect of listening will be addressed again in the Ethical Dimension feature.

These questions are only the tip of the iceberg when it comes to evaluating a speech. But they identify the fundamental concerns during critical listening. With some practice, listening with these questions in mind will become a habit that allows you to better engage your classmates and community members. For now, work on building the skills of attentive, comprehensive, and critical listening outlined here so that you can provide meaningful feedback to your colleagues.

Taking Notes

You can easily serve the purposes of comprehensive and critical listening by taking notes during speeches. Effective note taking should follow the same principles as your listening. Taking *comprehensive* notes does not mean trying to write everything down but instead capturing the statements and evidence that are crucial for understanding the speech as a whole. Think again about your experiences listening to a classroom lecture; if you try to write everything down, you will fall behind and you might have trouble distinguishing between main points and supporting details. Likewise, taking *critical* notes is more about raising questions for further discussion than about generating objections that will shut down discussion.

A few key techniques can put these principles into practice. First, set up a system to *organize your notes*. Over time, you may develop your own system; meanwhile, the system in Figure 3.1 is intended to help your comprehensive and critical listening skills and to generate feedback on content as well as delivery. Under this system, take notes about the content of a speech in the middle of your page. On one margin, leave enough room for notes about the delivery of the speech; on the other margin, include notes about the content of the speech and any questions you have for the speaker. This system makes it easy to keep your own ideas separate from the speaker's message while still allowing you to refer to the specific parts of the speech when giving feedback.

A second technique that is relevant to organizing your notes is to *use rough outline form*. You might not be able to have a perfect letter and number system, but you should try to distinguish major points from supporting material. Indent supporting material under the major points, and keep items of equal importance at the same level on your outline. In some instances, you may be able to identify the major points during the introduction of the speech. Placing these points on your outline right away can help you to establish outline form and enhance your comprehension of the speech.

For example, a speech on domestic abuse might include introductory material like this:

> In this speech, I want to inform you about four broad types of domestic abuse. First, I will define domestic abuse and discuss its prevalence, giving attention to how both men and women are victims of abuse. Then I will talk about four main types: emotional abuse, sexual abuse, economic abuse, and physical abuse. For each, I will define what this abuse is and share the words of survivors. By the end of my speech, I hope you will better understand what domestic abuse looks like and feels like.

Then your initial rough outline notes might look something like this:

DOMESTIC ABUSE
   —definition
   —prevalence

TYPES OF ABUSE
   1. Emotional
   2. Sexual
   3. Economic
   4. Physical

FIGURE 3.1 Taking Notes on a Speech

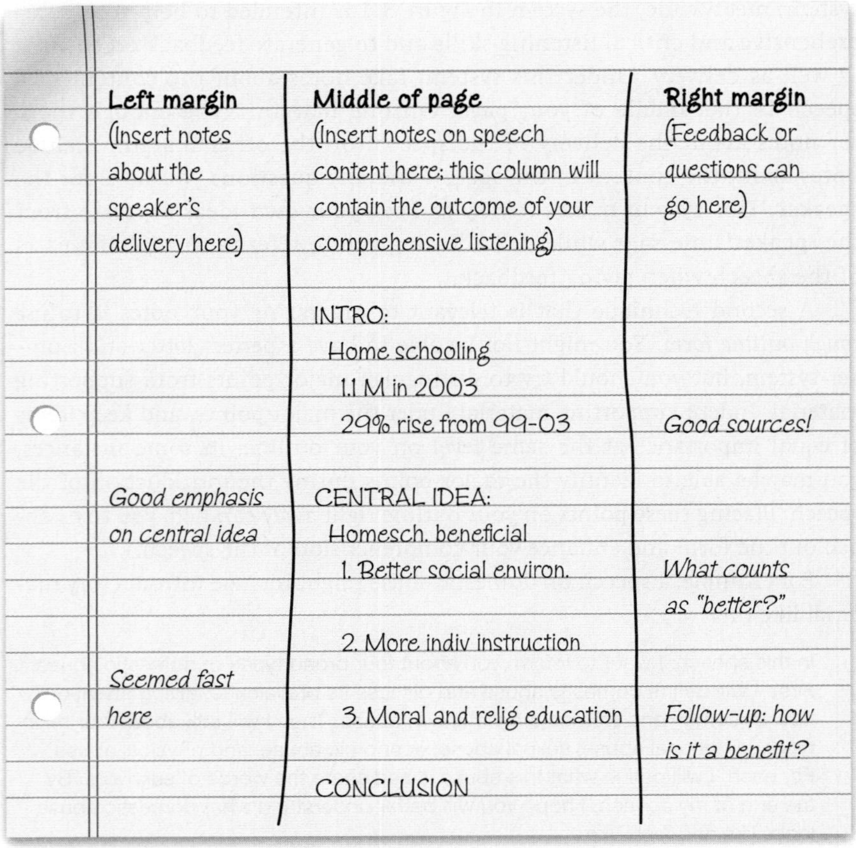

Left margin	Middle of page	Right margin
(Insert notes about the speaker's delivery here)	(Insert notes on speech content here; this column will contain the outcome of your comprehensive listening)	(Feedback or questions can go here)
	INTRO: Home schooling 1.1 M in 2003 29% rise from 99–03	Good sources!
Good emphasis on central idea	CENTRAL IDEA: Homesch. beneficial 1. Better social environ.	What counts as "better?"
	2. More indiv instruction	
Seemed fast here	3. Moral and relig education	Follow-up: how is it a benefit?
	CONCLUSION	

This type of outline form—indenting subpoints, numbering a series of points where possible—can help you to grasp the speech as a whole and see the relationships between main points and subpoints. If your instructor allows the use of a laptop computer or netbook, you might consider using the automatic outlining function in your word processing program.

Third, *leave adequate space* for taking notes. If you are able to identify major points right away, put plenty of white space between those major points. Likewise, give yourself enough room in the margins for your own feedback and comments. As shown in Figure 3.1, consider using the margins (or drawing your own margins) to the left and right of where you take notes on the speech itself. If you are using a computer to take notes, you could use some of the special editing features (such as Track Changes or Comments) to separate notes on the content of the speech from your own comments and feedback.

Finally, *use key words and short phrases* when taking notes on a speech. Keep in mind the uses for these notes. They will serve the purpose of jogging your memory and helping you to give productive feedback after the speech. You do not need to generate a word-for-word transcript of the speech; just jot down enough words that you can capture a speaker's primary idea at a particular moment.

Giving Feedback

After listening to a speech, it is appropriate to applaud the speaker's effort. But what then? Perhaps you agree so strongly with the speaker's ideas that you want to say, "Right on!" Maybe you want the speaker to say more about how this is relevant to your everyday life. Perhaps you were so surprised by new information and ideas that you want to thank the speaker for sharing those ideas. Or you might have been offended by comments that seemed to stereotype certain groups of people and want to make sure that those ideas do not go unchallenged.

All of these responses are appropriate for the feedback session that should follow a public speech. The opportunity to provide feedback and share your responses is vital in many ways:

- First, providing feedback allows speakers to learn how audiences perceive their speeches. Without a formal feedback session, speakers will have an extremely limited basis for judging their own performance and learning what went well and where there are areas for improvement. As one group of scholars suggests, "Feedback also helps the other person understand the effect of his or her communication. It's another chance to correct errors and misconceptions. It's also a chance for him or her to get a fresh and valuable point of view—yours" (McKay, Davis, and Fanning).

- Second, providing feedback allows audience members to participate in the ongoing public discussion of issues that are important to them. Without this, the public sphere can be dominated by people in positions of power or expertise—people who are more likely to be asked to speak in public settings. Feedback makes the public sphere more democratic.

- Third, providing feedback allows for the examination of important ideas and assumptions. Without feedback, an offensive remark or inaccurate piece of information may continue to circulate. In this way, feedback enhances the critical character of the public sphere.

As with the skills of listening, this section of the chapter focuses on a few of the basic skills involved in giving feedback. More skills will be added in the context of preparing for other speeches later in the book. These basic skills involve describing your response, asking questions, and offering suggestions.

Describing Your Response

Descriptive feedback, or a response that shares an individual's reaction to a speech, is especially useful in the classroom and other venues where participants are focused on the speaking process itself. The purpose of descriptive feedback is to let listeners describe how they reacted to various aspects of the speech rather than passing judgment about the quality of the speech itself or telling the speaker what to do. Descriptive feedback has the advantage of delaying judgment of the speech so that the speaker can learn about the range of responses from audience members. You can think of the descriptive feedback session as a focus group, in which the participants offer their reactions and the leader—in this case, the speaker—listens attentively to the responses and makes his or her own judgments about the performance.

From the standpoint of a listener, this difference between describing your reaction to the speech and passing judgment on the speaker manifests itself in how you state your feedback. The following guidelines for formulating descriptive feedback can help you to moderate the intensity of your feedback. This will be more helpful to most beginning speakers than harsh, negative criticism, and it can help to minimize speech anxiety and promote confidence (Kopecky, Sawyer, and Behnke; Smith and King). In particular, three guidelines can help you to phrase your responses in the spirit of descriptive feedback.

Speak for Yourself It is impossible for you to know how others will react to a speech. You might think a speech is fascinating while others might find it to be "old news." You might not have understood the connection between a narrative and the central idea, but it might have been obvious to others. The speaker's rate might be too fast for you but just fine for others. Because of these differences in perception, your feedback should reflect that they are your personal responses and not universal reactions to the speech.

To ensure that you speak for yourself, use **I-language**, which is wording that phrases your feedback so that it describes only your individual response, not an assumption about the response of others. Let other audience members speak for themselves.

Poor feedback: Your conclusion was difficult to understand.

Notice how this statement implies that the conclusion itself is the problem. Perhaps the conclusion was clear but this particular listener was distracted. A more accurate description would limit the listener's comment to his or her own perception of the conclusion.

Better feedback: I was confused by the conclusion of your speech; I wasn't sure if the point was just to reinforce the benefits of homeschooling or to argue that homeschooling is superior to traditional schooling.

In addition, try to avoid I-language that hides a blanket judgment about the speech.

Poor feedback: I think you should eliminate your fifth major point about the flat tax.

Let the speaker make the decision about whether to change the speech. Instead, use your I-language to clarify your concern about that point.

Better feedback: I started to lose interest by the fifth major point, and I didn't see how that point advanced your central idea.

This I-language gives the speaker a sense of what's going on in an audience member's mind. If other listeners have a similar response, then adjusting or eliminating the fifth point might be a good idea.

Focus on the Speech, Not the Speaker This guideline is rooted in what you have learned about anxiety or nervousness. As you know, the act of speaking can create anxiety as speakers put themselves and their ideas on display for others. Consequently, feedback on a speech often can seem as though it is feedback about a person. It's no wonder that for some speakers, the feedback session can be more worrisome than actually delivering the speech.

To minimize this anxiety for your fellow speakers, use language that describes the speech itself rather than the person speaking. As much as possible, avoid the use of the word "you," especially when it could seem as though you are accusing the speaker of doing something wrong. Instead, try to detach the speech itself from the person giving the speech

Poor feedback: You didn't provide a preview of your main points.

Notice how this statement personally accuses the speaker of an error. The feedback could be improved by redirecting the focus to the speech itself and perhaps softened with some I-language.

Better feedback: I didn't hear a preview of your main points. Did I miss them?
Better feedback: Did the introduction include a preview of the main points?

However, even statements with I-language might still fail to focus on the speech rather than the speaker.

Poor feedback: I felt that you were ignoring this side of the room.
Better feedback: I felt that the other side of the room was getting more attention than we were.
Better feedback: I'm not sure about others over here, but I didn't get much eye contact.

These examples show how even a minor wording change can take the edge off critical comments. Even though it is important for the speaker to take responsibility for his or her words, speakers might not be receptive to feedback if they feel personally attacked. So if you have comments that might be perceived negatively, they can be more effective if you make them about the speech rather than the speaker.

Be Specific Your first attempts at giving descriptive feedback might lead to very general statements. Even if feedback is phrased with I-language and focuses on the speech itself, general statements do little to help the speaker understand why a listener is responding in a certain way. Therefore, be as specific as you can to give useful feedback. When you describe your reaction, try to include what precisely you are reacting to in the speech.

Poor feedback: I really liked your introduction.

In response, a speaker could solicit specifics by asking, "What in particular did you like about the introduction?" or "Why did you like it?" Perhaps there was an opening story that captured the listener's attention.

Better feedback: I found your opening story to be very shocking. It definitely grabbed my attention and made me want to listen to the rest of the speech.

Taking good notes can help you to pinpoint these specific details. Then your feedback will sound less like a gut reaction to the speech and will give the speaker guidance on parts of the speech that merit a second look.

> *Poor feedback:* I had a hard time following the speech.
>
> *Better feedback:* I didn't catch the third main point. Was there a transition there?

When you use I-language and provide feedback on specific aspects of the speech itself, your responses are much more likely to be perceived positively by the speakers and to generate useful information for them as the speakers continue to work on their speaking skills.

Asking Questions

Even the most attentive listener is bound to miss something or forget a key point during the presentation of a speech. When listeners are processing information and focusing on evidence, they might not grasp all the connections that a speaker is trying to make. They might start thinking about a related topic or issue. They might hear information or arguments that conflict with beliefs and values they hold. In all of these situations, asking questions is a form of feedback that can help both speaker and listener to improve their understanding of the topic that the speaker is addressing.

Formulating good questions is another one of those skills that takes time to develop. As a starting point, consider the following basic purposes for asking questions.

Ask Questions to Get Information Ask questions to ensure that you have understood the speaker's message accurately or to get additional information about an idea that interests you and merits more attention.

> Could you please restate the third major point?
>
> Who was the source for that statistic about the number of students being homeschooled?

In the classroom or in a workshop setting, you might also ask information-oriented questions to learn about the process of public speaking. Often, the best opportunities to increase your knowledge and skills related to public speaking come from hearing speeches and interacting with speakers, so consider asking a question about some aspect of the speech process.

> I found your gestures to be very natural. Did you practice them ahead of time?
>
> I thought your speech had very reputable sources. How did you locate them?

THE ETHICAL DIMENSION

Listening as an Ethical Practice

The practices of listening and then giving feedback are rooted in broad ethical principles about the process of communication. In a 1994 speech, communication scholar Lana Rakow identified three ethical principles or ground rules for communication that show how even the acts of listening and feedback have ethical dimensions. These principles are inclusiveness, participation, and reciprocity.

Inclusiveness refers to an openness to diverse viewpoints and a willingness to listen to others regardless of their race, gender, socioeconomic status, religion, age, or sexual orientation. **Participation** refers to a right of all people to have the opportunity to voice their opinions, to be heard by others, and "to have their opinions count in public decision making." Consequently, the principle of **reciprocity** is grounded in a sense of equality among participants, indicating everyone has the opportunity to speak and to listen in a particular communication situation.

These principles provide an ethical justification for why you should engage in the listening and feedback practices described in this chapter. Inclusiveness requires attentive listening to all speakers regardless of their point of view or the preconceptions that you might have about a particular speaker. Even if you disagree with a speaker's viewpoint on an issue, it is imperative to include that speaker's viewpoint in public discussion and that you as an audience member are at least willing to listen to what the speaker has to say. After all, if you were speaking, you would want your audience to listen attentively so that you would feel included in the community. The principle of inclusiveness, then, implies reciprocity or taking turns. Including and listening to all viewpoints require that we take turns in the role of speaker and listener. And by taking turns, we serve the overall purpose of promoting participation in the public sphere.

These principles help to explain why the practices of descriptive feedback are so important. Speaking only for yourself allows others to express their own

A well-functioning public sphere allows listeners to take their turn as speakers.

opinions in the discussion. Likewise, focusing on the speech rather than the speaker keeps feedback from getting personal or suggesting that the speaker as a person should not be involved in the discussion. Even if a speaker advances a questionable idea or a troubling position, that person still has a right to be included. Thus, inclusiveness and reciprocity reinforce the principle of participation.

WHAT DO YOU THINK?

1. What can you do in your public speaking class to ensure reciprocity?

2. Is it ever ethical to "heckle," or interrupt, a speaker?

3. Examine the following YouTube clip from a town hall meeting about health care reform during the summer of 2009:

   http://www.youtube.com/watch?v=J-Bpshk5nX0&feature=fvw

Which principles apply to this situation? How would you evaluate the different kinds of listening and feedback by this audience?

Questions about process are less appropriate in situations in which the focus is on the public dimensions of public speaking rather than on the speaking dimensions. In these situations, questions generally should be oriented toward the content of a speech.

Ask Questions to Understand Connections   Questions also can help you and the speaker to clarify connections that might not be fully stated in the speech. Not only does this help you to understand the speaker's message, it gives the speaker some clues about where and how to adjust the speech.

> I really liked the suspense you built in your opening story, but I didn't understand how it related to your central idea. Could you please explain what you see as the connection between them?
>
> In the middle of the speech, one claim was that a flat tax would eliminate the capital gains tax. To me, the implication was that that's a good thing. Could you elaborate on why that's a good thing?

Both of these questions do involve getting additional information from the speaker. However, in contrast to just asking for a fact or a piece of evidence, these questions ask the speaker to elaborate on the message and its logic. By asking questions like these, you might discover some of the hidden assumptions that are at work in the speech, which can help you to determine whether you accept or reject the speaker's message.

Ask Questions to Express Doubts   A third type of question poses a challenge to some aspect of the speech. Questions that express doubts about a specific point or the overall message are very useful for testing ideas and puzzling through conflicting pieces of evidence or competing points of view. However, they can be phrased in ways that seem to attack the speaker or put the speaker on the defensive. Neither of these is a beneficial form of feedback.

Instead, questions that express doubts should be posed in a way that allows both speaker and listener to understand the basis of the listener's doubt or disagreement. Often, you can accomplish this by referring to the portion of the speech that raises concerns for you before posing the question.

> *Poor question:* How can you say that the flat tax is fair?
>
> *Better question:* One of the main points of your speech argues that the flat tax promotes fairness because it shifts the tax burden. Could you explain how it is fair if the middle class ends up bearing a higher proportion of the tax burden?

ASKING QUESTIONS
At public meetings, listeners often ask questions to better understand an issue or to express doubts about an official's position.

Or you might introduce a competing point of view so that that speaker understands why you disagree.

> *Better question:* In my economics class, we learned that flat taxes tend to be regressive. If that's true, how does it affect the argument that the flat tax is fair?

Note how each of these "better" questions provides substantive feedback and poses a question directly related to that feedback. Remember, questions like these should seek to continue discussion in order to clarify the issue rather than shut down the discussion by attempting to stump the speaker or merely air the listener's disagreement.

Offering Suggestions

It is always tempting to offer suggestions to a speaker. It fulfills our desire to help others, and it reinforces the belief that we are knowledge-able and caring people. However, this temptation should be balanced by the guidelines for descriptive feedback: Speak for yourself, focus on the speech, and give specifics. It is extremely easy to forget about these guidelines when offering concrete suggestions for changes and improvements. Since you are speaking for yourself, your suggestions should be just that: suggestions that would be helpful for *you*, not absolute commands to the speaker.

> *Poor feedback:* You should use more gestures.
>
> *Better feedback:* I would like to see a few more gestures in your next speech.

Should you wish to offer some suggestions, phrase them in the language of descriptive feedback and, where possible, phrase them constructively—as positive actions or alternatives that the speaker might consider, not as a list of criticisms.

> *Poor feedback:* You should get rid of all those statistics.
>
> *Better feedback:* I was overwhelmed by all the statistics about the demographics of homeschoolers. I'd appreciate a few examples that show the diversity among homeschooling families.

Using the language of descriptive feedback to frame your suggestions can be a bit awkward at first. You might find that the I-language gets old rather quickly, and phrasing comments to focus on the speech rather than the speaker can be difficult in some situations. Use your best judgment as to what sounds appropriate, but do make the effort to adapt your speech so that you and your classmates can develop a positive and respectful public sphere in your class.

Finally, be mindful of how different occasions call for different kinds of feedback. The feedback that is illustrated in this chapter is typical for a public speaking classroom. In the broader public sphere, appropriate feedback has some similarities to these comments as well as some differences. On one hand, it is completely appropriate to use I-language, focus on the speech itself, and provide specific details as you offer feedback to speakers. On the other hand, feedback about delivery and suggestions for improving one's public speaking is usually misplaced in most public settings. People are not likely to appreciate someone who uses the city council or volunteer board meeting as an opportunity to critique another person's public speaking skills. Instead, your feedback should focus on the issues and ideas that the speaker is discussing.

CASE CONCLUSION

Kelly Evaluates Her Classmates' Speeches

After class, Kelly started to figure out why she had had such a difficult time processing Maya's speech. It really had little to do with the speech and more to do with the internal and external distractions that kept Kelly from listening attentively.

Kelly woke up late that day and rushed out of her apartment without having anything to eat. On her way to campus, she had to stop to put gas in her car and was shocked to see how much it cost. Her day certainly had a hectic start! Kelly arrived at class just in time for Maya's speech. As Maya began speaking about Africa in her introduction, Kelly thought to herself, "This doesn't really matter to me." Her ears perked up when Maya started to mention oil, which led Kelly to start thinking about those gas prices. But Kelly stopped herself from thinking about all the other expenses in her life. Instead, she listened for the main points in Maya's speech and learned how need for oil has affected ordinary people living in Africa.

Kelly had better luck when it was time to listen to Nathan's speech. She remained focused and used the listening skills she was learning to formulate feedback on Nathan's speech about Shanghai:

Nathan, you were terrific. I really liked your introduction; it had everything you needed in it. But you should make it shorter because we were all waiting to hear your central idea. Once you got into the body of the speech, it rocked! All the examples were really great. I thought the description of the fish market in particular was really vivid. It made me feel like I was really there!

I did have one question about your speech. You were obviously trying to persuade us that Shanghai is a great place to live, but isn't it crazy to think that it's easy to live in such a huge city? Your speech would work better if you talked about some of the drawbacks of living in a city the size of Shanghai.

Questions:

1. Identify the different types of feedback Kelly used in her response.
2. Which statements are effective forms of feedback? How would you revise or reword statements that are less effective?

Summary

THE CHALLENGE OF ATTENTIVE LISTENING

- Attentive listening is the foundational type of listening. Working on this skill involves overcoming internal distractions such as thinking about personal concerns or jumping to premature conclusions about a speech.
- External distractions such as other people or other verbal and visual messages also can affect attentive listening, especially as listeners allow those external distractions to provoke internal distractions.
- To improve your concentration, be proactive in identifying external and internal distractions before a public speaking situation, and fill the processing gap by summarizing, taking notes, and formulating questions about the speech.

COMPREHENSIVE AND CRITICAL LISTENING

- Comprehensive and critical listening direct attention to the central idea, major points, and supporting materials of a speech.

- The idea of comprehensive listening suggests that audience members should try to understand how these components contribute to the overall message of a speech.

- Critical listening requires suspending judgment as well as formulating questions about the comprehensiveness of major points, the accuracy and credibility of evidence, the adequacy of evidence to support major points, and the adequacy of major points to support the central idea.

- Taking systematic notes in a rough outline form can assist in both types of listening.

GIVING FEEDBACK

- Giving feedback helps speakers to learn how their audience understood and reacted to the speech, and it promotes democratic discussion of issues.

- Three key guidelines for descriptive feedback include speaking for yourself using I-language, focusing on the speech rather than the speaker, and being specific in your response.

- Feedback also involves asking questions for the purposes of acquiring information, understanding connections, and expressing doubts.

- When offering suggestions to a speaker, use the guidelines for descriptive feedback to phrase those suggestions in a constructive and respectful way.

Key Terms

comprehensive listening, p. 62
critical listening, p. 62
discriminative listening, p. 63
appreciative listening, p. 63
empathic listening, p. 63
attentive listening, p. 63
internal distractions, p. 63
external distractions, p. 63

processing gap, p. 63
rhetorical listening, p. 70
descriptive feedback, p. 74
I-language, p. 75
inclusiveness, p. 78
participation, p. 78
reciprocity, p. 78

Comprehension

1. Why is effective listening important for civic and political engagement?

2. What is the processing gap? How is it related to attentive listening?

3. Name four internal distractions.

4. What is a premature conclusion?

5. What things should you listen for if you are engaged in comprehensive listening?

6. What are three questions you should ask if you are engaged in critical listening?

7. Why should listeners focus on the speech and use I-language when giving feedback?

8. What are three purposes of asking questions?

Application

1. During a class, make a note of thoughts that are unrelated to the class. See whether any patterns emerge about the kinds of things that distract your attention.

2. Develop a written plan to help you focus your attention prior to classes when you will be listening to speeches. Share and compare your plan with classmates.

3. Find a speech of a famous person or political candidate on YouTube. Use the critical listening questions to evaluate the speech.

4. When rehearsing your speeches with classmates, use this opportunity to practice giving feedback. Assign the descriptive feedback guidelines to different people, and ask that they observe and comment on how well listeners follow those guidelines.

Developing Topics for
the Public Sphere

4

CHAPTER OUTLINE

Understanding the Rhetorical Situation
Determining Your Topic
Assessing Your Audience
Crafting Your Purpose Statements and
    Central Idea

This chapter is intended to help you:

- Understand the idea of the rhetorical situation
- Develop a topic that has public significance
- Learn about different types of audiences
- Craft your purpose and central idea

As you consider speaking about public issues, you need to think carefully about the connections between your topic, your audience, and your purpose. This chapter introduces the concept of the rhetorical situation as a lens for seeing these connections and helping you to make sound choices as you invent your speeches.

Thinking about the rhetorical situation will direct your attention to the public significance of your topic. As was discussed in chapter 1, "public significance" simply means the importance of your topic for civic life or political decision making; this chapter gives you additional ideas for developing a publicly significant topic. No matter what kind of speech you are giving, it is important to show your audience why your topic is significant to them. By

Sara's Speech: Developing a Topic

Sara racked her brain trying to come up with a speech topic. Her own experiences traveling around the world led her to be interested in global issues. Human trafficking, the drug trade, and pandemics were just a few of the topics that fascinated her. She hoped to work or volunteer internationally after she finished college, too, so she looked for every possible opportunity to explore these topics.

But she also knew that most of her classmates had not been outside the United States and would not be interested in topics that did not have a direct impact on themselves. As a result, she struggled to identify a good topic. Should she pursue something that she thinks is important, regardless of what her audience cares about, or should she focus on things that her classmates talk about, even if those topics do not interest her or seem very significant?

doing so, your speech becomes more than just a class assignment—it connects your listeners to the world outside your class and encourages them to become active members of their community. ■

Understanding the Rhetorical Situation

Speeches that address public issues can involve a diverse range of topics. In your community, a city official might speak to inform a high school class about plans for a new skate park or to persuade members of a local business association to contribute money toward a new swimming pool. On campus, a student might speak to inform new students about counseling services that are available at the college or to persuade faculty members and administrators to change grading policies.

Regardless of the topic, these situations have several features in common:

- A significant issue motivates someone to speak.
- An audience of listeners exists and is able to play a role in addressing the issue.
- The speaker has some purpose or goal in mind as he or she speaks.

The concept of the rhetorical situation connects these features and provides a useful starting point for the invention of a public speech.

A **rhetorical situation** can be defined as "a situation that presents issues that can be resolved meaningfully through speech and writing" (Hauser 45). Rhetorical situations emerge when speakers perceive some significant issue that needs to be addressed through political participation or civic engagement. Amid ongoing controversies and the circulation of public discourse, rhetorical situations are specific moments when people can use their public voice to address important issues (Asen).

Rhetorical situations have three main features:

- The exigence, or issue
- The audience
- Constraints

These features are part of every rhetorical situation, but they are not always obvious or clear-cut. In fact, to some extent, the speaker can shape them. While this makes understanding rhetorical situations complicated, it also means that you, as a speaker, can exercise some power in those situations. Thinking about these aspects of the rhetorical situation can help you to think creatively about your topic.

Exigence

In rhetorical theory, a common definition of **exigence** is "an imperfection marked by urgency" (Bitzer). In other words, an exigence is what motivates a speaker to speak. For example, in a persuasive context, the exigence might be a problem that needs to be solved, whereas for a eulogy, the exigence is the grief experienced by the audience. Regardless of the context, the aspect of the rhetorical situation that leads someone to respond with speech is the exigence.

For the purpose of developing your topic, you can think of the exigence as *a significant public issue that is timely for your audience.* No matter what your purpose, significant issues and challenges that are urgent for your audience are often the primary motive for public speaking. As one classic public speaking textbook states, "problems usually represent the reasons we speak" (Walter and Scott).

However, problems are not always obvious or straightforward. For example, is a forest fire a public problem? The fire itself is not necessarily a problem. Some fires may be beneficial for the long-term health of a forest. Other fires may pose little threat to the land or to structures built near the forest. But a forest fire can become a public problem when people begin to discuss the damage that fires can do and the choices we might make to minimize that damage.

The point of this example is that public problems are constructed through effective rhetoric—through public speaking and other forms of rhetoric that define particular conditions as public problems (Vatz; Smith and Lybarger). The idea that public problems are constructed through effective rhetoric has two important implications for the invention stage of public speaking. First, *many damaging or harmful conditions might not be recognized by other people as problems* (Edelman). So you do not need to limit your speech topics to familiar

IDENTIFYING PROBLEMS
Many controversies are debates about whether something is a problem. Are violent video games a problem? Or are they symptoms of some other problem?

problems. Be on the lookout for damaging conditions that you believe deserve status as an exigence. Examples from the past and present—slavery, date rape, global warming—remind us of conditions that were not immediately recognized or discussed as problems. It took persistent public advocacy to shift attitudes and convince decision makers that these were urgent problems that needed to be addressed.

A second implication is that *many controversies focus on defining which conditions are the primary or most significant public problem.* So be open-minded as you explore your topic; do not assume that you already know what the "real" problem is. Think again about the topic of forest fires. For much of the twentieth century, forest fires on public lands in the United States were suppressed very quickly because fire was perceived as an obvious and significant problem. But scientists, advocacy groups, and citizens challenged that idea over time. Forest fires have a natural cycle, and suppressing fires for several decades interrupted this cycle and led to much larger fires; so one might view fire suppression as the real exigence. Others claimed that environmental restrictions on logging led to more fire-prone forests; they viewed those restrictions as the central problem. In some places, people have built homes very close to forests and expect those homes to be protected from forest fires. Is the problem inadequate fireproofing by property owners? Or is the problem their expectation that local fire departments can and must protect their structures? Perhaps the problem is insufficient resources for those fire departments.

Later in this chapter, you will see the practical implications of this way of thinking about public issues. When people disagree about the primary or most significant problem, you have found a topic of public significance. Your specific purpose and central idea will depend on whether your audience already recognizes the problem and is doing something about it or whether they are unfamiliar with the problem.

Audience

When most people think about an audience for public speaking, they are thinking of the **immediate audience**, that is, the people who gathered to hear the initial presentation of a speech. During the process of inventing your speech, however, you want to think of your immediate audience in a unique way. You want to develop your topic in such a way that your immediate audience will come to see itself as a rhetorical audience.

A **rhetorical audience** can be defined as "those persons who are capable of being influenced by discourse and of being mediators of change" (Bitzer 8). This simply means that you want your audience to be *open-minded* and *empowered* in relationship to your topic. You want your audience to be open to new information and opinions, and you want your audience members to understand their capacity to do something about the problem. For example, if you planned to give a speech on childhood obesity, you would want your audience to be receptive to information about the causes of childhood obesity. You also would want them to understand that they can have some impact on the prevalence of childhood obesity—for example, by changing their children's eating and exercise habits or by supporting changes to the types of food and beverages that are available in local schools.

Being open-minded and feeling empowered might seem to be out of your control, but there are strategies for helping your audience to see themselves in this way. If you expect that your audience will not immediately be open to your point of view, you might elicit some openness if you show that their peers or people they respect agree with your viewpoint. Likewise, audiences might feel disempowered if they think that a problem is too big to solve. You might need to redefine the problem so that it feels more manageable to your audience.

In fact, one scholar has defined the entire art of rhetoric as "the adjustment of ideas to people and people to ideas" (Bryant 413). This means that public speaking involves adapting your ideas in light of the beliefs and values of your audience and encouraging your audience to be the type of people who would find your ideas compelling. You can do this effectively by identifying the constraints in your rhetorical situation.

Constraints and Opportunities

In public speaking, a **constraint** can be defined as any factor that might influence the audience's receptiveness to the speech. During the invention of the speech, a speaker should focus on the cultural, political, and psychological constraints that might make an audience more or less open to his or her message. Preexisting beliefs, attitudes toward the speaker, commitments to particular values, and traditions, norms, and laws all can influence how an audience might respond to a speech.

Although the word "constraint" might suggest only what a speaker should *not* say, a constraint also can be an *opportunity* for generating ideas about how to address an issue creatively. In other words, a constraint is a starting point for invention. For example, an audience of college students might be opposed to more general education requirements but also believe that good writing skills are crucial for getting a job. Both of these ideas are constraints, but the latter suggests an opportunity for showing students why additional writing requirements might be a good thing. Or these constraints might suggest that a speech should avoid proposing new requirements and instead advocate that individuals choose writing courses as electives. Identifying constraints can help a speaker to figure out what to talk about, what to avoid, and how to approach certain topics.

Thinking about constraints and opportunities can be especially helpful in determining your topic and identifying its public significance. Think again about the forest fire topic. Many people perceive forest fires with fear, so that is a crucial constraint. It might be difficult to persuade them that federal agencies should reduce their firefighting capabilities. However, if your audience is strongly committed to the idea of small government and fiscal responsibility, those commitments provide other constraints that could help you to define the problem. You might be able to craft a speech that defines the exigence as overspending among federal agencies that fight forest fires.

Do not shy away from particular topics or problems just because there seem to be difficult constraints. Often, the best and most memorable speeches are the ones that address constraints in a creative way. More broadly, speaking in situations in which there are significant constraints enables open-mindedness, an important virtue for democratic audiences. Seeing constraints as opportunities for creative rhetorical invention can help you to address—and even enjoy—the most challenging rhetorical situations.

Determining Your Topic

The rest of the chapter will show you how to put these ideas about the rhetorical situation into practice. As you read through this section, you might want to take notes about how these ideas apply to topics that you are considering for your speeches. (One note before proceeding: This chapter was written with the idea that you may address the same topic for both your informative and persuasive speeches. Even if you do not do so, the ideas that we discuss will still be useful for developing a topic and purpose that has public significance.)

Brainstorming Topics

Often, students in a public speaking class struggle to develop a topic. In part, that's because your material for the speech comes almost exclusively from outside the class—from research, from your own experience, from events in your community. It requires extra work on your part beyond what you are reading and discussing in the class. It is also a struggle because your options are almost unlimited. In other rhetorical situations, you might have little choice about the topic; other people might specify the topic, or the situation might make your topic obvious. But in a public speaking class, you generally have freedom to craft a topic around your own interests and concerns.

To help you get started, consider some of these techniques and sources for brainstorming potential speech topics. The first few are very open-ended; the latter few will direct you to topics that are likely to have public significance, an important feature of a good public speaking topic.

Personal Experience Look back to chapter 2. Write down things from your own life—unusual experiences, jobs you have had, challenges that you (or family members of friends) have faced, problems that you have seen. Remember that with brainstorming activities, you should not count anything out for now. Even the most unusual thing might have some public significance. Just from the prompts listed above, my list would look like this: traveling in China, working on a pesticide-spraying crew, dealing with high cholesterol, and having inadequate health insurance.

Your Knowledge Make two columns on a sheet of paper. In one column, list topics with which you are already familiar or that you discuss regularly with others. In the other column, list topics with which you are less familiar or that spark your desire to learn more. If you are feeling especially anxious about speaking, you might lean toward topics in that first column. For example, I might start my list with the following:

Familiar Topics	Less Familiar/Want to Learn More
Child care	Bilingual education
Environmentalism	Biodiversity
International travel	Urban transportation
Saving for retirement	Social Security

Browsing If you do not regularly read newspapers or magazines that look at public issues, take a trip to the library, to the magazine and newspaper section of a local bookstore, or to a news-oriented website, and see what catches your interest. Many periodicals are now available electronically. You can type the name of a newspaper or magazine into a search engine such as Google, or you can consult the Internet Public Library's collection of online newspapers and magazines at http://www.ipl.org/div/news/.

Daily Lists/Journaling As you go through your day, keep a journal of things that catch your interest. This could stem from things you read, conversations you have, films you see, or events on campus or in your community. When possible, clip or print something that you can keep in your journal. Identify key words and phrases to help you brainstorm related topic ideas.

Focused Freewriting This is brainstorming with a focus. For example, these sentences might help you to think about potential topics for informative and persuasive speeches:

> I wish people knew more about . . .
> An important issue in my community is . . .
> I wonder what my classmates think about . . .
> I think it is wrong when . . .
> Our society would be better if . . .
> Something should be done about . . .

Clustering This involves brainstorming around a set of categories. If you are having a difficult time coming up with broad topic areas, these categories can be useful ones for inventing speech topics about public problems:

> Places
> Products
> Problems
> Plans/policies

Similarly, you can cluster topic ideas by thinking in terms of location:

> Campus problems
> Community problems
> State and regional problems
> National problems
> Global problems

Or consider subcategories or unique aspects of the following broad topic areas:

> Health and medicine
> Education and schooling
> Nature and environment

Work and jobs

Consumption and leisure

Gender and sexuality

Life and death

War and peace

As you review your lists of potential topics, recall the rhetorical power of the stories you heard during the first round of speeches. Typically, the best speeches are ones that connect the speaker's life and interests to the needs and interests of the audience. That principle can be an important guide in developing the topic for your informative and persuasive speeches. The best topic is one that sustains your interest while also engaging the lives of others. Since you will be spending a lot of time thinking about this topic, it is important to select a topic that will hold your interest—and the interest of your audience.

Inventing Topics of Public Significance

You have already learned that *public significance* designates the importance of your speech for civic life or political decision making. Chapter 1 suggested that there are several ways in which a speech might have public significance. These dimensions can be used later as a set of criteria to evaluate your finished speech. During the invention stage, though, we can use the idea of public significance to develop a good topic, a compelling purpose, and a clear central idea.

Consider the following dimensions of public significance as you develop your topic. The topic does not need to have all these features, but if it is lacking most of them, you might want to think about other topics.

- *The topic calls attention to damaging conditions.* Such conditions hurt individuals, degrade social relationships, or harm physical environments. Speeches that raise warnings about current or potential problems fit here (Hove). Speeches on war, water pollution, school violence, and sexism all point to significant damaging conditions.

- *The topic calls attention to shared interests or common concerns.* This is a traditional way of defining what makes an issue "public" and is why the decisions and actions of government entities are typical topics for public speeches. In fact, any topic that reflects concerns shared by many or the interests of a broad swath of the population—such as income taxes, infectious diseases, or Internet regulation—can have public significance. However, be aware that focusing on common concerns has often led societies to downplay problems that are experienced by disempowered groups or a minority segment of the population. Recall the examples of slavery and the massacres of Native Americans. Do not let the notion of "common concern" prevent you from addressing important topics that seem to affect a small number of people.

- *The topic calls attention to shared values.* Another way of talking about shared interests and concerns is with reference to values. If it is difficult to persuade audiences that conditions are damaging, you might instead show how conditions or actions undermine values that everyone cherishes. Conversely, a topic that allows a speaker to celebrate particular values or advocate a position that is based on certain value commitments can have public significance. For example, much of the public advocacy surrounding counterterrorism measures in the United States revolves around the values of liberty and security.

- *The topic calls attention to the exercise of power.* Remember that the role of the public sphere in a democratic society is to promote lively discussion and scrutiny of the exercise of power. As a result, decisions and actions by citizen groups, government entities, and corporations comprise topics of great public significance. Speeches on these topics might inform other people about the exercise of power or persuade audiences to support, challenge, and engage in the exercise of power. A campus's rules about curfews, an organization's lobbying efforts or campaign contributions, or the checks and balances between different branches of government are all topics that draw attention to the exercise of power.

- *The topic improves the audience's understanding of other points of view.* By exposing your audience to new ideas, unusual opinions, and different cultures—perspectives that differ from their own, in other words—you encourage an attitude of open-mindedness. For a predominantly white U.S. audience, for example, topics such as China's economic growth, discrimination against Hispanics, or the emergence of alternative political parties might usefully expand your audience's horizons.

- *The topic contains the possibility for civic or political action.* If your audience ultimately cannot take meaningful action in relation to the topic—if they cannot become a rhetorical audience—then you are not likely to go very far with the topic. Even informative speeches, which should not call for action, can be oriented toward helping audience members make informed decisions or take action in the future. This makes local topics such as campus issues or community challenges great choices for a speech, but even global topics such as war contain opportunities for civic engagement—such as volunteering to write letters to soldiers or help refugees—as well as political engagement.

Beyond public significance, there are some general criteria for speech topics that apply regardless of the specific situation:

- *The topic should be relevant to the audience.* Remember that a topic is not relevant on its own, just as a condition is not a problem on its own. For example, an audience of college students in their early twenties might not immediately see the relevance of a speech about pensions, since retirement is probably not a central concern in their lives. It is your task as a speaker to show your audience how the topic has relevance to their lives.

- *The level of discussion should fit the audience.* The topic should not be too technical or require expert knowledge if you are speaking to a group of ordinary citizens. If your audience does not know much about pensions, for example, a speech detailing the financial turmoil of a federal pension insurance program will probably be too technical for them as well as appearing irrelevant.

- *The scope of the topic should be limited.* The topic needs to be limited enough that you can address it adequately in the time available but not so narrow that it is of interest only to a specialized audience. For example, in a typical classroom speech, you won't be able to discuss all possibilities for retirement savings, but you might be able to clarify basic differences between pensions and 401(k) plans.

PUBLIC SPOTLIGHT

Erin Davies

One college student who has raised awareness of a topic of public significance is Erin Davies. In 2007, Erin's Volkswagen Beetle was vandalized by being painted with anti-gay graffiti. Instead of having them removed, Erin left the graffiti on her car and used them as the basis for her campaign against homophobia and anti-gay violence, which she called "FagBug." Not only has she driven the car around the country to speak at college campuses, she also made a documentary about her experiences while on tour.

Erin's advocacy highlights how a topic can have public significance. By drawing attention to oppression faced by gays and lesbians, she is raising awareness of damaging conditions and highlighting our common interest in a less violent society. In the process, she also improves the audience's understanding of other points of view. And by explaining to audiences how they can promote tolerance in their communities, she engages possibilities for civic action. Erin's example shows how a difficult personal experience can become the springboard for addressing significant public issues in a unique way.

 Social Networking Spotlight

Erin has a website at www.fagbug.com. The Facebook page for her film is http://www.facebook.com/pages/Fagbug/115706695114489?ref=ts

The Gay and Lesbian Alliance Against Defamation (GLAAD) is an organization that is very interested in the words and images about gay, lesbian, bisexual, and transgendered people that circulate in the public sphere. Their mission is to "amplif(y) the voice of the LGBT community by empowering real people to share their stories, holding the media accountable for the words and images they present, and helping grassroots organizations communicate effectively." Consequently, they take advantage of websites and social media to circulate these stories and challenge negative media representations. Check out

http://www.facebook.com/GLAAD
http://www.glaad.org/
and
http://www.youtube.com/user/glaadmedia

Developing Your Topic

During the invention of your speech, use the phrase "developing your topic" (as opposed to "choosing" or "selecting" a topic) to remind yourself of several things. First, choosing one of the topics you brainstormed is just the first step in the process of determining your topic. Now you will narrow the topic to something that will be manageable and meaningful for a series of short speeches. For example, it is difficult to address a broad topic such as global warming in five minutes and say something beyond very general statements. Developing your topic, then, involves an ongoing process of refining it so that it fits your rhetorical situation.

Narrowing Your Topic   Globalization provides an excellent example of the need to narrow a speech topic. This massive topic has many dimensions—economic, legal, social, and environmental, just to name a few—and can be viewed from a variety of perspectives. Rather than addressing them all, you might limit your speech to the dimensions that can be covered adequately in your allotted time.

> *Overly broad topic:* Globalization
>
> *Narrower topic:* The social impacts of globalization

Or you might narrow this topic by thinking about how globalization affects your own life or your audience's everyday experiences. For instance, one student introduced the topic like this:

> If you want to learn about globalization, just take a trip to our campus bookstore. Yes, there are plenty of books on the shelves about this important current issue. But walk past the book section and take a look at the sweatshirts. Did you know that of the $30 you paid for that sweatshirt, just five cents go to the young woman in Bangladesh who sewed it? Learning about globalization on our campus means facing the problem of sweatshop labor.

This introduction not only connects the issue to the audience's everyday experience; it also narrows the complex topic of globalization to sweatshop labor, an issue that is still complex but not quite as broad. The case study in this chapter narrows this topic even further.

Inventing a Distinctive Topic   "Choosing" or "selecting" a standard topic is like choosing an item off a menu; it limits you to whatever the restaurant decides to serve. So although you certainly might consider a familiar topic, also consider how you can creatively *invent* a new topic. A good example of this on a large scale is the environmental justice movement. Instead of seeing "environment" and "social justice" as two different topics, people observed that racial minorities and poor communities are more likely to be exposed to environmental hazards than white and affluent communities. Consequently, activists and scholars invented the topics of "environmental racism" and "environmental injustice" to help audiences see connections that they had not seen before.

You can also consider taking a distinctive approach to a more familiar topic. In the classroom, the same topics arise again and again. Marijuana legalization, gun control, and homelessness are a just few of these commonly chosen topics. (Some instructors may declare such standard topics off limits for your class.) No matter what topic you pursue, develop a fresh, new, or unusual approach. For example, rather than giving a speech that informs or persuades about restrictions on gun possession, you might give a speech that focuses on the more narrow topic of carrying concealed weapons.

> *Standard topic:* Gun control
>
> *Distinctive topic:* "Concealed carry" laws

By trying to invent a unique angle on your topic, you will not only make your speech more interesting to your audience, but you also might discover new ways of thinking about familiar problems, allowing you to make a distinctive contribution to the public sphere.

Refining Your Topic   Finally, feel free to adjust your topic as you learn more about it and get feedback from your audience. As chapter 6 will show, the research process not only generates supporting material for your speech; it also helps you to invent the central idea and main points of your speech. So as you learn new things during the research process, refine your topic to reflect that new knowledge. In addition, one of the best things about taking an entire course in public speaking is that you get several chances to learn from your audience and adapt your future speeches on the basis of what you learn.

For example, you might learn from your research that there is a wide range of recycling programs used by different types of organizations, and you might find out that your audience is very interested in what they can do on a local level to influence recycling practices. You could then further narrow your topic as follows:

> *Initial topic:* Types of recycling
>
> *Refined topic:* Recycling programs in our community

With this topic, you might invent a speech around different institutions in your community: your campus, city government, and private businesses. An informative speech could show how recycling is practiced or not practiced by these institutions; a persuasive speech could advocate a change in one or more of these institution's practices.

These suggestions about topic development—narrowing your topic, inventing an unusual topic, and refining your topic—reinforce a general rhetorical principle that was mentioned earlier: Public speaking requires a balance between your own interests and concerns and the interests and concerns of others. This balancing act between the speaker and the audience lies at the heart of every rhetorical situation. To find the right balance in developing a topic, it can be helpful to think in terms of the public significance of your topic.

Assessing Your Audience

Once you are satisfied with your general topic, you can begin to refine it in light of the potential audiences for your speech and the purposes you have for speaking. As you have already seen, speakers constantly need to adapt purpose and audience to one another. As you learn more about your audience's beliefs and desires, you may adjust your purpose, and as you learn more about your topic and further refine your purpose, you might need to take a different approach to making that message resonate with your audience. So the rest of this chapter and chapter 5 will move back and forth between purpose and audience to help your thinking move back and forth between purpose and audience.

To refine your topic and begin to identify a purpose, start with the idea of the rhetorical audience discussed earlier in this chapter. Remember that speeches in the public sphere should *encourage the immediate audience to become a rhetorical audience.* Because you are trying to create an audience that is open-minded and empowered, you want to consider whether or not your audience already has these characteristics. Public speaking that can overcome closed-mindedness, and a sense of disempowerment is not only likely to be effective—it is likely to be ethical, too.

Several factors can affect whether an audience will be resistant to speeches about public problems. As a result, you are likely to face various types of audiences. One traditional way of thinking about audiences divides them into partisans, neutrals, and opponents (Bryant and Wallace). In this context, **partisans** are people who support your position or have a favorable attitude toward your topic. A presidential candidate who is accepting the nomination at the party convention is speaking to a partisan audience. **Neutrals** are people who neither support nor oppose your position; they might be uninformed, apathetic, or well informed but undecided about your topic. **Opponents** are those who disagree with your position or have an unfavorable attitude toward your topic.

These three audience types can be further divided by examining the basis of these attitudes toward your topic (See Table 4.1). Understanding the basis of your audience's attitudes toward your topic will help you to revise your topic accordingly and identify an appropriate purpose for your speech. Classroom speeches typically assign you to pursue a particular purpose, but in other situations, you need to understand the basis of an audience's attitudes to determine whether informing or persuading is an appropriate purpose.

TABLE 4.1 Assessing Your Audience's Attitude

Audience Attitude	Basis of Attitude	Purposes to Consider
Partisan/Sympathetic Audience	Informed analysis	Persuade (intensify commitment, ask for specific action)
	Habitual association	Inform (enhance knowledge, illustrate and vivify)
Neutral/Undecided Audience	Informed analysis	Inform (introduce new facts or perspectives) Persuade (strengthen commitment)
	Lack of motivation	Inform Empower Persuade
	Lack of knowledge	Inform (overcome audience's selective attention and exposure)
Oppositional/Hostile Audience	Informed analysis	Inform (introduce new facts or perspectives)
	Habitual association	Persuade (weaken commitment)

Sources: Adapted from Bryant, Donald C. "Rhetoric: Its Function and Its Scope." *Quarterly Journal of Speech* 39 (1953): 401–24; Redmond, Mark V., and Denise Vrchota. *Everyday Public Speaking.* Boston: Allyn & Bacon, 2007; Simons, Herbert W. *Persuasion in Society.* Thousand Oaks: Sage, 2001.

Keep in mind that although these labels can be used to characterize an audience in general terms, not all members of your audience will have the same attitude, feel the same intensity of attitude, or give the attitude the same salience or importance as others do (McCroskey). Still, if most people in your audience are neutral because they lack information or are opposed on the basis of thoughtful analysis, then that should play a major role in your thinking about your topic and purpose.

Neutral Audiences

The typical introductory public speaking classroom is probably a neutral or undecided audience on most topics. As Table 4.1 shows, there are several bases for this attitude. Some audience members might *lack knowledge* on a topic. They simply might not have sustained exposure to public discussion about the topic or time to become knowledgeable about every topic under the sun. Other audience members might *lack motivation* with regard to your topic. Regardless of what they know about the topic, the bigger problem is their lack of interest in your topic. They might fail to see its relevance to their life, or they might see themselves as disempowered, with little or no chance of influencing decisions regarding that topic.

Sometimes it can be difficult to figure out whether lack of motivation or lack of knowledge is the main basis for a neutral attitude. For example, someone in an urban setting might not pay attention to news about farm subsidies, while a rural person might not be motivated to follow debates about mass transit. The source of these attitudes might seem to be lack of motivation, but perhaps additional knowledge would help these people to overcome their lack of motivation. Similarly, a person who doubts that he or she could have influence on foreign policy might not feel a strong need to learn about that topic.

Finally, a neutral audience might be undecided on the basis of **informed analysis**, or thoughtful and critical reasoning about a topic based on sound evidence. These audience members are knowledgeable about the topic. But in some instances they might not yet have made a decision. Perhaps they are awaiting additional information that would tip them one way or the other. In other instances, audiences might have a strong commitment to a neutral position based on informed analysis. Think of voters who register as Independent; one voter might not have figured out whether his or her interests align with a particular party, while another might have studied the positions of the major parties and chosen not to support any of them. Both people are neutral but for different reasons. Informing audiences with new facts or persuading them to see things from a new perspective will be required to shift the attitude of an informed, neutral audience member.

When trying to refine your topic and purpose, then, think about the reasons why listeners might be neutral. Do they lack motivation because they lack knowledge? Or do they lack motivation because they do not see the connection between your topic and their lives. Do they not feel empowered to do anything about this topic? Or do they need further information in order to make up their minds? Figuring out the answers to these questions can help you to determine whether your primary task should be to inform your audience or to motivate and persuade your audience.

Partisans and Opponents

Partisans and opponents are two sides of the same coin. Both have a clear position on an issue; however, partisans support your position and have a positive attitude toward your topic, while opponents disagree with your position and have a negative attitude toward your topic. Although these attitudes are clearly relevant to preparation for persuasive speaking, be mindful of them as you prepare for informative speeches too. Even if you are merely trying to inform your audience about immigration, people with strong opinions might dispute your facts or question your sources.

As with neutral audiences, the basis of partisan and opponent attitudes might be informed analysis. An attitude that is rooted in informed analysis suggests an open-minded audience member. Even if the person's attitude reflects a strong personal commitment, that attitude has been formed on the basis of sifting through evidence and comparing different points of view. In these instances, your purposes generally involve strengthening the commitment of supporters or weakening the commitment of opponents. Introducing new facts and addressing objections are typical strategies in informative or persuasive speeches to informed opponents.

In contrast to informed analysis, partisan and opponent attitudes might be grounded instead in **habitual association**, a pattern of "persistent exposure to ideas and situations" that reinforces an attitude (Bryant and Wallace 289). In other words, audience members' attitudes might be the result of having the same beliefs and values reinforced over a long period of time without thoughtful, critical reflection on those beliefs and values. For example, if an audience member grew up in a setting in which conservative beliefs about family life were taken for granted, then it would not be surprising for that person to exhibit conservative attitudes about family issues. If someone was surrounded by people who were strong supporters of immigration, that person might not be exposed to facts and opinions that raise critical questions about immigration policies.

These habitual associations are due to many factors; two especially important ones are selective exposure and selective attention. **Selective exposure** is the tendency to seek out messages that reinforce existing attitudes and avoid messages that conflict with those attitudes. Even if people are exposed to a diversity of messages, they might focus on certain aspects of messages more than others. This pattern, called **selective attention**, is the tendency to focus on simple or reassuring ideas and ignore complexity or troubling ideas. Both selective exposure and selective attention can significantly affect an audience's open-mindedness toward a topic because they reinforce the belief that one's own opinion *must* be correct.

Whether you are speaking to supporters or opponents, attitudes rooted in habitual association present serious challenges. For example, at first glance, the partisan or supportive audience might appear to be the easiest audience to address, but often you need to think more carefully about your purpose with this audience than with others. Ethically, it is inappropriate to merely exploit the audience's habitual associations; essentially, this is manipulating the audience's prejudices to reach your desired outcome rather than encouraging the audience to make an informed decision. Instead, your purpose might be to expand and improve their knowledge or to inoculate them against opponent messages that they have ignored in the past.

An oppositional audience also presents a daunting challenge, but a few points can help you to keep this challenge in perspective. First, it is virtually impossible to produce a significant shift in attitude in this audience with one speech. As you will learn in chapter 13, you should seek more moderate, limited goals. Second, remember that selective exposure and selective attention affect us all. If you are speaking to an audience that you think is misinformed, your speech will surely backfire if you treat the audience as ignorant fools and cast yourself as the one who will set them straight. None of us can avoid being selective, given limits on our time and the sheer amount of messages that circulate today. Third, recognize that habitual associations do not necessarily reflect ignorance. They might result from having different needs and interests than you have, from prioritizing values differently, or from seeing the world through cultural, political, or religious perspectives that are different from your own. While you want to speak with confidence that your facts are accurate and your opinions are well-founded, you also want to have a sense of humility and open-mindedness about your own views.

Often, you can get a sense of where your audience stands through informal conversation or from preliminary research. If you are invited to speak to a group, you might consult with the person who invited you to find out more about your audience. By getting a basic sense of the disposition of your audience to your topic, though, you will be prepared to figure out the purpose and thesis of your speech.

Crafting Your Purpose Statements and Central Idea

Now that you have thought about the rhetorical situation, developed your topic, and assessed your audience, you are ready to make your first attempt to state the general purpose, the specific purpose, and the thesis statement of your speech. In chapter 2, you learned about the difference between the general purpose of your speech and the specific purpose, which connects the general purpose to your topic and audience. You also learned about the central idea, the single sentence that expresses the main idea or position of your speech. In this section, you will learn more about the differences and overlap between the general purposes of informing and persuading, the two main categories of general purpose focused on in this book. In addition, you will see several tips on how to write a specific purpose statement and central idea.

Your General Purpose

Speaking to inform means that your primary aim is to describe, explain, or demonstrate something to your audience. You want to share knowledge so that your audience has a better understanding of the world by the end of your speech. Speeches that attempt to describe a proposal, explain the causes of a problem, or demonstrate how some process works all have the general purpose of informing an audience.

Speaking to persuade means that your primary aim is to influence the attitudes and commitments of your audience. You want to offer a viewpoint that is supported with evidence and appealing to listeners so that your audience's commitments to your topic have evolved in ways that you desire. Speeches that attempt to criticize some proposal, shift an audience's support of some idea, or encourage the audience to act in one way rather than another all have the general purpose of persuading an audience.

Of course, the real world of public speaking is a little more complicated than this. Many speeches will try to inform *and* persuade their audience. For example, a speech that is intended to show your audience that global warming is a public problem will require you to describe and explain the scientific positions on climate change and to encourage the audience to see these conditions as serious and urgent. Speeches that ask the audience to see some conditions as problems would be in the middle of a continuum that has informative and persuasive speeches at its poles.

There are other general purposes that you might pursue or observe in other rhetorical situations. For example, speeches on ceremonial occasions

SPEAKING TO PERSUADE
The forum for speaking influences whether your purpose will be to inform, persuade, or entertain.

often have the general purpose of praising some person, group, or practice. Speeches on national holidays often praise individuals or groups who played a significant role in the history of a country. In doing so, they also reinforce some of the important myths and values that speakers might use when trying to persuade an audience. These types of speeches will be discussed in chapter 15.

In your class, your general purpose probably will be designated by your speech assignments, so be sure to clarify your purpose with your instructor as you develop your speech. Beyond this class, you can benefit by thinking about the audience types listed above and the rhetorical situation to determine an appropriate general purpose for your speech. For example, if you believe that your audience lacks knowledge about a topic, then an informative speech will probably be a good choice. For an unmotivated audience, you might need to determine whether their apathy results from a lack of knowledge or because they perceive constraints on their ability to take meaningful action. The first situation calls for informative speech; the latter might call for a more persuasive set of strategies.

Your Specific Purpose

Your specific purpose should take shape according to your audience and the situation. Keep in mind that both the general purpose and the specific purpose state what you want to achieve *in relation to an audience*; you are trying to inform or persuade *them*, not yourself. The specific purpose should elaborate the general purpose in two ways: It should describe your audience, and it should further clarify the topic. These two additions will remind you of what you are really trying to accomplish in your speech.

Clarifying the Topic For example, consider the broad topic of climate change. The easy way out might look like this:

> *Topic:* Climate change
>
> *General purpose:* To inform
>
> *Specific purpose:* To inform my audience about climate change

The first sign of a problem here—one that your instructor would easily notice—is that the speaker has simply put the topic and the general purpose together to create a specific purpose. Unfortunately, this does not help the speaker; the statement does not describe the audience, and it does not narrow the topic. The speaker probably has not thought about the rhetorical situation or the audience, and as a result, neither the topic nor the specific purpose is very specific.

How could we improve the specific purpose statement? First, be sure to narrow the topic. Climate change is a huge topic that could be addressed in many different ways. So narrow the topic, and state the specific purpose so that you can cover the topic adequately during your speech. For example:

Topic: The effects of climate change

General purpose: To inform

Specific purpose: To inform my audience about the effects of climate change on coastal cities.

This speech intends to focus on the effects of climate change rather than on its causes, policies intended to influence climate change, or steps that individuals might take to influence climate change. Then the specific purpose narrows the topic even further to focus on coastal cities. This significantly reduces the scope of the speech and will make it easier for the speaker to conduct his or her research.

Adapting the Specific Purpose to the Audience The specific purpose could be made even better by adapting the general purpose in light of this particular audience. For example, if you perceive that you have an apathetic audience of people who don't believe that climate change has an impact on them, you might state the specific purpose like this:

Topic: The effects of climate change

General purpose: To inform

Specific purpose: To inform my audience how the effects of climate change affect their daily lives.

With just a small change in wording, you remind yourself that your speech needs to go the extra mile to have an impact on this particular audience.

Other adaptations related to the audience might reflect the specific type of informing or persuading that you hope to accomplish. For example, for an audience that lacks knowledge on the topic, you might use this specific purpose:

Specific purpose: To share knowledge with my audience about the three main effects of climate change.

For an audience that is skeptical of climate change, owing to habitual association, you might use this specific purpose:

Specific purpose: To raise my audience's awareness that there is widespread scientific agreement about the sources of climate change.

For an oppositional audience, you might use this specific purpose:

Specific purpose: To weaken my audience's opposition to market-based policies for reducing carbon emissions.

In each of these cases, the purpose of the speech is identified by narrowing the topic and determining the goal that the speaker desires for a particular audience.

Your Central Idea

After identifying your specific purpose, you can start thinking about the central point of your speech, which we will refer to as the *central idea* of your speech. Composition classes often call this your thesis statement, but in other classes that emphasize public speaking and oral argumentation, you will probably hear phrases such as "central idea" or "main claim." As the primary point of your speech, the central idea is a clear, one-sentence statement that you want your audience to accept by the end of your speech. In other words, it is the bottom line of your speech.

Your central idea is closely linked to your specific purpose. Ask yourself this question: *If you accomplish your purpose, what should the audience ultimately believe?* The one-sentence answer to this question is the central idea of your speech. It is the take-away message that you want your audience to remember even if they don't remember all the details. The answer to this question is more than just a restatement of the specific purpose. In many cases, you will not say in the speech what your specific purpose is. But you *will* state the central idea—perhaps even more than once to make sure your audience understands and retains it. Your central idea, then, should go beyond the specific purpose to include material that will form the main points of the speech.

Look first at the easy way out, using one of the examples from earlier in this section:

> *General purpose*: To inform
>
> *Specific purpose*: To inform my audience how the effects of climate change affect their daily life.
>
> *Poor central idea*: Climate change can affect your daily life.

This is a classic example of just restating the specific purpose. A better option is to give the audience a preview of the main points that you will address in the rest of your speech:

> *Better central idea*: Climate change can affect our supply of food, our exposure to disease, and our opportunities for recreation.

In some cases, restating the specific purpose statement could come off as a little blunt or condescending. For example:

Specific purpose: To inform my audience that there is considerable scientific agreement about the effects of climate change.

Poor central idea: Contrary to your opinion, there is considerable scientific agreement about the effects of climate change.

No audience would respond well to that! Instead, keep in mind this question: *If I accomplish my purpose, what should the audience ultimately believe?* That belief should be the basis for your central idea.

Better central idea: Scientists agree that climate change leads to significant disruptions of biological and social systems.

Later chapters will ask you to revisit your purpose and central idea in light of audience analysis, additional research, and the expectations for specific types of speeches. For now, though, keep in mind the following basic criteria for good central ideas:

- *A good central idea is clear.* Avoid broad statements and vague words that do not guide the audience to a specific idea. For example, "Climate change is a complicated topic" may be true, but it does little to identify the focal point of your speech. "Carbon dioxide and methane emissions significantly affect climate change" is more specific and concrete.

- *A good central idea is concise.* Always look for ways to condense your central idea into something that you can easily restate several times during your speech and that will be memorable for your audience. Focus on key words and phrases that you want to emphasize, and get rid of the rest. For example, the statement about carbon dioxide in the previous point is much more concise than "Carbon dioxide and methane emissions, which are two of the most important greenhouse gases, significantly affect climate change that is affecting people worldwide."

- *A good central idea is controversial.* In this context, "controversial" simply means that the central idea could be open to dispute or revision. A central idea does not have to be outrageous or unpopular to be controversial. Even informative speeches can have a central idea that is open to dispute. For example, a speech about the facts of climate change might be open to dispute if there are conflicting pieces of evidence. In addition, having a controversial central idea does not mean that your idea is weak. As long as it can be supported by sound evidence and reasoning, a controversial central idea is appropriate for public speaking. It shows that you are willing to engage something that entails public discussion rather than something that is obvious to everyone. In that way, having a controversial central idea makes it likely that your speech will have public significance.

THE ETHICAL DIMENSION

Scapegoating

When speaking about public issues, you have the opportunity to shape people's perception of problems. This opportunity has ethical implications because it requires you to make value judgments. If you are speaking about a public problem, then you are making a judgment that something is wrong and needs to be changed. Your choices and judgments about the source of that problem are ethical choices.

One rhetorical choice that is widely viewed as unethical is **scapegoating**. This tactic involves blaming some individual or group as the source of problems that are actually shared by a larger group or society as a whole. Commonly, the scapegoat gets demonized in public discourse as the hidden source of a society's demise. In its more extreme forms, the scapegoat is depicted as pure evil or as sub-human in order to justify taking extreme measures against the scapegoat. Perhaps the most powerful example of this is found in the rhetoric of Adolf Hitler and other Nazi leaders. Nazi rhetoric used scapegoating as it projected Germany's economic and social problems in the 1930s and 1940s onto Jewish people. But this scapegoating completely ignored other, more accurate ways of assessing the state of German society, and ultimately, it rationalized the violence of the Holocaust.

When addressing public issues, be mindful of the lure of scapegoating. Blaming specific individuals or groups for problems might not only produce inaccurate explanations of the problem

Scapegoating was a major rhetorical strategy for the Nazi regime.

but also can lead to unethical treatment of others in your community.

WHAT DO YOU THINK?

1. What groups do you see being scapegoated for particular problems in your community or society? How does public discourse depict these groups?

2. How can you distinguish between accurate or legitimate blame for a problem and scapegoating? Come up with a speech topic that accurately blames but does not scapegoat.

CASE CONCLUSION

Sara's Speech: Developing a Topic

To develop her topic, Sara first thought about her rhetorical situation. She knew that her exigence needed to be defined so that it was directly connected to her listeners' everyday lives. She also knew that most of her acquaintances believed in fairness, so that was a constraint that she could turn into an opportunity; they might be open to a speech that illustrated some sort of global inequality. But she wasn't quite sure how her audience might see themselves as empowered to influence or change inequality.

Then one day on campus, Sara observed a group that had been demonstrating and distributing information about sweatshop labor. After browsing through some magazines and websites, she found out that sweatshop labor was a big issue on college campuses. She guessed that most of her classmates probably owned clothes that were made by companies targeted for sweatshop labor, so she thought that might be a good topic.

Here is her initial topic:

Sara's topic: Sweatshop labor in the clothing industry

After talking with several of her classmates, Sara came to the conclusion that her audience was mostly neutral about sweatshop labor. Other than a couple of people who were adamantly opposed to sweatshops, most of Sara's classmates did not know whether their own clothing was made in sweatshops. Nor did they seem ready to take action related to sweatshops. They had never really thought about whether they could influence the practice of sweatshop labor.

After assessing the rhetorical situation, identifying her topic, and thinking about her audience's disposition toward sweatshops, Sara generated the following purpose statements for possible speeches for her class:

Topic: Sweatshop labor in the clothing industry

General purpose: To inform

Specific purpose: To inform my audience how major U.S. clothing companies use sweatshop labor

General purpose: To persuade

Specific purpose: To persuade my audience to support a ban on the importation of sweatshop clothing in the United States.

Questions

1. What are the bases for the attitudes among Sara's audience?

2. If Sara had a choice, would you encourage her to give an informative speech or a persuasive speech to this audience? Why?

3. For an informative speech, how else might Sara adapt the specific purpose to her neutral audience?

4. If Sara were trying to persuade an oppositional audience—one that did not perceive a problem with sweatshop labor in the clothing industry—what might be an appropriate specific purpose statement?

5. What would be appropriate central ideas for speeches based on the specific purposes that Sara generated?

Summary

UNDERSTANDING THE RHETORICAL SITUATION

- A rhetorical situation emerges when a speaker gives public voice to a significant issue.

- Defining the exigence and determining the constraints of your rhetorical situation will help you to invent the content of your speech.

- Speakers need to encourage listeners to be open-minded and to observe what they can do about the issue.

DETERMINING YOUR TOPIC

- Reflecting on your knowledge, browsing periodicals, freewriting, and clustering are useful ways of brainstorming topics.
- The public significance of your topic can come from its connection to damaging conditions, shared interests and values, the exercise of power, the circulation of alternative viewpoints, and the potential for civic or political action.
- Always seek to refine your topic and approach it in a distinctive way.

ASSESSING YOUR AUDIENCE

- For speeches addressing public issues, it is critical to assess whether your audience is neutral, a supportive partisan, or an opponent in relation to your central idea.
- For neutral audiences, it is especially important to determine whether they are neutral because they lack information or because they lack motivation.
- For all audiences, it is important to determine if their opinions are based on informed analysis, or habitual associations that are reinforced through selective exposure and selective attention.

CRAFTING YOUR PURPOSE STATEMENTS AND CENTRAL IDEA

- The general purpose of your speech is often dictated by the occasion. Your specific purpose should be tailored to your particular audience and should clarify your topic.
- The central idea of a speech addressing public issues should be a clear, concise, and controversial statement of the message that you want your audience to take away from your speech.

Key Terms

rhetorical situation, p. 86
exigence, p. 87
immediate audience, p. 89
rhetorical audience, p. 89
constraint, p. 89
partisan, p. 98
neutral, p. 98

opponent, p. 98
informed analysis, p. 100
habitual association, p. 101
selective exposure, p. 101
selective attention, p. 101
scapegoating, p. 108

Comprehension

1. What are the three parts of the rhetorical situation?
2. What is the difference between a condition and a problem? What role does public speaking play in that difference?

3. What are two important characteristics of a rhetorical audience?

4. In what ways might a speech have public significance?

5. What are some of the reasons why an audience might be apathetic about a particular speech topic?

6. How is the specific purpose of your speech related to the central idea?

Application

1. Pick a local problem (on your campus or in your community) that has public significance. Using news media reports (newspaper, magazine, radio, internet sources), identify how different speakers have tried to show that the condition is a "problem."

2. Discuss with your colleagues whether the following events and topics have public significance or how you might encourage an audience to see them as having public significance.

   - Underage students are drinking in their dorm rooms.
   - Your campus, which is located in a diverse community, has no racial or ethnic minorities in leadership positions.
   - A famous actor has been arrested for drug possession.
   - An elected official has been arrested for drug possession.
   - You are unable to get a building permit to add onto your house.

3. Consider the following topics and audiences. For each topic, imagine that you are asked to give a speech on that topic to each of the audiences. Take a position on the topic, and then discuss what type of audience each is likely to be: uninformed, misinformed, apathetic, supportive, or hostile. (The same audience might be described differently depending on the specific topic. You might need to do some research on these groups.)

Topic	Audience
Panhandling	Your local chamber of commerce
Gun control	Members of the Libertarian Party
Suburban sprawl	Members of the Christian Coalition
Gay and lesbian rights	Members of the Sierra Club
Immigration	Your public speaking class

4. As directed by your instructor, determine a general purpose, specific purpose, and central idea for any of the topic–audience combinations in the previous exercise.

Understanding Audiences

This chapter is intended to help you:

- Understand demographic characteristics of your audience
- Identify your audience's opinions
- Gather useful information about your audience
- Implement general tips for using audience analysis in your speeches

As you have learned so far in this book, attention to your audience's opinions and concerns is crucial for effective speaking in the public sphere. A focus on the audience distinguishes the social act of *public* speaking from the mere physical act of speaking. Even with excellent delivery skills and powerful supporting evidence, a speech will not be effective if it fails to engage its audience. This chapter is devoted to helping you understand your audience so that you can adapt your ideas to them as well as encourage them to become a rhetorical audience. **Audience adaptation** is the term for this process of modifying both your message and your audience's identity to achieve a message that resonates with your audience.

Han's Uncertainty about His Audience

Han was interested in speaking to his audience about U.S. foreign policy, but he wasn't quite sure how his audience might respond to such a speech. As a new student at his university, Han knew little about the student body and their culture. He did not know whether the students tended to hold liberal or conservative opinions or how much they knew about current issues. Han also was unsure how his audience felt about him.

From the first few days in class, he could not tell whether his predominantly white audience would be especially interested in or especially skeptical of someone whose voice and skin suggested that he might be from a different culture. He also wasn't sure how they would respond to his religious identity as a Muslim. He knew that he would have to overcome some cultural obstacles with at least a few people in his audience.

This chapter goes into greater detail than previous discussions of audience and gives you several tools for analyzing your audience. In chapter 4, you learned that an initial assessment of audience members should determine whether they are neutrals, partisans, or opponents with regard to your topic. In this chapter, you will learn about several other categories that facilitate audience analysis, and you will be shown practical strategies for obtaining this information. Chapter 4 also illustrated how to adapt your purpose and main claim in light of basic audience characteristics. This chapter will expand on how audience analysis can be used to adapt your speech as a whole.

Ultimately, the goal of this chapter is for you to become an **audience-centered** speaker—one who considers the needs of the audience during both speech preparation and delivery. By learning how to better understand your audience and by gaining tools that will help you to gather information from audiences, you will be well on your way to becoming an audience-centered speaker. ∎

Identifying Audience Demographics

Pete had had enough of all the bicyclists. Nearly every day, he encountered multiple bicycles whizzing by him on the way to class, and while driving around town, he saw many bicyclists riding on the wrong side of the street and ignoring stop signs. After one of his best friends got hit by a bicyclist, Pete decided to give a speech that would call attention to the problem of bicyclists in his community. He figured he would have a sympathetic audience, since he had seen a few letters to the editor in the campus newspaper complaining about biker behavior.

"You're probably as sick of the bikers as I am," Pete started. "They obviously don't care about anyone but themselves. They don't care about the rules of the road, and most of them have run over someone on campus.

Since it's only the hippies and a few old fogeys who ride bikes anyway, I think our campus should ban bikes, and my speech will tell you why."

Pete started to feel a little uneasy when he got a few dirty looks during the rest of his speech. During feedback, he discovered that many of his listeners were bicyclists who felt that they followed the laws. None of them had had an accident with a pedestrian. Most objected to being called hippies, and one of the middle-aged students asked Pete whether he thought she was an "old fogey." Even the non-cyclists were put off by Pete's attitude toward cyclists.

By forgetting to engage in audience analysis, Pete missed a golden opportunity to intervene in the public sphere. Pete assumed that everyone in the audience was like him and saw the world in the same way that he did. Even if he had important observations and criticisms of bicyclists' behavior, his expression of those ideas failed to resonate with his audience.

Audience demographics, or information about relatively stable characteristics of audience members, are a good starting point for thinking about constraints and opportunities for your speech. Especially if you are asked to speak before an audience of people with whom you are not familiar, inquiring about demographic characteristics is essential to avoid significant failures of adaptation.

When used properly, audience demographics can help you to avoid several tendencies that can hurt your effectiveness and interfere with building positive relationships with your audience:

- First, speakers need to guard against **egocentrism**, the habit of privileging their own knowledge and interests above all others. As Pete's example shows, egocentrism can manifest itself by assuming that everyone has the same experiences and attitudes as you do. By acknowledging demographic differences between yourself and your audience members, you can identify specific areas in which audience analysis is needed.

- A similar tendency is **ethnocentrism**, the habit of assuming that your own cultural standards are, or ought to be, shared by others. Customs and value judgments that you might take for granted are not necessarily shared if you are speaking to a culturally diverse audience. Assuming that all audience members celebrate Easter and believing that support for women's equality is universal are examples of projecting one's own culture onto the audience.

- Finally, careless use of audience demographics can lead to **stereotyping**, or the habit of overgeneralizing about the characteristics of a group. Assumptions that all bicyclists are hippies, all women are feminists, and all computer enthusiasts are socially inept are examples of stereotypes. Stereotyping is dangerous because it denies individual differences and because it often reinforces negative images of particular groups of people.

The challenge for effective and ethical audience analysis is to draw conclusions that aid the process of audience adaptation without unfairly stereotyping your audience. By thinking of demographic factors as simply the starting points for your audience analysis, you are reminded that several factors can influence audience identity and attitudes. This can check the tendency to draw stereotypical conclusions about your audience. In the last section of this chapter, we'll examine ways to apply this demographic information as you prepare your speeches.

Age

Age differences among audience members pose one of the first challenges for speaking in the public sphere. Your audience's knowledge base is one constraint that is likely to vary according to age. For example, most college-aged students are familiar with technologies such as iPods, MP3 players, and Xbox videogames and have used social networking sites such as Facebook, whereas at least some of those technologies may be less familiar to older listeners. As a result, you might need to explain references in more detail if some people in your audience are unfamiliar with those terms.

Your audience members' interests often will shift as they age. If your topic is loans, younger listeners might be most interested in the availability of loans for college costs, while older students might be more interested in mortgages and home equity loans. Remember, though, that this constraint is not always negative; it could also present an opportunity to enrich your invention of a topic. For example, a speech on college loans could easily address current college students as well as parents of high school students and grandparents. Similarly, younger audiences might be interested to learn how employers use social networking sites to research job candidates, while older audiences might be interested in how those sites facilitate unwanted interaction involving their children.

Sex, Gender, and Sexual Orientation

The differences between sex, gender, and sexual orientation point to areas that are rich with possibilities for audience adaptation but also with potential for stereotyping. In this context, **sex** refers to one's identity as male, female, or intersexed based on biological and physical characteristics. **Gender** refers to a person's enactment of his or her sex in relation to cultural norms and expectations, often described with words such as "masculine" or "feminine." In other words, sex is determined by biology, while gender is a cultural performance, in which individuals interact in ways that are more or less acceptable within particular cultures (Butler). **Sexual orientation** refers to one's romantic and erotic desires, most often as heterosexual, gay or lesbian, or bisexual. Because these categories do not overlap perfectly and involve human choice as well as biology, they create great potential for misunderstanding and stereotyping; as a result, it is necessary to pay close attention to the differences between them.

Recognizing the difference between gender and sex will help you to avoid making hasty assumptions about your audience. For example, the interests of an all-female audience are not limited to the contents of either *Cosmopolitan* or *Ms.* magazines, just as the interests of an all-male audience are not necessarily football and motorcycles. Because people perform their gender differently, speakers need to look beyond sex alone to determine their audience's attitudes and interests; other demographic factors must be taken into account as well.

Sexual orientation also creates potential for stereotyping. Just as members of a single-sex audience will not all share the same gender patterns, they also might not share the same sexual orientation. As a result, be on the lookout for **heterosexism**—the assumption that all people desire an opposite-sex romantic partner—and the use of **heteronormative language**—words and phrases that assume that everyone's romantic partner is of the opposite sex (Cooper). For example, if you are a woman speaking to other members of your same-sex residence hall, the term "partner" rather than "boyfriend" or "future husband" will avoid stereotyping and be more inclusive of listener perspectives.

As knowledge and attitudes have changed over time, it is increasingly inaccurate and inappropriate to assume that there are simple equations between sex, gender, and sexual orientation. Sensitivity to the differences between these categories will help you greatly in the process of audience adaptation.

Race and Ethnicity

Race and ethnicity are fundamental aspects of most people's identity. In part, that is because many people identify strongly with their heritage. It is also because those categories have often functioned to rationalize unequal treatment and discrimination. As a result, one's race and ethnicity are particularly powerful components of one's identity.

Multiracial and multiethnic audiences pose challenges and present opportunities in public speaking. Differences mean that you cannot presume that your audience members all have the same attitudes, interests, and experiences. But differences also can encourage you to examine issues from multiple perspectives and give these perspectives broader circulation. For example, a speech on immigration that gives voice to a recent Hispanic or Filipino migrant's perspective can circulate that perspective among audience members who might not have heard or understood that point of view.

Religion

Your audience members' religious beliefs contribute another dimension to their identity and attitudes. Religion is likely to influence their perspective not

only on issues such as prayer in school and public funding of faith organizations but also on issues such as poverty, media regulation, and environmental protection. As a result, religion is important to consider during audience analysis even when you are addressing issues that are not explicitly about religious practices.

As with other demographic categories, be wary of stereotyping based on religious identity. For example, since September 11, 2001, much public discourse has equated Muslims with terrorists, which stereotypes Muslim people and implies a distorted understanding of Islam as a religion (Morey and Yaqin). Although this is a particularly extreme form of stereotyping, it reflects what can happen if we draw conclusions too quickly from one aspect of identity. We can see this on other issues in the public sphere; not all Catholics oppose birth control, not all Christians are politically conservative, and not all atheists hate religion. These differences stem from personal decisions as well as the fact that religious traditions have long histories of internal disagreements over their meaning and application to public life.

Rather than making assumptions about specific beliefs and positions that your audience members might hold on the basis of religion, consider appealing to broader values and principles that can help you bridge differences across religious identities—even with those who do not affiliate with a faith tradition. For example, many religions have some version of the Golden Rule as an ethical guideline that incorporates notions of justice, equality, and compassion. A precept like that can help you to appeal to religious values while also establishing common ground.

Class and Economic Standing

The class position and economic standing of your audience members are probably some of the more difficult demographic factors to analyze. In the United States, there is less attention to class than there is in many other countries; consequently, many of your audience members might not think about their own identity or their beliefs and values in terms of class. In addition, class is a complicated mix of family history, income, and job status. For example, how would you describe the class and economic status of a plumber who makes $80,000 a year and those of a college professor who makes $50,000 a year? Does it make a difference if the plumber came from a family full of doctors and lawyers or if the college professor's father was a mechanic?

Still, the status of your audience members plays a significant role in the experiences, the knowledge, and the interests that they have. That can and should influence how you choose your topics and how you discuss those topics. For example, the economic standing of your audience members may affect their interest in the topic of the alternative minimum tax, since that tax has more direct effect on more affluent families. However, changes in those taxes could have an impact on public services or the taxes on lower-income families. As with other aspects of audience adaptation, use class position and economic standing as categories to brainstorm ways to show the relevance of your topic to your audience.

Place

An often-overlooked demographic factor is the place where people live (Kemmis; Snyder). Is your campus in a large urban area or in a small rural town? Is your environment dominated by mountains, prairie, desert, or ocean? Do most students commute to their classes, or do they live and study and work mostly on campus? These and other questions can spur you to think about how your audience's physical environment shapes their daily life, their interests, their concerns, and their desires.

One of the easiest ways to adapt your speech to your audience's place is by discussing local issues. Campus and city matters that directly affect your audience are perfect topics for classroom speeches. Conversely, you can make broader issues come alive by connecting those issues to the specific places where you and your audience live. For example, the topic of skin cancer could be introduced by talking about a popular lake, river, or beach that is known by your audience as a summer recreation spot.

In addition, consider your audience's sense of place, that is, the feelings that they have toward the natural and social environments that surround them. The mood of a place—the hustle and bustle of a big city or the serenity of a small coastal village—is recognized in people's everyday talk about where they live. Tapping into this sense of place can promote identification among your audience members, and it can direct their attention to the things that they most value. For example, if you are discussing the pros and cons of a new Walmart, your audience's sense of place will affect whether they are disposed to see the new store as a needed boost to a town with a flagging economy or as a threat to family businesses in a close-knit community.

Identifying Audience Opinions

In addition to broad demographic categories, it is helpful to learn what your audience thinks and feels about the topic of your speech. Analysis of **audience opinions**—their beliefs, attitudes, and values related to your topic—gives you details about your audience's engagement with the topic and the possibilities for inventing your speech. Identifying opinions helps you to learn the composition of your audience as partisans, opponents, and neutrals, as described in chapter 4. More important, opinions indicate *why* some members of your audience are partisan, *for what reasons* they might oppose your position, or *what prevents them* from committing to a particular position on an issue. Understanding these opinions can help you to find the most effective ways to inform and persuade your audience.

Beliefs

A **belief** is a statement that expresses what an individual thinks is true or probable. Whatever an individual *thinks* is factually correct about the past, present, or future counts as a belief, even if that belief actually is incorrect. What was the primary cause of the Civil War? Does capital punishment deter crime? How much is the global mean temperature likely to increase in the next fifty years? Your audience's answers to these types of questions constitute their beliefs about these issues.

A speaker needs to understand an audience's beliefs, whether or not those beliefs are actually true. That is because incorrect beliefs can be a major barrier to an audience's reception of your message. If you were trying to inform an audience of young people about Social Security, for example, it would be crucial to know whether they believe that Social Security has no impact on them right now. In fact, that belief is false; Social Security directly affects them through their paycheck, and it indirectly affects them if it influences their grandparents' quality of life. As a speaker, you probably need to address that belief if you want your audience to sit up and listen to your speech.

While almost any idea can be made to sound like a belief by adding the words "I believe that ...," for our purposes, the category of belief is limited to factual matters. Your audience might believe that "abortion is wrong," that "the Red Sox are the best team in baseball," or that "the United States should invade Canada." However, none of these statements are factual beliefs. They might be based on facts, but they are not assertions about facts alone. To describe these more complicated opinions, it is necessary to talk about values and attitudes.

Values

A **value** is a relatively stable commitment about the quality or merit of objects, actions, or ultimate goals (Inch, Warnick, and Endres). Commitments about what is morally appropriate, aesthetically pleasing, or desirable for individuals or groups fall into the category of values. Often, a value can be summarized in a word such as "equality," "justice," "stability," or "consistency." The meanings that listeners attribute to these words form the basis of value judgments about specific things or practices. For example, someone who values "fairness" is likely to evaluate a campus policy or a school bond proposal on the basis of how fairly the costs and benefits of those actions are distributed.

Compared to beliefs, values are difficult to change. Because values develop over a long period of time and are grounded in personal experience as well as instruction from parents, churches, schools, and other social institutions, they are constantly reinforced as a relatively coherent value system (Rieke, Sillars, and Peterson). For example, people who value "fairness" probably learned that value early in life, when they were taught to share with others, and were probably reminded of that value as they experienced unfair situations throughout their life, such as losing the big game after a referee's call or not having the same opportunities as their friends.

Because values tend to be stable and enduring, they are a significant constraint in any rhetorical situation. On one hand, the stability of values means that no single speech is likely to produce a major shift in a person's values. On the other hand, deeply held values present great opportunities for a public speaker. Because values are central to people's identities—both who they are and the kind of person they hope to be—tapping into those values can show your audience the significance and relevance of your speech for their own lives.

One way to understand your audience's values is to identify their **value hierarchy**, which is the relative importance of different values within an individual or group's value system. In particular situations, specific values may come into conflict, pushing people to make difficult choices based on which values have greater importance or higher priority. For example, initiatives to enhance national security—such as surveillance of telephone conversations and screening procedures at airports—have sparked public controversy because they appear to violate our assumptions of privacy. People's judgments about the initiatives may be rooted in how they prioritize values. Supporters of the initiatives might place a higher value on "security" than on "privacy" in these situations, while opponents might reverse that priority. Whenever possible, adapt your message to listeners' values, and show the relevance that different values may have in a particular context.

Attitudes

An **attitude** is an expression of an individual's preferences. Like beliefs, attitudes express someone's opinion, but these opinions are not about facts alone. They include an implicit or explicit value judgment. As a result, you can think of an attitude as a preference that is based on an individual's beliefs and values. Attitudes are usually stated in a way that expresses a *favorable or unfavorable* disposition toward an object or idea or that evaluates a policy or practice as *desirable or undesirable*. For example, consider these attitudes:

> I don't like taking the bus.
>
> Our university does an excellent job of helping students find internships.
>
> Stem cell research is a good thing.
>
> I think the United States needs to cap immigration at current levels.

All of these statements express an attitude about some object, idea, policy, or practice. The first two statements express a personal opinion about whether something is favorable or not, while the latter two share judgments about policies or practices that are desirable.

Learning your audience's attitudes about your topic is one of the primary goals for audience analysis. You need to know whether your audience favors capping immigration levels if you want to give an effective speech on the topic. In turn, because attitudes are based on beliefs and values, you might need to determine those underlying beliefs and values to discover why someone holds a particular attitude. An unfavorable attitude about taking the bus might be based on beliefs (whether accurate or inaccurate) about the bus system: The bus is dirty; it doesn't arrive on time; it's crowded. But that attitude also might be related to the person's values, such as convenience, affordability, and flexibility.

Investigating the beliefs and values that underlie attitudes can help you to pinpoint opportunities for informative and persuasive speaking that will resonate with your audience. If your audience perceives that the bus is usually late or has limited routes, an informative speech might help to alter some of those beliefs. A persuasive speech might encourage the audience to value the affordability of taking the bus over any minor inconveniences it might pose.

Taken together, attention to audience demographics and attention to audience opinions related to your topic are absolutely necessary for effective public speaking. The next section offers some practical tools for gathering this information about your audience.

THE ETHICAL DIMENSION

Pandering

Especially for beginning speakers, it can be very enticing to tell your audience what they want to hear. If you are anxious about speaking, you might want to do whatever it takes to get the audience on your side. In a classroom setting, you might feel that a positive response from your classmates will lead to a good grade from your instructor. The more general desires to be liked and to avoid conflicts might also push you to embrace whatever opinions your audience holds.

Agreeing with one's audience on all issues or merely telling them what they want to hear has come to be known as **pandering**. This ethical issue related to audience adaptation has concerned rhetoricians for thousands of years. In his dialogue *Gorgias*, the ancient Greek philosopher Plato criticized teachers of public speaking for encouraging their students to merely reinforce their audiences' opinions rather than showing audiences what is in their best interest. Today, political candidates often get accused of pandering when they tell every interest group that they share the group's concerns and will make these a top priority if elected. Some political commentators pander to particular viewpoints to keep a loyal fan base rather than promoting effective deliberation.

The ethical problem with pandering is that it creates an inauthentic relationship between speaker and audience. Rather than honestly acknowledging differences of opinion, a speaker hides his or her opinions in order to appear in complete agreement with the audience. You can imagine what happens once the speaker's actual opinions surface. What if a classmate were to campaign for student body president on a platform of opposing tuition hikes but in fact believes that some tuition increases are beneficial and actually supports some increases while in office? People who voted for the candidate might feel that they were used to gain votes. They and others probably would find the president untrustworthy and might not be willing to support his or her other initiatives. Paradoxically, pandering can create barriers between speakers and audiences rather than bringing them closer together.

WHAT DO YOU THINK?

1. Can you think of a prominent speaker who has gone out of his or her way not to pander to the audience?
2. How does pandering inhibit the full range of voices from being heard in the public sphere?

Analyzing Your Audience

Gathering information about your audience can be more or less systematic depending on the availability of two things: time and access to your audience. If your preparation time is limited, you might not be able to gather in-depth information about the basis of your audience's attitudes. Likewise, if you are not able to interact with your audience while you are preparing your speech—typical for most speeches in the public sphere—then you might not even know the demographic composition of your audience until you begin to speak.

However, you can still make some educated guesses about your audience in these situations. Your method for audience analysis will be *indirect*. Instead of asking your audience directly about their demographic characteristics and their opinions on your topic, you will infer as much as you can from observations and external sources that provide clues about your audience.

Indirect Methods

First, *examine past statements* by your audience members. In the classroom, for example, you have probably learned some audience demographics if classmates have talked about growing up in a poor neighborhood, the importance of their synagogue, or their experiences of discrimination. Beyond the classroom, established organizations—such as a group that assists teenage mothers, the Republican Party in your county, or a nearby branch of the Sierra Club—usually have made statements or taken positions in the past that might provide clues about their opinions.

Second, you can *talk with third parties* who know something about your audience. If you are invited to speak before a group, you could have a conversation with the person who invited you to gain insight into the people who are likely to attend your speech and why they are interested in your topic. Similarly, you might speak with a representative of the group who serves as a stand-in for the type of people who are likely to attend your speech. Or you might seek out other people who have spoken to this audience to learn about their experiences and the audience's reactions.

Third, *explore mass media and social media* that are connected to your audience. In particular, popular magazines tend to target very specific groups. For example, *Essence* aims to reach black women, and *AARP The Magazine* goes to older people who are members of the American Association of Retired Persons. Both *Commentary* and *Tikkun* address Jewish readers, but they do so from contrasting political perspectives. Magazines like these succeed in part because their staffs do intensive market research about the interests, desires, and opinions of their target audience. Essentially, these sources have already done a significant amount of audience research for you. Websites and Facebook pages that serve organizations also can be useful indicators of the topics and issues that concern your audience.

Keep in mind that indirect strategies will never represent the exact demographics and opinions of your particular audience, so use them with caution. When you have the opportunity, supplement these strategies with more formal and direct methods of audience analysis.

Interviews

When you have easy access to your audience, such as with your public speaking class, use direct methods such as *interviews* and *surveys*. These methods can yield more focused and specific information than indirect methods can. The rest of this section will use examples related to the topic of organic food to illustrate how to use direct methods.

Interviews can reveal audience opinions that are not apparent through observation. For example, if you observe someone eating what you think is unhealthy food, that does not necessarily tell you anything about the person's opinions about organic food. To adapt a speech on this topic effectively, you need to discover your audience members' beliefs and attitudes about organic food as well as underlying values that might be relevant to their food choices (e.g., health, affordability, concern for the environment). Therefore, try to generate questions that explore each of these categories:

Beliefs:	Do you think that organic food is more healthy than nonorganic food?
	What does the "USDA Organic" label mean to you? What does it tell you about your food?
Attitudes:	If the federal government were to propose more subsidies for organic food production, would you be likely to support it, oppose it, or be neutral?
Values:	What are your top three considerations when buying food?

Interviews give you the flexibility to engage in dialogue to elicit underlying opinions. For example, you could ask interviewees why they hold a particular position on subsidies in order to elicit additional beliefs (e.g., "The government can't afford it"), attitudes (e.g., "I think small farmers deserve more support"), or values (e.g., "The free market is superior to government action"). The main disadvantage of interviews is that they take a lot of time. For most speeches, it is probably not feasible to interview every audience member. You might try to interview just a few members of your audience, but be mindful of whether they are representative of your audience as a whole. If you do consider interviewing, look ahead to the next chapter to find out more about preparing and conducting an interview.

Surveys and Questionnaires

A more efficient method of direct audience analysis is a **survey**, a systematic attempt to gather information about a particular population. The tool for demographic and opinion surveys is called a **questionnaire**. Think of the survey as the overall effort and the questionnaire as the actual document of questions that each individual will answer. To make a questionnaire worth your time and your audience's time, think carefully about what you need to know in order to construct and improve your speech.

Planning the Questionnaire First, *determine the relevant demographic characteristics*. Some demographic items might not be related to your topic. Your audience's economic standing probably would not matter much to a speech on illegal steroid use among Olympic athletes, but it might significantly affect their perception of issues surrounding work and careers, trade, and taxation.

Demographics also can help you think about the perspectives and voices to include in your speech. A largely male audience might need to hear from a well-respected male about the prevalence of domestic violence or might need to hear the voices of women who have experienced violence. Rather than just producing a laundry list of demographic questions, figure out which ones can tell you something meaningful about your audience's relationship to your topic.

Second, *determine the audience opinions you want to understand.* For an informative speech, questions about beliefs and attitudes can illuminate areas in which additional information could be useful for your audience. In effect, questions about beliefs are like questions on classroom tests. For example, you might ask one or more true/false questions to get at basic knowledge: "The USDA Organic label means that there are no genetically modified organisms in the product. True or false?" Knowing whether your audience holds true or false beliefs can help you to determine the amount of time and supporting material you will need to address a particular aspect of your topic.

To get at attitudes, ask a series of questions that first identify an attitude and then elicit underlying beliefs and values. For example, you might first ask whether respondents prefer to buy organic food. Additional questions could inquire about beliefs (such as cost or availability) or values (such as health or safety) that ground their attitudes.

Values can be evoked in multiple ways. As was shown above, a question that probes the reasons behind an attitude may elicit audience values. You also can access values directly by asking respondents to rank a set of value terms that are relevant to the topic. On the topic of organic food, you might ask, "What are the three most important factors in your food purchasing decisions?" and provide a list that includes items such as health, taste, affordability, and proximity. These values can then be used to generate appeals that will be persuasive to your audience rather than ones that you yourself find to be persuasive.

Third, *determine a reasonable length for your questionnaire.* This might seem minor, but you get the benefits of a questionnaire only if respondents are willing to fill it out. People are bombarded with survey research—online, through the mail, over the telephone, and in shopping malls—so they might not be enthusiastic about filling out a questionnaire. Even if it is required for your class, respect your classmates' time, and keep the questionnaire to a one-page document that takes no more than ten minutes to complete.

USING A QUESTIONNAIRE
Questionnaires are extremely useful for learning about your audience's demographics and opinions. Plan ahead to determine exactly the information you need to know so that you can keep the questionnaire at a reasonable length.

Composing Good Questions Writing a clear question is more difficult than it might seem. Ambiguous wording, leading questions, and inflexible choices all can distort the actual opinions of your audience. Professional survey researchers have developed standard types of questions and have noted several pitfalls; awareness of these pitfalls that can help beginners to come up with good questions. For starters, try to compose questions that fit the following categories.

Closed Questions Closed questions yield definite answers within a predetermined set of choices. These are sometimes called forced-choice questions, since they force the respondent to answer only from the alternatives that are listed. You are probably familiar with true/false and multiple-choice questions, but others are extremely useful for learning about your audience.

- *Demographic questions.* These are easily written as closed questions.

  Where You Live:

  On-campus   City   Suburb   Rural

- *True/false or yes/no questions.* These are useful for testing basic beliefs, gauging familiarity with an issue, and evoking simple attitudes and preferences.

  The average food product travels 1,500 miles to get to your table.

  True   False

  Do you know who decides which foods can be labeled "organic"?

  Yes   No

  Would you favor your local supermarket carrying more organic food?

  Yes   No   Undecided

- *Multiple-choice questions.* These give respondents a wider range of options than yes/no questions and provide a more detailed understanding of beliefs and attitudes.

  Which statement do you think describes the relationship between organic food producers and industrial agriculture most accurately?

  a. Organic producers and industrial agriculture are mostly separate entities.
  b. Organic producers and industrial agriculture are relatively equal competitors in the market.
  c. Many of the main organic producers are owned by industrial agriculture companies.

  Which statement most closely reflects your opinion about industrial agriculture? You may circle more than one answer.

  a. Industrial agriculture is positive because it provides a wide range of food choices.
  b. Industrial agriculture is positive because it provides food at affordable prices.
  c. Industrial agriculture is negative because it harms our environment in the long term.
  d. Industrial agriculture is negative because it tends to produce less nutritious food.
  e. Overall, the benefits and harms of industrial agriculture are about equal.

- *Scale questions.* These questions can reveal the intensity of an opinion or the relationship between different items, such as with a ranking.

  > Identify your level of agreement with the following statement:
  > "It is easy to purchase locally grown food in my community."
  >
  > **Strongly agree   Mildly agree   Neutral   Mildly disagree   Strongly disagree**
  >
  > On a scale of 1 to 5, rank where you are most likely to shop for food. Use 1 for most likely and 5 for least likely.
  >
  > __National supermarket chain (e.g., A&P, Safeway)
  > __Locally owned grocery store
  > __Discount or wholesale store (e.g., Super Wal-Mart, Costco)
  > __Natural food store
  > __Farmers' market

Closed questions are useful in two ways. First, they give you feedback on very specific audience opinions. This allows you to tailor your speech more closely to the opinions of your audience and avoid vague generalizations. Second, the limited range of answers makes it easy to compare responses across audience members. For example, look at the scale question above. If instead you had asked an open-ended question such as "How easy is it to purchase locally grown food in your community?" some respondents might have replied with a vague answer such as "Sort of," while others might have given you a long story about their latest visit to the farmers' market. Such answers make it more difficult to identify trends and patterns in your audience.

Closed questions do have disadvantages. Because answers are limited, they can make respondents answer in ways that are not truly accurate. The multiple-choice questions above do not exhaust all the possible audience opinions. Demographic-related questions, such as race, can force an inaccurate answer if a person's complex heritage does not fit one of the categories. Yes/no questions can oversimplify one's position. For example, even if several people answer No to the question "Should organic producers get more government subsidies?" some of them might want to express that what they really oppose are subsidies but that they strongly support the production and availability of organic food.

Open Questions An **open question** permits your respondents to answer in their own words. Sometimes, the closed questions that you pose will overlook issues that are at the heart of your audience's relationship to the topic. For example, you might believe that price is a key obstacle to people purchasing organic food and generate several closed questions to confirm that belief. But if you are unaware that availability is an obstacle, you will not see that issue come up in answers to your closed questions. Open questions, then, can open you to new ideas and insights about your audience and topic.

You can think of open questions as being on a spectrum, with some questions being more broad and other being more focused. Here, "focused" does not mean that the question is completely closed. Respondents still get to answer in their own words, but the question will ask them to discuss something more specific.

- *Broad questions.* A broad question can get at an individual's overall impression or "gut reaction" to a very general idea, object, or action.

  What comes to mind when you hear the phrase "industrial agriculture"?

  What is your opinion of this year's Farm Bill?

- *Focused questions.* These questions restrict the scope of the participant's response so that he or she is less likely to give you unimportant or irrelevant information. Even though they are open, focused questions can ask for specific information but without giving the respondent a set of prescribed choices.

  What do you know about the impact of fertilizers and pesticides on water quality?

  Who or what type of person would you perceive as credible on the topic of organic food?

It can be tempting to use lots of open questions, hoping that you will learn a great deal of rich information about your respondents. But keep in mind the reasonable length guideline when adding open questions. After a few open questions, respondents might grow tired of filling out your questionnaire and give shorter and less-detailed answers.

Avoiding Poor Questions Survey results are commonly criticized because of how questions are worded. If your classmate were to ask you, "You prefer organic food, don't you?" you might feel some pressure to answer Yes. This kind of question, a **leading question**, assumes a shared perspective and encourages the answer that is desired by the questioner rather than an honest response.

Even a subtle change in wording can help you to avoid leading questions:

Leading question: Don't you think it's time to eliminate farm subsidies?

Better question: In your opinion, should farm subsidies be eliminated?

The better option allows the respondent to express his or her own attitude freely.

Similarly, a **loaded question** uses descriptive language in ways that could influence how a respondent sees the available choices.

Loaded question: Do you prefer healthy, flavorful organic food to the overprocessed dreck produced by the corporate-industrial food complex?

Better question: Overall, which do you prefer: organic food or conventional food?

Notice how the loaded question uses adjectives to make one option seem more favorable than the other.

Double-barreled questions force two ideas into the same question when they should be treated separately. Answers to these questions might reflect a response to only one part of the question or fail to reflect contrasting opinions about the different ideas. As a result, questioners are unlikely to get accurate and useful answers.

> *Double-barreled question:* Do you favor increasing subsidies for organic food and decreasing subsidies for conventional food?

How you would interpret a No answer to this question? Perhaps it means that the respondent is opposed to both positions. Or perhaps it means that the respondent favors one position but not the other and felt compelled to answer No to the whole question since there was no way to answer No to just one part. Instead of using double-barreled questions, ask separate questions or rephrase the question in a way that explains the relationship between the two positions more clearly.

> *Better question:* Do you favor increasing subsidies for organic food?
>
> *Better question:* Would you support an increase in subsidies for organic food if it meant decreasing subsidies for conventional food?

Finally, be mindful of asking **private questions**, which might elicit information or provoke emotions that respondents would prefer to leave undisturbed. For example, people might find questions about sexual orientation or religion intrusive and unnecessary. Likewise, questions about unpleasant or traumatic personal experiences (e.g., death of a loved one, getting fired from a job) or illegal behavior (e.g., drug use) can be off-putting and might generate unreliable results. So when developing your questions, be sure to consider your respondents' possible reactions, not just the information that you would like to have.

Using Audience Analysis in Your Speeches

Once you have gathered information about your audience, what do you do with all of this material? Putting your audience analysis to work in your speeches takes some creativity. This section shows you how to move systematically through your audience research and identify opportunities for general audience adaptation. Later chapters will offer more detailed advice about using audience analysis in the specific contexts of informative and persuasive speaking.

Using Audience Demographics

Recall the tendencies of egocentrism and ethnocentrism described in the first part of the chapter. Speakers cannot assume that their audiences share their personal interests or their cultural background. Consequently, an exploration of audience demographics is necessary to see where your identity and experiences align with your audience and where they differ. Here are three practical ways to use demographics in the process of audience adaptation:

- *Use audience demographics to adjust your topic and purpose.* Where there is uniformity in a particular demographic category, define your topic and purpose in a way that highlights their relevance to that group of people. This does not mean that you should avoid topics that you think will not interest your audience. Rather, your task is to make significant topics interesting.

  For example, the topic of methamphetamine use in rural areas might not be of obvious interest to a largely urban audience, but it might have relevance for that audience if it is discussed in terms of shifting priorities for drug enforcement. In other words, use demographics to adapt, rather than abandon, your topic and purpose.

- *Use audience demographics to identify similarities and differences between you and your audience.* If you are similar to your audience in certain ways, you can emphasize those similarities early in your speech to establish common ground. Mentioning shared experiences (e.g., commuting to work) and cultural references (e.g., movies, TV shows) are an easy way to display your similarity to your audience.

  When significant differences exist between you and your audience, first consider whether those differences are likely to matter to your audience. For example, your ethnicity might not really matter to an audience that is trying to determine whether a new park should be built in their neighborhood. If differences do matter, however, explore two basic strategies: seek common ground elsewhere, or use difference to establish expertise or a unique perspective. For example, an African-American man speaking to a predominantly white audience about racial profiling might incorporate the following passage in his speech:

  > No matter what our personal opinions, I think we can all agree that as a society, we need to be able to talk candidly about race. [Here, the common ground is an attitude. Next, the speaker uses demographic difference as well as personal experience to show why he is a particularly credible speaker on the topic.]
  >
  > Today, I want to share with you my personal story about being pulled over on my way home from work last month. Hopefully my experiences as a black man—along with some startling statistics and testimony from white and black folks alike—will help you understand the problem that our society calls racial profiling.

- *Use audience demographics to remind you of the need for inclusive and empowering language.* Evidence of diversity in your demographic analysis should heighten your sensitivity to language that might denigrate or disempower audience members. Overt forms, such as sexist, racist, and homophobic language and ethnic and religious slurs, have no place in public speech. More subtle forms, however, can be just as alienating and can damage a speaker's credibility.

Consider the well-meaning student who gave a persuasive speech about "the need for Americans of all different cultures" to support non-discriminatory policies in the workplace. Even though her speech was intended to bridge cultural differences, she ignored the fact that several classmates were not U.S. citizens or did not identify themselves as Americans. While these listeners might have supported her overall purpose, they might have felt that the speech was not really addressing them.

Using Audience Opinions

As with demographics, audience opinions can help you with several big-picture issues that arise at the beginning of the speech process. Consider the following ways of applying your knowledge of audience opinions:

- *Use audience opinions to adjust your topic and purpose.* For example, if an audience believes that heart disease is primarily the result of choices about diet and exercise, you might focus your speech on factors such as genetics and family history. An audience that values privacy would likely be interested in topics ranging from Internet privacy to credit card companies' use of personal information. The audience's level of prior knowledge or personal experience with Internet use or credit cards could help you to decide which topic is more appropriate.

- *Use audience opinions to determine the depth of your speech and the supporting material you need.* Audiences with substantive knowledge of a topic might be bored by a speech that intends to give a broad overview of that topic. Conversely, audiences with little knowledge might be overwhelmed by speeches that cover too much or are filled with technical jargon. For example, you might try to use stories to inform the latter audience only about how cookies work rather than developing a detailed explanation of three types of XSS vulnerability.

- *Use audience opinions to identify areas of consensus and areas of disagreement within your audience.* Your audience might have very similar values but have wildly divergent beliefs and attitudes about the perennial public speaking topic of marijuana legalization. If the audience is split on whether marijuana's health effects are largely positive or negative, you might orient an informative speech as a mutual inquiry into the latest medical research on this topic.

PUBLIC SPOTLIGHT

Wangari Maathai

Upon receiving the Nobel Peace Prize in 2004, the Kenyan activist Wangari Maathai delivered a lecture in Oslo, Norway, that appealed to a wide range of audience members. Her situation made audience adaptation extremely complicated. Her immediate audience comprised Norwegian royalty, diplomats from around the world, and fellow Kenyans. An even broader global audience would likely hear reports about her speech. In many ways, her speech is a model of how to adapt to diverse audiences in an increasingly global society.

Maathai's own work with the Green Belt Movement in Africa provided the basis for a rhetorical strategy to appeal to multiple audiences. For Maathai, the issues of environmental sustainability, democracy, and peace are all interconnected. As a result, discussing her work on each of these issues helped her appeal to those who might be involved with one issue but not the others. In the middle of her Nobel Lecture, she summarized these connections:

Global activists such as Wangari Maathai must continually adapt their messages to diverse audiences.

> The Norwegian Nobel Committee has challenged the world to broaden the understanding of peace: there can be no peace without equitable development; and there can be no development without sustainable management of the environment in a democratic and peaceful space. This shift is an idea whose time has come.

Maathai also used inclusive and empowering language to build a sense of connection among her diverse audiences. In addition to discussing her own experiences, she encouraged others to see themselves as engaged in the same kind of work that won such a prestigious award:

> Although this prize comes to me, it acknowledges the work of countless individuals and groups across the globe. They work quietly and often without recognition to protect the environment, promote democracy, defend human rights and ensure equality between women and men. By so doing, they plant seeds of peace. I know they, too,

are proud today. To all who feel represented by this prize I say use it to advance your mission and meet the high expectations the world will place on us.

By using empowering language and showing the connections between diverse topics, Maathai's speech reached beyond the elites in her immediate audience, stretching the public sphere to include and recognize ordinary citizens enacting positive change in their communities.

 Social Media Spotlight

The Green Belt Movement has an active presence on Facebook at
http://www.facebook.com/group.php?gid=4031089747

Videos of recent Nobel Peace Prize lectures can be found at
http://nobelprize.org/nobel_prizes/peace/video _lectures.html

Additionally, the film *Taking Root: the Vision of Wangari Maathai* and an excellent set of related resources about her work can be found at
http://www.pbs.org/independentlens/takingroot /film.html

Using Demographics and Opinions Together

Audiences often will have some diversity even if they appear to be demographically homogeneous. Since it is impossible to adapt your speech to each individual listener, one of your primary tasks as a speaker is to *constitute your audience as a group.* Using both audience demographics and opinions, you can encourage your audience members to see themselves as sharing at least some characteristics.

- *Use audience demographics and opinions to constitute your primary audience.* The **primary audience**, sometimes called a target audience, is the portion of your audience that you most want to engage with your speech. Communication campaigns show the importance of identifying a primary audience. Rather than trying to persuade everyone, campaigners will orient their messages to listeners on the basis of their level of knowledge about and interest in the topic. A good example of how to think about different target audiences can be found in the "Six Americas" studies that identify different audiences for climate change communication (Maibach, Roser-Renouf, and Leiserowitz).

  For public speaking, try to identify opinions and demographic characteristics that would include a strong majority of your audience, and consider these listeners to be your primary audience. For example, consider an audience with a diverse racial composition that also places a high value on academic achievement. It might be most effective to constitute the audience as a unified group by talking about academic achievement among minorities in general rather than by trying to target a particular minority group as the primary audience. For example, your speech might focus on the role of race in your college's admissions policies or on student services geared toward minority groups. Thinking in terms of a primary audience helps you to maintain a clear sense of purpose in your speech.

  At the same time, you should not ignore your other listeners. Let's say that in the audience described above, the majority supports affirmative action policies but several listeners oppose them. A persuasive speech that targets the majority to bolster its support should not ignore the concerns of opponents. Even if you do not aspire to persuade the opponents, you might hurt your credibility with your primary audience if you appear dismissive of others in the audience, and you might make opponents even more staunch in their opposition.

  In addition, there is a fine line between appealing to your primary audience and pandering to your audience. The Ethical Dimension feature earlier in the chapter addresses this persistent challenge in public speaking.

- *Use audience demographics and opinions to constitute your audience as a "public"* One important feature of a public, as you know, is that it brings people together on the basis of both similarity and difference. In your speaking, then, use your audience analysis to display similarities and differences among your audience members with the larger goal of helping them to see how they are a public.

For example, any topic with a connection to taxes—whether it has to do with their collection or their redistribution through government programs—reflects this tension between similarity and difference. Everyone is affected by taxes, but there are differences: different rates, different types of taxes, and different exemptions and credits create an endless variety of tax situations. And taxes help to provide different types of benefits. Because we all are affected by taxes and we all are affected differently by taxes, a speech on taxes would do well to recognize those similarities and differences, perhaps showing how a particular tax proposal might affect different people in the audience.

Constituting your audience as a public, then, is a way of saying that audience analysis should be used to demonstrate the public significance of your issue. Directly identifying the aspects of an issue that unite us and separate us can help your audience to understand the broader importance of that issue.

CASE CONCLUSION

Han's Uncertainty about His Audience

The more Han thought about his audience, the more he realized that there was not one obvious way to approach his topic. He knew that an all-out criticism of U.S. policy might not fly with his audience, but he also suspected that not everyone held the "my country, right or wrong" attitude. So Han decided that he should explore his audience's beliefs and attitudes about recent policies related to terrorism as well as their broader values. Learning these things might help him to clarify his topic and speak on something that would be relevant to his audience.

Han read *Newsweek* and *Time* to get a sense of the conventional wisdom on his topics. Then he started to develop a questionnaire for his audience that included the following questions:

Do you support the Patriot Act?
**Yes   No   Undecided   Don't know
                              enough about it**

True or False: Freedom should be valued more highly than security.
What do you think is the perception of the United States in predominantly Muslim countries?

As Han worked on his questions and interviewed a few of his classmates, he thought further about how to refine his topic.

Han learned several important things from his audience analysis. First, he learned that "national security" was a key value for his audience. However, he also learned that his classmates thought that there should be something to balance the excesses of the government. This gave him a good sense of his listeners' attitudes and values. In addition, he found that his listeners knew very little about the Patriot Act.

As a result, Han made a significant decision to adjust his topic. Instead of focusing on foreign policy, he decided that his speech should focus on the value of "freedom" and raise awareness of potential threats to freedom. This focus would help him to establish an area of common ground with his audience early in the speech. His audience analysis also helped him to determine that he would need to spend a fair amount of time explaining the Patriot Act and showing his audience how it might affect them. Han hoped that by doing so, he would be able to show his audience that the domestic policies that directly affect them are connected to the foreign policies that were initially his main concern. By shifting his speech in this way, Han was not pandering to his audience; he was inventing a topic that had significance for his audience while also being consistent with his own values.

HAN'S SPEECH OUTLINE

First Draft

I. Introduction: Speaking to people who are mainly concerned with national security.

  A. "They that can give up essential liberty to obtain a little temporary safety deserve neither liberty nor safety." — Benjamin Franklin
    Constitution provides system for security but also freedom and liberty. What is this system?

  B. Checks and balances

  C. Current policies threaten this system

  D. Central idea: The Patriot Act compromises our system of checks and balances.

  E. Preview.

II. Checks and Balances

  A. Where this idea comes from

  B. How it applies in practice

III. The Patriot Act

  A. Background on the act

  B. Examples of how the act compromises checks and balances
    1. Wiretapping examples
    2. Detention examples
    3. Information-sharing examples

IV. Solutions

  A. Congressional action

  B. Judicial action

V. Conclusion

Summary

IDENTIFYING AUDIENCE DEMOGRAPHICS

- Close attention to the demographic composition of your audience can help you to craft a speech that resonates with their identity and avoids egocentrism, ethnocentrism, and stereotyping.

- Depending on the subject of your speech, you might consider these demographics: age, sex, gender, sexual orientation, race and ethnicity, religion, class and economic standing, and place.

IDENTIFYING AUDIENCE OPINIONS

- Analysis of audience opinions—their beliefs, attitudes, and values related to your topic—gives you details about your audience's engagement with the topic and the possibilities for inventing your speech.

- A speaker needs to understand an audience's beliefs regardless of whether those beliefs are actually true. Incorrect or mistaken beliefs can be a major barrier to an audience's reception of your message, or an opportunity for developing a useful informative speech.

- Values are relatively stable commitments about quality and merit. While they are not likely to be changed by one speech, they can be used to show your audience the importance of your topic to their own lives.

- Attitudes are an expression of a listener's preference based on one's beliefs and values. Investigating the beliefs and values that underlie attitudes can help you to pinpoint opportunities for informative and persuasive speaking that will resonate with your audience.

ANALYZING YOUR AUDIENCE

- In some speaking situations, your ability to analyze your audience might be limited to indirect methods—observation or interaction with persons or media that are connected to your audience in some way.

- Direct methods, such as interviews and questionnaires, can give you much more focused and detailed information. An efficient tool for audience analysis is the questionnaire, which uses a mix of closed and open questions to elicit demographic information as well as beliefs, attitudes, and values from audience members.

USING AUDIENCE ANALYSIS IN YOUR SPEECHES

- Knowledge of audience demographics can be used to adapt your speech in several ways: to adjust your topic and purpose, to identify similarities and differences, and to choose inclusive and empowering language.

- Knowledge of audience opinions can be used for those purposes, too, as well as for determining your need for supporting material and the possibilities for crafting an inclusive group identity for your audience.

Key Terms

audience adaptation, p. 112
audience-centered, p. 113
audience demographics, p. 114
egocentrism, p. 114
ethnocentrism, p. 114
stereotyping, p. 114
sex, p. 115
gender, p. 115
sexual orientation, p. 115
heterosexism, p. 116
heteronormative language, p. 116
audience opinion, p. 119
belief, p. 119

value, p. 120
value hierarchy, p. 120
attitude, p. 121
pandering, p. 122
survey, p. 124
questionnaire, p. 124
closed question, p. 126
open question, p. 127
leading question, p. 128
loaded question, p. 128
double-barreled question, p. 129
private question, p. 129
primary audience, p. 133

Comprehension

1. What are the three tendencies or habits that demographic analysis can help you avoid?

2. What is the difference between audience demographics and audience opinions?

3. How are attitudes different from values? From beliefs?

4. What are the advantages and disadvantages of interviews as a method of audience analysis?

5. Is a multiple-choice question open or closed?

6. What sort of information can be generated by a scale question?

7. Why should we not trust the answers to loaded questions?

8. What is a primary audience?

Application

1. What demographic factors would you want to know about if you were considering a speech in the following topic areas?

   Adoption

   Hate crimes

   Medicare

   Public transportation in your community

   The U.S. prison system

2. Choose two of the topics listed above, and determine what beliefs, values, and attitudes it would be helpful to know from your audience.

3. Identify a group in your community to whom you would like to speak. Which direct and indirect methods of analyzing that audience would you choose? Why?

4. Using the topic you have identified for your next speech, construct one example of each type of closed question described in this chapter (demographic, true/false or yes/no, multiple-choice, scaled). In class, share these with a colleague, and have him or her construct two open questions on your topic. Then discuss the quality of your questions with your classmate.

Researching Public Problems

This chapter is intended to help you:

- Understand the need for different types of supporting materials for your speeches
- Learn the strengths and weaknesses of different types of sources
- Find supporting material in your community, in your library's resources, and on the Internet
- Explore ethical questions about the process of doing research

If the word "research" makes you feel anxious, you are not alone. If you have had little training about research or few experiences doing research, it is reasonable to feel uneasy about it. Research can be confusing and overwhelming. Most college libraries have thousands if not millions of volumes as well as access to hundreds of electronic databases. A Google search for "economic impacts of ski areas," which identifies only material available on the Internet, turns up 1.98 million hits!

In addition to these practical challenges, research can create anxiety because it opens you to the possibility of changing your mind. As you learn new facts and get exposed to new viewpoints, you might revise your own thinking

CASE SCENARIO

Jamie's Ski Resort Speech

Jamie was excited when she first heard about a new ski resort that was being proposed in her state. She loved snowboarding and was looking forward to an alternative to the smaller ski hill just outside of town. But apparently not everyone in the area felt the same way. After reading her campus newspaper's article about the ski resort, she heard about a group that was trying to prevent the U.S. Forest Service from allowing national forest land to be used for the resort. She saw bumper stickers and letters to the editor about the proposed resort, and she heard radio ads promoting the resort even thought it hadn't been approved.

Jamie soon learned that the Forest Service was revising its management plan for the area where the resort was being proposed. No wonder she was hearing so much about the resort! The Forest Service is required to listen to public comments on the proposed plan; all of these voices were trying to shape public opinion about the resort. Because Jamie knew that many of her classmates were avid skiers and snowboarders, she thought it would be a great topic for her public speaking class. But she didn't feel that she knew enough to speak with authority about it. If she wanted to help her classmates make an informed judgment about the issue, she knew that she needed to dig deeper than a few newspaper articles and a bumper sticker.

about an issue. One study of public speaking students found that students were more likely to report an attitude change on the issues about which they gave speeches than on the issues raised by other speakers in the class (Gayle). In other words, the act of researching and constructing your own speech is more likely to shift your attitude than is listening to someone else!

All these sources of anxiety are rooted in uncertainty—about the research process, about how to make sense of research resources, and about what you might conclude from your research. To help you reduce some of this uncertainty, this chapter shows you how to develop a **research plan**, a systematic process of locating sources that is manageable and efficient. The plan in this chapter encourages you to *think strategically* before you head to the library or start typing phrases into an Internet search engine.

The main sections of this chapter will follow the three main steps of this research plan: determining your research needs; locating and accessing sources; and producing support for your speech ■

Determining Your Research Needs

The key to doing research efficiently is establishing a clear idea of what you're looking for *before* you begin any in-depth work to locate sources. Consider the following example:

Antonio decided that he wanted to give a speech on the minimum wage. Having worked at a minimum-wage job before attending college, he felt that his personal experience would be a good source of information about what it's like to live on a minimum-wage income. But Antonio was not familiar with the history of the minimum wage or hard data about how changes in the minimum wage affect employers and employees. He knew that if he was to give an effective speech about the minimum wage, he would need to talk about more than just his own experiences.

Antonio kept an eye out for books about the development of the minimum wage and for sources of government data that track the effects of the minimum wage on the economy over time. He was less concerned with the many newspaper and magazine articles that focused on an individual or family's personal story, although he found a few of these to add variety to his speech. Rather than trying to find everything on the topic, Antonio focused his research to locate specific types of supporting material that he knew would be necessary for an effective speech.

Determining your research needs, then, involves applying a few basic ideas to your own circumstances and goals as a speaker. This section will briefly show how engaging in the following tasks can help you to determine your research needs:

- Identify the issue.
- Do background research.
- Revise the issue and generate key terms.
- Specify the supporting material.

Identify Your Issue

In chapter 4, you learned how to develop the specific purpose statement and the central idea of a speech. These two statements should be the starting point for your research, since they remind you of the boundaries of your speech. If you were interested in the topic of sex education, for example, you might start with a central idea like this:

Central idea: The two main approaches to sex education in the United States are abstinence-only and comprehensive.

This statement might become more specific during the research process. But as a starting point, it clarifies that your research will look for supporting material about these two approaches. It also should remind you to be on the lookout for other approaches during your research. Remember that one of the critical listening questions discussed in chapter 3 asks, "Does the speech omit any relevant major points?" Perhaps there are other important or emerging approaches to sex education. Be open to the possibility that your research will reveal new ideas that might lead you to alter your purpose statement or main claim.

Do Background Research

After identifying your issue, do some background research to help you answer basic questions about your issue. How many people work at minimum-wage jobs? What do people mean when they talk about "comprehensive" sex education? How are people in my community addressing these problems? The purpose of background research is not to gain exhaustive knowledge about your topic but to familiarize yourself with the important ideas, terms, and people related to your topic.

Use a Database While you are in this course, you may have access to MySearchLab (access code required), which provides databases of high-quality source material, including EBSCO. If your topic has a strong business or economic dimension to it, you might also consult the *Financial Times* database, also found within MySearchLab. Your college library likely subscribes to other electronic databases that can give you access to a wide variety of scholarly and popular sources.

Browse in Newspapers, Magazines, and Books Reading your local newspaper can show you how people in your community are addressing the issue of sex education. National newspapers such as the *Washington Post* or *Los Angeles Times,* magazines such as *Time* or *Newsweek*, and political opinion periodicals such as *National Review* or *The American Prospect* often provide analysis of broader trends and may refer to prominent spokespeople or organizations that represent different points of view. (Most publications also have

BACKGROUND RESEARCH

Informal reading and conversations can help you to explore the range of opinions on a current public issue.

online versions.) Finally, browse books to see how authors are discussing your issue. Scholarly books can be a great treasure, since they typically contain citations of related sources.

Talk to Professionals and Interested Citizens Discussing your topic with professionals and interested citizens allows you to ask questions, clarify meaning, and explore ideas that you find interesting. For example, talking with a professional scientist at your university would allow you to check your own understanding of climate change to make sure that it is accurate. Your informants also may talk about "hidden" problems or the "real" issues that are not getting public attention. Your speech could then introduce these concerns into the public sphere. Finally, these sources may provide insight into issues that affect your community. Talking to school principals, health care professionals, or school board members about sex education would be crucial for understanding how that issue is playing out in your community.

Consult Reference Works If you are looking for specific facts—such as the minimum wage in your state or rates of sexually transmitted disease in other countries—use *reference works,* publications that are designed to collect and organize raw information in a way that is easily accessible for quick use. In contrast to regular books and articles, reference works typically contain little context and usually are not trying to build an overall argument or narrative.

Most libraries have a special reference section, where these works are separated from the regular collection of books. Some standard reference works are the following:

- *Encyclopedias* provide comprehensive information about a variety of topics or a particular topic. Examples are *Encyclopedia Britannica* and *World Book Encyclopedia;* more specialized encyclopedias include *Latino Encyclopedia* and *Encyclopedia of Rhetoric.*

- *Yearbooks and almanacs* assemble statistics and other basic data in various subject categories. The *United National Statistical Yearbook,* for example, contains economic, social, and environmental data on more than 200 countries around the world.

- *Compilations* collect various types of sources and organize them around topics so that readers can get an overview of an issue and the range of viewpoints on that issue. For example, *Editorials on File* collects staff editorials from newspapers around the United States. There are also several book series that compile previously published work about a broad topic area; each book in the series focuses on a single topic. Some well-known series are *Contemporary World Issues, Opposing Viewpoints,* and *Taking Sides.*

These references are especially useful for familiarizing yourself with the topic in the early stages of research. Depending on your topic, other reference works such as *biographical references, quotation books,* and *atlases* could come in handy later.

You may have noticed that these suggestions do not include using Internet search engines such as Google or Yahoo! While Internet sites for established newspaper and periodicals can be good sources for finding background information, a broad Internet search is not going to be very useful at this stage. Later in the chapter, you will learn more about effective and efficient online research.

PUBLIC SPOTLIGHT

Michael J. Fox

Michael J. Fox has been a prominent public advocate for research on Parkinson's disease. As someone who has the disease, Fox has used the power of public speaking to raise awareness and influence the broader public discussion about the disease and potential treatments. In 1998, Fox famously testified before Congress without taking medication, which gave public visibility to the physical symptoms of the disease. Since then, Fox has been especially active in writing about his life and in advocacy for stem cell research that could lead to cures for the disease (Fox, *Always Looking Up*).

Fox has become a prominent voice on this issue not only because of his personal situation, but also because of his ongoing research on the disease. As he learns about the disease from doctors and about potential cures from scientists, he brings that information into his speeches and books. Fox also has gained insight from others who are afflicted with Parkinson's disease. As he says in his memoir *Lucky Man,* "My greatest teachers now came from within the P.D. community itself. My coming out had an impact on their lives, as it turned out, but even before that, their stories, gleaned from what I read on P.D. web sites suddenly lit up with conversation, had at least as profound an impact on mine" (230).

Michael J. Fox incorporates both research and firsthand experience in his public advocacy about Parkinson's disease.

 Social Networking Spotlight

The Michael J. Fox Foundation for Parkinson's Research focuses on funding the scientific research that has the greatest potential for treating and curing Parkinson's disease. One way in which the foundation communicates with supporters and donors is through a monthly *FoxFlash* e-newsletter, which can be found along with other organization publications at http://www.michaeljfox.org/about_publications.cfm

Another organization, the Parkinson's Disease Foundation, takes advantage of Facebook to circulate educational information about the disease, promote fundraising activity, and engage in advocacy and activism: http://www.facebook.com/parkinsonsdiseasefoundation

Revise the Issue and Generate Keywords

If your background research has led you in a slightly different direction, you might want to make minor changes to your specific purpose statement or main claim. Take Antonio's minimum wage speech as an example. Initially, he stated his specific purpose like this:

Specific purpose: To inform my audience about the effects of raising Arizona's minimum wage.

In his background research, Antonio learned that hundreds of studies have debated the effects of changes in the minimum wage. He also learned that a key issue surrounding an increase in the minimum wage is the impact on small businesses. He reformulated his specific purpose statement as follows:

Specific purpose: To inform my audience how a change in the minimum wage might affect small businesses in Arizona.

Rather than talking about all the effects or trying to evaluate all those studies, Antonio narrowed the scope of his topic to something that was more manageable yet still significant to himself and his audience.

Background research also can lead to a unique approach to a popular issue. For example, a typical central idea for an informative speech on sex education might look like this:

Central idea: The two main approaches to sex education in the United States are abstinence-only and comprehensive sex education.

But your audience might already know that. From community research, you might learn that the most important issue about sex education is not the curriculum but its timing. The central idea might turn into this:

Better central idea: Teachers, school board members, and local parents hold divergent beliefs about the appropriate timing of sex education in our public schools.

In addition, use your background research to generate a list of key words that you will use when looking for specific sources. For example, terms such as "abstinence," "age-appropriate" and "curriculum" might be key words about sex education. Also, identify synonyms for words and phrases in your specific purpose statement or main claim. Pollution, carbon dioxide, and greenhouse gas are not exactly the same things, but searching on each of those terms could yield different sources.

Specify the Supporting Material

The last part of determining your research needs is identifying the types of supporting material that you will need. As Antonio's minimum-wage example suggests, an effective speech usually relies on different types of supporting material. In some instances, a statistic is necessary to make your point, while at other times, testimony will be the most effective form of support. By thinking ahead about the types of supporting material you will need, you can improve the efficiency of your research.

This section serves as a brief introduction to five basic types of supporting material: common knowledge, personal experience, examples, testimony, and statistics. Because the main work with supporting materials comes when you incorporate them into your speeches, later chapters will discuss their use in more detail. For now, you just want to become familiar with the different types so that you can think about what you need for your speech and recognize them when they appear in your research.

Common Knowledge Widely shared beliefs and values of a society can be thought of as **common knowledge**. This type of knowledge is not cited as a formal piece of evidence, since we all "know" it to some degree, but people you find in your research may rely on these ideas to support their points. Some beliefs are basic facts; for example, in U.S. society, it is common knowledge that there are fifty states and three branches of federal government. Other beliefs are opinions, less stable than facts but still widely shared. Again, in the United States, there is a tendency to believe that government power should be resisted and that individuals are responsible for their own behavior.

Common knowledge may take the form of values that are shared widely even if people disagree about their precise meaning or their priority. For example, liberty, security, and freedom of speech and religion are shared values in liberal democracies, even as citizens debate their relative importance in a particular situation (McGee; Condit and Lucaites).

Personal Experience As you saw in chapter 2, personal experience can provide a basis of support for other ideas in a speech. Your own observations and experiences offer a useful starting point for discussing issues that matter to you. In addition, you may learn about the personal experiences of others through interviews or articles that share firsthand accounts of events. But remember that they are only one person's perspective on events and should be supplemented with other supporting materials.

Examples Examples are specific instances that are used to illustrate a more general point. In your research, you are likely to see *brief examples* that can be described in a sentence or two, *extended examples* such as the narratives we discussed in chapter 2 or the case studies in this book, and **hypothetical examples** that ask an audience to imagine a specific scenario. A brief example about sex education might simply mention several topics that are taught in order to illustrate the idea of comprehensive sex education:

Comprehensive sex education consists of lectures about anatomy, descriptions of different types of contraception, and role-playing to promote effective communication about sex.

An extended example might describe a role-playing exercise in detail so that an audience could see what these exercises actually do. A hypothetical example might ask an audience to imagine themselves in the role of a student or a school board member trying to make a decision. Any of these types of examples from your research could be used in a speech.

Testimony In it simplest form, **testimony** is the words of others that are used to support a point. Your speeches will use testimony when they include a quotation or a paraphrase from a particular person or organization that you find during your research. For example, a speech on global warming might quote James Hansen, a NASA scientist who has been a prominent public voice on global warming for decades. This is an instance of **expert testimony**, words that get rhetorical power from the person's specialized knowledge or training. A speech on sex education might include a summary of the local PTA's position that you gained during an interview with the group's president. This is an instance of **citizen testimony**, words that get rhetorical power from the person's own knowledge and direct experience. Of course, these categories are not necessarily distinct; experts may also speak as citizens, and citizens may bring some unique knowledge to the public sphere (Bean; Tesh). Still, it is important to understand how different kinds of voices can help you to support your own ideas.

Statistics **Statistics** are numbers that add up specific instances and express relationships. The most basic type of statistic is a **raw number**, which merely counts specific instances. The statistic that approximately 1 million teenage girls have unintended pregnancies in the United States annually uses a raw number. Another useful statistic is a **percentage**, which explains a relationship between an entire population and some subset of that population. For example, what is the retention rate at your college? This rate is the percentage of students who return for classes from one semester to the next; the percentage expresses the relationship between the number who return and the total number who attended during the previous semester. A **ratio** is the measure of relative sizes of two populations; for example, the ratio of minimum-wage workers to managers at a local fast-food restaurant might be 9 to 2.

Central tendencies are statistics that characterize some set of data by looking toward the middle of the data. The **mean**, or average of a data set, is calculated by adding all the items and dividing by the number of items in the set. Most grade point averages, for example, are calculated by adding your credit points and dividing by the number of credits you take. The **median** also expresses a central tendency by referring to the middle item in the set when the items are ordered numerically. Income data are often reported in terms of the median income in a population. Later chapters will discuss how to analyze these statistics and use them accurately in your speeches.

Locating and Accessing Sources

You are now ready to engage in systematic research on your issue. Think in terms of three broad research categories that will guide you to different types of sources: community research, library and database research, and web research. Because this book is focused on political and civic engagement, think first about doing research in your community.

Research in Your Community

Why do community research? Because effective engagement with local issues cannot happen by burying your head in a book or surfing the Internet. To get a feel for local issues, you need to talk to people in your community. Jamie's speech on the new ski resort, for example, is an ideal one for community research. Even if you have not selected a local issue, someone in your community may have had an unusual experience or special expertise on your topic. At least three groups of people should be considered as potential sources for your research:

- *People who are affected by the issue.* By talking to people who are affected by an issue and sharing their ideas with your audience, you are strengthening the public sphere. For example, colleges that are looking to expand their campuses might need to buy property from nearby residents. Research for a speech on this topic should consider who will be affected by the issue: residents, students who might rent from those residents, and members of the college community who might benefit from additional space on campus.

- *People with local expertise on the issue.* If you are discussing the pros and cons of giving tax breaks and passing zoning changes for a company that wants to locate in your community, professionals in your community should be able to tell you about the likely economic and environmental impacts. Even if you do not pursue a local issue, you still can benefit from talking to experts in your community. For a speech on childhood obesity, you might talk to local pediatricians or dieticians or faculty members in child psychology or nutrition at your college.

- *People involved in the decision-making process.* If your issue involves a clear decision point for a public agency, a private organization, or a group of elected officials, those decision makers are another potential source. These people have been examining the issue themselves, so they will be useful sources of information about your issue. Also, as was suggested in chapter 1, the positions of decision makers should be the object of public discussion. Identifying where decision makers stand on an issue is an important part of effective political and civic engagement.

The primary way to do community research is to interview people. The rest of this section will discuss basic guidelines for preparing questions for the interview, conducting the interview, and compiling notes about the interview.

Preparing for the Interview Just like your speech as a whole, the interview process should begin with an attempt to *clarify your purpose*. Why do you need to interview someone? By the end of your interview, what do you hope to have learned or accomplished? Your time and the time of your respondents (or interviewees) are precious, so use interviews to obtain supporting material that you cannot find elsewhere. Interviews can elicit personal experiences, examples, and testimony that may emerge only from talking with someone face to face.

In addition to determining the purpose of the interview, *identify your interviewees* on the basis of the three groups mentioned in the list above. If your first choices for an interview are unavailable, ask them who might be willing or interested to discuss the topic. A bit of persistence will pay off and could even lead you to sources who provide unexpected insights.

Once you have identified respondents, *schedule your interviews promptly*, since the timing is dependent on other people's schedules. Contact respondents several days ahead of time to explain who you are and why you wish to have an interview. Be brief, but show the person that you are familiar with the issue and that his or her insights are vital. You will be more likely to get the interview if the respondent knows that you have done your homework.

Next, *prepare your questions* ahead of time so that you will achieve your stated purpose. Usually, interviews begin with easy, nonthreatening questions to build trust with the respondent before moving to more complex or controversial issues. In addition, use closed questions and open questions that you learned about in chapter 5 to elicit different types of information from respondents. For interviews, closed questions are useful for clarifying factual information or the respondent's position on an issue:

> Can you give me an example of how the current sex education curriculum is inadequate?

Closed questions can be useful for eliciting specific items, such as statistics, examples, potential main points or subpoints for your speech, or other details that corroborate supporting material from other sources.

Open questions give the respondent the opportunity to explain their beliefs, attitudes, and positions. In this way, open questions can help you to learn what the interviewee thinks is important or worth mentioning about the issue.

What do you think about the proposed sex education curriculum?

Open questions, then, are useful for generating testimony and quotations as well as personal experiences that illustrate the motives and feelings that are behind a respondent's viewpoint.

A third type of question that makes interviews so dynamic is a *probe* (Stewart and Cash). Probes are essentially "follow-up" questions that clarify meaning and elicit additional information. For example, use a more specific *informational* probe when the respondent provides a vague or incomplete answer or an answer that implies an attitude or feeling that you want to understand.

Why is your support for abstinence-based sex education so strong?

To clarify an interviewee's response, use a *reflective* or mirror probe. This type of probe allows you to confirm the words of your respondent or their meaning.

If I were to summarize, your main objection is that comprehensive sex education sends a mixed message to students. Is that a fair statement?

A reflective probe is especially useful if you intend to paraphrase or summarize your respondent's statements.

Conducting the Interview   In many cases, you may be interviewing someone while at their job, so treat the interview as if you were going to work yourself. Your personal appearance and dress should be professional, and you should arrive on time. Bring all the materials you need—pens or pencils, a notebook, recording materials, documents—and have them ready to use when you arrive. If you are planning to use an audio or video recorder, test it ahead of time and arrive early enough to set it up.

When you meet your respondent, introduce yourself and remind him or her of the purpose of your interview and the approximate length of the interview. You can use this opportunity to encourage the respondent to focus on certain issues or perspectives.

I know there are a lot of different personal opinions about sex education, but for this interview, I'm really interested in your knowledge as a psychologist.

If you wish to use recording equipment, ask permission at the beginning of the interview, and have the person say and spell his or her name so that you can use it accurately in your speech. It is good practice to tell the respondent that you will be the only one to use the recording and that you will destroy it or delete it at the end of your class unless the respondent consents otherwise.

Throughout the interview, recall the listening skills from chapter 3. Be an attentive listener, and use the probes discussed above to follow up on interesting or unclear statements. While you should follow your interview schedule, be open to the possibility of following up on new ideas that you had not considered during your preparation. At the end of the interview, be sure to thank the respondent for his or her time.

Afterward, *organize your notes immediately*. Schedule some time after your interview to review your notes and identify the highlights—main points from the interview and details that might serve as supporting material in your speech. Use a blank copy of your interview schedule as a guide, but follow your original notes closely so that you are sure to include insights that went beyond your own questions. After you have gathered information from other sources, you can use your interview notes to create note cards on specific points that you want to include in your speech. (For more on this, see the section titled "Reading and Taking Notes" near the end of this chapter.)

Research in Libraries and Electronic Databases

The digital information revolution is both a blessing and a curse. Although it offers access to lots of information, the diversity of sources and the dizzying array of tools to access those sources make it difficult for students to do research systematically. The terms that are commonly used to explain the research process do not always fit this constantly changing environment. For example, like most major newspapers, the *New York Times* is a "print" source, but it also exists in several electronic forms that are constantly updated, archived on the *Times*'s website, and stored in different databases.

As a result, there are several ways in which you could research and access material from the *New York Times*. You might use a search engine, the search tool on the *Times* website, a periodical index, or a database search tool. It is easy to get confused about the complicated relationships between search technologies, databases, and sources. To do research efficiently, you need to understand the difference between a **source**—the actual material you will use in your speech, such as an article, chart, or photograph—and **research tools**—the databases, catalogs, search engines, and other aids that collect, organize, or direct you to source material. Remember that *your goal in research is to find sources. Research tools merely help you to find sources.* Keep this difference in mind throughout the speech process. Not only will it help you during research, it will also keep you from citing "Google" or "Lexis-Nexis" rather than the actual sources during your speech.

Because your ultimate goal is finding sources, search systematically for different types of sources (rather than merely "getting on the Internet" or

TABLE 6.1 Using Research Tools to Find Sources

To Find This Type of Source:	Use This Type of Research Tool:	Examples of Good Tools Are:
Books	Library catalog	Your college's library catalog
		WorldCat
Newspapers	Specialized database	Newsbank
		Lexis-Nexis Academic
	Newspaper index	Inter net Public Library
Popular magazines	General database	Readers' Guide Full Text
		Academic Search Premier
		ProQuest
Scholarly and professional journals	General database	Academic Search Premier
		Web of Knowledge
	Discipline or topic database	PubMed
		EconLit
Government publications	Government-sponsored website	GPO Access
		Fedstats.gov
	Specialized database	Lexis-Nexis Congressional
Websites	Search engine (advanced)	Google
		Ask.com
	Subject directory	Librarian's Index

"going to the library") to execute your research plan. This section explains different types of sources and the strengths and weaknesses of those source types. Refer to Table 6.1 to see which research tool will help you to access those sources.

Books Books in your college library can be excellent sources. Compared to books in public libraries or bookstores, they are more likely to contain extensive supporting material and bibliographies. Also, most scholarly books also go through a formal review process by other experts in the field, whereas public libraries and bookstores tend to include more books that were written for commercial purposes. While you can find good sources elsewhere, you are more likely to find reliable sources in an academic library.

A key limitation of books is their recency. Even a book that has just been published was actually written six months to two years before publication, which might not be recent enough for you to claim that you have the most current evidence in your speech. For recent evidence, newspapers or periodicals might be a better choice.

Another limitation of books is their length, which can make it difficult to find needed information quickly. So take advantage of the search tools contained in the book itself. The *title page verso*, which appears on the back of the title page, lists the date of publication and the subject headings for the book. If these look promising, check the *table of contents* and the *index* to see whether there is overlap with your topic. These tools can help you to determine whether the book or parts of it are worth examining in more detail.

Newspapers and Magazines Popular periodicals are publications that come out on a regular basis (e.g., daily, weekly, monthly, quarterly), are written for a general audience, and are produced for commercial purposes. You probably know them as newspapers and magazines. Some are considered national or international, such as the *Wall Street Journal* or *Newsweek,* while publications such as the *Atlanta Journal-Constitution* or *High Country News* have a more regional focus. Even topic- or lifestyle-focused publications can be written for a broad audience; periodicals such as *Sports Illustrated, Ms.,* and *Jet* fall into the category of popular magazine. Many cities have a daily newspaper as well as "alternative weeklies" and magazines that cover local issues and events in the community.

The strength of these sources is that they are concise and current. As a result, they often make direct connections to immediate public problems and potential solutions. While a book may produce an in-depth analysis or provide historical background for an issue, newspapers and magazines tend to focus on what is happening now and what people believe should or will happen next.

However, their recency and focus on "what's next" typically mean that they include *limited analysis*. For example, some critics have argued that news organizations focus on too much political tactics (e.g., how will a bill make it through Congress? What does Candidate X need to do to win the primary?) to the detriment of analyzing substantive issues (Jamieson). Also, there is a tendency to *oversimplify issues* by presenting only dominant perspectives and omitting voices and issues that are too complicated to cover concisely. Finally, many politically oriented periodicals exhibit *bias,* an implicit or explicit favoring of one position over another. This topic will be discussed in chapter 7.

Scholarly and Professional Journals Periodicals containing articles written by academic researchers or professionals in a field are referred to as scholarly and professional journals. In contrast to popular periodicals, journal contributions are written for an audience of other experts in their field. For example, scholars who are interested in public speaking and the public sphere contribute to *Rhetoric and Public Affairs,* while medical researchers and practicing physicians might contribute to the *Journal of the American Medical Association.*

Scholarly journals typically have a stringent peer review process that strengthens the quality of articles that get published. Other experts and editors provide feedback on submissions, and not every submission gets published. Scholarly journals also tend to be more narrowly focused than popular periodicals are. For example, there are journals such as the *International Journal of Offender Therapy and Comparative Criminology* and the *Journal of Supramolecular Chemistry*. But this narrow focus can make it more difficult for someone outside that specialization to fully grasp the articles or their practical implications. Professional journals may be more accessible and often discuss how scholarly research applies to practical settings.

Government Publications Government sources can be extremely useful for obtaining information about public issues. At the federal level, each branch of government produces publications that analyze issues, record official business, or justify decisions. The President and leaders of Cabinet departments and federal agencies give speeches that address public policies, and courts issue opinions about cases that come before them.

Particularly useful for speeches on public issues are the hearings and reports from Congressional committees and agency reports. *Committee hearings* are public meetings at which the committee invites people to give testimony on a particular issue or piece of legislation that the committee is considering. Hearings often involve people with different perspectives, so the hearing transcript can be an excellent source for observing differences of opinion. *Committee reports* are issued after committees have researched an issue. Staff members are charged with synthesizing that research and writing a report that makes the best argument for a position or proposed legislation. *Agency reports* may compile data about the extent of some problem that the agency is addressing, describe the agency's performance in a particular area, or provide a rationale for agency decisions.

Some government sources, such as the Government Accounting Office (GAO) and the Congressional Budget Office (CBO), are explicitly dedicated to providing nonpartisan information for use in decision making. These sources in particular have a good track record for minimizing political bias in their work. But other government sources may produce material for the purpose of advancing a political agenda rather than merely providing information. Understanding whether a document is intended to inform people about facts, defend a position, or persuade people to accept a particular point of view becomes especially critical in looking at committee and agency reports. Also, recognize that government publications in the United States tend to focus on what is possible within the current political system. These sources are less likely to incorporate marginalized viewpoints or radical criticisms of political and economic systems.

GOVERNMENT PUBLICATIONS
Many university libraries are depositories for federal government documents.

Research on the Internet

In many ways, the Internet is like a huge garage sale of information. You may find some good stuff, but you might have to comb through lots of useless and flawed items to find it. You might pick up some junk along the way. Even if you find something that seems good, your choices are limited. You might need to look elsewhere to find the options that will better serve your needs.

This analogy between the Internet and a garage sale is intended to encourage you to think carefully about what you are doing when you search the Internet. The Internet is constantly changing, and the sources that you find through an Internet search can be wildly different in terms of their purpose and their quality. Whereas a database of scholarly journals will produce the same type of source, an Internet search usually generates very different kinds of sources (see Figure 6.1). While the "one-stop shopping" of a Google search might seem easy, in many ways it makes it more difficult to conduct your research efficiently and systematically.

Because your goal in research is to find sources, keep the following guideline in mind when it comes to Internet-based research: *Use the Internet to locate specific sources, not to do a general search.* Instead of making it the starting point for your research, do Internet research at the end of the process, after you have identified gaps in your research and can execute narrowly tailored

FIGURE 6.1

THE WILD WORLD OF THE WORLD WIDE WEB

A Google search for "sex education" yielded an eclectic set of websites among its first ten results:

- AVERT, an international AIDS charity

- A Wikipedia entry on sex education

- A collection of links about sex education produced for a graduate course at Arizona State University. The site also has links for dental plans, casino games, and reverse mortgages, and the site's designer owns an escort service in Phoenix.

- Scarleteen: Sex Ed for the Real World, focusing on "the realities of teen sexuality"

- A National Public Radio story from February 2004 about national opinion polling on sex education.

searches. The rest of this section examines several types of websites you are likely to encounter when doing research for your speeches. Although you can find "good" and "bad" examples of all these types of sites, this list starts with sites that are generally the most reliable and ends with sites that you should be most wary of using.

Print Source Sites As was mentioned earlier, many newspaper and popular magazines also maintain websites that contain some or all of the articles from the print versions. These sites also may have unique features, such as slideshows or interactive forums, that are not found in the print version. The websites maintained by these publishers typically can be considered as reliable as the print source, since in many cases, the content is the same as that in the print source.

However, because websites permit more interaction between readers and journalists, be sure to know what part of a site you are examining. News articles and opinion pieces written by staff members typically have been reviewed by editors before being published, while interactive forums, blogs, and readers' letters are rarely if ever checked for factual errors.

Government and Education Sites Sites that are sponsored by educational institutions and government at all levels can be useful sources of information. These sites are designated by their **domain**, the last three letters in the site's **URL**, the uniform resource locator (or web address). Educational institutions end with .edu, while government agencies and offices end with .gov. Some examples are the following:

The University of Colorado: www.colorado.edu

Rice University's Department of Hispanic Studies: hispanicstudies.rice.edu

The White House: www.whitehouse.gov

State of Montana's Department of Agriculture: agr.mt.gov

The reliability of information on government and education sites depends on the level of scrutiny that is given to the original source material. For example, a faculty member at an educational institution might post a scholarly journal article that has been peer-reviewed or a committee report that has been discussed and written by other faculty members and administrators. These would be more reliable documents than that same faculty member's thoughts about fly-fishing or personal reactions to current events. In other words, be sure to distinguish formal research and institutional documents from personal items. For government sites, try to determine whether the page is primarily informational and nonpartisan or whether it is advocating a partisan position.

Electronic Periodical Sites Because of production costs and changes in readership, many periodicals now appear only in electronic form. Some electronic periodicals are scholarly journals such as the *American Communication Journal* and the *Electronic Journal of Sociology*, while others are similar to popular magazines. For example, on U.S. politics and public culture, sites such as Salon.com and Slate.com are well-established sites that have stable editorial staffs.

It can be difficult to judge the reliability of online-only sites. Unlike a site that is based on a long-running print source, most online-only sites have a short history. So try to determine whether your source is a recent invention and whether it has a consistent pattern of publication. Many sites are started and then abandoned (but left posted for you to stumble across) if interest wanes or money runs out. For online scholarly journals, be sure to determine whether the journal is peer-reviewed. If not, the site might just be an outlet for work that did not meet the standards of a regular scholarly journal. Remember, *anyone* can create a website, so you must determine whether a site is merely one person's pet project or an ongoing commitment that is recognized by others as a respectable publication.

Organizational and Commercial Sites Like .edu and .gov sites, organization and commercial websites are designated by domains: in this case, .org and .com. Although these domains are meant to distinguish between nonprofit organizations and for-profit businesses, in practice there is some overlap. They are grouped together here because most of these sites will discuss issues from a very definite point of view. Advocacy groups, think tanks, and nongovernment organizations may advocate their positions on .org websites, just as a company may promote its products and services on a .com website.

The reliability of organizational and commercial sites, then, must be judged with reference to the sponsoring organization or company. Objectivity should be your primary concern. When a page advocates a strong position on an issue or tries to sell you something, you would do well to (1) think about how self-interest may influence the objectivity of the advocate's arguments and (2) find other sources to determine whether the site's claims are reliable.

Wikipedia Entries Wikipedia is a web-based encyclopedia project that includes millions of entries and is published in more than 100 languages. The popularity and ease of using Wikipedia have made it a magnet for students doing research. Perhaps Wikipedia's most unusual characteristic, compared to most other sources, is that entries are always "in progress." That is because entries are written collaboratively; the "Wiki" in Wikipedia is a term that refers to a collaborative website that allows anyone to add material to the site or edit an entry. You could log onto a Wikipedia entry right now and edit an entry for your school, your city, or yourself—or almost any other entry!

This collaborative way of producing an encyclopedia creates significant reliability problems. Entries might not be finished as they are in a paper encyclopedia and therefore may have significant factual errors, contradictory information, and omissions or distortions of key points. Even the creators of Wikipedia recognize that its entries are susceptible to "vandalism" and may exhibit a "heavily unbalanced viewpoint" and that the quality of entries can be highly variable ("Wikipedia: Researching"). As a result, Wikipedia entries are generally less reliable than are the other types of sources discussed in this chapter.

Remember, too, that because Wikipedia is functionally an *encyclopedia,* it should be treated as a starting point for research, not a significant source in itself. Even the Wikipedia introduction states, "In most academic institutions, major references to Wikipedia, along with most encyclopedias, are unacceptable for a research paper" ("Wikipedia: Researching"). In other words, feel free to consult Wikipedia, but move beyond it, using it as a tool to help you find source material that you will actually use in your speech.

For more guidance, check out Purdue University's resource on Online Research (Purdue), and see Figure 6.2 for tips on evaluating websites.

Accessing Websites You have probably used Google to search for websites. Google is by far the most popular general *search engine,* a research tool that searches a database of billions of pages collected from the Internet. As large as Google is, most librarians and information specialists advise that you use multiple search engines if you are looking for a source. Other good search engines are Yahoo and Ask.com.

A somewhat different type of search tool is a *directory,* which identifies common categories and subcategories and organizes web pages under them. For example, the category Health might include subcategories such as Alternative

FIGURE 6.2

SPECIAL TIPS FOR EVALUATING WEBSITES

Because of the wide diversity of sources and ease of publishing on the web, evaluating those sources can be more challenging than evaluating other types of sources. Here are some additional tips and questions for evaluating the reliability of websites:

What kind of site is it? Look back to the "Research on the Internet" section, which describes different types of sites. Reliable sites exist within all domains, but sites connected to real-world organizations and institutions tend to be more accountable than personal sites. Remember, too, that .com and .org sites typically reflect a particular point of view, which can influence their objectivity.

Can you contact the author or organization? Reliable websites should have links such as "About Us" or "Who We Are" among other links for navigating the site. Many will also have "Contact" links or email addresses so that you can write to the author. If you cannot determine authorship and the site makes it impossible to contact the author or organization, they are not taking responsibility for the information on their site. Do you really want to use such information in your speech?

Does the site clearly display its recency? Reliable websites should include a "last updated" or "last modified" line at the bottom of every page. If this line is missing or if the page has not been modified in the past year, the site might not receive much attention by its creator and therefore might not be a reliable or sufficiently recent source for your speeches.

Does the site include footnotes and links to other sites? A site with footnotes and links to other websites shows that the authors have researched the topic and understand that other people are working on the topic. It also shows that they are willing to have you compare their site to others.

An excellent guide that develops these and other techniques for evaluation websites can be found at http://www.lib.berkeley.edu/TeachingLib/Guides/Internet/Evaluate.html

Medicine, Long Term Care, and Weight and Obesity. The Librarian's Internet Index is a subject directory compiled by public librarians that includes short descriptions of each site in the directory. The key advantages of a directory over a general search engine are that search terms have already been identified and sites have been prescreened by other people. As a result, you are more likely to find more reliable sources, but you have somewhat less control over your search.

With either tool, use the search terms that you generated earlier in the research process. To make your search efficient, execute a *Boolean search* or use the "advanced search" option of the search engine. Both will improve the precision of your search; a Boolean search uses words and symbols, while the "advanced search" gives you options for adjusting the search. With a Boolean search, for example, you might do the following:

- Use quotations marks to search for an exact phrase, such as *"sex education curriculum."*

- Use NOT to exclude pages that have a particular word. For example, to learn about lesser-known greenhouse gases, you might search for *greenhouse gas NOT carbon dioxide*.

- Use OR to find pages with synonymous terms, such as *global warming OR climate change*. This will expand the number of results.

- In contrast, use AND to require that pages have both terms. such as *sex education AND abstinence*. This will reduce the number of results.

Look at the "help" link on your search engine to understand how it accepts Boolean logic. In some cases, it is easiest to do an "advanced search" and use the limiters it provides. These limiters go beyond search terms to help you limit the language, the date of publication, and the domain to be searched. For example, you can limit your search to only .gov sites, or you can have it exclude .com sites. If you are bilingual or multilingual, you can search sites in more than one language.

THE ETHICAL DIMENSION

Researching Diverse Viewpoints

Research might not seem like an activity that involves ethical concerns. Research appears to be very practical and straightforward; there do not seem to be any hard choices or dilemmas, and except for interviews, research does not really affect anyone else—right? In fact, the research phase is one of the most important times to consider ethical issues. Your choices during the research process are ethically significant because they affect your own ability to be adequately informed on your topic. And they are significant because ultimately your audience will be affected by those choices.

The principle of *inclusiveness*, which was discussed in chapter 3, indicates how the research process has an ethical dimension. In the context of research, inclusiveness translates into a "willingness to listen" to diverse viewpoints. This enhances the democratic values of equality and access to the public sphere. Willingness to listen also fulfills your responsibility to be an informed speaker. This is a responsibility that you owe to your audience for their benefit: "As we speak, we must realize that for the moment we are the source of knowledge for our audience about ideas and occurrences" (Walter and Scott 17). If your research is not inclusive, then you risk losing the trust of your audience, which can hurt your effectiveness.

Inclusiveness does not mean that you will include every possible perspective in your speech. It does mean that you research and consider a broad range of viewpoints before drawing a conclusion. In contrast, the stance that you should avoid is **rationalization**, in which you take a position before examining the evidence and seek only sources that support your position. Instead, look at the whole range of sources on the issue, and develop a reasoned position based on the available evidence.

Researching diverse viewpoints, then, has both a practical payoff and ethical importance. By applying the principle of inclusiveness to your research, you can build an ethically sound foundation for effective public speeches.

WHAT DO YOU THINK?

1. If you are opposed to abstinence-only sex education and you seek out sources that point out its strengths, is your research a rationalization of that position? Why or why not?

2. How might you demonstrate to your audience that you have researched and considered a broad range of viewpoints before drawing your conclusions?

Producing Support for Your Speech

As you are gathering sources, start thinking about how those sources can be used to build your speech. First, *develop a working bibliography* that lists the full citation of sources you are considering for use in your speech. Do this while you are gathering sources so that you do not waste time trying to track down citation information later. Second, pose some basic questions to *evaluate the quality* of your sources. Once you have screened your sources, you can focus on *reading and taking notes*.

Develop a Working Bibliography

A working bibliography is a list of citations of potentially useful sources. Your working bibliography may list sources you do not ultimately use in your speech. But it provides a starting point for your reading and can come in handy if you decide to pursue further research or speeches on the topic at a later time.

The working bibliography can take the form of note cards or a typed list that you maintain as a digital file. The advantage of note cards is that you will have one card per entry, allowing you to take notes about that source or set it aside if you discover that it is not useful. The advantage of a typed list is that all your sources are in one document and ready to be compiled for your final bibliography. Some electronic databases allow you to download citation material or send it via email, which makes it easy to put that material into a document.

Several pieces of information are needed to cite the source correctly. This includes the author, title of the article (for periodicals), title of the publication, date of publication, volume and issue numbers, and page numbers. For books, you should also note the publisher and the library call number. Figure 6.3 shows bibliographic entries for books, periodicals, and websites using MLA style. (Other citation styles are available in MySpeechLab.) The bottom of each card provides access information, which can be helpful for doing additional research.

Evaluate Your Sources

Next, skim your materials to identify "red flags" that raise questions about the overall reliability of your sources. This can be especially challenging for web sources, so refer to Figure 6.2 for specific questions regarding online sources. Subsequent chapters will explain how to think critically about the language, evidence, and arguments in your sources; for now, consider the following issues when you initially evaluate your sources.

FIGURE 6.3 Examples of a Working Bibliography

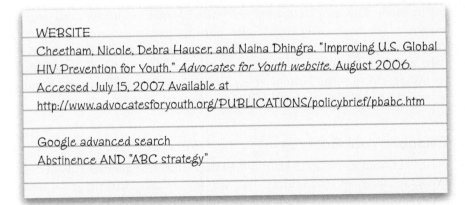

BOOK
Pollin, Robert. *The Living Wage: Building a Fair Economy.* New York: New Press, 2000.

University Library
Call #: 331.23 P774L 2000

PERIODICAL
Santelli, John S., Laura Duberstein Lindberg, Lawrence B. Finer, and Susheela Singh. "Explaining Recent Declines in Adolescent Pregnancy in the United States: The Contribution of Abstinence and Improved Contraceptive Use." *The American Journal of Public Health* 97.1 (Jan 2007): 150-156.

Education Professional Collection database
Subject= sexual abstinence; peer-reviewed

WEBSITE
Cheetham, Nicole, Debra Hauser, and Naina Dhingra. "Improving U.S. Global HIV Prevention for Youth." *Advocates for Youth website.* August 2006. Accessed July 15, 2007. Available at http://www.advocatesforyouth.org/PUBLICATIONS/policybrief/pbabc.htm

Google advanced search
Abstinence AND "ABC strategy"

Authority Who is the speaker or writer responsible for the source? What qualifications or expertise does this person have that makes him or her a reliable source of information on this topic? If the publication is sponsored by an organization, what is its mission and their agenda? Does it have a track record of high-quality work, or have others consistently questioned the organization's research or findings?

In many popular publications, information about the author will be displayed prominently—at the end of an article, on the dust cover of the book, or via a link to the publication's staff or contributors. If you are unable to find information on the author, try a Google search or use a biographical reference work to find out more. For academic researchers, you might search a database of journals in the scholar's field to see whether he or she has published other articles on the topic.

Recency Does the source reflect the current state of knowledge about a particular issue? There is no absolute rule about how recent a source needs to be; it depends on the topic and issues under discussion. For example, if you want to address the philosophy behind the minimum wage, a book probably does not need to be brand new. But if you want to discuss trends in the minimum wage in the first decade of the twenty-first century, it might not be adequate if it were published in 2003. For that, a government document or a periodical would be a better choice.

When using electronic sources, be sure to note the date of actual publication as well as the date you accessed the source. Because electronic sources can be changed so easily, you might have accessed a source that has since been updated. Websites should display both their original date of creation and the date of the most recent modification.

Objectivity Discovering the authorship of a source can help you to think about its objectivity. For example, a publication sponsored by Planned Parenthood may have strong evidence and support that you can use in your speech, but you should recognize that the evidence in the publication is most likely to be consistent with pro-choice arguments. Similarly, the Family Research Council is a strong advocate for sexual abstinence outside of marriage; to find arguments for condom use, you might need to look elsewhere.

Also, consider the author's self-interest. If the author stands to gain something by advocating a particular position, he or she might not acknowledge alternative positions or contradictory evidence. This does not mean that you should automatically reject the source; rather, you should understand its limitations. If your audience believes that your sources are one-sided, they might not see you as a credible, fair-minded speaker.

Read and Take Notes

While there are many different strategies for reading and note taking, a few techniques are particularly relevant for speech research. These techniques will help you not only to identify supporting material for your speeches, but also to creatively invent ideas and main points for your speeches.

Read for Main Points You especially need to understand the central idea so that you can represent the source fairly and accurately in your speech. For example, if an author supports raising the minimum wage but you quote his or her description of the opposition's arguments, it might appear that the author is an opponent of the wage increase. To make sure you are representing the author correctly, prepare an annotation that summarizes the author's overall point in one or two sentences on a note card.

In addition, use main points to organize your note cards. State a main point in your own ideas at the top of the card in a short phrase. Then include a brief version of the citation that refers you to the full citation on the working bibliography. Leave enough room that you can include supporting material on the rest of the card.

Read for Organizing Strategies Good sources will break down a complex issue or idea into several parts. For example, a source might mention "five key factors that contribute to global warming." As you read, note these mini-lists, and see whether other sources break down the issue in the same way or whether they have points that might be added to another source's list. These lists can help you to generate your own way of organizing part of your speech.

Read for Supporting Material As you read, keep in mind the different types of supporting materials—common knowledge, personal experience, examples, testimony, and statistics—and include the type as an identifier along with the actual supporting material on your note cards. By including identifiers, you can quickly see whether you have adequate variety in your supporting materials.

There are two ways to transcribe supporting material onto your note card. One is as a *paraphrase*, in which you summarize the material from your source in your own words. The other, a *direct quotation,* restates the exact words from your source and puts quotation marks around them. For both paraphrases and direct quotations, you must cite your source if you incorporate that material in your speech. Later chapters will further explain how to avoid plagiarism as you incorporate source material into your speeches.

Read for Visual Aids Be on the lookout for visual aids as another type of supporting material. A powerful photograph, a simple chart or graph, or a model of some process can be highly effective for sharing information and shaping perceptions. Rather than trying to reproduce the visual aid on your note card, simply write, "Visual Aid" as an identifier, and then briefly describe the type of visual aid and the information or ideas it depicts. Print, photocopy, or save an electronic copy of the visual so that you can easily consult it later and decide whether you want to use it in your speech. Chapter 12 will discuss how to use visual aids.

Read for Differences of Opinion As you know, public issues emerge when there are disagreements and differences of opinion about some public problem. As you read, pay attention for places in which an author refers to an opposing point of view, questions common knowledge, or challenges an opponent. Identifying a clash of opinions can help you to invent your speech in several ways. It can direct you to an important factual question that might be the basis for an informative or persuasive speech; for example, you might give a speech that sorts out conflicting evidence about the effectiveness of abstinence-only sex education programs. Or a disagreement might point you to an important clash of values or goals that underlie a policy dispute.

CASE CONCLUSION

Jamie's Ski Resort Speech

Jamie found that following the research strategy in this chapter not only helped her work efficiently, but also led her to some unexpected sources. First, she conducted background research. By browsing through back issues of her local newspapers, she found an article that included an extended interview with the resort developer that explained his point of view in great detail. She learned that the developer already had cut several ski runs on his own property but needed access to the adjacent Forest Service land in order to have a viable ski area. She then contacted the Forest Service to find out about the decision-making process, opportunities for public participation, and what the agency saw as the main issues. She discovered that one issue of concern that had not been covered in the newspaper articles was the need for water that would be generated by the resort—for snowmaking, for the resort village, and for new homes near the resort.

As Jamie started talking about her speech with friends, she was encouraged to seek out one of the forestry professors on campus, who was concerned that a rare tree species might be disturbed by development of the ski area. One friend mentioned a book she had seen about the relationship between ski areas and real estate development. Jamie found the book at her library, and after some skimming, she discovered interesting similarities and differences between the examples in the book and the proposed resort.

After thinking about everything she had read, Jamie decided to focus on the economic and environmental impacts of the resort. She contacted the forestry professor for an interview, and she found a couple of books about the environmental impacts of ski areas through a search of her library catalog. She also found some good articles about ski area development in her region of the country, which she thought would provide good comparison points. Finally, she did a focused Google search to identify how the ski industry approached these issues. She found a great site at http://www.nsaa.org/nsaa/environment/the_greenroom/. With this material, Jamie began to sketch a working outline that noted where she would include certain material.

Questions

1. What suggestions would you give Jamie to improve her overall research process?

2. If you were going to be an audience member for Jamie's speech, what kinds of sources would you want to see? Which sources would be most credible? Why?

JAMIE'S WORKING OUTLINE

Purpose: To inform

Specific purpose: To share knowledge with my audience about potential environmental and economic impacts of a new ski resort

I. Introduction

    A. Attention-getter about the fun of skiing

    B. Central idea: The proposed resort is likely to have significant environmental and economic impacts

    C. Preview of main impacts

II. Environmental Impacts

    A. Impact on tree species (interview from forestry prof.)

    B. Impact on elk habitat (research articles)

    C. Impact on water (interview with Forest Service, evidence from industry site)

III. Economic Impacts

    A. Benefits of ski resorts (testimony of resort developer, local tourism bureau)

    B. Disadvantages of ski resorts (evidence from book, articles about other resorts)

IV. Conclusion

Summary

DETERMINING YOUR RESEARCH NEEDS

- Start by doing some background or informal research that helps you to sharpen your specific purpose.
- Then identify which types of supporting material will be the most effective for your speech.

LOCATING AND ACCESSING SOURCES

- Consider interviewing community members who are affected by your issue, who have relevant expertise, or who are involved in decision-making processes.
- Systematically search the sources available through your library and electronic databases, such as books, periodicals, scholarly journals, and government publications.
- Use Internet searches to fill in research gaps and find specific sources.

PRODUCING SUPPORT FOR YOUR SPEECH

- While you are researching, develop a working bibliography that has all relevant citation information.

- Base your initial evaluation of sources on their authority, recency, and objectivity.

- Read sources to help you invent key aspects of your speech: main points, organizational strategies, supporting material, visual aids, and differences of opinion.

Key Terms

research plan, p. 140

common knowledge, p. 146

hypothetical examples, p. 146

testimony, p. 147

expert testimony, p. 147

citizen testimony, p. 147

statistics, p. 147

raw numbers, p. 147

percentage, p. 147

ratio, p. 147

central tendency, p. 147

mean, p. 147

median, p. 147

source, p. 151

research tools, p. 151

domain, p. 156

URL, p. 156

rationalization, p. 160

Comprehension

1. What are the three basic steps of the research plan?

2. What activities might be part of background research?

3. What are three categories of people that might be good interview sources?

4. What is the difference between a source and a research tool? Name some examples of each.

5. What are some of the differences between a popular magazine and a scholarly journal?

6. Why should you avoid using the web for a general search?

7. What are three guidelines for evaluating the reliability of sources? What special considerations should you have when using those guidelines to evaluate web pages?

8. In addition to identifying supporting material, how can reading your sources help you to invent your speech?

Application

1. Identify a regional or national issue that may have some impact on your campus or community. How would you go about your background research on this issue? What sources would you consult to figure out the community angle, and what sources would you examine to understand the broader issue?

2. Discuss your topic with your classmates or friends, and brainstorm potential interview sources in your community.

3. Pair up with a classmate, and identify two electronic databases that would be good starting points for each of your topic.

4. Locate an .edu site, an .org site, and a .gov site that would be a good source for your speech. Discuss your findings with your classmates, and look for any patterns to the type of material you find on each of those domains.

5. Bring one of your sources and the bibliographic entry or note card for that source to class. Exchange material with a classmate, and check whether the classmate's note card contains accurate citation information for the source, and a fair summary of the source.

Criticizing and Crafting Public Discourse: The Power of Language

CHAPTER OUTLINE

Understanding Public Discourse

Using Effective Language in Your Speeches

Using Appropriate Language in Your Speeches

This chapter is intended to help you:

- Understand some of the basic units of public discourse
- Use language that is concrete, familiar, and active in your speeches
- Incorporate figurative and rhythmic language in your speeches

Language can make a speech come alive. Well-chosen words can capture an audience's attention, shape how audience members think, and inspire them to action. A carefully crafted phrase or sentence can leave a lasting impression with an audience.

As a result, effective public speakers need to develop two broad skills relative to language. First, speakers must be able to critically analyze the language of other people. Second, speakers must be able to produce effective and appropriate language of their own. This chapter takes up both dimensions of language so that you can make sense of the voices and messages that emerge from your research and can improve the quality of the language in your own speeches. ■

CASE SCENARIO

Dave Examines the Language of Marriage Advocacy

Dave had been hearing a lot about same-sex marriage in the news and thought that it might be an interesting topic for his speech. After researching it, he decided that the opposing camps on the issue were living in different worlds. Some advocates were saying that same-sex marriage would mark the end of civilization, while others were saying that it was a fundamental human rights issue. The stories they told about gay relationships were completely at odds. Dave wasn't ready to take a stand himself just yet; he wanted to find out a bit more about why there was such disagreement.

Understanding Public Discourse

As you learned about the public sphere in chapter 1, you need to understand what other people are saying and the issues involved before you enter the "conversation" on a public issue. The rhetorical theorist Kenneth Burke describes this need to understand the ongoing conversation with the following story:

> Imagine that you enter a parlor. You come late. When you arrive, others have long preceded you, and they are engaged in a heated discussion, a discussion too heated for them to pause and tell you exactly what it is about. In fact, the discussion had already begun long before any of them got there, so that no one present is qualified to retrace for you all the steps that had gone before.
>
> You listen for a while, until you decide that you have caught the tenor of the argument; then you put in your oar. Someone answers; you answer him; another comes to your defense; another aligns himself against you, to either the embarrassment or gratification of your opponent, depending upon the quality of your ally's assistance. However, the discussion is interminable. The hour grows late, you must depart. And you do depart, with the discussion still vigorously in progress (Burke).

Contemporary scholars of rhetoric offer several concepts that can help us to better understand public discourse. These concepts can direct your attention to specific aspects of language that can shape how you think about public issues. By identifying these units of discourse, you will be in a better position to critically analyze public messages and compare those messages to others that circulate on your topic.

Ideographs

An **ideograph** is an important cultural value term that is regularly used to justify public decisions and actions (McGee). Advocates of a particular public issue often rely on ideographs as a way to connect controversial proposals to widely shared values. Words such as "liberty," "equality," and "progress" and phrases such as "national security," "freedom of religion," and "private property" are ideographs. They represent the core commitments of a society and are generally viewed positively by audiences.

By associating an ideograph with a specific idea or proposal, a speaker can shape an audience's perception of that idea. Generally, speakers use ideographs to evoke positive feelings and associations. For example, a speaker might support a scholarship program with the following words:

> Our state is committed to equal opportunity for all of its residents. Nowhere is that more important than in higher education. That's why contributing to the University's scholarship fund is so important. Students with financial need can apply for these scholarships and reduce the financial burden of attending college.

Here, equal opportunity is the ideograph that is used to depict the scholarship program in a positive light and connect it to a goal that everyone shares.

An ideograph can shape meaning in other ways. It may spur listeners to think more about the broader value and less about the specific details of the proposal. Or ideographs may encourage listeners to perceive an opponent's argument less favorably.

> The current system of graduation requirements doesn't allow us much choice, but if we adopt this change, we will have greater freedom of choice.

An appeal to "freedom of choice" may be hard to resist. In the United States, who does not want freedom of choice? But some people may infer that opponents of the proposal are opposed to choice or wish to limit freedoms. This might not be the case, but the strongly positive associations of ideographs often promote a distorted view of public controversies.

Therefore, ideographs are an important type of language that merits critical examination. When you come across ideographs in use, keep in mind the following questions:

- *What does the ideograph mean in practice?* "Freedom of choice" may sound appealing, but what are the available choices? If you are free to choose *any* courses to graduate, there might be so many options that it becomes impossible to make sound choices.

- *What other ideographs are relevant?* Other values may be relevant in a situation even if a speaker ignores them. Giving students unlimited freedom to choose their courses probably will not lead to "broad learning" or a "comprehensive liberal arts education."

- *How does the ideograph conceal its opposite?* Unlimited freedom to choose might make you more dependent

IDEOGRAPHS IN PRACTICE
Freedom of choice might be illustrated by the practice of voting.

on other people to help you pick good courses. In the realm of foreign policy, the broad goal of freedom may be used to justify actions that actually lead to domination or oppression of other people.

- *How does the ideograph shape perception of other voices and ideas?* As was noted above, advocates can use ideographs to create the impression that opponents are against some time-honored value. It's more likely that the opponent has a different meaning for that ideograph or finds other ones equally important.

Myths

You know from earlier chapters that narratives, or stories, can be a potent resource for public speaking. While narratives generally tell a story about a unique situation, another kind of narrative tells a more general story that is widely recognized in a culture. This type of narrative is a **myth**, a common cultural story that reinforces values or political lessons.

A myth is *not* a false idea or an urban legend that can be easily disproven. Instead, think of a myth as a parable that tells us something true about a culture and its values. The following parables or myths have been identified as central to U.S. culture. Even as they reinforce certain meanings and values on a national level, you may find versions of these myths popping up even in discussion of more local issues (Reich; Brock et al.)

Mob at the Gates   This myth tells a story of a virtuous nation or group that faces a world full of threats and must do whatever is necessary to protect itself. The threatening mob may be external (e.g., "international terrorists") or internal (e.g., "immigrants). But the threat is serious, and the mob is depicted as absolutely opposed to your core values.

As you might imagine, this type of myth shapes meaning by focusing on the worst aspects of the so-called mob and deflecting attention from any flaws of the virtuous group. It also emphasizes the ideograph of "security." So be attentive to how this myth exaggerates differences between groups, avoids common ground, and encourages strong measures to ward off threats.

The Triumphant Individual   Sometimes referred to as the Horatio Alger myth or the American Dream, this myth creates a story of an individual who comes from humble beginnings, struggles against adversity, and achieves success through perseverance and hard work. The story of Oprah Winfrey's rise is often told as a triumphant individual myth, in which Oprah rose out of poverty and overcame childhood abuse and racial barriers through sheer determination (Cloud).

This myth is a standard of American political discourse. It shapes meaning by focusing on individual action and downplaying inequalities and systemic barriers to success. As a result, it emphasizes the ideographs of "hard work" and "freedom." Be aware of how the myth can work to motivate audiences to act while obscuring the struggles of those whose lives do not fit this story line.

The Benevolent Community In contrast to the Triumphant Individual, the Benevolent Community puts a group at the center of the myth. This story depicts people coming together to improve their community, achieve a common goal, or help other people who are in need. Whenever a collective effort is needed—to support victims of a natural disaster, for instance, or to build a playground at a local school—the appeal to the Benevolent Community is likely to emerge.

This myth reminds people of the importance of social bonds and draws attention to the positive aspects of community. It emphasizes values such as "equal opportunity" and the "common good" At the same time, the myth may deflect attention from the ways in which communities that see themselves as benevolent can shun outsiders and minority groups within a larger population.

Rot at the Top This parable tells a story of leaders who were once trustworthy and principled but are now corrupted by money and power. This is a myth is commonly voiced by people who are outside a system of decision making and by opponents of those who are in positions of power. The myth is intended to delegitimize the establishment and pave the way for change.

Because this is such a popular myth in political discourse, it is important to understand how it is regularly used to exaggerate the importance of even mundane influences on decision making. The ideographs of the "public interest" and "the people" are often valorized to suggest that the people who are at the top ("the powerful") are merely out for "personal gain." Give careful attention to the specific situation to which this myth is applied before deciding whether the charge should be taken seriously.

Characterizations and Connotations

Language also can shape perception through **characterizations**, or common descriptions of people, actions, or things that reinforce particular meanings and associations. Essentially, characterizations are stereotypes, but keep in mind that they are not necessarily negative. Whether positive or negative, characterizations are powerful because they are repeated so much that they are taken for granted.

Different characterizations can be used to shape competing perceptions of the same people. For example, depictions of "welfare queens," "fat cat businessmen," and "dirty hippies" are probably familiar to you. But so are more positive characterizations, such as "working mother," "pillar of the community," and "free spirit." Language can be used to characterize things other than people, too. Universities are sometimes depicted as "ivory towers," a fraternity might be called an "Animal House," and a course you are taking might be a "snooze," a "blast," or a "piece of cake."

Characterizations typically rely on the connotative meaning of words. The **connotative meaning** is the range of meanings and associations related to a word that easily evoke attitudes in listeners; the **denotative meaning** of a word is the literal meaning. When speakers and writers are attempting to shift attitudes, take a position, or persuade, they are more likely to use characterizations that tap into the connotative meanings of some words. For example, if a speaker refers to someone as "different" from others, that word probably does not evoke strong emotions or attitudes. But if that speaker were to call the person a "deviant" or a "rebel," that term may call up a range of associations for you. Similarly, calling a personal injury lawyer an "ambulance chaser" does not mean that the lawyer literally runs after ambulances. Instead, it is typically used to evoke negative connotations of a greedy lawyer who thrives on the suffering of others.

Characterizations and connotations play a significant role in shaping perceptions. Critical listeners and readers not only need to assess the accuracy of such language strategies. They also should pay attention to the attitudes and emotions that these words and phrases evoke, making sure that there is good evidence for such feelings beyond these popular labels and phrases.

Finally, other features of public discourse can play into our understanding of public issues. The Appendix to this book discusses two important parts of the public sphere—the range of public voices (at least as they exist in the United States), and the framing of news stories by media outlets. Learning more about each of these areas can help you be a more discerning analyst of public discourse and a more fluent speaker on public issues.

Using Effective Language in Your Speeches

As you have seen, public discourse has a big impact on how issues are framed and understood. Consequently, your own speeches on public issues need to be attentive to how you use the language of others in discussing those issues with your audience. In addition, you need be attentive to micro-level language choices and the style of language you use. **Style**, or the rules and practices of composing effective discourse, is a vital topic for all public speakers.

For beginning public speakers, it is especially important to recognize that oral style for speaking has both similarities and differences relative to the written style you use in papers and reports. Good writing and speaking both use active, concrete, and familiar language for maximum impact. But in speaking, your language choices must be adapted to the ear rather than the eye. Instructors can often tell when a speech is simply an essay that was submitted to another class. Not only is that a form of academic misconduct; it also will not be as effective as a work that is designed to be a speech from the beginning.

Ultimately, once you have invented and organized your speech, you need to state your ideas in the most effective and compelling way possible. This is different from simply having "clear language," a phrase that itself is not very clear! When listeners say they want "clear" language, they often mean something much more specific. The rest of this section illustrates different types of language that can help you to attain the clarity that audiences desire.

Concrete Language

The words you use in your speeches will be a mix of concrete language and abstract language. **Concrete language** refers to tangible, specific things, such as "raft," "robot," or "Rascal Flatts," while **abstract language** refers to more general ideas or concepts, such as "motherhood," "majesty," or "morality." Of course, this distinction between concrete and abstract language is relative. You might think of it as a continuum with varying degrees of concreteness or specificity.

Abstract————————————————————————Concrete
   "Equality"   "Equal rights for women"   "Title IX"

General——————————————————————————Specific
   "Woman"   "mother"   "teen mother"   "Kristin"

Your decision to use concrete or abstract language will depend on your purposes as well as the topic you are discussing. Earlier in this chapter,

CONCRETE LANGUAGE
The slogan "Equal Pay for Equal Work" is a concrete statement of a demand for equality.

for example, you learned about one type of abstract language: ideographs. Freedom, progress, and national security are abstract ideas that may mean different things in different contexts. As a result, ideographs can be useful for establishing common ground and inspiring action based on shared goals.

But abstract language also can leave listeners wondering what you "really" mean. Concrete language can solve this problem by giving your audience more tangible and specific information. To understand this difference, compare the following two passages that discuss "progress" on campus:

1. Progress is important here. We are committed to improving academics, strengthening our faculty, and growing our campus. With an eye toward the future, we are confident that we can be one of the premier campuses in the area.

2. Here at Excellence University, we are committed to real signs of progress. Provost Jones has implemented a plan for incorporating more writing instruction and requiring capstone courses in each department. The university is hiring ten new faculty members in the natural sciences, social sciences, and humanities to strengthen departments such as Physics and English. And Vice President Delgado has identified donors for three new buildings. Excellence University is poised to be a top 10 regional university by 2015.

The first passage relies on abstract language, while the second passage uses much more concrete language. The type of language in the first passage is sometimes referred to as **boilerplate language**, which is standardized language that could be used in different contexts without significant changes. In contrast, the second passage shows specifically how academic programs will be improved and which areas will be strengthened.

Concrete language makes a speech more interesting and lively for listeners. It evokes connections and associations to real things rather than intangible ideas. This does not mean that you should avoid abstract language entirely; it is appropriate at times, but be attentive to how concrete language can help abstract ideas to become more meaningful for your audience.

Familiar Language

In chapter 5, you learned that audience analysis can help you to determine the depth and complexity that are appropriate for addressing a particular topic with a particular audience. As you begin to craft the language of your speech, use words and phrases that will be familiar to your audience without "dumbing down" the overall content of the speech.

For starters, audience analysis can help you to determine whether to use or avoid **jargon**, language that is specific to a profession or field and rarely understood outside that field. For example, suppose one of your friends who is a science major said the following about an article she was reading:

> It's about complex dielectric permittivity measurements from ground-penetrating radar data to estimate snow liquid water content in the pendular regime.

An easier way to explain it, using more familiar language, would be as follows:

> I'm learning how scientists use radar to determine the water content of dry snow.

This language certainly would be more familiar to a general audience. If you were giving a speech on the topic, you might start with a sentence like that to convey a general idea in familiar terms and then incorporate more specific or complex ideas later. Remember that *familiar* language does not necessarily mean "simple" language. If your friend were speaking at a conference or in a seminar to other geoscientists, the first passage would be familiar and probably more effective.

Using familiar language also can help you to avoid complicating a topic unnecessarily. This often happens among beginning speakers who believe that they need to sound like an expert on a topic. Instead of adapting to their audience with an effective oral style, they often use **pretentious language**, wording that is pompous and not part of a person's everyday vocabulary, or **clutter**, excess wording that does not aid audience understanding. Both are present in the following example:

> The symbiotic interaction of an organized communal cotillion can ameliorate anomie and overcome the atomization of postmodern sociality.

A long sentence filled with unusual words can present challenges for both the speaker and audience members. The speaker might stumble over words, and listeners might struggle to figure out the speaker's meaning. As a result, the audience may miss important points in subsequent sentences or perceive the speaker as a less-than-credible source. A far more familiar and direct statement might look like this:

> Social dance can build community!

This statement cuts to the chase. It is more memorable, and it avoids both the pretentiousness and the clutter of the first passage.

Active Language

Oral style differs from some forms of academic writing by using active rather than passive language. In this context, **active language** or an **active voice** refers to the use of active verbs and a subject–verb sentence structure. By using active language, you can generate a more lively style that economizes words and engages your listeners.

Using subject–verb sentence structure can prevent sentences from having lots of clauses that create confusing relationships. Although you may have some introductory clauses (like this one!), sentences that are organized with subject–verb structure simplify those relationships for your listeners. This structure is simply "A does B," while passive language takes the structure "B is done by A."

> *Passive:* Speaking at the meeting about the new health center were some passionate students.
>
> *Active:* Students spoke passionately at the meeting about a new health center.

Here, the active voice keeps the subject and verb closer together; it creates a more vivid picture of what happened. You could keep this basic structure even if you wanted to include an opening phrase that aided a transition:

> Later in the meeting, students spoke passionately about the new health center.
>
> Regarding the health center, students spoke passionately in support of it.

Attention to active verbs also can fix clutter and pretentiousness problems in some cases. Again, speakers often use extra words to sound more formal or bureaucratic, but just as often, those words hinder effective expression of an idea.

> *Poor example:* The reduction of accidents between bikers and pedestrians can be accomplished by the implementation of new paths for use by bikers.

This sentence is filled with **nominalization**, or the process of turning verbs into nouns. A verb such as "reduce" becomes "reduction," and "implement" becomes "implementation." Nominalization makes a sentence more complicated and more passive than it needs to be. For example, the first part of the sentence could be improved slightly.

> *Somewhat better version:* Reducing accidents can be accomplished by implementing new paths for bikers.

This sentence gets rid of some words, but shifting to active voice would be even better:

> *Even better version:* New bike paths can reduce accidents involving bikers and pedestrians.

Notice how this sentence eliminates unnecessary action words ("accomplished" and "implementing"). Instead, it focuses on the most important action—reducing accidents—and rearranges the sentence after locating the subject of that action.

Finally, use active voice when you are taking a position or stating previews, summaries, and transitions. This means using "I" in your speech when it is appropriate. If you have been trained to use the passive voice, this can be a hard habit to break.

> *Passive voice:* First, past recessions will be reviewed. Then, an overview of causes of these recessions will be covered. Finally, the speech will end with a presentation of solutions.

But remember that your job as a public speaker is not to present objective findings that could be replicated by others. Instead, you want to develop a personal connection with your audience and offer your unique perspective on issues.

> *Active voice:* In the first section of the speech, I will review past recessions. Then I will explain the causes of these recessions. I will conclude by presenting several potential solutions.

Certainly, you can go overboard with the use of I-language in a speech. For example, it is not necessary to start every sentence with "I believe" or "I think." Also, avoid introductions that "narrate" the process of developing your speech, such as "I had a difficult time identifying a topic, so I started reading some magazines about new computer technology. This really appealed to me, so I did more research." This sort of I-language is not all that interesting to listeners, so just jump right into your topic.

Figurative Language

Figurative language alters or turns the usual meanings of words to create novel perceptions and associations among listeners. Like concrete and active language, figurative language can make your speech more lively and vivid. It can help your audience to see what you are talking about. But figurative language also can help your audience to see things from a new perspective and to think creatively about your topic.

You are probably familiar with **metaphor**, a type of figurative language that compares two objects or ideas that are generally perceived as dissimilar. Rhetorically, metaphors bring the meanings and associations of one thing into contact with another. Martin Luther King, Jr.'s "I Have a Dream" has achieved its status as a great speech in no small part because of its rich and diverse use of metaphors. In that speech, King used a metaphor that most could identify with easily—cashing a check. King's metaphorical device uses common words like "check" and "promissory note" to represent the assurances made by the authors of the Constitution and the Declaration of Independence when they promised that all men—regardless of race or ethnicity—would be guaranteed the "unalienable Rights" of "Life, Liberty and the pursuit of Happiness."

King continued the metaphor as he spoke about how America has since defaulted on that note through the unfair treatment of black Americans. The check metaphor brings familiar ideas about banking and applies them to the idea of seeking civil rights. In this instance, the metaphor creates a perspective on this abstract idea by connecting to something concrete. Seeking civil rights is essentially seeking the fulfillment of an obligation, one that we take for granted when we write and cash checks.

In creating a perspective, metaphors can guide thinking and make a speaker's conclusions appear reasonable. This occurs as speakers and audience members develop the implications of metaphors. For example, in the next passage of the speech, King plays out the implication that just as a bank should pay when someone wants to cash a check, Americans have the right to expect their nation to make good on the promises made by the founding fathers. King maintained that the "great vaults of opportunity of this nation" could indeed fulfill those initial assurances by the founding fathers and had the funds to cash the promised check of equality.

By using an extensive metaphor as a language strategy, King's conclusion seems logical, plausible, and reasonable. Just as we don't expect banks to be bankrupt or to have insufficient funds, we should not think that America lacks justice and opportunity. It is reasonable that the metaphorical check should be paid. You can read the complete text of King's speech online at www.thekingcenter.org.

Some scholars contend that metaphors are actually part of our fundamental structures of thought. Consequently, it is crucial to reflect constantly on the implications of your metaphors. For example, people commonly use war metaphors in talking about personal and public conflicts. These metaphors can escalate conflict and narrow our perceived range of choices in a situation.

Other metaphors, however, can expand possibilities for thinking and action. For example, rather than using a war metaphor to speak about a struggle, you might instead use metaphors of running a marathon or climbing a mountain. These metaphors can help listeners observe different aspects of the struggle. You might focus on the preparation that is needed ahead of time; or, you might discuss the persistence that is needed to overcome challenges and obstacles. The mountain climbing metaphor might help you discuss coordination within a group, while the marathon metaphor might allow you to focus on overcoming mental barriers. And both metaphors can help your listeners visualize successful completion of a goal.

As you can see, metaphors do not necessarily need to involve unusual language. Simply using familiar ideas and common experiences as a lens for seeing other ideas can help you bring new meanings and perspectives to your audience.

A closely related figure of language is a **simile**, which draws a comparison using the words *like* or *as*. Similes are comparable to metaphors, but the inclusion of *like* or *as* usually makes a simile somewhat less artistic and somewhat more specific. For example, if King were to have said that seeking

THE ETHICAL DIMENSION

Metaphors and Their Implications

Metaphors work by transferring meaning from one realm of life to another. While this can be valuable for creating new meanings and associations, it also can open the door to some troubling ethical challenges. When metaphorical implications make it possible to degrade or deny the legitimacy of other interests and voices, then speakers need to reevaluate their use of metaphors.

Extreme metaphors have become commonplace in depicting reality. For example, war metaphors are used to describe just about any type of conflict. Your roommate's failure to do the dishes may lead to a "skirmish" or a "battle," or it may be a "powder keg" waiting to "explode." Legislators may "fire" an "opening salvo," "dig in their heels" during debate, agree to a "truce," or threaten the "nuclear option." From a practical perspective, such metaphors can make it more difficult to find common ground or possibilities for compromise.

As scholars Josina M. Makau and Debian L. Marty explain, "Because metaphors have the potential to significantly shape beliefs, and because this power is often hidden, metaphors challenge decision makers to carefully assess their appropriateness, acceptability, and value" (149).

Andre Bauer, the Lieutenant Governor of South Carolina, apologized for comparing welfare recipients to stray animals, saying that he wished he had used a better metaphor.

WHAT DO YOU THINK?

1. Consider the ethical implications for how the words we use and read about influence the way in which we perceive and interact with opponents. For instance, what are the implications if discussion in the public sphere uses the terms "dance" or "game" rather than the word "war"?

---

freedom is like cashing a check, that would suggest that the comparison is limited. How is it like cashing a check? In what ways is it different? Consider the similes in this passage from Hilda Solis's acceptance speech for a JFK Profiles in Courage Award:

> In the community that I represent, there are numerous examples of environmental hazards. If you were to take an aerial tour, it looks like a war zone. The mining industry has created enormous gaping holes, including a 500 acre pit, which from the air, makes the cities I represent look like Swiss cheese.

Using similes of a war zone and Swiss cheese is appropriate here because they acknowledge the limits of the comparisons. Solis is not saying metaphorically that her community *is* a war zone, with all of the implications that come with that metaphor. Instead, she is simply saying that *one aspect* of her community—the mining impacts—makes it look similar to these things.

Finally, be aware that figurative language can sometimes hamper your effectiveness. In discussion of public issues, one language figure to avoid in most cases is **euphemism**, a mild or vague description of something troubling or unpleasant. Euphemisms are especially prevalent in public discourse about war. For example, the phrase "enhanced interrogation techniques" has circulated in public discourse to describe the troubling practice of torture, and "targeted killing" serves as euphemism for assassination.

Similarly, euphemisms might be used to soften the impact of an unpleasant action or to minimize stigma. On campus, a grading option might be "credit/no-credit" instead of "pass/fail," and "academic dismissal" is a way of describing expulsion. As all of these examples suggest, the benefits and drawbacks of euphemism are not always clear. In terms of effectiveness, however, know that you will lose credibility with listeners who perceive that euphemisms are intended to deceive or thwart understanding.

Rhythmic Language

Rhythmic language is language that uses the sounds of words and phrases to create a pleasing or memorable effect. As with other forms of language discussed in this section, rhythmic language should not be used simply for its own sake. Think about how you can use it to your advantage to attract attention, emphasize ideas, and build momentum in your speeches.

A common use of rhythm is **alliteration**, the repetition of initial sounds to connect related words and phrases. Alliteration can be useful for stating a series of points:

> Our proposal should be judged on three criteria: cost, clarity, and comprehensiveness.

Here, the preview of upcoming points allows the speaker to introduce the three points in a memorable way and makes it easier for the audience to remember those points as they are reinforced later in the speech.

Alliteration also can be used to attract attention to artistic or clever phrases. Some of the most famous examples in contemporary U.S. political rhetoric come from former Vice President Spiro Agnew:

> In the United States today, we have more than our share of the nattering nabobs of negativism.

But alliteration needs to be used sparingly; otherwise, it becomes a gimmick. The clever "alliteration speech" in the film *V for Vendetta* reflects this excessiveness:

> The only verdict is vengeance; a vendetta held as a votive, not in vain, for the value and veracity of such shall one day vindicate the vigilant and the virtuous.

On another level, **anaphora** is a type of rhythmic language that repeats entire words or phrases. Anaphora is especially useful for building momentum and amplifying an idea. President George W. Bush used anaphora to link a series of points in his 2006 State of the Union speech. In the middle of the speech, he started a series of sections with the same phrase, offering details about specific initiatives:

> Keeping America competitive begins with keeping our economy growing. . . .
>
> Keeping America competitive requires us to be good stewards of tax dollars. . . .
>
> Keeping America competitive requires affordable energy. . . .

You will learn more about this strategy, sometimes referred to as parallel structure, in chapter 9.

Finally, the technique of **antithesis** uses parallel structure to heighten the movement or contrast between ideas.

> We observe today not a victory of party but a celebration of freedom, symbolizing an end as well as a beginning, signifying renewal as well as change (Kennedy).
>
> As we take these steps together to renew our strength at home, we cannot turn away from our obligation to renew our leadership abroad (Clinton).

Antithesis is not only memorable for audiences. It also can aid a speaker's invention process, encouraging reflection on contrasting ideas and alternative perspectives. Thus, this type of rhythmic language is not just a catchy ornament to a speech; it can spur the very creation of the speech itself.

Using Appropriate Language in Your Speeches

As you have learned throughout this book, audience and situational factors are central to making sound decisions about public speaking, and decisions about language are no different. For example, turn back to chapter 5 to review the crucial audience-related issues of egocentrism, ethnocentrism, and stereotyping. Language that privileges your own background and viewpoints, denigrates others, or makes hasty generalizations about groups must be avoided.

In addition, speeches should use wording that reflects contemporary usage patterns for naming ethnic, cultural, and religious groups. Table 7.1 provides a starting point for avoiding outdated language, but you should recognize that these trends can change quickly. The underlying principle is that speakers should use names that the groups in question would prefer the speaker to use. The same name may be perceived as derogatory depending on who is saying it. For example, some African-American friends may refer to one

PUBLIC SPOTLIGHT

Terry Tempest Williams

It is not surprising that author Terry Tempest Williams has a way with words. She was awarded a Guggenheim Fellowship and a Lannan Literary Fellowship and won awards from the Wilderness Society and the Western American Literature Association. Her biography describes her as "a writer who speaks and speaks out eloquently on behalf of an ethical stance toward life" (Steven Barclay Agency). Her commencement speech at the University of Utah in 2003, when she received an honorary doctorate, truly is an eloquent plea for an ethical stance toward life in a democratic society.

Williams opened her speech with a description of her own experience as an undergraduate at Utah with a wonderful line of alliteration: "I realized that in American Letters we celebrate both language and landscape, creating an empathy for all life." In the middle of her speech, she developed the theme of her speech through a compelling mix of anaphora, parallel structure, and occasional alliteration. This passage magnified her theme and elevated the key values she wanted to emphasize in the speech.

What does the open space of democracy look like?

In the open space of democracy there is room for dissent.

In the open space of democracy there is room for differences.

In the open space of democracy, the health of the environment is seen as the wealth of our communities. We remember that our character has been shaped by the diversity of America's landscapes and it is precisely that character that will protect it.

Cooperation is valued more than competition.

Prosperity becomes the caretaker of poverty.

The humanities are not peripheral, but the very art of what it means to be human.

In the open space of democracy, beauty is not optional, but essential to our survival as a species.

And technology is not rendered at the expense of life, but developed out of a reverence for life.

Reverence for life.

Coming less than two months after the U.S. invasion of Iraq, Williams's speech was a bold speech defending core public values at an important historical moment. It was not easy. Later, she wrote that after speaking the above passage, "I was halfway through the speech with my heart still pounding. It was difficult to establish eye contact" (Williams). Yet through powerful language, Williams gave an eloquent defense—and example—of freedom of speech.

 Social Media Spotlight

Freedom of speech is a potent issue for social media. For example, how should Facebook and Twitter deal with posts that are perceived as harassment or bullying? To what extent should these media be policing the political and organizational activity of their participants? The following two articles explore some of these issues:

http://www.nytimes.com/2010/12/13/technology/13facebook.html?_r=1&ref=business

http://www.ibtimes.com/articles/91259/20101212/will-facebook-twitter-continue-to-back-free-speech-online.html

another informally as "Negro," but that term would be offensive coming from speakers from other ethnic groups.

Finally, speakers need to consider situational factors in order to develop appropriate language. Even if the speeches you currently give are all addressed to college students, your language choices may vary as the

TABLE 7.1 Using Appropriate Language to Name Groups

These trends can change rapidly and vary according to location, so consider discussing this figure with your colleagues.

Past Usage	Contemporary Usage
Ladies	Women
Mankind	Humanity or humankind
Hispanic	Hispanic or Latina/o
Indian	Native American or tribal affiliation (e.g., Blackfeet)
Negro	African-American
Oriental	Asian or country of origin (e.g., Korean)
Homosexual	Gay and/or lesbian

and other informal language needs to be minimized as you move into more formal settings. A persuasive speech to your classmates may take on a different tone than a speech that is intended to motivate action at a demonstration.

The guidelines for appropriate language for different audiences and situations can take you only so far. To become a savvy speaker, you need to become a voracious consumer of speeches—not only listening to speeches, but also reflecting on language choices and evaluating those choices in light of current public discourse and the constraints of the rhetorical situation. As you give more attention to the language of skilled speakers, your own language in speaking will improve.

CASE CONCLUSION

Dave Examines the Language of Marriage Advocacy

Dave began seeing some key ideographs in his research. Some voices were saying that same-sex marriage is fundamentally immoral and that our culture needs to honor the traditional principles and family values that marriage represents. Proponents of same-sex marriage tended to emphasize equality and justice, and talked a lot about unfair discrimination.

Even though Dave read several articles about the legal strategies of the opposing groups, he realized that he needed to avoid legal jargon with his audience.

Instead, he decided to discuss how different kinds of same-sex partnerships would be similar to or different from opposite-sex relationships, and he found himself using many similes in his speech.

Finally, Dave found some opinion pieces that included derogatory language about their political opponents. He was turned off by these kinds of remarks, and thought his audience would be too. The issues themselves were fascinating enough that this sort of unfair language would only detract from his speech.

Summary

UNDERSTANDING PUBLIC DISCOURSE

- Effective public speakers need to be able to critically analyze the language that other people use to discuss public issues.
- Ideographs, myths, and characterizations are some of the key units of public discourse that shape perception of public issues.

USING EFFECTIVE LANGUAGE IN YOUR SPEECHES

- Effective style in public speaking requires adaptation of language to an oral context.
- Concrete, familiar, active, and figurative language can enhance effective style.

USING APPROPRIATE LANGUAGE IN YOUR SPEECHES

- Speeches should use wording and style that reflect contemporary usage patterns for naming groups and that are sensitive to situational differences.

Key Terms

ideograph, p. 170
myth, p. 172
characterization, p. 173
connotative meaning, p. 174
denotative meaning, p. 174
style, p. 174
concrete language, p. 175
abstract language, p. 175
boilerplate language, p. 176
jargon, p. 176
pretentious language, p. 177

clutter, p. 177
active language (or active voice), p. 177
nominalization, p. 00
figurative language, p. 179
metaphor, p. 179
simile, p. 180
euphemism, p. 182
rhythmic language, p. 182
alliteration, p. 182
anaphora, p. 183
antithesis, p. 183

Comprehension

1. What are some contemporary examples of ideographs?
2. Is a myth a false story? Why or why not?
3. What is the difference between connotative meaning and denotative meaning?
4. What is the difference between active voice and passive voice?

5. How does nominalization affect style? How should speakers change nominalization?

6. What is euphemism?

Application

1. Examine the website of your senator or representative or another prominent national political candidate. On what ideographs does this person rely to explain his or her positions on issues?

2. Examine a recent State of the Union address or speech of response from the opposing party. What myths are used in these speeches? How do they attempt to alter perception of issues?

3. Develop a one-minute speech that exhibits the characteristics of effective language described in the chapter. Your speech should attempt to describe one of the following:

   A college football game
   Your college's student center
   A night at your favorite restaurant
   Your favorite season of the year

8

Inventing Your Informative Speech

This chapter is intended to help you:

- Identify the purposes of informative speaking
- Explore and generate ideas for your speech in a systematic way
- Understand the strengths and limitations of different types of supporting material

As you learned in chapter 2, invention is the process of generating ideas for your speech. That chapter gave you several prompts for thinking about topics and ways to address those topics. But specific types of public speaking can take advantage of particular systems for invention. This chapter focuses on strategies for informative speaking.

The big challenge of effective informative speaking is to get beyond the "data dump." You have probably heard speeches that are dull lists of facts, dates, and other information that do little to spark your interest. But an informative speech does not have to be dull. As with any type of speaking, it is important to use information creatively to build a speech that serves your purpose and connects with your audience. After discussing the specific purposes that a

> ### CASE SCENARIO
>
> ## Maloree's Speech on Sonar
>
> For her informative speech, Maloree was interested in raising awareness about the effects of sonar blasts on marine life. She had recently found out that the use of sonar had been linked to whale deaths and wanted to explore the issue further. From earlier audience research, she was aware that her audience knew next to nothing about this issue and did not have an informed opinion about it. But most of all, she didn't really know whether this topic would matter to her classmates. There certainly was not much public discussion about it in her community. She would need to think carefully about how to approach this speech so that it would be relevant to her audience.

speaker might pursue in informative speaking, this chapter shows how to use audience research and supporting material to creatively invent the substance of an informative speech. ■

Purposes of Informative Speaking

Recall from chapter 4 that speaking to inform means that your primary aim is to describe, explain, or demonstrate something to your audience. By the end of an informative speech, your audience should have learned something new or have a better understanding of your topic. Even if you put that information to use later for persuasion, the ultimate purpose in informative speaking is not to tell the audience what to do or what choices they ought to make. Instead, you are trying to help the audience to become a rhetorical audience—one that is open-minded and feels empowered to act wisely.

Effective informative speaking enhances these qualities in an audience so that they feel prepared to make sound choices in the future. This means that you need to consider the broader *civic and political purposes* that you want to join your audience in pursuing as well as the typical *constraints* that may influence your audience's perception of your speech.

Civic and Political Purposes of Informative Speech

Both civic engagement and political engagement generate opportunities for informative speaking. Whether you are volunteering for the local blood drive or working for a campus political group, you can serve your community through informative speaking in order to communicate with other group members, spread the word about your group, and share ideas that advance the mission of your group (Ahlfeldt). Three purposes of informative speaking, listed in Table 8.1, are especially important for civic and political engagement: raising awareness, sharing knowledge, and explaining alternatives.

TABLE 8.1 Adapting Your Speaking Strategies to the Audience and Your Purpose

Informative Purpose	Audience Obstacles	Adaptation Strategies
Raising awareness	Lack of prior exposure Perceived irrelevance	Minimize complexity Heighten personal relevance
Sharing knowledge	Boredom/overexposure Integrating new and old knowledge	Highlight new facts and perspectives Begin with familiar knowledge, then replace or add new knowledge
Explaining alternatives	Aware of only limited options Commitment to one option	Begin with known options, then add new ones Compare several options and clarify their differences

Raising Awareness Addressing an unrecognized or misunderstood issue through informative speech is a great way to promote awareness. For many civic organizations, this is a central part of their mission. For example, to raise awareness among others in the community, a group that is interested in helping refugees may produce informative speeches that describe the challenges faced by newcomers to the country.

In the political realm, citizens and advocacy groups may disseminate information to raise awareness of an issue while also working to persuade decision makers to adopt particular policies. For example, a group such as Mothers Against Drunk Driving might sponsor speakers who inform young people about the effects of alcohol or inform elected officials about the problems of drunk driving in their communities. Consequently, the informative purpose of raising awareness can easily become persuasive. For the purposes of classroom speaking, be mindful to avoid a value judgment or a call for action in speeches to raise awareness; let the audience members make up their own minds.

For speeches that attempt to raise awareness, the primary obstacles that the speaker needs to overcome are as follows:

- The audience's lack of prior exposure to information about your topic
- The audience's perception that the issue is irrelevant to their lives

As you saw in chapter 4, these two obstacles often go hand in hand. Therefore, *speeches that attempt to raise awareness should minimize complexity and maximize the personal relevance of the issue.* For instance, obsolete consumer electronics from the United States are regularly shipped overseas to be dismantled by workers in China and India. If your audience is unaware that this "e-waste" is a health issue for those workers, you may lose them if you try to explain all the scientific evidence linking various metals to disease. Instead, you might begin by comparing e-waste to a more familiar topic—such as lead in toys or mercury in fish—to explain the hazard. Or you might get the audience members thinking about all the electronic items that they use. That would help to demonstrate the relevance of the topic to their daily lives

Sharing Knowledge Another reason for informative speaking is to fulfill an audience's need for facts, observations, and interpretations of data that can help people make good decisions. Civic audiences need information for a variety of reasons. For example, other students in your major might want to learn about the main factors affecting employment in your field. Or your religious organization might ask you to figure out ways to reduce its environmental impact and to give a report of your findings. Political organizations—such as parties, staffs of elected officials, or interest groups—also need knowledge to strengthen their decision making. They rely on informative briefings to make decisions about positions they might take on a particular issue, and they use informative speech when they bring evidence to elected officials about conditions and problems that affect them.

RAISING AWARENESS

If you are trying to raise awareness of a problem such as electronic waste, try to highlight how that problem is connected to your listeners' everyday lives.

In contrast to speeches that raise awareness, speeches that attempt to add knowledge to the decision-making process typically are presented to audiences who are at least somewhat familiar with the topic and already recognize its importance. The key obstacles for these audiences are boredom with a familiar topic and lack of understanding how new knowledge relates to their prior knowledge.

Even if audiences recognize the importance of an issue, they might have already heard so much about a topic that they resist hearing more. (For this reason, some public speaking instructors will even ban speeches on supposedly "overdone" topics such as capital punishment, abortion, and gun control.) For an informative speech to have an impact, then, *the speaker should highlight new facts or provide a fresh perspective on existing knowledge.* For example, a typical informative speech about energy might merely describe different types of energy sources. A potentially more interesting informative speech might highlight the emerging evidence about the limitations and inefficiencies of corn-based ethanol. Such a speech would be more interesting than basic descriptions of energy sources because it would offer new information and a new perspective for thinking about our energy choices.

Explaining Alternatives Helping people to understand alternatives is another type of information sharing that deserves special attention. As was noted above, informative speakers can aid public deliberation on an issue by introducing new facts and interpretations of evidence to the discussion. In a speech that explains alternatives, however, the speaker's explicit goal is to show how facts and interpretations compare to one another so that audiences can better understand the available options.

All kinds of civic and political matters can be addressed by explaining alternatives. A civic group that is interested in helping underprivileged children might need help deciding which activities are likely to have the greatest impact. In your classroom, a speech on volunteer opportunities at local hospitals might highlight the differences in the purposes, styles, and time commitments of various opportunities so that your audience members can decide on the ones that fit their own needs and desires. For political issues, a speaker's clear explanation of alternatives is crucial to help the audience make good decisions about policy. Whether the issue is changing your college's general education requirements or changing how health insurance works, audiences can make better decisions if they understand the likely consequences of alternative courses of action.

The obstacles that a speaker faces for a speech that explains alternatives include the ones discussed in the previous sections (lack of prior exposure, perception of irrelevance, boredom with the topic, and failure to see how it relates of prior knowledge), but in this case, the obstacles faced by the speaker depend on the specific context and audience:

1. *Lack of familiarity with alternatives.* In these situations, the speaker should aim to fully explain the available alternatives. For example, many speeches at freshman orientation and other events for new students are intended to explain the various possibilities for housing. Similarly, a student who is facing an unintended pregnancy could benefit from hearing about the range of options and resources available to her for dealing with the situation. In both situations, hearing informative speech about alternatives can empower the audience; instead of feeling that there are no choices, listeners can begin to see alternatives and make choices that are consistent with their own values and goals.

2. *Commitment to a particular alternative.* A more informed audience poses somewhat different obstacles to the speaker. Even if the audience sees alternatives, they may see only some of them or may favor one alternative already. In this situation, the challenge for the speaker again is to integrate knowledge of new alternatives with what the audience already knows. Starting with familiar options and moving to the less familiar can help to expand the audience's perspective. An informative speech about conservative politics in the United States, for example, might begin by discussing the Republican Party and then move on to discuss particular

factions or third parties such as the Libertarian Party or the Tea Party movement, describing the similarities and differences these groups have with the better-known group. This technique empowers audience members by expanding the range of available options and clarifying those alternatives so that audiences can make an informed choice.

Other Purposes of Informative Speech

While the types of speeches listed above are focused on helping the audience deliberate on an issue in some way, other types of informative speeches are less connected to civic or political decision making. Yet they are still critically important. One study found that faculty and college alumni agreed that informative

---

PUBLIC SPOTLIGHT

Coleen Rowley

Coleen Rowley found herself becoming a prominent figure in the public sphere as a result of her career. Rowley was an FBI lawyer in Minneapolis and had been involved in the investigation of Zacarias Moussaoui several weeks before the September 11, 2001, attacks. Although agents in Minneapolis had reason to believe that Moussaoui was connected to terrorist activity, agents at FBI headquarters blocked further investigation. Rowley believed that the 9/11 attacks could have been prevented if FBI headquarters had taken the terrorist threat more seriously.

As many people in the public sphere tried to analyze the security failures related to the attacks, Rowley spoke out to inform the discussion in several ways. In testimony before the Senate Judiciary Committee, she *shared knowledge* about the actual events surrounding the investigation of Moussaoui, showing that some people in the FBI had blocked the Minneapolis agents' actions. She *raised awareness* of some of the broader problems within the FBI bureaucracy and how they might affect national security. She also *explained alternatives* for some of the potential ways of solving those problems, putting several ideas on the table without advocating for one.

Rowley's informative speaking helped the FBI and other agencies to learn from their mistakes. But she also recognized that informing the public about these issues was an ethical obligation too. As she put it:

Foremost, we owe it to the public, especially the victims of terrorism, to be completely honest. I happen to be pretty well acquainted with the Minnesota family of a young man who was killed in the Khobar Towers terrorist bombing and have been able to glimpse a little of their feelings in the years that have transpired since that 1996 event. I know that theirs is an ongoing struggle to learn and try to understand what happened to their son/husband. I can only imagine what these crime and terrorism victims continue to go through. They deserve nothing but the complete, unfettered truth.

 Social Media Spotlight

By speaking out about some of the problems with the FBI's actions, Rowley has been identified as a whistleblower by some observers. Whistleblowers bring allegations of misconduct to public light and often face retaliation by their employers or co-workers. As a result, whistleblowers often seek more confidential routes for discussing their allegations first. However, organizations that assist whistleblowers actively use websites and blogs to provide these routes and to circulate information and success stories.

For example, The National Whistleblowers Center has a presence on Facebook, Twitter and YouTube, where they discuss their activities and campaigns to strengthen whistleblower protection laws. Their website allows individuals to submit confidential reports and get referrals to legal assistance in their community. All these media can be accessed via http://www. whistleblowers.org

speaking is the most important public speaking skill (Johnson and Szczupaki-ewicz). Keep in mind these other reasons for engaging in informative speaking.

Publicizing Your Organization Speaking to inform other people about your civic or political organization is a type of awareness-raising activity. Speeches that publicize your organization are generally designed to expand recognition of the organization and its activities and to set the stage for subsequent persuasion (e.g., for donations, volunteers, and members). This type of informative speaking is fundamentally a form of public relations in which you attempt to generate positive regard for the organization based on vivid descriptions of its members, its actions, and its effects on individuals and the community.

For example, as a participant in the National Breast Cancer Awareness Month campaign, you might speak to the Biology Club or a residence hall on campus to inform the members about the purposes, activities, and impacts associated with that campaign. Like other awareness-raising speeches, publicity speeches must overcome lack of knowledge and motivation among audience members. Gauging your audience's existing knowledge and perceptions of your organization is a must, as is depicting how your organization has relevance to your audience.

Describing Processes Giving directions and discussing procedures are specific types of information sharing that are often achieved through oral presentations. Although these speeches are typically not focused on informing decisions, they still have a clear outcome or goals that should orient the entire speech. For example, a set of directions about how to put on a fund-raiser should clarify the ultimate tangible outcomes of those processes so that the audience can understand how all parts of the process fit together.

The audience's prior knowledge of processes and outcomes is a fundamental constraint on these speeches. New organization members might need more detail about the specific elements of the process, while more experienced members might have grown complacent or apathetic and need reminders about the importance of the overall goal. Indeed, in many organizational settings, such speeches should include some motivational content to achieve the informative purpose.

Narrating a History For informative speaking, the purpose of narrating a history is to improve understanding of some set of events or to demonstrate connections between past, present, and future. Within an organization, for example, sharing the history of the group can help new members to learn what the organization is all about. Narrating a history also can show trends and changes that help listeners to understand their current situation in a more complex or nuanced way. For example, after hearing a narrative speech about the history of al-Qaeda, listeners might be better able to make sense of the threats that that group might pose.

Therefore, it is critical that speakers highlight the relevance of this history to the present situation. Some listeners may find the history of a college interesting for its own sake, but others might need more of a reason to listen. Perhaps listeners can learn why the college currently emphasizes certain programs or how current initiatives have struggled to overcome obstacles in the past. Putting the relevance of a speech in the foreground can help the audience to see the information not merely as a history lesson, but as a usable history that informs their current thinking.

Clarifying Your Informative Purpose

You can incorporate what you have learned about the purposes for informative speaking with what you learned in chapter 4 about narrowing your topic and adapting to the particular audience as strategies for clarifying your specific purpose.

For example, if your audience research showed that many students already know what depression was but are unfamiliar with its prevalence on college campuses, then you have already identified one possible way of narrowing your purpose.

Topic: Depression among college students

General purpose: To inform

Specific purpose: To raise awareness about the increasing rate of depression among college students in the United States

Note how the specific purpose has been written to remind the speaker that the precise goal is to raise awareness. Rather than merely informing an audience, the purpose statement implies that *for this audience*, the real goal is to overcome the audience's lack of awareness.

Look at this slightly different purpose:

Topic: Depression among college students

General purpose: To inform

Specific purpose: To share knowledge about how antidepressants interact with alcohol and recreational drugs

This specific purpose focuses on knowledge that might be particularly relevant to a college audience. Instead of a standard speech about the causes of depression, this informative purpose shares knowledge that might shape personal choices as well as collective decisions about campus health campaigns or the regulation of drugs.

Another way to clarify your purpose is to consider whether a speech to share knowledge can be crafted as a speech that explains alternatives. For example, consider these two specific purpose statements:

Specific purpose: To share knowledge about ways of treating depression

Specific purpose: To explain differences among three standard methods for treating depression

The latter purpose emphasizes that the goal is to compare the alternatives and illuminate their differences. This gives the latter purpose statement a stronger focus. While both speeches will share knowledge with

THE ETHICAL DIMENSION

Informing or Persuading

At several points, this chapter has emphasized the importance of maintaining a clear distinction between informing and persuading. This distinction, however, can become complicated in practice, and some communication scholars have rejected this distinction in public speaking (Gring). It raises difficult conceptual and ethical issues that you should consider as you think about your own speech as well as the speeches of others.

General David Petraeus's testimony to Congress in 2007 is an excellent case for exploring these issues. Petraeus informed his audience about the progress of U.S. military operations, described the state of social and political conditions in Iraq, and offered recommendations for future action. The latter part of his testimony blurred the distinction between an informative presentation and a persuasive speech. Afterward, there was significant discussion of whether Petraeus's testimony was merely informative or whether he attempted to persuade Congress and the public to support a particular course of action. For example, follow the link below to an article about his testimony as well as video and a transcript of the hearing. http://www.washingtonpost.com/wp-dyn/content/article/2007/09/10/AR2007091000806.html?hpid=topnews

The Petraeus example shows that the line between informing and persuading is not entirely within your control; it is partly determined by your audience. Ethically, this highlights the notions of participation and reciprocity mentioned in the Ethical Dimension feature in chapter 3. To speak ethically *and* effectively, you need to recognize that other people may perceive your informative speech as trying to subtly persuade your audience. Therefore, it is your task to monitor your speech for statements that your audience might interpret as supporting one side of an issue.

In addition, the line between informing and persuading is determined partly by your situation. That

General David Petraeus.

is because speaking situations create basic audience expectations that must be honored if participants are going to be equals in the situation. If audiences expect an informative speech, they might begin to mistrust you if you seem to favor one viewpoint. Being open-minded, acknowledging conflicting evidence and alternative points of view, and refraining from value judgments are some of the practical ways in which you can honor the expectations of the situation. (You might examine how well Petraeus's testimony does these things.)

WHAT DO YOU THINK?

1. Is the distinction between informative and persuasive speech completely within your control? Is it completely outside your control?

2. Do ethical concerns obligate you to strive toward a purely informative speech? Do you have leeway to consider your particular audience's expectations and the situation?

their audiences, the latter purpose statement gives more guidance as to what kind of knowledge should be shared and how it should be shared.

Your purpose statement may undergo further refinement as you start thinking about the supporting materials you have gathered and the perspectives you have gained during the research process. This is when you begin to invent the primary content of your speech.

Strategies for Inventing Your Informative Speech

Even if you have already identified your topic and purpose, it can be difficult to figure out exactly what you should say in your speech. For some beginning public speakers, the challenge is overcoming the feeling that you have nothing to say. For others, the challenge is having all kinds of ideas but not knowing how to narrow down those ideas or discuss them coherently. In both of these situations, it can help to have a topical system for invention—a set of general categories or topics that can provoke new ideas and suggest ways of organizing ideas (Herrick). The rest of this section develops this topical system in connection with what you have learned from previous chapters.

Using Audience Research

The final section of chapter 5 discussed basic ideas for adapting your speech in light of audience research. Those ideas focused on broad-scale adaptations, such as adjusting your topic and purpose and establishing initial connections with and among your audience members. In addition, you can use audience research to help you invent specific components of your speech, including main points, transitions, and supporting materials.

Inventing Ideas from Demographic Research As you have seen, it is necessary to consider the composition of your particular audience to successfully adapt your speech. But you also can use demographic categories to brainstorm ideas about your topic. Think of the characteristics as lenses that help you to see different aspects of your topic that you might not have thought about previously. Consider how these characteristics can highlight questions and issues that might be explored in an informative speech on adoption:

- *Age.* Does the age of the adoptive parents or an adopted child affect decisions about adoption? Do adoption agencies have formal or informal rules about the age of adoptive parents? Also, the age of your particular audience might suggest issues that you need to emphasize or provide extra support. For example, an older audience of adoptive parents might know a lot about adoption but not be familiar with recent laws or trends in international adoption.

- *Sex, gender, and sexual orientation.* Do parents have a choice in selecting the sex of an adopted child? What factors influence the selection of a girl over a boy or vice versa? To what extent is the adoptive parents' sexual orientation an issue in adoption? The composition of your particular audience might encourage you to address certain perspectives; for example, a largely female audience might be interested in issues that are relevant to single mothers or lesbian couples.

- *Race/ethnicity.* What are the various perspectives on the benefits and disadvantages of interracial adoption? Are there cultural differences in adoption practices? Are there specific racial or ethnic issues that are raised by interracial adoption? In terms of your particular audience, racial or ethnic differences might suggest a purpose of explaining alternatives or might be used to transition between main points that describe adoption agencies and resources that focus on different groups.

- *Religion.* How do different religious denominations address adoption? How does adoption fit into their broader theology and ethics or their doctrines about related issues such as procreation and abortion? On these topics, your particular audience's familiarity with various religious traditions as well as their personal faith commitments would play a significant role in the amount and types of supporting material to include in your speech.

- *Class.* Are there class differences regarding who tends to adopt and who tends to provide babies for adoption? To what extent do the financial costs of adoption affect who has the ability to adopt? What adoption practices equalize or exacerbate class differences? For your particular audience, again consider what information is most likely to be relevant to their connection to the adoption system.

- *Place.* From what regions or countries do most adopted children come? How do adopted children cope with relocation? Within a country, are there any tendencies or trends toward local adoptions versus distant ones? As always, the places that your audience members call home provide opportunities for illustrating the personal relevance of your topic and for demonstrating the diversity of your audience.

On virtually any subject, you can use this tool to brainstorm ideas and identify areas that need extra development. The key is to remember that demographic characteristics are useful both for generating ideas and for adapting those ideas to your specific audience.

Inventing Ideas from Opinion Research Understanding the beliefs, values, and attitudes of your audience is just as important in informative speaking as it is in persuasive speaking. In both situations, your audience brings a set of ideas to the situation that will affect their receptiveness to your

INFORMATIVE SPEAKING: GIVING A TOUR
Speaking to a tour for the general public might focus on providing a coherent whole and emphasizing relevance, while a tour for experts would need to be tailored to the specific reasons why they are visiting.

speech. Chapter 4 referred to these factors as *constraints* and noted that they represent opportunities for making your message resonate with your audience as well as barriers to the audience's comprehension.

For most informative speeches, the main constraints are the existing beliefs of your audience. Whether you are trying to raise awareness, share knowledge, or explain alternatives, in informative speaking, you are aiming to present your audience with a set of facts that enhances their understanding of some topic or issue. So paying special attention to the existing beliefs of your audience is necessary for determining the purpose and the specific tactics for any informative speech.

To get a handle on the opinions of your audience, consider how their beliefs about your topic might be categorized in one of the following ways. We'll use NASA's space program as a running example.

- *Deficiency.* Your audience lacks basic knowledge about your topic or holds incorrect beliefs. If they do not know much about space exploration or they believe that the space program is primarily about the space shuttle, then an informative speech probably should focus on raising awareness and sharing knowledge rather than explaining alternatives.

    In these situations, invention should aim to provide a *coherent account* of your topic and to make main points *vivid*. In other words, help your audience to see the big picture rather than all the details or complications. For example, an informative speech could use NASA's mission statement ("to pioneer the future in space exploration, scientific discovery and aeronautics research") to establish three main points that provide a coherent overview of the organization. You could make these points vivid by discussing concrete examples of how the space shuttle contributes in each of those areas.

• *Abundance.* Your audience has some substantive knowledge about your topic. For example, an audience of physics students might be familiar with the technical aspects of the destruction of the Space Shuttle Columbia in 2003. An informative speech could build on this knowledge by providing *new information* or an *updated account* of that knowledge. Perhaps there is an *alternative or transformative explanation* of the knowledge that your audience already presumes (Rowan). There may be *upcoming decisions or choices* that rely on that knowledge. Or there may be *applications* of that knowledge in new situations.

  The purpose of an informative speech might be to raise awareness of the Columbia accident investigation, share knowledge about organizational factors that contributed to the accident, or explain how the lessons learned from Columbia are affecting current space missions. All these strategies begin, either explicitly or implicitly, by recognizing the existing beliefs of your audience and then introducing new knowledge.

• *Relevance.* Your audience has some knowledge about the topic, but audience members do not see any real connection to their lives. They might know about the space shuttle program but also believe that space exploration is extremely expensive and does not produce any tangible benefits for most people.

  The key to making your topic relevant is to *identify and amplify matters that your audience does find relevant and important.* In these situations, research on your audience's beliefs—and your own creativity—can be far more important for successful invention than your topic research. For example, if many of your classmates are flying somewhere during an upcoming break, this might be more relevant to their lives than the International Space Station or the climate on Mars. You might use that everyday concern as a basis for a speech about how NASA's work on technologies has improved de-icing and helps commercial aircraft avoid turbulence.

• *Commitment.* Your audience's beliefs, whether correct or not, provide the basis for definite attitudes about your topic. The same audience that thinks space research is irrelevant might also believe that NASA's budget is skyrocketing out of control. As a result, the audience might have a largely negative attitude toward NASA (e.g., "it's a waste of money") and might be skeptical about information that contradicts their beliefs. (In your audience research, you might want to consider whether these beliefs that underlie attitudes are simply taken for granted or whether they have been reinforced by explicit messages.)

If your audience's preexisting commitments could make them skeptical about your topic, your invention process should first *determine whether their commitments are rooted in beliefs or values*. For example, an opponent of NASA might not be familiar with how that agency's budget is allocated. That is a factual matter that can be addressed with informative speech. In contrast, a value judgment that NASA's money would be better spent on education is not an appropriate issue for a purely informative speech.

In addition, your invention process should *recognize why certain beliefs are "common sense"* before introducing contradictory information. If an audience opposes NASA because they believe it is irrelevant, you might need to acknowledge some seemingly irrelevant space research before you explain its hidden relevance or introduce other types of research that has more obvious relevance. (Again, during your audience research, you might want to gather instances that already resonate with your audience and use those as starting points for invention.)

Using Topic Research

After focusing on your audience, reflect on the materials you gathered while researching your topic. The last section of chapter 5 showed how research can help you to identify potential organizing strategies, visual aids, supporting materials, and differences of opinion, all of which contribute to the invention process. In addition, there are several themes that speakers address no matter what the specific subject matter of their speeches. These **common topics**, general themes and relationships that are common to all types of public speaking, provide another useful set of categories for generating the substance of your speech (Aristotle). Try to observe how these common topics might be relevant to your specific subject and rhetorical situation. For these topics, let's use free speech and censorship as our examples.

- *Existence.* Is there such a thing as free speech? How do we know that it exists? What does a society look like when free speech is nonexistent? What evidence suggests that censorship exists? These sorts of questions use the notion of **existence** to explore the most basic features of a particular subject.

   Speeches that are intended to raise awareness about an issue definitely need to establish where that issue exists in the real world. This is especially true for abstract ideas such as "free speech" or "discrimination." For example, you might talk about your campus's regulations regarding public speech or demonstrations, or you might discuss an instance of a political or religious group that believes their rights of free speech are being violated. Speeches about alternatives may also require attention to existence. For example, what alternatives actually exist for removing carbon dioxide from the atmosphere? Some alternatives might be available already, while others might not be workable for several years.

- *Definition.* In some instances, establishing the existence of something requires that you first provide a **definition** of what that thing is. What counts as freedom of speech? What does it mean to be censored? During your research, you should keep an eye out for any definitions of key terms and any definitional disputes in which people disagree on the meaning of a term or on what counts as an example of a term.

  There are several ways to invent a speech around definitions. Dictionary definitions and etymology, or the history of a word's meaning, are relatively straightforward strategies, but they do not always resonate with an audience. You might consider using them along with other strategies. The *genus/species* strategy, in which you define something by showing its relationship to a more general class of items, can be useful if other items or the larger class is more familiar. For example, millet belongs to a class of items called cereals, which include corn, rice, and wheat. Another strategy is to *operationalize* the term—describe its observable properties or what it looks like in practice. It might be difficult to identify a precise dictionary definition for "feminism," for example, but you could develop an entire speech around examples of feminist organizations or illustrations of feminist action to enhance your audience's understanding of feminism. Finally, the *essence* strategy attempts to distinguish the essential characteristics of some concept from its accidental characteristics. For example, a speech about college education might focus on how students gain a broad exposure to a liberal arts curriculum, not whether the university has a successful football team.

- *Comparison.* For informative speaking, consider the ways in which your research points to **comparison**, noting similarities and differences that can be used to enhance understanding of your subject. What are the similarities and differences between government censorship and corporate control of the media, for example? How does censorship in the United States compare to that of other countries? How do current laws regarding censorship compare to past laws?

  Comparison is useful for informative speaking in part for purposes of audience adaptation. Complex ideas, for example, can be made more comprehensible through *analogies* that compare the idea to a past situation or something more simple. The "greenhouse" analogy, for example, is one that scientists use to explain how carbon dioxide emissions contribute to global warming.

- *Causality.* Exploring **causality**, or the relationships between cause and effect, is another way to examine your subject. What factors lead to censorship? What caused the Founders to include free speech rights in the

U.S. Constitution? What effects have speech codes had at various universities? What has caused such codes to be upheld or overturned in court?

The topic of causality is relevant to all informative speeches, and is especially worth exploring in speeches that attempt to explain alternatives. If the members of your community organization are interested in exploring options for fund-raising, they will want to think about the consequences of pursuing those options. Does one option cost more money than the organization can afford? Will one option require the organization to find additional volunteers?

- *Correlation.* Showing the **correlation**, or relationship between two co-existing events or phenomena, can help your audience have a more comprehensive view of a situation. For example, is there a relationship between censorship and other forms of government repression? Is there a correlation between the level of free speech in a society and the quantity of civil society or nongovernmental organizations?

  In informative speaking, correlation is a great way to expand a single idea into several ideas. For example, a speech about successful elementary schools might focus on the importance of parental involvement. But research on this topic probably would suggest that several other factors contribute to student success. Instead, an informative speech might describe how each of these factors is correlated with measures of student performance.

- *Time and space.* How have censorship practices changed over time? Are there particular times when governments exercise significant limitations on free speech? What are the times or places that have seen free speech issues come into public prominence? How do different spaces enable or constrain public speech?

  Thinking in terms of time and space not only helps you to generate ideas, but also can point you toward specific organizational patterns. For example, a speech about changes in censorship practices probably would be organized most clearly by discussing those changes chronologically. Or an informative speech about student transportation choices might focus first on students who live on campus, then on students who live within a mile of campus, and then on students who live more than a mile away. Chapter 9 will discuss these organizational patterns in more detail.

Providing Support for Your Informative Speech

Once you have determined the basic ideas for your speech, you can zero in on the other key part of invention: generating support for those ideas. You learned about the different types of supporting materials in chapter 6, and if you were able to find appropriate types of support as you researched your topic, you have a firm foundation for this phase of preparing your speech.

But why do you need to provide supporting materials? Isn't it enough just to tell people what you know to be true? It's not. Supporting materials are necessary for effective speeches for at least two reasons. First, *supporting materials help to maintain your audience's attention*. It is easy to speak in generalizations about virtually any topic, but the mark of a good speaker is the ability to move beyond generalizations to specific, unique, and insightful statements that make the topic come alive for an audience. For example, your classmates might quickly get bored with a speech that begins like this:

> Why is drunk driving an important issue? Well, drunk driving affects a lot of people. It can end in serious injuries or even death. Thousands of people are killed every year in drunk driving accidents. It is especially a problem for young people, which is why I am talking about it to you today.

These general statements say little that is new about this common classroom speech topic. Beyond the classroom, too, audiences may grow impatient with speeches that merely repeat basic knowledge and fail to address the personal relevance and practical importance of your topic.

Instead, an effective speech requires that your supporting material shed new light on the issues. Consider this:

> Many of you probably know that the drinking age was raised to 21 primarily to reduce drunk driving fatalities. But did you know that a higher drinking age also may make our society smarter? Research over the past decade has shown that our brains continue developing well into our twenties and that the use and abuse of alcohol in our teens and twenties can have significant effects on our cognitive ability. If you have joked that drinking will "kill a few brain cells," listen to some of the following studies about the dangerous and even permanent effects of underage drinking. They will show you that it's no joke at all.

This passage starts with a well-known idea but quickly pivots to a new idea backed by supporting material that is detailed and personally relevant to a college audience. This is not just any speech about the drinking age, but one that grabs audience attention by giving them something unique.

Second, *you need supporting materials so that your audience will accept, or at least consider, what you are saying to be true*. As you are speaking, thoughtful audience members will ask themselves, "Why should I believe that?" or "What's the evidence for that?" For a speech about the drinking age, you might provide testimony from an experienced doctor or results from a study published in a peer-reviewed journal. Providing supporting materials is a way of answering audience questions ahead of time and satisfying the audience's desire for knowledge.

The rest of this section returns to the five types of supporting material described in chapter 6. It briefly reviews each type of material and then expands on the strengths and weaknesses of those types of material. Just as magazines and websites have their strengths and weaknesses as sources, different types of supporting materials each have particular characteristics that should guide their use in your speeches. This section will use the topic of immunization to examine these issues.

Common Knowledge

Basic facts, beliefs about how the world works, and widely shared values are all examples of common knowledge. Because this knowledge is common and not disputed, there is no need to provide citations or external sources. And even though you will want to move beyond common knowledge in your speech, it can be a good starting point for discussing various ideas. Consider this way of introducing a discussion of vaccines:

> As you know, vaccines are products used to promote immunity to diseases. Several vaccines can be given to children before the age of two, while others are intended for older people.

This passage uses a simple definition to activate shared knowledge about the topic. You might also consider appealing to a shared value:

> How many of you would like to be sick? How would you feel if you contracted a life-threatening disease? Obviously, our health is a fundamental concern for everyone in this room. That's why understanding the facts surrounding immunization is vitally relevant—not just for parents, but for all of us.

As you can see, common knowledge is useful for

- developing audience identification
- establishing common ground before introducing more controversial ideas

In most speeches, it is imperative to establish common ground between you and your audience early so that your audience will be receptive to your subsequent ideas. However, common knowledge has limitations, too. Because common knowledge is taken for granted, it is not necessarily examined critically, so it might not be accurate. For example, a speaker who claims, "We all benefit if everyone gets a flu shot" might seem to be stating a piece of conventional wisdom. But in fact, people with certain kinds of allergies may have significant negative reactions to the shot. Audience members also might not have the same level of agreement on shared values. Saying, "I'm sure you would do anything to be healthy" might overstate the value that they put on health. So keep these limitations in mind as you use common knowledge in your speeches.

Personal Experience

Personal experiences are observations and narratives drawn from your own life. By using personal experiences in a speech, you show your audience that you have a direct connection to your topic, and you give them a glimpse into why this issue might matter to you.

> Vaccines not only protect your state of health, they can also protect your state of mind. I learned this the hard way when I studied in Brazil several years ago. I had traveled to South America previously, and knew I had updated all my standard shots. But I forgot a very important shot: the one for yellow fever. Even though I never got sick, for four months every mosquito I saw made me anxious.

Here, the personal experience—a specific instance supports the general idea that vaccines do more than just protect your bodily health. By using a personal experience, a speaker's very presence, as well as his or her words, functions as a form of support.

Personal experiences are especially useful for

- creating identification with your audience
- demonstrating connections between private life and public issues
- illustrating general ideas
- making ideas vivid and emotional

For example, the yellow fever story is unique, yet it taps into the sense of worry and anxiety that is a normal part of travel. It also vividly illustrates an idea about vaccines and conveys emotions that the speaker felt. In addition, the story could be elaborated or connected to public issues such as global pandemics or the resurgence of malaria. In all these ways, personal experiences give life to broader ideas.

For informative speeches, then, personal experiences enhance the meaning of otherwise straightforward information. At the same time, personal experience has limitations as a form of supporting material. Most important, your own experience is never the final word about an issue. For example, suppose you managed to avoid chicken pox in spite of never getting a vaccination for it; that does not necessarily demonstrate that the vaccination is unnecessary. A single personal experience like this can be useful for creating identification and making ideas vivid and emotional. But if you are trying to support a more general point, try to supplement personal experiences with other forms of evidence.

Examples

Examples are specific instances that illustrate a larger point. Recall that chapter 6 described three different types of examples. A personal experience such as that related by the student who traveled to Brazil is an *extended example*—a description of an instance that runs for several sentences. In contrast, a *brief example* merely mentions one or more specific instances to make an idea more concrete. A *hypothetical example* develops an imaginary scenario to transport the audience to a different time or place. Each type of example can serve the purposes of informative speaking.

Brief examples (shown <u>underlined</u>) provide a way to immediately clarify or specify an idea:

> Vaccines work in different ways. Some contain inactive versions of a virus, <u>such as the influenza vaccine</u>. Others contain an attenuated, or weakened, version of a virus. <u>The measles, mumps, and rubella vaccine</u> is probably the most prominent example of an attenuated vaccine.
>
> In spite of the widespread availability of vaccines, outbreaks of infectious diseases are not historical oddities of your grandparents' generation. <u>For example, in 1998, the San Francisco Bay Area saw an outbreak of pertussis, or whooping cough, that led to the death of two infants.</u>

Brief examples are primarily intended to give a quick point of reference for an audience—a concrete instance or a short list of items that fit within some larger category.

Extended examples are useful when you are trying to *explain* something rather than merely specify it. For instance, you might develop an extended version of the San Francisco pertussis example to explain why the disease continues to be a concern.

> Outbreaks of infectious disease are not a thing of the past. The Bay Area pertussis outbreak shows one reason why: conflicting beliefs about the benefits and risks of vaccination. In the spring of 1998, two infants in the area died from pertussis, and the state epidemiologist reported 198 cases of the disease during the first half of the year, mostly concentrated in the Bay Area. Health officials attributed the outbreak to the fact that many parents in the region resist having their child vaccinated; in Sonoma County, up to half of schoolchildren are not vaccinated. But some parents defend their choice by pointing to evidence of seizures and significant brain damage that is correlated with vaccination.

This shows how extended examples can be used to provide detail and explain ideas that cannot be captured in a sentence or two. Similarly, a vivid story that describes a child suffering from the terrible coughing would be much more compelling than the plain statement "Pertussis is a horrible disease." Or a hypothetical example could be used to help your audience envision a family member experiencing the disease. Hypothetical examples are useful if your audience believes that the topic is not personally relevant. You can follow a hypothetical example with a real example or other evidence of the actual condition to effectively convey both the relevance and the reality of your topic.

Examples are a crucial part of any public speaker's repertoire. They are useful for

- illustrating general ideas
- clarifying ideas by making them tangible and concrete
- explaining ideas in detail (extended examples)
- framing situations as relevant to your audience (hypothetical examples)

The well-worn adage "Show, don't tell," reminds public speakers that they should use vivid examples and not just rely on plain descriptions or generalities to make their points. At the same time, examples are limited as sources of support. Some examples may be extremely unusual or not representative of the typical case. When possible, use multiple examples to illustrate your points, as well as statistics and testimony that reinforce the truth of your examples.

Testimony

Any time you use the words of others to support your points, you are using testimony. If your audience is likely to find those words more authoritative, credible, or eloquent than your own, then you should use testimony for support. *Expert testimony* is provided by people who have specialized, in-depth knowledge about your topic. *Citizen testimony* comes from those who have direct experience or firsthand knowledge of an issue.

Your use of testimony should be guided by an assessment of which kind of testimony is most relevant to your topic and most likely to be perceived positively by your audience. In particular, expert testimony is useful for enhancing your credibility and addressing controversial issues:

Although many pregnant women are understandably reticent about introducing chemicals into their body, getting a flu vaccine is a different story. In the eyes of Dr. Sarah J. Kilpatrick, a committee chair in the American College of Obstetricians and Gynecologists, the greater risk comes from getting the flu and then getting treated for it. "The antiretroviral drugs commonly prescribed to combat the flu have not been tested for safety and efficacy in pregnancy, and their effects on the fetus are unknown. Pregnant women who are using these drugs should do so with caution. Your best bet is to avoid the flu altogether, and vaccination can help you do that."

Expert testimony allows you to show that an idea is not just your personal opinion but is shared by those who have greater knowledge or training than you have.

Citizen testimony is useful for demonstrating how a problem or issue affects ordinary people. In some situations, it can indicate limitations of other forms of support. For example, consider claims about a possible connection between autism and thimerosal, a preservative that is used in some vaccines.

Citizen testimony may raise important questions about the current state of scientific knowledge, but audiences are not likely to perceive it as being as authoritative as expert testimony. However, other citizen testimony—such as a parent's account of caring for an autistic child—might be an extremely compelling way to describe and explain autism to your audience.

Testimony, then, is useful for

- enhancing your own credibility
- providing support on especially complicated or controversial topics
- giving audiences a firsthand look at an issue

On the other hand, testimony typically represents only one person's point of view. As with personal experience and examples, try to identify additional pieces of evidence, other persons who back up the testimony you use, or testimony that represents the conclusions of multiple, diverse voices. The Financial Crisis Inquiry Commission report or the Intergovernmental Panel on Climate Change reports exemplify the latter. Also, be mindful of how some advocates will produce testimony that advances their own personal or economic interest through deliberately misleading or partial accounts. You have an ethical obligation to fully identify any person whose testimony you use in your speeches so that your audience can evaluate the potential bias of your source. You will learn about strategies for citing sources orally in chapter 12.

Statistics

The usefulness of statistics comes from their capacity to describe a large amount of data quickly and precisely. A speech about immunization against the human papillomavirus (HPV), for example, may need to discuss the prevalence of infection in the U.S. population. It would be impossible, not to mention unethical, to list all 20 million Americans who currently have the infection, but that statistic can get the job done quickly. In addition, the statistic lends precision to your attempt to describe the scope of a problem. Rather than just saying, "HPV is a significant problem," you can use statistics to show that nearly 75% of Americans between the ages of 15 and 49 have been infected during their life.

Raw numbers are especially useful for illustrating the sheer impact of some occurrence or practice:

There are approximately 100 different strains of HPV.

The direct costs of treating symptoms of HPV are estimated to be $1.6 billion per year.

Percentages or ratios illustrate impact but also give audiences a sense of the prevalence or distribution of something. This can help them to think about probability, risk, and other judgments about the likelihood of something happening.

> Approximately one third of all new STD infections are cases of HPV.
>
> Half of all sexually active people will contract an STD/STI by age 25.

Central tendencies such as mean and median also get at distribution, but they do so by focusing our attention on the middle of some set of data.

> In one study, the median duration of HPV infection was 7.5 months.
>
> The average time from infection to cancer is approximately 20 years.

Statistics like these are typical in both informative and persuasive speeches. Beginning speakers often have a tendency to rely heavily on statistics, assuming that they are the "strongest" or "most factual" supporting material possible. But statistics are particularly prone to being misunderstood and misused. Rather than focusing on the inherent mathematical problems involved with compiling statistics—which are important—the rest of this section simply asks you to follow a few simple guidelines when you use statistics in speeches:

- *Use statistics from reliable sources.* The best way to avoid many of the inherent problems of statistics is to rely on people who know how to use them accurately and fairly. A dorm survey of students about HPV or statistics from a company that sells an HPV vaccine are not likely to be the most reliable supporting materials. Instead, look to individuals and organizations that have a good track record of producing accurate and unbiased information on your topic. On this topic, it might be public health professionals such as the Centers for Disease Control and Prevention or an association of medical professionals such as the American Academy of Pediatrics.

- *Consider alternative interpretations of your statistics.* Ask how other people might interpret your numbers or whether other statistics would be more relevant. The issue here is not their accuracy but their implications. For example, if the direct costs of treating HPV are $1.6 billion, what are the indirect costs? Perhaps using the $1.6 billion statistic underplays the significance of the problem. Statistics also can be used to exaggerate. For example, most of the 20 million people who are currently infected will never exhibit symptoms and will clear any disease naturally. Perhaps that statistic creates a misleading impression about the problem. In both of these instances, a speaker would do well to think about the material that will best support the claim and to think about the kinds of main points that can be supported by the available evidence.

- *Always put statistics into a context.* Numbers do not speak for themselves; it is your job to make a statistic meaningful to your audience. Suppose the rate of HPV infection in your community went up 10% last year. That piece of data means little by itself. Does it represent a big increase? Is it the same rate as past years? Are other people relieved or alarmed at this? Similarly, it can help to translate statistics onto a personal or local scale. If there are 5.5 million new HPV cases per year, how many of them will be on your campus? How many new cases will there be per day?

- *Avoid the "avalanche" or "wall" of numbers.* Providing too many statistics, especially in rapid succession, generates information overload rather than a well-formed speech. In your research, try to identify those few statistics that best capture the essence of your issue. A single, well-placed statistic that is illustrated by vivid examples and bolstered by powerful testimony is much more likely to be remembered by your audience than any statistic from a speech that is overloaded with numbers.

All of these points are intended to focus on the *meaning* of your statistics. As was discussed in the first part of this book, your task as a speaker is to participate in meaning making with your audience. Even though the speech you are currently inventing is traditionally called an informative speech, it is much more than the mere transfer of information. Inventing an informative speech requires that you keep communication, rather than information, at the forefront of your thinking.

CASE CONCLUSION

Maloree's Speech on Sonar

Maloree decided that because her audience knew little about sonar and its impacts on marine life, her speech would aim primarily to raise awareness. From her audience analysis, she learned that many of her classmates self-identified as environmentally concerned, but even they did not see sonar as a particularly important issue. So not only would she need to provide a *coherent* and *vivid* account, she also would need to make it *relevant*.

Maloree developed main points around *defining* what sonar is and then talking about how sonar has *caused* significant problems for marine life, especially whales. To make the problem vivid, she relied on brief examples and explanations from experts that would help to illustrate both how sonar worked and what impacts it has had. But Maloree struggled to incorporate a wider variety of research in her speech. For example, the nature of the topic made it nearly impossible to incorporate personal experience into the speech. As a result, she decided that at least for this speech, she would use a hypothetical example in her introduction to put her listeners into the situation and encourage them to see the issue as relevant.

MALOREE'S WORKING OUTLINE

Purpose: To inform

Specific Purpose: to raise awareness about the effects of sonar blasts among marine life

I. Introduction

    A. Attention-getter: Imagine a sound so loud that it blew out your eardrum

        1. leaves you unable to communicate

        2. pushes you out of your home

        3. interrupts basic biological functions

    B. This scenario is occurring among marine species in the vicinity of sonar blasts

    C. Central idea: Sonar blasts are significantly disrupting marine life.

    D. Preview

II. Understanding Sonar Blasts

    A. Early uses of sonar

    B. Power of sonar

    C. Current use of sonar

III. Effects of Sonar Blasts

    A. Disruption of migratory routes

    B. Disruption of communication patterns

    C. Disruption of surfacing movements

IV. Conflict about Sonar Blasts

    A. Military readiness needs

    B. Marine Mammal Protection Act

V. Conclusions

Summary

PURPOSES OF INFORMATIVE SPEAKING

- Informative speeches in civic and political contexts often focus on raising awareness, sharing knowledge, or explaining alternatives.
- Other purposes of informative speech include publicizing organizations or events, describing processes, and narrating histories.

STRATEGIES FOR INVENTING YOUR INFORMATIVE SPEECH

- Demographic categories suggest unique approaches to a topic as well as ideas that will resonate with a speaker's particular audience.

- Audience beliefs about the topic should determine whether a speech focuses on providing simple and vivid accounts of a topic, transforming existing knowledge, or heightening the relevance of the topic.

- Common topics of existence, definition, comparison, causality, correlation, time, and space all can help a speaker elaborate ideas on a particular subject.

PROVIDING SUPPORT FOR YOUR INFORMATIVE SPEECH

- Common knowledge, personal experiences, examples, testimony, and statistics each have certain strengths and weaknesses as supporting material. Speakers need to be attentive to these weaknesses and use multiple forms of evidence to make up for them.

Key Terms

common topics, p. 201
existence, p. 201
definition, p. 202

comparison, p. 202
causality, p. 202
correlation, p. 203

Comprehension

1. What are the three main civic purposes of informative speaking?

2. What are the primary audience obstacles for speeches intended to raise awareness? What adaptation strategies should a speaker use to deal with these obstacles?

3. How can you use general demographic characteristics to generate ideas about your topic?

4. How are the audience's attitudes and commitments relevant to inventing an informative speech?

5. List the common topics.

6. How might you use the units of public discourse to generate ideas for an informative speech?

7. What are the strengths of common knowledge as a form of supporting material?

8. What weakness is shared by both examples and personal experience?

9. What is the difference between expert testimony and citizen testimony?

10. What guidelines should you follow when using statistics?

Application

1. For the following broad topics, come up with specific purpose statements that would serve each of these three purposes: raising awareness, sharing knowledge, and explaining alternatives.

   Tuition   Business ethics   Ecotourism   Iran   Zoning

2. In a group of your classmates, share the topic for your informative speech. Then use the demographic categories to brainstorm different angles you might take on that topic.

3. For your speech topic, determine whether deficiency, abundance, relevance, or commitment is the most important aspect of your audience's opinions. Then identify which of the common topics are the best ones for engaging those opinions.

4. Select a newspaper article on an issue that interests you. After reading the article, come up with two ideas for an informative speech that would go beyond the information in that article.

5. Attend a public lecture given by a faculty member or a visiting scholar. Identify the types of supporting material that he or she uses most often. Consider why one type is used more often than others and how the speech would have had a different effect if other types were used more often.

Organizing Your Informative Speech

This chapter is intended to help you:

- Gain strategies for organizing an informative speech
- Understand principles for wording and arranging your main points
- Identify patterns for integrating supporting material in your speech

You might be puzzled about the best way to turn all of your ideas for supporting materials into an effective speech. A coherent organizational pattern, chosen strategically to serve your purpose, will help you to move from merely having good ideas to having a great speech. Organization is important for both listeners and speakers. For listeners, a well-organized speech that follows a recognizable pattern of thought will be easy to follow. It will enhance listeners' understanding and sustain their attention. Some organizational patterns can help an audience to see how information is related to decisions and issues in the public sphere. A strategic organizational design does not just convey information; it puts that information into a context that audiences find meaningful.

From the speaker's perspective, a well-chosen organizational strategy will enhance the speaker's ethos, or credibility with the audience. Think about the

Emily's Speech on the Western Hemisphere Institute for Security Cooperation

Emily had decided to speak about the Western Hemisphere Institute for Security Cooperation (WHINSEC), formerly known as the School of the Americas, a military training school for Latin American soldiers located in Fort Benning, Georgia. Emily knew that a campus organization had been critical of the institute, but she didn't know why. Her research about the institute revealed a long and complicated history as well as strong arguments both for and against its activities. Because she did not yet have a strong opinion about the institute, she thought it would be a good topic for an informative speech.

After doing some audience analysis, Emily felt sure that her audience knew less about WHINSEC than she did. So during the invention stage, she decided that her main purpose would be to raise awareness about the institute and its training programs. But how would she decide which ideas should be her focus? There were so many things to discuss that it was difficult to narrow down her main ideas. And since her audience knew so little about the topic, she wasn't sure how she could make it relevant to them or give the topic a sense of urgency. Pulling her thoughts and her research together was going to take some more thinking.

last time you heard a rambling speech or a disorganized lecture. In all likelihood, it not only made the speech confusing but also reflected poorly on your opinion of the speaker. A well-organized speech is more likely to indicate that you have planned your speech ahead of time and are in command of your subject matter. Sound organization also can help your delivery of the speech. If your main points follow a logical pattern, it will be easier for you to remember those points and make smooth transitions between them.

The rest of this chapter shows you how to think strategically about the organization of informative speeches. It illustrates several organizational patterns that can help you to overcome the usual rhetorical obstacles in informative speaking. After discussing the big picture of organizing an entire speech, the chapter turns to micro-level issues related to organization: wording your main points clearly and integrating your supporting material effectively. You will build on these skills when you start outlining your speech, described in chapter 11. ■

Identifying an Organizational Strategy

Excitement and anticipation often accompany the beginning of the academic year. While students look forward to seeing old friends and taking new classes, faculty and staff put new ideas into practice and initiate plans for the future. At many colleges, the president or provost will kick off the year with a convocation address that identifies the school's priorities for the coming year.

At one college, the president wanted to share his big plans with every-one on campus. He thought it would be a smart rhetorical strategy to start by praising various people and programs for their accomplishments during the past year, then talk about challenges that the college faced, and then lay out his goals and priorities for the future. Moving from past to present to future made good sense.

Unfortunately, good sense about organization stopped there. Even though his primary purpose was to inform his audience about priorities for the coming year, he spent so much time praising people and discussing challenges that he left little time to discuss those priorities. This problem was compounded by the fact that he had twenty-three specific items on his priority list! These items were not even grouped into categories representing different aspects of the college such as Academics, Student Life, or Build-ing Projects. As some audience members began to leave and others moved uncomfortably in their seats, the president skipped a few things on his list and cut the speech short. Afterward, hardly anyone could remember any of the items.

This scenario, based on a real event, reveals the importance of taking organi-zation seriously. The college president seemed to have a good overall organi-zational strategy. The speech started with the past, then moved to the present and finally into the future. It seemed appropriate for the situation, since pre-vious convocation speeches typically involved recognition of past accomplish-ments and an overall assessment of meeting college priorities.

But because it did not consider the audience obstacles or the primary purpose of the speech, this organizational strategy was not sufficient after all. Even the very best twenty-three-point speech would have been difficult for any audience to follow. Most audience members were not interested in hear-ing about all of these priorities; many of the ideas only affected a small por-tion of the campus. If the primary purpose of the speech had been to inform the audience about these priorities, the president should have reorganized the speech to (1) devote more time to discussing the priorities, (2) limit the num-ber of priorities, and (3) put the priorities into categories so that they would be easier to follow and remember.

Developing an effective organizational strategy, then, involves more than just identifying a series of main points. It is really an extension of your think-ing during the process of invention. By specifying your informative purpose, identifying audience constraints and opportunities, and assessing the rele-vance and importance of addressing your topic, you can begin to craft an organizational strategy that fits your rhetorical situation.

Sequential Strategies

Sequential strategies rely on natural patterns in the world to organize speeches in familiar ways. For informative speaking, sequential strategies are especially helpful when you are trying to share knowledge about a broad or

PUBLIC SPOTLIGHT

Misty Romero: Advocating for Alternative Spring Breaks

Misty Romero exemplifies how civic engagement can lead someone to a greater awareness of important political issues. During college, Misty got involved with an organization called Break Away, which sponsors "alternative" spring breaks involving community service. She went to Juarez, Mexico, during her sophomore spring break; participated in more alternative breaks; and eventually served on Break Away's national board of directors for six years. Her example was so important that Break Away instituted the Misty Romero Active Citizen of the Year Award to honor individuals connected to the organization who are committed to a life of active citizenship.

While on her breaks, Misty learned about the challenges that many people face in getting needed health care. "[Through alternative breaks] I learned about many social justice issues first hand while I became acquainted with people who had different life experiences and opportunities than I have had. These experiences taught me that it is our responsibility as humans to contribute to healthy communities from the level of family community to the level of world community"

Since college, Misty has completed nursing school and works as a registered nurse. But she also wants to promote political change that will result in dignified and affordable health care for all. Her experience has shown her the importance of good organization in public speaking. "Preparing a well-organized speech is important in order to accurately convey your message. And organizing your thoughts prior to speaking publicly definitely helps decrease any anxiety related to giving a speech." Misty's public speaking skills will help her to connect her personal concerns and professional experience to this important public issue.

unfamiliar topic. These patterns allow you to present the main points of your speech in a simple and systematic way. Two typical sequential patterns are chronological order and spatial order.

Chronological Order   The **chronological order** strategy organizes a series of points according to their occurrence in time. In most cases, the first point in the series will be the earliest event, and the most recent occurrence will be the last point. While chronological order can be used to structure the main points of your speech, it is also a common way to proceed through a series of subpoints. It is useful for describing processes and narrating histories as well as for raising awareness about an issue or problem that has developed over time.

A rather straightforward informative speech can use chronological order to simplify a broad topic and provide a useful overview for audiences that are newcomers to a topic. This example shows how a speaker might present the history of feminism in an understandable way:

Specific purpose: To share knowledge about important eras of feminism in the United States.

Central idea: Scholars divide the history of feminism into the first, second, and third waves.

Main points:

I. Feminism's first wave focused on political rights during the nineteenth and early twentieth centuries.

    II. Feminism's second wave addressed social and cultural inequality during the 1960s and 1970s.

    III. Feminism's third wave challenged traditional versions of feminism starting in the early 1990s.

These main points also show that chronological order is not merely a means to convey the dates of events but also a way to capture changes over time. Rather than a dry history, a speech with chronological order can offer your audience substantive knowledge about a topic.

Chronological order also can be used to heighten the relevance of a topic. To do this, organize your points so that they lead to a current situation or concern of your audience:

> *Specific purpose:* To share knowledge with my audience about changes in women's participation in the workplace.
>
> *Central idea:* Women's participation in the labor market is related to broader social trends and historical events.
>
> *Main points:*
>
>   I. During World War II, many women worked outside the home as part of the war effort.
>
>   II. Starting in the 1970s, demographic shifts and wage stagnation resulted in more women entering the labor market.
>
>   III. In the past decade, better educational opportunities and rising unemployment rates have slowed the entry of women into the labor market.

Here, chronological order shares knowledge about past events but also provides information that helps audience members to understand their own situation.

Spatial Order

A **spatial order** strategy organizes a series of points according to their location or direction. Like chronological order, spatial order can be used for structuring either main points or subpoints, and it is especially useful for simplifying a topic and exploring alternatives. Essentially, spatial order lends itself to looking at several "snapshots" on a particular topic.

For example, spatial order can show what a broad topic or phenomenon looks like in different locations. This example about energy consumption uses national boundaries to define locations:

> *Specific purpose:* To share knowledge with my audience about the major energy consumers in the world.
>
> *Central idea:* Three countries—the United States, China, and Russia—are the three biggest energy consumers in the world.
>
> *Main points:*
>
>   I. Russia is a heavy consumer of natural gas.
>
>   II. China is the largest consumer of coal.
>
>   III. The United States is the world's leading energy consumer, using more energy than China and Russia combined (U.S. Department of Energy).

For some topics, a spatial order that follows a natural direction can help the audience to anticipate the progression of your points, making your speech easier to follow:

Specific purpose: To share knowledge with my audience about household energy conservation measures.

Central idea: Energy conservation can be accomplished inside and outside your home.

Main points:

I. Inside your home, insulation and programmable thermostats can reduce energy use.

II. Between your home and the outdoors, caulking and weather-stripping can minimize wasted energy.

III. Outside your home, landscaping can act as a natural insulator to limit your need for energy.

Rather than overwhelming an audience with a long list of conservation measures that are not clearly related, a speaker can use spatial order to break down that list according to natural divisions in the world. In a different situation, these main points could be adapted to explore alternatives. If you belong to an organization that is trying to reduce its energy costs, for example, subpoints could be developed to inform your audience about the feasibility and benefits of different energy-saving options.

SPATIAL ORDER
Spatial order could be used to inform an audience about where oil reserves are located around the world.

Analytical Strategies

If the main points of your topic don't fit within a sequential organization, consider using an analytical strategy. **Analytical strategies** break down a topic into its related parts or components. Compared to sequential strategies, analytical strategies typically put more emphasis on connections, relationships, and structures. As a result, these strategies are especially useful when you are dealing with complex topics, such as trying to reveal distinctions or differences between similar things, or showing relationships between items or events.

Causal Order The **causal order** strategy is used for organizing main points according to cause-and-effect relationships. For informative speaking, describing causal relationships often occurs in the context of raising awareness about some problem or explaining alternatives. You might raise awareness of a problem by discussing its causes, or you might share knowledge about alternatives by discussing the likely effects of various alternatives.

In some cases, a speech that is organized according to causal order will be in chronological order, with the causes discussed in the first main point(s) and the effects covered next:

> *Specific purpose:* To raise my audience's awareness that legislation has had a significant impact on media choices.
>
> *Central idea:* The Telecommunications Act of 1996 substantially affected consumers' media choices.
>
> *Main points:*
>
> I. The Telecommunications Act of 1996 changed ownership and licensing regulations for radio, television, and telephone companies.
>
> II. The Act had a significant impact on consumers' media choices.
> A. First, the Act ushered in major media consolidation.
> B. Second, the Act reduced the diversity of viewpoints in the media.
> C. Third, the Act made cable television and local phone markets less competitive (Common Cause).

Even though the main points of this speech are arranged chronologically, the purpose of this speech is to show a causal relationship. A chronological speech, such as the one about national energy consumers above, does not necessarily show a causal relationship.

In other situations, a speaker may discuss the effect(s) first and then explain the causes. This is usually the strategy for helping an audience to understand what factors have led to some current, prominent issue or problem. If the issue is prominent, then it makes sense to start a speech with that familiar material and then look back to the sources of the problem:

> *Specific purpose:* To explain to my audience why cable television choices are limited.
>
> *Central idea:* Efficiency and franchising rules explain why cable television choices are limited.

Main points:

    I. Many people have raised concerns about the limited choices for cable television.

    II. We have limited choices because our city's local franchising rules give exclusive rights to one cable system (Sadler).

    III. The rights are exclusive because it is more efficient to have one system than multiple systems.

Topical Order Another analytical strategy is **topical order**, a strategy of organizing a series of points by identifying a set of categories, subtopics, or dimensions of the speech's topic. Topical order is the most general organizational pattern and often is used when none of the other patterns seem to fit the topic or purpose. However, it should not be just the default organizational strategy. Instead, use it when you want to simplify a complex topic or focus the audience's attention on a few important aspects of a topic.

A classroom lecture describing different theories or perspectives often takes a topical strategy:

Specific purpose: To share knowledge with my audience about different approaches to the study of media effects.

Central idea: Four main approaches to media-effects research are social effects, uses and gratifications, agenda setting, and cultivation.

Main points:

    I. Social-effects research examines whether media content promotes antisocial or prosocial behavior.

    II. *Uses and gratifications research* explores how and why audience members use different media types.

    III. *Agenda-setting research* investigates how news coverage affects the issues that the public thinks are important.

    IV. *Cultivation research* examines how media portrayals shape viewers' perception of reality.

In this example, the speaker's purpose is simply to divide a big topic into a few basic categories. This outline does not attempt to show relationships or draw comparisons between the main points. However, a lecture on this topic might arrange these same points in chronological order if the purpose was to sketch a history of media research or to explain how one type of research became more popular than an earlier type of research.

Another common use of topical order allows you to take different perspectives on the same topic:

Specific purpose: To raise awareness of the ways in which advertising shapes our society.

Central idea: Advertising is a significant part of our economic, social, and political systems.

Main points:

    I. Economically, advertising is a $650 billion industry.

    II. Socially, advertising reflects and transforms our beliefs, attitudes, and values.

    III. Politically, advertising plays a major role in electoral campaigns.

Comparative Order The **comparative order** strategy organizes main points by drawing direct connections between two or more things. Comparative order is similar to topical order, but here the topics are specific points that illuminate how different things compare to one another. As a result, the comparative order strategy comes in handy for displaying similarities and differences, raising awareness of unfamiliar ideas in terms of familiar ones, and explaining alternatives.

A comparative order strategy may take three different forms depending on your purpose and the primary obstacle to audience understanding (Rowan). First, a comparative order can serve the goal of *clarification*. If an audience is confusing closely related ideas or is likely to struggle with understanding the meaning of a new idea, you can use a comparative strategy to clarify the primary idea by distinguishing it from other ideas. For example, the following outline uses a comparative strategy to help an audience to understand the flu:

Specific purpose: To inform my audience how to distinguish the flu from other common illnesses.

Central idea: Having "the flu" is different from having a cold or an upset stomach.

Main points:

    I. The flu is defined as a respiratory infection caused by the influenza virus.

    II. The flu is often confused with the common cold.

        A. Like the common cold, the flu is spread by exposure to infected people and leads to a cough.

        B. Unlike the common cold, the flu usually leads to a high fever and body aches.

    III. The flu also is often confused with having an upset stomach.

        A. For example, nausea and vomiting are commonly referred to as "stomach flu."

        B. However, nausea and vomiting are typically caused by other types of viruses, bacteria, or food poisoning, not the influenza virus (U.S. Department of Health and Human Services; American Lung Association).

In this instance, the main audience obstacle is the common confusion between the flu and other types of illnesses. Rather than just defining the flu and outlining its symptoms, the speaker uses a comparative order strategy with a goal of clarifying the similarities and differences between these illnesses.

Second, the goal of *simplification* can be served by a comparative order strategy. If an idea is complex, comparative order can be used to describe that idea in relation to a simpler and more familiar idea. (This strategy uses a pattern of reasoning known as an analogy, which will be explained in more detail in chapter 15.) For example, informing your audience about a complex system with many parts is one informative purpose that can benefit from this strategy.

Specific purpose: To raise awareness in my audience about tensions between different parts of the U.S. health care system.

Central idea: Doctors, nurses, hospitals, and insurers are all trying to expand their power over other parts of the health care system.

Main points:

I. The health care system traditionally has worked like a honeycomb.
   A. Each part has a distinct place in the system.
   B. Strong walls separate each part.
   C. The builders of the system must respect this separation for the system to function properly.

II. In recent years, walls within the health care system have broken down.
   A. Doctors have taken a role more like that of a hospital administrator than of a caregiver.
   B. Nurses and other health professionals have expanded their practice into areas traditionally reserved for doctors.
   C. Hospitals are competing with specialized care centers and organizing themselves more like insurance companies.
   D. Insurance companies are taking more and more decisions away from health care professionals and their patients (Dworkin).

III. The health care honeycomb cannot function effectively if its builders are working against one another.

Here, the health care system is being described through a comparison to a honeycomb. The comparison not only simplifies the health care system, but also draws the audience's attention to aspects of the system that the speaker wants to highlight.

A third goal that can be served by a comparative strategy is the *transformation* of an audience's factual beliefs and assumptions (Rowan). In some situations, even an informative speech may share facts and explanations that contradict an audience's existing beliefs. In those situations, your audience is not likely to accept your contrary ideas right off the bat. It will be more effective to start by acknowledging the audience's beliefs and then comparing them to a more accurate or coherent explanation. Communication scholar Katherine Rowan suggests organizing this kind of speech with four main parts:

1. State or ask questions that elicit the audience's beliefs.

2. Acknowledge how those beliefs may be reasonable.

3. Demonstrate the inadequacy of those beliefs with familiar examples.

4. State the more accurate account and provide evidence.

For example, consider how this organizational strategy might be used to transform your audience's beliefs about alcohol use on college campuses:

Specific purpose: To share knowledge about the problem of "normal" drinking among college students.

Central idea: "Normal" drinking is a significant problem among college students.

Main points:

I. Many people think the biggest alcohol problem on college campuses is binge drinking.

II. Binge drinking can have immediate and severe consequences, such as alcohol poisoning and, in some cases, death.

III. However, binge drinking actually is the exception, not the norm, on college campuses.

    A. Statistically, binge drinking on campuses is going down.

    B. You have seen the posters around campus stating that most students have only a few drinks when they go out.

    C. In your own experience, are most people at the local bars or at a party binge drinking or are they drinking moderately?

IV. "Normal" drinking is a widespread problem on college campuses.

    A. The focus on rare but dramatic consequences of binge drinking leads us to ignore the problem of so-called normal drinking.

    B. By comparison, far more students engage in "normal" drinking.

    C. Far more alcohol-related problems—unwanted and unplanned sex, drunk driving, poor classroom performance—stem from "normal" drinking (Prevention Research Center).

Notice that the speaker does not just give the audience a bunch of information about "normal" drinking. Nor does the speaker completely reject the audience's beliefs. Instead, the speaker first acknowledges that the audience's concerns about binge drinking are plausible and then goes on to compare the two types of drinking and their effects. The comparative order strategy, then, provides an organizational pattern that can be useful when you want to inform your audience about something that they are not likely to believe at first.

Key Issues Order A fourth analytical strategy, the **key issues** strategy, organizes a speech around a set of questions that are relevant to decision making. Each main point poses a question or raises a key issue on the topic, and the supporting material provides information that answers those questions. Although this strategy is sometimes used to structure persuasive speeches, informative speeches with this strategy should withhold judgment while speakers and audiences explore the available evidence on the key issues.

If your audience is relatively unfamiliar with your topic, you might use a key issues strategy to answer the "frequently asked questions" about that topic. For an informative speech, remember to focus on factual questions rather than on value or policy questions.

Specific purpose: To raise awareness about the key facts surrounding race-sensitive admissions policies on our campus.

Central idea: Race-sensitive admissions policies on our campus are concerned with the composition of the student body, academic qualifications, and the likelihood that admitted students will graduate.

Main points:

    I. How do race-sensitive policies affect the proportion of minority students on our campus?

    II. How do race-sensitive policies affect the qualifications of students admitted to our college?

    III. To what extent do these policies admit students who are likely to graduate?

As you can see, this speech does not dive into value-oriented questions. It does not state that diversity is a good thing. Nor does it address policy questions, such as whether the campus should eliminate race-sensitive policies. But the evidence from this speech could inform subsequent arguments about those questions.

If your audience is more familiar with a topic and recognizes that there are multiple viewpoints, you can use a key issues strategy to highlight opposing viewpoints. Here, the main points of the speech are the key areas of agreement and disagreement, especially the questions for which people have different answers. In these situations, it may be appropriate to *identify* key issues that are value- or policy-oriented as well as factual. But remember that *you should not take a position on these issues or advocate for one viewpoint.* Your purpose is simply to inform the audience about those viewpoints, focusing the audience's attention on the points about which people disagree. For example, this speech identifies the key issues of dispute surrounding Puerto Rican statehood:

Specific purpose: To share knowledge about the controversy over Puerto Rican statehood.

Central idea: The controversy over Puerto Rican statehood focuses on questions of political rights, economic benefits, and cultural identity.

Main points:

    I. Puerto Ricans have had an ongoing debate over remaining a U.S. commonwealth or becoming the 51st state.

    II. One key issue is the political impacts of statehood.

        A. Proponents of statehood emphasize that Puerto Rican residents would be able to vote in U.S. federal elections (Williams).

        B. Defenders of the commonwealth say that Puerto Rico would lose some of its autonomy.

III. A second area of dispute is statehood's economic benefits.
    A. Proponents of statehood argue that the poor would have better access to federal aid programs.
    B. Defenders of the commonwealth remind that Puerto Rican residents would no longer be exempt from federal income tax.

IV. Finally, advocates question how statehood would affect Puerto Rican culture.
    A. Proponents of statehood believe that Puerto Rico has a strong cultural heritage that will not be influenced by becoming a state.
    B. Defenders of the commonwealth believe that statehood will make Puerto Rico even more like the mainland United States (Rubinstein).

You might have noticed that the key issues strategy essentially combines the topical and comparative strategies to organize the speech around fundamental differences. Because the key issues strategy often highlights different points of view, it can be very easy to "stack the deck" in favor of one viewpoint or slip into a more persuasive mode of speaking. (Again, this strategy is a standard way to organize persuasive speeches; we will return to it in chapter 14.) You can fulfill your ethical obligations when using the key issues strategy in an informative situation by following a few simple guidelines: Avoid value judgments, phrase your main points fairly, and address only those issues that everyone involved in the controversy recognizes as important.

Table 9.1 summarizes the organizational strategies described in this section and suggests situations when those strategies might be appropriate. Once you have determined your overall strategy, you can further develop your main points.

TABLE 9.1 Organizational Strategies

	Organizational Strategy	Guiding Principle	Potential Uses
Sequential Strategies	Chronological order	Occurrence in time	• Narrate histories • Provide broad overviews
	Spatial order	Location or direction	• Provide "snapshots" of an issue • Show movement
Analytical Strategies	Causal order	Cause-and-effect relationships	• Show impacts of an action • Identify underlying factors
	Topical order	Categories and subtopics	• Simplify complex topics • Show different perspectives
	Comparative order	Similarities and differences	• Explain complex ideas • Present counterintuitive ideas
	Key issues order	Agreement and disagreement	• Clarify facts, decision points, and opposing viewpoints

Developing Your Main Points

Producing effective main points is partly a matter of structure and partly a matter of individual creativity. You have already seen that your organizational pattern, specific purpose, and central idea will dictate the kinds of main points that will make sense. But the content of those main points will depend on your own sense of the ideas that are important and relevant to your audience.

Several principles can help you with the arrangement and wording of your main points. These include logic, balance, primacy versus recency, simplicity, and parallel structure.

Logic

Logical divisions in your topic naturally suggest your main points. In fact, the chronological, spatial, and topical strategies already use logical or natural divisions to develop an overall pattern for your speech. When you craft your main points, then, be sure to follow the logic of those patterns.

Less Effective	More Effective
I. You can volunteer for Red Cross in our community.	I. You can volunteer for Red Cross in our community.
II. You can work for Red Cross in our state.	II. You can work for Red Cross in our state.
III. You can work for Red Cross internationally.	III. You can work for Red Cross nationally.
IV. You can work for Red Cross in another state.	IV. You can work for Red Cross internationally.

Here, the less effective outline stops following the logical pattern between points III and IV. The speaker could eliminate point IV or try the other example outline.

Logic is sometimes less obvious for speeches that are organized by topical order. There might not be a clear logic to the order of points in a topical strategy. However, at least make sure that the points fit logically with the other points.

Less Effective	More Effective
I. The Red Cross provides disaster services.	I. The Red Cross provides disaster services.
II. The Red Cross provides blood services.	II. The Red Cross provides blood services.
III. The Red Cross provides health and safety services.	III. The Red Cross provides health and safety services.
IV. Many countries have a similar organization called the Red Crescent.	

Point IV may be interesting and relevant in an informative speech, but it does not fit with the other main points that describe particular services. Depending on the purpose, a more effective set of main points would focus only on the services; or they might describe the different parts of the Red Cross and Red Crescent movement.

Balance

Effective main points will also reflect balance so that each point receives roughly equal treatment. If one point comprises 80% of the body of your speech and the other two points each receive 10%, your audience might feel that they have not heard enough about the latter two points. Or they might think that those two points are not very important and wish that you had focused solely on the first point. In either case, it is worth reconsidering what your main points should be.

Here is what such an imbalanced speech on your college's athletic program might look like, along with a more effective example:

Less Effective	More Effective
I. Our football team is the primary focus of the athletic program. (80% of the speech)	I. Football is the primary focus of the athletic program. (50% of the speech)
II. Men's basketball also receives significant financial and academic support. (10%)	II. Other revenue-generating sports receive slightly less but still significant attention. (30%)
III. Women's basketball gets significant attention, too. (10%)	III. Non-revenue-producing sports have significant participation but get little attention. (20%)

In this case, the less effective example is unbalanced. If a speaker has that much to say about football and very little to say about the basketball teams, then the points about the basketball teams are not really "main" points. A more effective speech would set aside the points about the basketball teams and focus only on football. Alternatively, the speaker could adjust the main points to achieve better balance, as in the more effective example. Even though the points are not exactly equal in the more effective example, they are much better balanced and still convey a sense of proportion, pointing out that football gets more attention than non-revenue-producing sports do.

Primacy versus Recency

Another consideration in developing main points is whether to put the most important point first or last. Scholarly research does not provide a conclusive answer to this question. Some research shows a **primacy effect**, by which people are most influenced by the first message they hear about a topic. Other research shows a **recency effect**, by which the last message people hear has a greater impact than earlier information (Murphy, Hofacker, and Mizerski). Although it is not clear whether primacy or recency is the stronger effect, we can conclude from these studies that the middle items often get lost in the shuffle.

The lesson for informative speaking, then, is that if one idea is not particularly strong, it should go in the middle. (The lack of a conclusive answer to the primacy/recency question is why this principle is in the middle of this section!) Key issues and topical strategies can benefit from this lesson; likewise, chronological speeches might be most effectively organized if the first and last events in the series are more important than the middle events.

Simplicity

When possible, try to simplify your main points. Psychological research suggests that recall of sentences is aided by simplicity in both length and structure. This is especially important in speaking situations, in which your audience does not have the opportunity to go back and review, as they do with written texts. Short sentences or questions with simple subject–verb structure tend to make the best main points.

Look at the different ways in which a speaker might construct main points in a speech about gambling:

Less Effective	**More Effective**
I. Compared to the rest of the population, the problem of gambling is a greater one among college students.	I. Gambling disproportionately affects college students.
II. The chance that your grades will drop goes up if you are a problem gambler.	II. Problem gambling can hurt classroom performance.
III. It's no surprise that when you gamble in a compulsive way, you may find yourself without money for tuition.	III. Problem gambling can threaten financial well-being.
IV. Your health can be affected by problem gambling.	IV. Problem gambling can lead to health issues (Oregon Department of Human Services).

Visually, these examples show what the word count proves: The more effective example is much simpler than the less effective example. It has fewer than half the words of the first example, and its sentences are composed in a very simple structure using active voice. The subject comes first, followed by an active verb and a direct object. In contrast, the main points in the less effective example have more complex sentence structures: clauses in points I, II, and III and passive voice in point IV.

Be aware that this emphasis on simple sentences is not meant to apply to every sentence in your speech. Using only short sentences will make your speaking seem short and choppy. Furthermore, audiences will appreciate variety in your sentences. It makes your speech easier to listen to, and it will help those short main points to stand out from the rest of your speech.

Parallel Structure The gambling example shows another attribute of effective main points. **Parallel structure** is use of the same grammatical pattern of wording to phrase a series of ideas. Phrasing your main points with parallel structure is not just a clever or fancy way to state these ideas. It also helps your audience's understanding: It signals movement from one main point to the next, and it reinforces that the points have the same level of importance. You can also use parallel structure to phrase a series of subpoints.

The more effective gambling example shows one way in which parallel structure can work. Each sentence begins with the same noun phrase ("Problem gambling") and then has a similar pattern for the verb phrase ("can hurt," "can threaten," "can lead"). Similarly, the example about energy conservation in the spatial order section above uses prepositional phrases ("Inside your home," "Between your home and the outdoors," "Outside your home") to introduce each main point.

If you are not consciously trying to use parallel structure, it is easy to start with it and then drift off into other forms.

Less Effective	More Effective
I. Three key issues can help us to assess our community's support for senior citizens.	I. Three key issues can help us to assess our community's support for senior citizens.
A. Did past programs and informal support serve the needs of our seniors?	A. Did past programs and informal support serve the needs of our seniors?
B. Do current programs and informal support serve the needs of our seniors?	B. Do current programs and informal support serve the needs of our seniors?
C. The main future needs of our seniors lie in health care and financial planning.	C. Are local entities planning for the future needs of our seniors?

Point C in the less effective example departs from the pattern of parallel structure established in points A and B. Rather than a question, the speaker presents a statement. This might not jump out for the audience as a main point, since the earlier main points build an expectation for another question as the third key issue. In addition, this break from parallel structure hurts the logic of the outline. Even though it follows chronological order, point C does not focus on community support as the previous two points do. The more effective example shows how using parallel structure for point C would keep the speaker focused on the actual purpose of the speech.

THE ETHICAL DIMENSION

Information or Persuasion? The Dilemma of Omission

The discussion of organizational strategies can help us to think further about the distinction between informative and persuasive speaking. In chapter 8, the Ethical Dimension feature suggested that "being open-minded, acknowledging conflicting evidence and points of view, and refraining from value judgments and calls to action are all ways in which you honor the expectations of the situation." These ethical guidelines are directly relevant to various organizational strategies. If you are using a key issues strategy, you need to avoid encouraging your audience to take one side in the controversy. Likewise, with a comparative order strategy, you should avoid making connections that are intended to cast some idea in a completely positive or negative light.

A more difficult ethical challenge arises even if you avoid explicit attempts at persuasion. When you develop your main points, you cannot escape the dilemma of *omission*. In the context of organizing an informative speech, omission means leaving out important main points. The reason you cannot escape this dilemma is because you always have to select a few main points to discuss in your speech; therefore, you will always leave out points that are relevant to your topic. In this view, every informative speech is a partial and incomplete discussion of a topic.

Several of the examples in this chapter show that even well-organized speeches may omit important material:

Your choice to cover or omit certain issues is an important ethical issue in informative speaking.

- *Chronological order*. The example about the history of feminism omits events in the 1930s through the 1950s that set the stage for second-wave feminism.
- *Spatial order*. The example about household energy conservation completely ignores a family's transportation choices, which could make up a significant share of their energy use.
- *Causal order*. Speeches inevitably omit some causal factors in order to focus on the most obvious or primary causes; certainly, there are other forces shaping cable television choices than the ones mentioned in the example for causal order.

- *Topical order*. This strategy gives a lot of leeway to the speaker; surely, there are more than three areas in which advertising influences our society.
- *Comparative order*. This strategy may ignore or omit relevant differences; the health care system does not have a queen bee organizing its honeycomb, after all.
- *Key issues.* In most controversies, there are far more key issues than any speaker can cover. For example, many other questions could be asked to determine the impact of race-sensitive admission policies besides the questions used in the example for key issues order.

THE ETHICAL DIMENSION Information or Persuasion? *(continued)*

Just because all speeches inevitably leave out some important material does not mean that they are all biased in a sinister way. It simply means they are partial and limited. The ethical question is whether those limits impair or distort an audience's ability to make sense of the topic. From a listener's perspective, this question should lead you to think about the relevant issues that are absent from a speech and why they may have been omitted. From a speaker's perspective, this question should encourage you to be mindful of the choices you make when deciding on your main points.

To respect your audience's expectations for an informative speech, keep in mind the following ethical guidelines:

1. Select aspects of your topic that your audience would not dispute as being important.

2. Be wary of ignoring or excluding aspects that are widely recognized as important.

3. Address these issues directly by telling your audience the scope of your speech.

For example, you might acknowledge that your speech sets aside questions about alcohol abstinence in order to focus on "normal" drinking and binge drinking. Or if your speech omits an obviously important issue (such as the energy conservation speech that omits transportation), you might say that while others have recognized that important issue, your speech examines some overlooked aspects of energy conservation. Ultimately, if you reflect on what your speech omits, both during the construction and during the delivery of your speech, you will be more likely to avoid giving a speech that is subtly biased in a harmful way.

WHAT DO YOU THINK?

1. Identify an important campus issue as a potential speech topic. What do you and your classmates think are such important aspects of that topic that they should not be omitted from a speech on the topic?

2. Should an informative speech omit areas of controversy on a topic, in order to not seem persuasive? Why or why not?

Organizing Your Supporting Material

By the time you have decided on an organizational strategy and crafted your main points, you should have a good sense of what your speech will ultimately look like. But the specific contours of your speech will take shape as you integrate your supporting material, and you want those contours to be smooth. Just as your main points should fit together logically to advance your purpose, your supporting material should fit together sensibly to provide backing for your main points. If that material is in the wrong place or out of order, the contours of your speech won't be quite as appealing to your audience.

Using Sequential and Analytical Patterns

The sequential and analytical patterns described above in the section on identifying an organizational strategy also work well for presenting supporting material. For example, consider how this portion of a speech on arts education organizes supporting points using topical and cause-and-effect order.

II. Arts education influences several aspects of human development

    A. Spirit

        1. Arts education gives students a vehicle for self-expression and reflection.

        2. As a result, arts education promotes spiritual and moral development.

    B. Mind

        1. Arts education requires students to think with precision and abstraction.

        2. As a result, arts education enhances higher-order thinking skills.

    C. Body

        1. Arts education fosters feelings of empowerment and an improved self-image.

        2. As a result, arts education contributes to mental and physical well-being (Gee).

Here, subpoints A, B, and C are organized topically, and for each subpoint, the supporting points are arranged in a cause-and-effect order.

Using multiple strategies in that way is appropriate, but notice that within a series of related points, the speaker uses only one pattern to organize those points. If you change your organizational pattern, it will make it more difficult for your audience to understand how a set of points is related.

Less Effective	More Effective
I. Several states have resisted parts of the No Child Left Behind (NCLB) Act.	I. Several states have resisted parts of the No Child Left Behind (NCLB) Act.
A. Texas resisted performance standards for special education students.	A. Texas resisted performance standards for special education students.
B. Utah ordered schools to follow state accountability standards rather than NCLB standards.	B. Utah ordered schools to follow state accountability standards rather than NCLB standards.
C. In 2005, the state of Connecticut went to court over NCLB's testing requirements.	C. Illinois sacrificed some federal funding rather than accepting NCLB sanctions.
D. In 2007, the Department of Education proposed improvements to NCLB.	D. Connecticut went to court over NCLB's testing requirements (National Education Association).

In the less effective example, the pattern clearly starts with spatial order. In supporting subpoint C, however, the speaker also includes a date. While this is reasonable in itself, it leads the speaker into chronological order moving from subpoint C to subpoint D. In subpoint D, the speaker focuses on the next important event in the chronology rather than providing evidence about another state that resisted NCLB. As a result, the supporting material in subpoint D does not actually support the main point. The more effective example adheres to one pattern through the series of subpoints.

Using Inductive, Deductive, and Hourglass Patterns

In addition to these patterns, think about the particular supporting materials and their relationship to your audience and your purpose. Which materials will be the easiest for your audience to understand? Which materials will the audience most likely accept? Which are likely to have the greatest impact? Do you intend to emphasize the quantitative or the qualitative aspects of your topic? Do you intend to provide a comprehensive overview or a more detailed picture of your topic? These are some of the considerations that can help you to integrate your supporting materials effectively.

Generally speaking, you can think about organizing your supporting material in an inductive, a deductive, or an hourglass pattern (see Figure 9.1). **Inductive order** starts with specific instances or examples and uses them to build a more general or abstract point. In contrast, **deductive order** starts with general statements and then provides specifics to back up those statements. The **hourglass order** places the most significant pieces of evidence at the beginning and end of a series and puts the least important material in the middle.

Inductive Order Using an inductive order can be especially useful if you are trying to raise awareness about an issue or address an unfamiliar aspect of your topic. In these instances, audiences can quickly get confused if you jump right into a series of statistics or definitions. They might not have enough context for making sense of this material. Instead, try starting with *concrete* supporting material before moving on to the more complex aspects of your issue.

For example, you might start with an attention-grabbing example or a personal experience, then follow up with a definition or testimony that is connected to that example.

> I'm starting to learn a few lessons about credit cards. Last year, I had $2,000 on my credit card. Since then I've been paying a lot more than my minimum payment for over a year now, and I still have well over $1,000 left to pay. What gives?
>
> What gives is your credit card company. They give you additional debt if you don't pay off your entire bill all at once. What's more, they give you more money, by allowing you to continue charging things even as you pay down your balance. This gift that keeps on giving is known as "revolving" debt, a type of debt that lets you borrow a set amount of money again and again. Let me explain revolving debt a bit further and show how it differs from nonrevolving debt, or installment debt.

FIGURE 9.1 Patterns for Integrating Supporting Material

Inductive Order

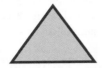

Begin with specific, narrow information

Follow up with general, broad statements

Deductive Order

Begin with general, broad statements.

Follow up with specifics, details

Hourglass Order

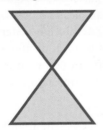

Begin with material you want to emphasize.

Put the least important material in the middle.

End with material you want to emphasize.

Here, the speaker begins with a concrete personal experience to introduce the more complicated idea of revolving debt, following up with a brief definition. Note too that the speaker previews a comparison of revolving and installment debt. For an audience that is unfamiliar with the world of finance, this strategy probably would be more effective than starting with two abstract definitions of these concepts.

Similarly, try inductive order if you think that your audience will resist one of your larger points. If you lead with a potentially controversial point or one that your audience is hesitant to accept, the audience might get hung up on that point and miss the supporting evidence that follows. Instead, begin with concrete pieces of evidence that are less debatable. For example, if you were trying to raise awareness among die-hard football fans about the problem of concussions, your listeners might not be receptive to that main point right away. Instead, you could start with a few examples of injured players to build support for the main point.

In addition to explaining how inductive structure works, this section is intended to remind you that informative speaking is not necessarily

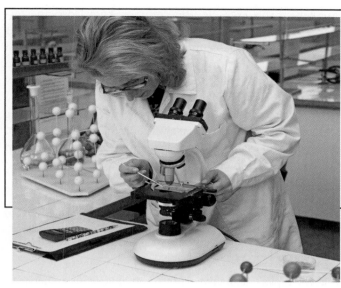

INDUCTIVE ORDER

One example of an inductive pattern is the scientific method. Scientists will first observe specific instances and then draw general conclusions or principles from them.

uncontroversial. Explaining evolution to a fundamentalist audience or even telling your organization about its financial problems is a daunting informative challenge. Start with points that are not debatable, and think carefully about how to proceed.

Deductive Order If your audience is already familiar with your topic or if you are trying to share new knowledge and details about your topic, you might consider deductive order. Unlike the audience that is just beginning to learn about a topic, an informed audience probably does not need to be led inductively to most main points. As was described in chapter 8, it might be easier to start with broad or general statements that reinforce a common understanding about the topic and then share new knowledge. Common knowledge, definitions, or testimony can serve this purpose:

> As you know all too well, credit card companies are using all available means to reach the lucrative college market. According to Dr. Robert Manning, Director of the Center for Consumer Financial Services at the Rochester Institute of Technology, changes in the law and high profit rates in the college credit market have led to "an unprecedented national marketing campaign that targeted increasingly younger and inexperienced consumers" (Manning and Kirshak, p. 40).
>
> But what you might not know is that credit card companies aren't the only ones profiting in the college credit market. University entities also make money through exclusive contracts with those companies. And while you would think that universities would have a clear policy regulating this activity, our university does not. Instead, different entities on campus have their own policies, which vary in how aggressively they can pursue student accounts (U.S. General Accounting Office).

The first paragraph in this example uses common knowledge and testimony to reinforce a commonly held, general idea: Credit card companies are a significant presence on college campuses. Then the second paragraph becomes more specific. It focuses on this particular campus as an illustration of the broader trend. It also moves beyond the general idea to provide new knowledge about how credit card companies are operating on the campus.

A deductive strategy also can be useful when you want to maximize the impact of supporting material that focuses on a very specific aspect of an idea. A startling statistic, a powerful example, or an eloquent piece of testimony can be an effective way to end a section of your speech.

> Federal spending has increased in several areas during the past decade. The biggest contributors are defense and homeland security. But new entitlement programs, such as prescription drug coverage for senior citizens, also contributed to the increase. Discretionary spending plays a role, too. You might be surprised to find out that between 2001 and 2006, federal financial aid for college students went up a whopping 400% (Riedl).

No matter what the topic, a deductive pattern can guide your audience to something very specific on your topic.

Hourglass Order   An hourglass order is another strategy for emphasizing a certain piece of supporting material. Here, the idea is to take advantage of both primacy and recency effects by placing the material you want to emphasize in the first and last positions in a series. For example, if you are trying to emphasize the quantitative aspects of some topic, you might organize three pieces of evidence like this: a statistic, some other form of evidence, and another statistic.

> How can we get a handle on the significance of consumer credit in our society? Start with the number 1.6 trillion. Such a staggering number is normally associated with the federal budget or the GDP of major countries. But let that hefty number sink in today—let it sink right into your wallet. $1.6 trillion is the total amount charged annually on bank credit cards. The reasons? "American families are facing financial hardship not experienced for generations," according to Tamara Draut, Director of the Economic Opportunity Program at Demos, a think tank (ConsumerAffairs.com). "Households are turning to high-cost credit cards to keep afloat." And the picture for households is not pretty. The average outstanding credit card balance for a two-adult household that doesn't pay off their card each month? $13,000. Even if you paid off $1,000 a month, it would take well over a year to pay it off.

Here, the two statistics work like anchors to support this point. All the pieces of evidence are important to showing that consumer credit is a significant issue, but putting the statistics at the beginning and at the end helps the speaker to frame the issue in quantitative terms. Conversely, you could do the same with anecdotes about individuals who are struggling to pay off debt, using those as your first and last pieces of supporting material and putting in between them a statistic about the number of debtor households in the United States.

CASE CONCLUSION

Emily's Speech on the Western Hemisphere Institute for Security Cooperation

Emily assessed her organizational options. Chronological order might work well, since she could talk about the history of what is now the Western Hemisphere Institute for Security Cooperation (WHINSEC) and the current controversy, but she had not found much supporting material about the future of the institute. Spatial order also could work; she could use several Latin American countries as main points, but again her material did not really focus in any particular countries in detail. Also, this strategy would do little to overcome the audience's lack of knowledge about the school itself.

Causal order had possibilities too. It made sense to talk about the institute's training as a cause of both positive and negative effects in Latin America. On the other hand, Emily didn't feel that her evidence was strong enough to discuss cause and effect; it might seem more like a persuasive speech if she tried to claim that those connections were obviously true. Topical order might be the best route, she thought. Yet there were also some key issues that dominated her research and distinguished the arguments of the institute's supporters and detractors. Perhaps she could combine some of these strategies to give her audience a good start on understanding this topic.

Emily decided on a topical order for organizing her speech and then started working on her main points. Because she knew that she was going to focus on the history of WHINSEC, its purpose, and the controversy about it, she knew that she had three clear and separate main points. It made most sense to start with the history before getting into the current controversy, so she decided to start with that main point. Examine Emily's outline to see the way in which she ultimately organized her speech.

Each of Emily's main points hinted at the best way to organize her subpoints. For example, her first point about the history of the institute would be organized chronologically and identify important events in the institute's development. The second point about the two purposes of WHINSEC would have a topical order, and the third point about the controversy over WHINSEC would have a key issues order. For example, here are her first point and subpoints:

EMILY'S WORKING OUTLINE

Purpose: To inform

Specific purpose: To share knowledge about the history, mission, and controversy surrounding the Western Hemisphere Institute for Security Cooperation, formerly known as the School of the Americas.

I. Introduction

II. The history of WHINSEC spans more than 60 years.

    A. The School of the Americas was established by the United States in 1946 in Panama.

    B. In 1984, the school moved to Fort Benning, Georgia.

    C. In 2001, the school was transformed into the Western Hemisphere Institute for Security Cooperation (WHINSEC).

Notice how the subpoints are arranged chronologically.

Notice how the wording of the main points is simple and parallel. The subpoints here are arranged in topical order.

III. The mission of WHINSEC is to train Latin American military and police officials

    A. WHINSEC provides military training on issues such as counterinsurgency and interrogation.

    B. WHINSEC also provides courses on human rights.

Notice how the main point IV. signals a key issues order for these subpoints A and B.

IV. The controversy over WHINSEC focuses on whether it restricts or promotes violence in Latin America.

    A. Supporters of WHINSEC claim that it is a helpful tool in reducing Latin American warfare.

Notice how each of the subpoints A and B are arranged in deductive order, starting with the general position of supporters and critics first and then offering specific pieces of evidence for additional support. Then, within her discussion of the controversy over WHINSEC, Emily organized her points using a deductive order. She started with the general positions of defenders and critics of the institute and then offered specific pieces of supporting material to reinforce those positions.

        1. It provides military and law-enforcement training for several Latin American countries.

        2. It facilitates information and technology sharing between countries in the Americas.

        3. It has put emphasis on human rights training since the School of the Americas was transformed into WHINSEC in 2001.

    B. Critics of WHINSEC, however, focus on its connection to injustice and inhumane activities.

        1. Training materials used by the school discuss torture and execution.

        2. Graduates of the school have been leaders of secret police and death squads in several Latin American countries.

        3. Since 2004, four countries have announced they would stop training at WHINSEC: Venezuela, Argentina, Uruguay, and Costa Rica.

Summary

IDENTIFYING AN ORGANIZATIONAL STRATEGY

- Your choice of organizational strategy depends on your purpose as a speaker and the specific obstacles to audience understanding.
- Sequential strategies, such as chronological and spatial order, follow natural patterns for proceeding through a topic.
- Analytical strategies, such as topical order, causal order, comparative order, and key issues order, allow you to show connections and relationships.

DEVELOPING YOUR MAIN POINTS

- Keep main points logical, simple, and parallel in structure.
- Give each of the main points relatively equal treatment so that the body of the speech is balanced.

ORGANIZING YOUR SUPPORTING MATERIAL

- The sequential and analytical patterns for overall speech organization also work for organizing supporting material.
- Inductive, deductive, and hourglass patterns provide additional options for integrating your supporting points.

Key Terms

sequential strategies, p. 217
chronological order, p. 218
spatial order, p. 219
analytical strategies, p. 221
causal order, p. 221
topical order, p. 222
comparative order, p. 223

key issues, p. 225
primacy effect, p. 229
recency effect, p. 230
parallel structure, p. 231
inductive order, p. 235
deductive order, p. 235
hourglass order, p. 235

Comprehension

1. What two patterns of organization use a sequential strategy?
2. How is causal order different from chronological order?
3. What three goals can be served by using a comparative order strategy?
4. When using a key issues strategy to organize an informative speech, what should a speaker do to avoid making the speech persuasive?
5. What ethical guidelines help a speaker with the dilemma of omission?
6. According to the principle of balance, how should you treat your main points?
7. What is the principle of parallel structure?
8. Within a series of related points, how many organizational patterns should you use?
9. In an hourglass pattern for organizing main points, where should you place the pieces of supporting material you want to emphasize?

Application

1. Identify an important issue or topic on your campus. Then create four specific purpose statements for possible speeches on that topic, corresponding to speeches organized by using (a) chronological order, (b) spatial order, (c) causal order, and (d) key issues order
2. Examine the following list of topics, and think about the obstacles to audience understanding that might arise if you were to develop a speech on those topics. Then identify the goal you would try to achieve

when speaking on those topics, and prepare a set of main points for a speech that try to achieve that goal. (You might have to learn a bit about the topics to prepare the main points!)

Financial aid applications
The workings of the human heart
The types of taxes that are taken out of your paycheck
Nuclear waste
The fairness of the criminal justice system

3. Using one of the purpose statements from Question 1, generate a balanced set of main points and an unbalanced set of main points.

4. Using another one of the purpose statements from Question 1, generate a set of main points that exhibits parallel structure.

Beginning and Ending Your Speech

This chapter is intended to help you:

- Identify the functions that effective introductions and conclusions should serve
- Observe various techniques for introducing and concluding a speech
- Make effective, ethical choices in introductions and conclusions

A good movie trailer is a skillful piece of rhetoric. It grabs your attention with exciting action, memorable dialogue, or compelling visuals. It provides a glimpse of the basic plot of the film but saves the details for the film itself. And it sets the stage for the rest of the film, giving you a sense of what is to come. When done well, a trailer draws you in and entices you to view the entire movie.

A good speech introduction does many of those same things. As you learned in chapter 2, an introduction should attempt to arouse the audience's attention. It also should prepare the audience for the rest of the speech by previewing the main points and ideas, in much the way that a movie trailer suggests the basic plot. And it should create a desire in audience members to listen to the rest of the speech. This chapter will expand on what you learned in chapter 2 to help you invent effective introductions that are adapted to your purpose and audience.

CASE SCENARIO

Christine's Speech on Relay for Life

For several years, Christine had participated in Relay for Life, an event sponsored by the American Cancer Society in which teams raise money and then walk together. She knew quite a bit about the event from her personal experience with it and was motivated to share her knowledge, since she found participation personally rewarding. Christine figured that it would be easy for her to develop a good informative speech about the topic. After doing some research, she had plenty of information for the speech, but she wasn't sure how she could make the topic exciting to her audience. How would she get their attention at the beginning of the speech? And what options would she have for concluding her informative speech?

In addition, this chapter also expands on what you know about conclusions. It will illustrate several techniques for ending your speech in a way that leaves a memorable and positive impression on your audience. It will also describe how speakers can use the conclusion to encourage participation in the public sphere. Whether your speech has an informative, persuasive, or commemorative purpose, the conclusion is the last opportunity to explain why your ideas are relevant to public life. Effective conclusions are not just an ending to a speech but the launching pad for your audience to engage with the world. ∎

Crafting Introductions

Like a good movie trailer, a good speech introduction is catchy. It grabs hold of the listeners and leaves them wanting more. But capturing an audience's attention is only part of what speakers need to accomplish in the opening portion of a speech.

While the central point of a fictional film might be ambiguous or open to interpretation, an audience expects a speech to have a clear, specific central idea. Also, films often provide entertainment or an escape from everyday concerns, while public speakers are more likely to engage audiences about a significant real-world topic. As a result, speakers need to demonstrate the relevance of the topic to their audiences and build their ethos among audience members.

The many functions of an introduction, then, involve building connections between speaker, topic, and audience. You might visualize these connections as a triangle, as shown in Figure 10.1. By making sure that you focus a portion of your introduction on each side of the triangle, you will be on your way to crafting an effective introduction.

FIGURE 10.1 The Functions of an Introduction

Think of your introduction as a time to build three basic connections in your speech: between speaker and audience, between speaker and topic, and between audience and topic. Arousing your audience's attention can help to build all three of these connections.

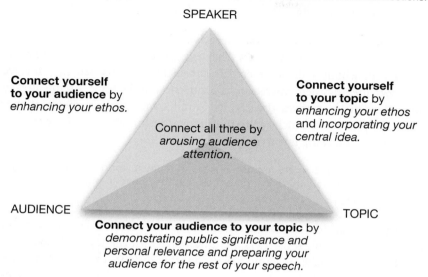

SPEAKER

Connect yourself to your audience by *enhancing your ethos.*

Connect yourself to your topic by *enhancing your ethos* and *incorporating your central idea.*

Connect all three by *arousing audience attention.*

AUDIENCE

TOPIC

Connect your audience to your topic by *demonstrating public significance and personal relevance and preparing your audience for the rest of your speech.*

Arousing Audience Attention

Your first task is to arouse your audience's attention with an **attention-getter**, a tactic to draw in the audience during the initial sentences of a speech. A public speaking course provides great opportunities for working on this aspect of introductions. Imagine if every speaker in your class started a speech like this:

Ineffective: "Today I would like to talk to you about the topic of . . ."

That opening line is boring in itself; it would be downright painful if it were repeated twenty or thirty times! Simply announcing your topic does little to excite or engage an audience.

A public speaking class poses an additional challenge if some of your classmates speak on the same topic. Adapting to this situation requires a little extra effort to show that you are taking a fresh approach to your topic. For example, laws regarding marijuana are a common topic in college public speaking courses. Inevitably, some students start their speeches by listing all the slang words or street names for the drug. Not only is this attention-getter stale, but it does nothing to show how your perspective on the topic will be unique and distinctive.

Arousing audience attention, then, can be a challenge. Yet it is also an opportunity to exercise some creativity. To spur your thinking, keep in mind the following attention-getting techniques. All of the examples in this section are from speeches about various food issues, so you can see how each technique can be used to highlight different aspects of a topic.

Personal Narrative **Personal narratives**, or stories about yourself or others, are excellent attention-getters. They engage audiences by providing characters with whom audience members can identify, and when they involve your own life, they demonstrate your connection to the topic. As you already know, personal narratives also can lend drama and highlight the emotional aspects of your topic, which can be useful for arousing attention. For example, consider the following line to open a speech:

> Food security is a very important topic in today's world. People in many countries are facing such high prices that they have to make difficult trade-offs.

This opener does capture a central idea, but it does little to capture an audience's attention. If listeners are unfamiliar with the topic of food security, this opener makes it sound like yet another distant, abstract problem. If listeners have heard of the topic, these lines are not particularly dramatic or provocative.

Now compare them to the introductory section of a speech by Sean Callahan of Catholic Relief Services, testifying before Congress about this issue:

> CRS staff around the world has heard stories of families who are stretched to the limit by the high price of food. Some are having to make do with eating less at each meal. Some are already skipping meals, or even not eating on a particular day. Few can afford to buy meat or chicken for any of their meals. The most desperate will sell off precious resources, such as a water jug, a hoe or even the tin roof of their home in order to buy food. Tragically, they may even have to decide which child or children may have the best chance of survival and which, already ill and weak, will be allowed to die. These are the agonizing choices the global food crisis is forcing the poor to make.

This set of statements goes beyond stating the central idea. It captures the audience's attention with concrete details about real people. These details do a much better job of dramatizing the challenges related to food insecurity. Callahan builds on this idea with even more specific stories:

> I was in eastern Ethiopia last month, and I saw how the people there are already suffering. I visited a feeding site run by the Ethiopian Catholic Church and the Missionaries of Charity in a largely Muslim area where, over the previous five weeks, 28 children had died of malnutrition. The conditions there are already dire. They are going through a "green drought," where there was just enough rain to allow stocks to sprout 3 to 5 inches, but there is no yield.

> I saw one Ethiopian parent bring a very sickly, lethargic child to the center for emergency treatment. The parent told the sisters, "I brought this child because I thought he could make it. My weakest child is at home." Nearby, a grandfather fed his grandson sips of milk every 30 seconds from a plastic syringe.

This extended opener takes us to a specific place, introduces us to specific people, and shows us what is happening in their everyday lives. Rather than hearing about an abstract issue, we get to see a concrete instance of how this topic is related to someone's life. This personal narrative does a far better job of arousing attention than a plain announcement of the topic can do.

Personal narratives also arouse attention when they show why you have a strong connection to your topic.

> Many of you have probably participated in our college's service connection with the local homeless shelter. I remember the first time I went to the shelter. It was an amazing sight, seeing dozens of college students providing meals to families that were less fortunate. I felt a profound sense of camaraderie and began to understand what service to one's community was all about. And in talking to people there, I started to realize that hunger was not just an individual problem, but a social problem.

This narrative is less detailed than the previous example, but it moves quickly to emphasize the impact that this experience had on the speaker. It provides an easy transition into the larger theme of the speech.

Be mindful of the length of your narrative as you compose your introduction. While an extended narrative can provide a rich, vivid opening to your speech, a narrative that drags on or includes lots of unnecessary details may fail to keep the audience's attention. It can also hurt your ethos if the audience believes that you are unprepared and just "winging it." No matter what the length of your narrative, keep it focused and directly connected to your specific purpose.

Quotation   Using a quotation—the words of another person—can be a compelling way to introduce a speech. But this technique is not merely something to use when you run out of ideas of your own. Instead, use a quotation strategically.

For example, you might use an eloquent or provocative statement to bring a fresh perspective to your topic.

> "One reason to eat responsibly is to live free." You might not think of eating as connected to your freedom, but these words of Wendell Berry should make us all think twice. For Berry, making conscious decisions about our food choices is an important part of being an informed, empowered citizen. As he puts it, "The condition of the passive consumer of food is not a

PERSONAL NARRATIVE
Like many other humorists and comedians, David Sedaris relies on personal narratives to draw listeners in.

democratic condition." In the next few minutes, I hope I can give you a glimpse into Berry's insights and show you how the idea of food democracy is having an impact on you with every bite you take (Berry).

The initial line from Berry works well as an attention-getter because it boils a complicated topic down to a core idea. And because the meaning of the quotation is not immediately obvious, it can draw in listeners who want to learn more.

Alternatively, you could use a quotation from a person that your audience knows or respects to strengthen the connection between the audience and your topic. Passages from texts with a strong cultural resonance—a constitution, a sacred text, or a revered piece of literature—can serve the same purpose.

> "There are people in the world so hungry, that God cannot appear to them except in the form of bread." Spoken by Mahatma Gandhi many decades ago, these words are equally true today.

> "And when ye reap the harvest of your land, thou shalt not wholly reap the corners of thy fields . . . thou shalt leave them for the hungry and the stranger." For millennia, this passage from *Leviticus* has provided a moral compass for Western societies. Food is not a possession to be hoarded but something to be shared with the least fortunate among us.

You might instead use a quotation from someone with expertise or experience in relation to your topic. As you have already learned, using these kinds of voices in your speech can enhance your own credibility as a speaker.

> "No substantial famine has ever occurred in any independent and democratic country with a relatively free press" (Sen). This bold claim from Amartya Sen, Nobel Prize–winning economist at Harvard University, tells us something important about the connection between food and democracy.

> "A silent tsunami that respects no borders" (Sheeran). That's how Josette Sheeran, executive director of the United Nations World Food Programme, describes the impact of rising food prices on the world's poorest people.

No matter what your quotation, it is crucial to select a quotation that serves the purpose of your speech and to connect it explicitly to that purpose. Even a provocative quotation can fall flat if the audience struggles to understand how it is related to the specific purpose of your speech.

Shock/Startle A **shock/startle** opener jostles an audience out of its comfort zone with a shocking or unusual statement to gain audience attention. This is a common and potent opening tactic, but it is a somewhat more risky choice than others. It can backfire if you are addressing an oppositional audience or an audience that has more traditional expectations about public speaking (McGee). In these situations, it is likely better to choose tactics that allow you to establish common ground.

Nevertheless, the shock/startle opener can be a useful tactic if you are trying to raise awareness of a topic or idea or provide a new perspective on your topic. Consider these two examples:

> How many people in the world face food insecurity, or hunger on a daily basis? Ten million? A hundred million? Five hundred million? Not even close. 840 million people fall into this painful category.

> 840 million people. It's a staggering number—approximately the number of people living in Africa, more than the total population of Europe, one seventh of the world's population. It's also the number of people worldwide who suffer from hunger.

As you can see, even a common attention-getter like this startling statistic can be presented in different ways.

The shock/startle technique does not necessarily need to occur in the first line of the speech. One effective way to set it up is by starting with one of the other tactics and then adding an unexpected twist. For example, look back to the homeless shelter example in the section on personal narrative. In that version, the audience likely assumes that the speaker volunteered in the shelter as a college student. But it could have taken a startling turn instead:

> I felt a profound sense of camaraderie and began to understand what service to one's community was all about. And in talking to people there, I started to realize that hunger was not just an individual problem, but a social problem. Yes, I remember my first visit to the shelter. It wasn't as a college student on a service project but as a 12-year-old waiting in line with her parents for a meal.

Ethically, be mindful of how shock/startle can sometimes be manipulative. Here, the principle of inclusiveness from "Listening as an Ethical Practice," the Ethical Dimension feature in chapter 3, provides a relevant guideline. A shocking idea or statistic that is used to narrow the audience's thinking to one point of view serves an exclusionary purpose and undermines rational thinking. Speakers can take a more inclusive approach by recognizing how their startling statement fits in or conflicts with other perspectives about their topic.

Suspense Building suspense can encourage audience members to become active listeners and connect to the topic of your speech. This tactic commonly takes the form of a riddle, as a speaker provides clues for the audience to consider and then reveals the answer.

> Its impact has rippled slowly but powerfully throughout the world. First, it wiped out 20 percent of the soybean crops. Then it affected corn output, making your corn flakes, your rib eye steaks, and even your soda more expensive. Now it is even threatening forests around the world. Is it a new pest, a superbug for the twenty-first century? Is it yet another effect of climate change?

Not exactly. The culprit is not some unstoppable plague but a conscious, deliberate choice we have made. Our decision to mandate biofuels has had some significant and unforeseen consequences.

A suspenseful introduction like this has the advantage of shifting attention to more exciting aspects of your topic. Instead of announcing a topic that your audience initially might find dry, your introduction structures their approach to the topic through a set of interesting puzzle pieces that need to be put together.

Suspense also can work in tandem with your conclusion. The introduction sets up a scenario that is relevant to your topic but is left unresolved while you deliver the body of the speech. The goal is to build suspense as your audience listens. Then you return to the scenario's outcome during the conclusion to provide a satisfying ending to your speech. You might think of this as a "sandwich" or "bookend" tactic for your introduction and conclusion.

Growing food is a difficult business. Donnie Fulks knows that all too well. He grew up on farms in Maryland and Virginia and experienced firsthand the challenges that farmers faced. His family struggled to grow crops in poor soil, they constantly fought bugs and crop diseases, and he himself often became ill from chemicals used on the farm. Something was not right on their farm, and Donnie and his father began thinking about alternatives. "We decided there had to be a better way" (Wechsler).

If you want to know their decision, you will have to wait in suspense until the section on conclusions!

Direct Address **Direct address**, or explicitly hailing the audience by using the words "you," "we," and "us," is a useful tactic for gaining the attention of listeners as well as building a sense of community among them (Beins). Direct address can be used along with other tactics or by itself. Often, you will hear direct address in the form of a *rhetorical question,* a question that is meant to generate silent thinking rather than a spoken answer. For example:

Can you imagine going to bed hungry? Can you imagine that people go to bed hungry every night, right here in our own community?

A speech by food policy activist Mark Winne uses a series of rhetorical questions:

Why, for instance, in the richest nation in the world do we have 38 million of our brothers and sisters frequently wondering where their next meal will come from? . . . Why do so many of us have before us an unprecedented abundance of accessible and diversified retail food outlets to choose from while a significant segment of our citizens live in what can only be called food deserts?

In these examples, the speakers use direct address to help connect the audience to a set of facts about the topic. Rather than just stating the facts, direct address positions audience members as if they are already involved with the topic. This can be a start to demonstrating the personal relevance of the topic, an aspect of introductions discussed later in the chapter.

Direct address is not just for questions; it can be used in statements, too:

> Shopping for food these days can be a challenge if you want to get the best price. You go to the supermarket and stock up on some staples: a box of rice, coffee, spaghetti sauce, and a few frozen pizzas. But when you go to the local food co-op, you find that you could have saved some money. That box of rice you got at the supermarket is much more expensive than the bulk rice at the co-op. Your spices and your favorite coffee are cheaper at the co-op, too. Why is there such a difference? My speech today will show you some of the reasons why—and, I hope, help you become a more informed food shopper.

Direct address also can be a useful technique if you need to enhance the speaker–audience connection. Many speakers will use direct address, for example, when they are facing a hostile audience to show that the speaker understands their opposition:

> Many of you are probably feeling a little strapped for cash these days. Between paying for tuition, covering your rent, and paying your bills, we are all facing the money crunch. The last thing you want is higher food prices. But if your health hinged on paying just a little bit more, would it be worth it?

By directly addressing your audience in a way that accurately reflects their beliefs and opinions, you help to build the bond between speaker and audience that is crucial for effective public speaking.

After you have captured the audience's attention, you need to offer the audience a reason to continue listening to an entire speech on you topic. Focusing on the relevance and significance of your topic and on establishing your ethos as a speaker are the next steps for creating these connections.

Demonstrating Public Significance and Personal Relevance

As you learned in chapters 4 and 5, audience members might not see your topic as being as important or interesting as you do. In some speaking situations, then, demonstrating the significance and relevance of your topic is a crucial task in the introduction. Especially if the audience comes to your speech uninterested or apathetic, you will want to demonstrate significance and relevance as soon as possible.

Public Significance To invent this part of your introduction, begin by reviewing the section on dimensions of public significance in chapter 4. Showing how your topic involves exposing damaging conditions, highlighting shared interests and values, illustrating issues of power, exposing your audience

THE ETHICAL DIMENSION

Starting Your Speech with a Hypothetical Example

You have done your research. You have composed your speech. You have rehearsed it repeatedly. But you have not yet found that perfect attention-getter to start your speech. And you know how important it is to get off to a good start with an effective introduction. Should you just make up a story or an example that fits your speech?

Using a hypothetical example, an imaginary situation that helps you to illustrate a larger point or principle, is a common way to begin a speech. It can be especially effective when real examples would be distant from your audience's experience (Rieke, Sillars, and Peterson). However, hypothetical examples can also be used in misleading ways. If you choose to begin your speech with such an example, be attentive to the following ethical guidelines:

- *Label your hypothetical example clearly*. It may be tempting to produce a hypothetical story about your own experience and then pass it off as a real experience. Who would know the difference? But doing so puts you in the position of either perpetuating a lie indefinitely or having to admit that lie. Both positions compromise the trust relationship with your audience. Instead, develop an example that does not involve you, and mark it clearly with a lead-in such as "Think about this scenario . . ." or "Imagine the following situation . . . ."

- *Create a representative example*. Starting your speech with an extreme or unrealistic example

may get the audience's attention. But it also may lead them to question your trustworthiness. The key is to remember that the purpose of an introduction is not merely to arouse attention; it is also to enhance your ethos. Instead of an extreme example, develop a more realistic scenario that reflects actual experiences or situations in the real world. For example, you might create a hypothetical story about health care for the elderly by developing a composite based on several real examples.

- *Support your example with evidence*. Another way to use hypothetical examples responsibly is to make sure that you have real supporting material that backs up your imaginary situation. This further shows how your example is realistic and representative.

WHAT DO YOU THINK?

1. If you introduced your speech with a hypothetical story about poor treatment in nursing homes, what types of supporting material would help you to show that your story is realistic?

2. Using a speech topic that you have heard in your class, think of two hypothetical examples that illustrate that topic: one that is realistic and representative and one that is misleading. Discuss with a classmate what makes the latter example misleading and how it violates ethical principles of public speaking.

to diverse viewpoints, or making connections to civic and political action can reveal the significance of a topic to your audience.

For example, this introduction highlights the shared interests that may be affected by an important decision:

> Whether or not you are a football fan, the university's decision about moving up to a Division I level team has significant implications. It will directly affect the budget, which could have big impacts on other programs at the university. It will lead to larger crowds on game day, which will affect the entire community. And it could help to increase student enrollments over the long term. This decision, then, is not just about football, but about matters that affect everyone in the community.

Some topics will be significant in several ways, so an introduction could use multiple appeals to heighten the importance of the topic:

> Why bother learning about chemicals in cosmetics? Beyond illustrating the potential health risks, the story of cosmetics also tells us something about the hidden world of consumer product regulation. You may be surprised to find out who really has control over the ingredients found in the products you use every day.

This introduction signals to the audience that damaging conditions (health risks) as well as issues of power (product regulation) will be at the heart of this speech.

Personal Relevance Even if a topic has public significance, some audience members may not find the topic relevant to their own lives. If you can show how the topic has a direct impact on your audience members, they will be more likely to continue listening to your speech. Consider some of the following ways to demonstrate relevance to your listeners:

- *Personal stake:* The topic affects them personally.

  If you think Social Security is relevant only to the elderly, think again. Six percent of every paycheck you receive will go into the Social Security system. And if you plan to be self-employed, more than 12 percent of your income goes in. With the possibility that these rates will rise during our lifetime, it is critical for our generation to become more engaged with these issues.

- *Family and friends:* The topic affects people close to them.

  Changes in Social Security benefits will have a widespread impact. If you have grandparents of retirement age, it could affect their ability to pay for their basic needs. If you have a family member or friend with a major disability, it will affect that person's income, too. And though none of us likes to think about it, Social Security will help your spouse and children in the event of your untimely passing. We owe it to all these people to make sure the system stays on a sound financial footing.

- *Local impacts:* The topic can be observed nearby.

  Our community should have a special interest in rising health care costs. As a hub for medical services, we are likely to see an influx of new residents who want to be closer to those services. But rising costs will put economic pressure on those families as well as on the medical service providers. Our city's economy over the long term is closely tied to how these changes play out. Consequently, all of us need to take this issue seriously.

As these examples show, demonstrating personal relevance requires thinking about those people, places, and entities that matter most to your listeners on an individual level. Through careful audience analysis, you can identify these links and connections early in the process of inventing your speech. These connections also can provide topics for invention for your speech as a whole. For example, you can highlight the "family and friends" connection in your introduction and then include supporting material to reinforce this connection in the body of your speech.

Enhancing Your Ethos

While relevance involves the connection between topic and audience, ethos connects you to your audience as well as your topic. Recall from chapter 1 that ethos involves three related factors: your knowledge about the topic, your honesty and trustworthiness as a speaker, and your goodwill toward others. By highlighting your knowledge and credentials, you show your connection to the topic. By demonstrating honesty and goodwill, you develop your connection to your audience. Although speakers should try to address all three factors in their introduction, a particular rhetorical situation may lead you to give special emphasis to one more than others.

Your Knowledge about the Topic If you are addressing a complex topic or one that involves specialized knowledge, your audience will especially want to be assured that you are well informed on your topic. Your expertise might come from education and training:

> My own interest in ballot initiatives began well before this speech. Last year, I took a seminar on state government and wrote my term paper on the pros and cons of ballot initiatives. During the summer, I had an internship at an organization that succeeded in getting an initiative on the November ballot. The connections I made through that internship helped me to find some current research on ballot initiatives for my speech today. There are many questions and misconceptions about these initiatives; I look forward to addressing these in my speech and answering any questions you may have afterward.

Alternatively, your knowledge of the topic might come from personal experience or long-term familiarity with the topic:

> Coal-bed methane is not just another speech topic about some abstract, distant issue. I have lived right in the middle of this issue for most of my life. My parents' ranch lies in the heart of methane development country. Our livelihood—the land we live on, the water we draw upon—could be significantly affected depending on the path that methane development takes. It's an issue that is hotly disputed in my hometown, and I have heard positions on all sides. While I will provide you with some facts and figures, I also hope I can give you a glimpse of this issue from the front lines.

Your Honesty and Trustworthiness as a Speaker The introductions in the previous sections stress the speaker's knowledge of the topic, which should enhance his or her credibility. They also reveal the speaker's personal connection to the issue, which is an excellent way of demonstrating honesty. If the speaker addressing coal-bed methane had not revealed her family's

connection, listeners might have felt deceived if they learned about that connection later. She may have strong feelings about the issue, but by being honest about her personal experience, she is letting her audience assess her biases, and in the process, she is building their trust.

If you are speaking on a highly controversial topic, trust is especially important to address in your introduction. You may want to state explicitly why your audience should give you a full and fair hearing. For an informative speech, you might discuss how you have tried to be even-handed while researching and inventing your speech:

> You have probably seen and heard a lot of information about each candidate's platform on energy. Today, I'd like to help us distinguish accurate information and fair criticisms from spin, and I've taken three steps to do this. First, I refer to each candidate's written statements about his or her own plan but not descriptions of his or her opponents' plan. Second, I use only other sources who identify themselves as nonpartisan. Third, I discussed my speech with two faculty members who are experts in energy or public policy. I cannot cover all the details in one short speech, but you should feel confident that I am presenting each position accurately and fairly.

Your Goodwill toward Others If your audience recognizes that you have a personal stake in the topic, you may need to show the audience that you are genuinely concerned about their interests, not just your own:

> Since many of you know I'm a stockbroker, it probably comes as no surprise that I have decided to inform you today about the capital gains tax. I won't deny that I have a definite opinion on this, but I recognize that each of us has different values and goals that might lead you to a different conclusion. For now, let's set aside those differences and focus instead on the facts. My speech will explain three different expert predictions of how lowering the capital gains tax will affect our economy. Armed with these facts, we can have a more productive discussion in the future about whether to change that tax.

No matter which appeals you use—and you might want to use more than one—the key to enhancing your ethos is to anticipate any concerns that the audience might have about you as a speaker. If you can show in the introduction that you are a knowledgeable, trustworthy person who has the interests of the audience in mind, you can go a long way toward enhancing your overall effectiveness throughout the rest of the speech.

PUBLIC SPOTLIGHT

Edward James Olmos: Community Activist

Starring in TV shows such as *American Family* and *Battlestar Galactica* and in movies such as *Selena* and *Stand and Deliver*, Edward James Olmos has made a name for himself as an actor. But his commitment to culture, diversity, and racial harmony also has led him to be a tireless community activist and public speaker. Olmos speaks regularly on these topics at schools and universities, at detention centers, and to youth organizations around the country.

Olmos's speeches are filled with many of the techniques that also work well in introductions and conclusions. Certainly, his speeches about racial harmony address a *publicly significant* topic. He usually develops the first half of his speech around his *personal experience* about growing up in the barrio. He also uses *direct address* to get his audiences involved in his speech and help them envision their future: "Forget everything about self and push yourself outward toward others. You start helping others and you will become one of the best people in the world you can be" (Gonzalez).

In addition, Olmos's *ethos* is a key factor in his effectiveness as a speaker. His life experience is a testament to his central idea; as he puts it, "I personify the fact that there's only one race, the human race." Most of all, he recognizes that dynamic, passionate speech is the best way to connect with an audience. "For me, inspired speaking is the only kind of speaking that I enjoy listening to and watching and feeling—and doing" (Keppler Speakers).

Edward James Olmos

ries that address important public issues, such as violence and its impact on young people. Olmos's websites share information about his many advocacy projects and report that his company will soon be producing content for new media markets.

 Social Media Spotlight

In addition to feature films and television projects, Olmos Productions has produced several documenta-

- Website: http://www.edwardjamesolmos.com/
- Facebook: http://www.facebook.com/EdwardJOlmos
- Twitter: http://twitter.com/edwardjolmos

Incorporating Your Central Idea

You are already familiar with how to phrase your central idea. Now you want to work on incorporating your central idea smoothly and effectively into your introduction so that you will effectively preview the important content your audience should listen for. Both verbal and nonverbal techniques can help your audience to easily recognize your central idea.

Verbal Techniques When crafting the actual wording of your central idea, try different lead-ins that signal to your audience the emergence of your central idea. The most straightforward lead-ins are short phrases that clearly identify an idea or opinion as yours:

> In this speech, I will explain how . . .
>
> My main goal in the next few minutes is . . .
>
> Today, I want to argue that . . .

A transition sentence also can work well as a lead-in. Here, your lead-in serves as a transition between statements that demonstrate relevance or enhance your ethos, and the central idea itself:

> Since all of us will soon be voting on the proposed athletics fee, we should look at the pros and cons and make an informed choice. [Central idea] In my view, the athletic fee should be adopted.
>
> Based on my research, I have identified three important impacts of climate change: [Central idea] Climate change can affect our supply of food, our exposure to disease, and our opportunities for recreation.

Nonverbal Techniques Nonverbal cues also help to signal the central idea to your audience. A *pause* before or after your central idea can set it off from other sentences in your introduction. Slightly slowing down your *speaking rate* also allows you to emphasize the importance of your central idea statement. Slight variations in *pitch* can add variety to the sentences around your central idea, too. No matter what techniques you use, the point is to make your central idea stand out as an important and distinct statement that your audience needs to remember.

Preparing Your Audience for the Rest of Your Speech

After stating your central idea, you have some choices as a speaker. You might want to further reinforce your ethos or the significance or relevance of the topic. For example, if your central idea focuses on specific effects of climate change, you could reinforce the significance of these effects with a brief statement like this:

> These effects are united in an important way: They all have an influence on your personal health.

Alternatively, you might want to include statements about relevance or ethos if you have not addressed those prior to the central idea. Where you decide to include those elements is probably less critical than the fact that you do include them at some point in your introduction. Beyond that, there are specific things that you can do to prepare the audience for the rest of the speech.

Preview Your Main Points Most important, this latter portion of the introduction should preview the rest of your speech. As was explained in chapter 2, a preview forecasts the main points or main sections of your speech. This can be as simple as stating those main points in the order in which they will appear in the speech:

> After a brief description of the purpose of Amtrak, the first part of my speech will explore how well Amtrak's current system serves that purpose. The second half of the speech will compare three current proposals for changing the Amtrak system.

> First, I will explain what a community development block grant is. Second, I will talk about how block grants are being used in our community. Third, I will show you how you can get involved with projects funded by those grants.

Signal Your Organizational Strategy In the process of listing your main points, good previews often will make the overall organizational strategy clear to the audience. Even though the organizational strategy might seem obvious to you, remember that your audience is hearing your speech for the first time and might not immediately pick up on your pattern. Signaling it with key words in your introduction can give the audience a structure for processing the rest of your speech and anticipating key points.

> First, I will discuss the origins of the NCAA. Next, I will describe how the NCAA first developed academic eligibility rules for college athletes. Then I will explain the current controversy over the NCAA's new eligibility rules. By the end of my speech, I hope you will have a better understanding of how the NCAA's concerns with academic performance have changed over time.

> The opening section of my speech describes the basic principles underlying all the efforts to reduce carbon dioxide emissions. Then I will turn to a comparison of the differences between two main proposals: cap-and-trade and a carbon tax. I will elaborate on this comparison by looking at the specific case of the Kyoto Protocol. Hopefully, drawing a contrast between proposals will show you why I think a carbon tax is a better choice.

In both of these examples, the preview reinforces the organizational pattern (chronological in the first, compare and contrast in the second) and shows how the purpose of the speech will be served by using that pattern of organization.

Crafting Conclusions

Think about movies one more time. You can see ninety terrific minutes of a film, but if the ending is a dud, you will probably leave the theater feeling disappointed. An abrupt ending, a confusing plot twist, or a scene that does not feel consistent with the rest of the film can leave viewers unsatisfied.

The conclusion of a speech is no different. Ending abruptly is jarring to listeners. Introducing a new idea or jumping to a new topic in the last thirty seconds will probably leave your audience confused. Likewise, speaking in a different tone or discussing opposing points of view can make listeners wonder exactly what they should be taking from your speech.

Instead, conclusions should be seen as the culmination of what you have said in the rest of your speech. As you learned in chapter 1, the two primary functions of a conclusion are to *reinforce your central idea* and to *indicate the end of the speech*. In doing so, you also want to maintain consistency with the body of your speech. No matter what your topic or purpose, attending to these two functions can make your conclusion a satisfying one.

Reinforcing Your Central Idea

After discussing details in the body of your speech, your conclusion should work to synthesize those details by returning to your central idea. Reinforcing the central idea in your conclusion should include restating that idea as well as amplifying it in a way that serves the specific purpose of your speech.

Restate Your Central Idea Repeating your central idea during the conclusion helps both you and your audience. Repetition of the central idea will help your audience to remember the bottom line or take-home message of your speech. It also encourages reflection on how well the various parts of your speech support that message. That reflection is important for you as a speaker, too. When you are developing your speech, forcing yourself to restate the central idea after you have composed the body can spur you to consider whether your main points and supporting materials are adequate.

For example, this restatement of a central idea is tied directly to main points in the speech:

> In conclusion, I hope the four main points of my speech have demonstrated how food democracy is concerned with the production of safe, nutritious, affordable, and sustainable food.

With this restatement, both you and the audience are reminded of the core themes that should have been addressed in the body of the speech.

In addition, restating your central idea *exactly* as you stated it in the introduction helps you to keep your conclusion focused. It can be tempting to introduce a new idea, expand the scope of your topic, or exaggerate your position to give your speech that extra boost during its final moments. Think about the food democracy example above; it might be tempting to conclude a speech on that topic with the following way:

> *Poor restatement:* As I have shown, food democracy is really important—so important that I want to end by telling you about my plan for boycotting big supermarket chains.

Whoa! This conclusion makes two important mistakes. First, it oversimplifies the central idea. Instead of reminding listeners about key aspects of food democracy, it makes the obvious statement that the topic is important. Second, the statement introduces a new idea that is very different from the original idea. This will only raise more questions for your audience—precisely when you do not have the time to answer them.

Amplify Your Central Idea Instead of changing your central idea, you want to amplify it. As a term of rhetoric, **amplification** does not mean speaking more loudly; it means giving extra emphasis to an idea through supporting materials and artistic language. In your conclusion, you can amplify your central idea in several ways.

First, always consider *summarizing your main points*. Because your main points all support your central idea, summarizing them all in one spot is a way of amplifying your central idea one more time. Here, creativity and detail can be used to your advantage, in contrast to the exact repetition of your central idea. For example, your audience might not be satisfied if you simply restate the preview from your introduction. By the end of the speech, listeners will have learned much more about your topic, so your conclusion should remind them of what they have learned.

A more compelling conclusion will weave together details from the body of your speech to make your summary substantive:

> *Poor summary:* I first described the purpose of Amtrak, then discussed the adequacy of Amtrak's current system, and finally looked at three proposals to change it.

> *Better summary:* As I have shown, the conflicting missions of Amtrak have led to a system that is insufficient in certain areas and inequitable overall. Proposals to improve the system differ as to whether intercity or rural routes need the most attention.

The better summary adds only a few words to remind listeners of what they heard in the speech and how those details fit together.

Second, consider *quotations, anecdotes, and personal narratives* that eloquently reinforce your main idea. These attention-getting devices that work well in introductions can function equally well at the end of a speech. So if you are trying to decide between several attention-getters, think about shifting one to your conclusion.

A concluding quotation, for example, can be a good technique for reiterating the importance of your central idea. Well-chosen quotations can elevate the idea to a higher plane, providing common ground on controversial topics or inspiring listeners to act on the basis of a lofty ideal:

> No matter what academic reforms you support in college athletics, I think we can all get behind the goal of a high-quality education for all. In the words of Mark Emmert, President of the NCAA, "Everything we do in intercollegiate athletics must be driven by an overriding commitment to the academic success of our student athletes" (Johnson).

Personal narratives or other anecdotes typically reinforce your central idea in the opposite way—by focusing on specific, concrete examples in contrast to lofty ideas:

> The story of a young man who I'll call Matthew shows how these grants can have a positive impact on our community. Matthew's teenage years were marred by drug use and run-ins with the police. But a mentor of Matthew's connected him with Second Chance, a program to help at-risk youth funded by a block grant. Matthew got to work on building affordable housing and picked up construction skills that he parlayed into a regular job with a local builder. Developing communities and building the capacity of its residents—that's exactly what block grants are meant to do.

Third, remind your audience explicitly of the *public significance and personal relevance* of your topic. After listening to lots of details and supporting materials in the body of the speech, listeners may need a reminder about the "big picture"—why all of it matters to themselves and to their community:

> Ultimately, coal-bed methane will be a significant part of the solution to our country's energy needs. With rapidly rising energy consumption, we all need to take a close look at every possible energy source at our disposal. Hopefully, my speech has shown you how we might weigh those needs against the need for a clean and healthful environment.

Indicating the End of Your Speech

As was described in chapter 2, some speakers will indicate the end of their speech with a brief organizational marker such as, "In summary . . ." or "Let me conclude . . . ." But this is only the first step in concluding your speech effectively. As you just read, you need to reinforce and amplify your central idea. In addition, you can use a few common techniques to lead your audience out of the speech and provide a sense of closure.

Indicating the end of your speech, then, is not simply a matter of telling your audience that your speech is nearly over. Ultimately, you want to make the entire conclusion a distinctive part of your speech so that your audience can feel that the speech is coming to a powerful and memorable ending.

Break the Suspense Remember how building suspense can be a great attention-getter? Breaking that suspense in the conclusion can help your speech to come full circle, implicitly signaling that the speech is coming to an end:

> For one final look at the benefits of sustainable agriculture, let's return to our friend Donnie Fulks. After he and his father learned how some of the fertilizers and pesticides had harmed the health of their soil, they changed their farming practices. They now grow certified organic corn, soybeans, and small grains, as well as pumpkins and strawberries using less harmful methods. In addition, their farm attracts thousands of visitors and student field trips who are interested in their practices as well as their products. "My biggest crop now is cars in the parking lot," says Donnie. His example shows that growing food sustainably can be a winner all the way around.

Returning to the opening story gives your speech a sense of closure as well as consistency. At its best, the concluding part of the story will provide yet another way to amplify the central idea.

Call for Engagement Speakers who are attempting to promote political or civic engagement should always consider including a direct call to their audience in the conclusion. Issuing a **call for engagement**—an explicit statement of how an audience can continue involvement after the speech—reminds the audience that the time for engagement does not end once your speech is over. Your conclusion, then, is the perfect opportunity for showing your audience members how they might act on the basis of what they have learned in your speech.

There are two very different types of engagement that you might ask from your audience. You are probably more familiar with the type of call that comes in persuasive speeches. These speeches often end with a **call for action**, when speakers advocate for a specific policy or a change in behavior and conclude by encouraging listeners to act in ways that are consistent with that advocacy. For example, if a classmate advocates a change to your college's investment practices, he or she might call for actions such as voting in a campus referendum, volunteering for an organization that is working on the issue, or attending a rally in front of the administration building. Upcoming chapters on persuasive speaking will look at this type of call in more detail.

But informative speeches do not advocate for a particular policy or change in behavior. Because informative speeches do not develop judgments about some policy or behavior, it would be unethical (and probably unpersuasive) to ask your audience to support a particular position on your topic. Instead, informative speeches may issue a **call for learning**—that is, your conclusion can show audiences what they can do to become more informed and knowledgeable about your topic.

For example, an informative speech on Middle East politics should not call for action in regard to a specific policy. Instead, it might direct listeners to additional sources of information on the topic:

Here on campus, we have a wealth of opportunities to learn more about the complexities of politics in the Middle East. Next Thursday, the International Student Association is sponsoring a panel discussion on the latest round of peace negotiations. Next semester, Dr. Skidmore is offering her Israel-Palestine seminar on Tuesday evenings. And the Foreign Film Series on Wednesday nights is showing two films this year on the subject.

While these statements do encourage listeners to act, the action does not involve picking a side or supporting a cause. Instead, the call simply encourages the audience to seek opportunities for additional learning. Recognizing that there are other sources of information also shows that you are interested in the audience's personal development, thereby enhancing your ethos.

Envision the Future Like a call for action, a *vision of the future* makes logical sense in a conclusion. It helps your audience to make the transition from your speech in the present to what comes next beyond your speech. A vision of the future provides yet another way to conceptualize political and civic engagement on your topic.

Again, informative and persuasive speeches will use this tactic in different ways. Persuasive speeches will use it to motivate action, showing how an action will lead to a better future or prevent an unappealing future. For informative speeches, visions of the future should be focused on *describing the ongoing relevance of your topic*. The point is not to say what you want the future to look like, but to show your audience how information about this topic will be relevant to future events.

For example, your conclusion might point to trends that will affect the information in your speech. This contextualizes your information and gives audiences a focus for engagement in the future:

As you have seen, the United States, Russia, and China are currently the three biggest energy consumers in the world. But in the coming years, keep your eyes on India. With a large population and a growing economy, it is already being mentioned in the same breath as China in discussions about future energy needs.

In a similar way, you might alert listeners to future needs for information that are related to your topic. For instance, decision makers are especially interested in what we don't yet know, as well as what we already know:

In summary, our college's financial aid policies need to take into account the demographic changes and initiatives by our competitors that I have described today. But there is another important factor that is still unknown: what impact the recession will have on families in our state. In the coming months, we will need to gather information and pay attention to this important question.

Informative speeches also can refer to the future in order to reinforce significance and relevance. Here, you show how your speech is not just providing information for its own sake, but offering something that will soon have a clear practical application:

Now that you understand the similarities and differences between a "roadless" area and a "wilderness" area, you will have a better idea of what's at stake in Senator Smith's proposal to create three new wilderness areas out of current roadless areas. The Senator's website has a copy of the proposal, and he is accepting comments on it through the end of the month.

Here again, note how this reference to the future is not being used to advocate a particular position, but to show that the information in the speech has a direct connection to a significant issue or a personal decision.

CASE CONCLUSION

Christine's Speech on Relay for Life

Christine knew that she needed to connect both herself and her audience to the topic as well as build some connections between herself and her audience. To accomplish the first two objectives, she decided that her attention-getter would use two techniques: direct address and personal narrative. She began by directly addressing the audience in order to connect the broad topic of cancer to them:

> Unfortunately, most of us probably have known someone diagnosed with cancer. It may be your parent or grandparent, sibling or acquaintance. Having a relationship with someone with cancer can have a tremendous impact on you.

Then, she turned to a personal narrative to connect herself to her topic:

> For me, the cancer victim who has most affected my life is Nat, a six-year-old boy who I met at Relay for Life last spring. I spent the first two hours of the Relay chasing him around the course in search of his name on a candle-lit luminary bag. Nat has been cancer-free for a year since Relay and is still healthy. But without the research funded by Relay for Life, he might not be with us today. That research helps people across the world—including your loved ones, and someday maybe even you— in the struggle against cancer.

Christine saved other material for the body of her speech and instead made sure to build the connection between herself and her audience. She did this by speaking about her personal experience with Relay for Life as a way of bolstering her ethos. She offered this credibility statement right after stating her central idea and before previewing the rest of the speech:

> Today, I want to share with you a behind-the-scenes look at Relay for Life, with the goal of explaining how organizational and individual support has made this event so successful. My knowledge comes not just from participating in the Relay in our community, but also from talking with local organizers and reading about the development of the Relay. In the rest of my speech I will first talk about the history of the Relay and what it has grown into today. Then, I will discuss the organizations that make it possible. Finally, I will talk about individual participation in the event.

For her conclusion, Christine saved a powerful statistic that amplified the success of the Relay for Life. She highlighted this even further by reminding the audience where the money goes. Then she ended the speech by encouraging her audience to think about future resources that will be needed, which indicated the end of the speech and reiterated the importance of her topic:

> As you have seen, both the organizational support and individual participation have made Relay for Life an extremely successful fund-raising event. Indeed, the organizational strength behind the Relay means that the $40,000 raised on our campus last year is just a drop in the bucket. Nationally, the Relay raised over $405 million! That money supports ongoing cancer research, as well as programs such as Great American Health Check, an awareness campaign about early cancer detection, and Camp Sunrise, an overnight camp for kids with cancer. As our society continues to seek resources to "fight for the cure," I hope you can better appreciate the efforts that go into raising some of those resources through the Relay for Life.

Summary

CRAFTING INTRODUCTIONS

- Effective introductions need to build connections between the speaker and the audience, between the speaker and the topic, and between the audience and the topic.

- The key functions of an introduction are arousing audience attention, demonstrating public significance and personal relevance, enhancing your ethos, incorporating your central idea, and preparing your audience for the rest of the speech.

CRAFTING CONCLUSIONS

- Conclusions serve two basic purposes. First, they should reinforce the central idea of your speech by restating that idea precisely and amplifying it with compelling pieces of supporting material or attention to the significance and personal relevance of the topic.

- Conclusions also need to signal the end of the speech. In the public sphere, speakers should always consider including a call for engagement that is appropriate in light of the overall purpose of the speech.

Key Terms

attention-getter, p. 245
personal narratives, p. 246
shock/startle, p. 248
direct address, p. 250

amplification, p. 260
call for engagement, p. 262
call for action, p. 262
call for learning, p. 262

Comprehension

1. What functions should a speech introduction serve?

2. If you want to strengthen the audience's connection to your topic with a quotation, what type of person should you quote?

3. What are some of the ethical concerns in using a hypothetical example in your introduction?

4. What nonverbal cues can you use to signal the central idea to your audience?

5. Why is it important to restate your central idea at the end of your speech?

6. What are the two different types of calls for engagement that you can make in your conclusion?

Application

1. Listen to the introduction of a lecture, either a classroom lecture or a public lecture. Which functions does the speaker fulfill successfully? Are there any reasons why the speaker might ignore some of those functions?

2. With a partner, have one of you come up with a list of three specific audiences and the other come up with three speech topics. Then brainstorm strategies you might use to connect each audience to each topic in an introduction to a speech on the topic.

3. Examine the conclusion of a presidential inaugural address, and compare the address you chose with those that your classmates have chosen. What kind of engagement does the conclusion call for? Are there similarities or differences? How do the conclusions envision the future?

Outlining Your Speech

This chapter is intended to help you:

- Develop a working outline that organizes your main points and supporting material into a coherent speech
- Use organizational markers that signal the structure of your speech to your audience
- Generate a speaking outline that enhances the delivery of your speech

Outlines can help anyone to be an effective speaker in the public sphere. If you are a beginning speaker, preparing an outline helps you to follow your organizational pattern so that your speech is clear to your audience. An outline also can jog your memory during the presentation of your speech, helping to minimize your anxiety. If you are a more experienced speaker, preparing an outline reminds you of your main points and can keep you from going off on tangents during your speech. Whenever you are addressing important issues in your community, you want to do whatever you can to enhance your coherence and credibility; an outline can be an important tool for those goals.

Making an outline, then, is not just academic busywork. It leads directly to real improvements in the delivery of your speech. In this chapter, we'll look first

Cole's Speech on Alternative Fuels

Cole is a car lover. He has several cars of his own and is always working on them. But he was not sure how enthusiastic his audience would be about a speech on cars. After doing his audience analysis, he learned that his classmates' interests in cars were mostly about fuel efficiency and the different kinds of hybrid cars that were available. As a result, he decided to focus his research on alternative fuels for cars. In his informative speech, he decided to use a topical organizational strategy to discuss three major alternative fuels: ethanol, natural gas, and hydrogen. These three topics would become the three main points in the body of his outline.

at how to develop a working outline, a tool that you will use to help you to organize your material and develop your speech. Then we will show how to create a delivery outline, a condensed version of your working outline that you can use during your presentation. ■

Developing Your Working Outline

A **working outline** is a complete, full-sentence outline of your speech. It includes all the material you plan to have in your speech: the introduction and conclusion; the main points, subpoints, and supporting material that make up the body of your speech; and the organizational markers that help the overall coherence of the speech. Most working outlines begin with your purpose statements and main claim, and they end with a bibliography or list of references.

A working outline is similar to an outline that you would make when developing an expository essay for other courses. By producing a working outline, you will be able to see the full scope of your speech, get feedback from others, and figure out whether any sections need revision or additional support. Start by putting down familiar material, and then work on parts of your speech that are less developed or that need extra attention. Follow the guidelines in the rest of this section to construct that outline.

State Your Specific Purpose and Central Idea

The specific purpose and central idea provide an anchor for your outline. Returning to the statements you formulated in chapter 4 as you develop the outline will help you keep your speech focused on achieving its intended purpose. Although these statements are not part of the lettering and numbering system that you use for the speech itself, many speakers find them to be a helpful way to ensure that the outline includes the essential information.

WORKING OUTLINE
Showing your working outline
to friends can help you get
feedback from an audience's
point of view.

Designate the Introduction, Body, and Conclusion

Before you get to the details of your speech, put these three headings in your outline. Place them in the center of the page, and leave space under each one. This will remind you of the basic speech structure that you learned about in chapter 2. By the time you have finished your outline, the body section should be the largest portion of your speech—typically, larger than the introduction and conclusion combined.

Transfer Your Organizational Pattern to the Body

From what you learned in chapter 9, you should have a clear idea of your main points and the organizational pattern that works best for your overall purpose. Using the organizational pattern you have chosen as a guide, put these main points into the body section of your speech first, as complete sentences. (If you are using a computer to write your outline, you might want to put these statements in bold or highlight them so that you can easily identify the main points as you proceed.) After stating your main points, begin to include subpoints and supporting material if you are ready to do so, making sure that your main points are clearly marked and in the right order.

For example, here is one portion of an outline of a speech using a topical organization in an early stage of development, with comments explaining how the outline is being assembled:

COMMENTS

The speaker's first main point is stated in a single sentence and is marked by bold type.

So far the speaker has three subpoints and might need to add supporting material.

The speaker has three sub-subpoints describing different types of diets. Here, the speaker has made a note for further development of the outline.

Second main point.

For the subpoints, the speaker has noted specific pieces of supporting material that will be incorporated in the outline later.

BODY

I. Veal is a unique type of beef.

Veal comes from calves, not adult cattle.

Most veal comes from male calves.

Special diets help produce veal.

Grain-fed

Grass-fed (*need full sentences)

Milk-fed

II. The process of raising veal has generated controversy.

Some people find problems with the calves' living conditions.
(PETA statistic)
(farmer quotation)

Health advocates find problems with the antibiotics given to calves.

(Evidence from Smith book)
(CDC testimony)

As you can see in this example, the main points, subpoints, and ideas for supporting materials build a skeleton of the outline. Once all your main points are included, you can see how the organizational pattern works as a whole. Then you can start to develop your subpoints and supporting material.

Fill in Subpoints and Supporting Material

Speakers take different approaches to incorporating the supporting material in their outline. One approach is to use notes or placeholders (as in the veal example) as you sketch the entire speech. You might note a specific piece of research, or you might just include a general marker of where you need additional supporting material. Then, after referring to your research, you can go back to fill in details. Another approach involves writing out only the main points first and then adding all the supporting materials for that point before moving onto the next point. No matter how you develop your subpoints and supporting material, the final version of your working outline should include all of those statements in complete sentences.

Apply a Consistent Outline Form

After you have put all needed material into the body of the speech, apply a consistent pattern of numbers, letters, and indentation to identify the relationships between different statements in the outline. A typical form of outlining follows this pattern.

I. MAIN POINT

    A. Subpoint

        1. Supporting material for subpoint A

        2. Supporting material for subpoint A

            a. Supporting material for sub-subpoint 2

            b. Supporting material for sub-subpoint 2

    B. Subpoint

        1. Supporting material for subpoint B

        2. Supporting material for subpoint B

        3. Supporting material for subpoint B

    C. Subpoint

        1. Supporting material for subpoint C

        2. Supporting material for subpoint C

II. MAIN POINT

    A. Subpoint

        1. Supporting material for subpoint A

        2. Supporting material for subpoint A

    B. Subpoint

        1. Supporting material for subpoint B

        2. Supporting material for subpoint B

            a. Supporting material for sub-subpoint 2

            b. Supporting material for sub-subpoint 2

    C. Subpoint

        1. Supporting material for subpoint C

            a. Supporting material for sub-subpoint 1

            b. Supporting material for sub-subpoint 1

        2. Supporting material for subpoint C

            a. Supporting material for sub-subpoint 2

            b. Supporting material for sub-subpoint 2

Your outlines will not necessarily follow this *exact* outline. For instance, a speech might have only two subpoints for the first main point, and you do not need exactly two pieces of supporting material for sub-subpoint B.2. The purpose here is to illustrate several principles of good outline form:

- *Coordination.* The principle of **coordination** requires that elements of equal importance should occur at the same level of the outline. For example, each main point above uses a Roman numeral, and each piece of supporting material for the numbered subpoints uses a lowercase letter. One technique that helps maintain the principle of coordination is the use of parallel structure, which was described in chapter 9. If you can phrase equally important points using the same grammatical structure, that is one sign of successfully coordinating those points.

- *Subordination.* The principle of **subordination** requires that within any point, your subpoints and supporting material should descend in order of importance. The system of indentation in a standard outline helps us to visualize these relationships between main points, subpoints, and supporting material. The main points, which are the most important level, are at the left margin, and the subpoints and supporting materials each move farther to the right. For example, in the outline above, the details of points a, b, and c are the least important of all.

- *Adequacy.* The principle of **adequacy** requires that if you want to divide any point of your speech, that point that should have *at least two* subordinate subpoints. After all, it is impossible to divide something into only one part. Either create a second subpoint or incorporate the subpoint into the next higher level of the outline.

- *Consistency.* The example above illustrates the most common system for outlining, but your instructor might ask you to use a different system. No matter what system you use, it is critical that you follow the principle of **consistency**; use the same system *consistently* during the entire outline. If you use Roman numerals for your main points, then *all* your main points should have Roman numerals. Also, do not skip a level when outlining. According to the letter and number system in the example above, the subpoints of the main points must be A, B, C; they cannot jump to 1, 2, 3 or a, b, c.

Now that you have seen what an outline should look like in general, let's look at some concrete examples. Compare the following outlines of speeches describing a college's academic departments. The outline on the right is much more effective in following these principles.

Less Effective	**More Effective**
I. Humanities Division	I. Humanities Division
A. Literature	A. History
II. Philosophy	B. Literature
III. Social Sciences Division	C. Philosophy
1. Economics	II. Social Sciences Division
2. Sociology	A. Economics
IV. Biology	B. Sociology
A. Chemistry	III. Natural Sciences Division
B. Physics	A. Biology
C. Natural Sciences Division	B. Chemistry
	C. Physics

The more effective outline follows the organizational structure of a college. Each division is represented by a main point, and the departments that are part of the division are represented by equal subpoints. In contrast, the less effective example violates the principles of good outlining in the following ways:

- *Coordination:* Neither Philosophy nor Biology is an entire division, yet the outline treats them as coordinate with the Humanities and Social Sciences Divisions.

- *Subordination:* The Natural Sciences Division is not subordinate to the Biology Department.

- *Adequacy:* Main point I has only one subpoint.

- *Consistency:* The subpoints of main point III skip the capital letters.

Even though the less effective example has the appearance of an outline, it does not serve the purpose of helping you to deliver a coherent, well-organized speech.

Add the Introduction and Conclusion

Once the body of the speech is fully outlined, add your introduction and conclusion. If you add these elements after you have worked on the body of your speech, it will be easier to make adjustments and ensure that they reflect the final version of your speech.

While the introduction and the conclusion each should be an organic whole, it can be helpful to set them up in outline form. Each main point corresponds to one of the functions of an introduction or conclusion and includes a few sentences that fulfill that function. For example, you might outline your introduction to a speech on religion in public schools like this:

INTRODUCTION

I. What does religious freedom mean to you? Is it the right to pray without interference from others? Is it the freedom to practice your religion in public buildings? Or perhaps it involves freedom from the religious practices of others? It means different things to different people, so there is often controversy around issues of religious freedom.
Arouse attention.

II. Prayer in public school is one of those issues. It cuts to the core of the meaning of religious freedom and the tension between church and state in our society. As a result, prayer in public schools is an important issue for us as a society. And it is probably important to many of you on a personal level. Polls consistently show that more than 90% of Americans believe in God, and more than half pray on a daily basis (Pew Forum on Religion & Public Life).
Demonstrate significance/relevance.

III. Because this is such an important issue, I have begun to examine the different perspectives on it, through library research as well as interviews with the superintendent of our local public school system as well as a law professor who specializes in First Amendment law. What I found in my research
Enhance ethos.

and what I want to share with you today are the main areas of disagreement between school prayer proponents and opponents.

State central idea.

IV. **Disagreements over prayer in public school focus on the meaning of the First Amendment and the types of prayer that are or should be allowed in public schools.**

Prepare audience for rest of speech.

V. In my speech, I will first discuss a brief history of the idea of the separation of church and state. Then I will explain how advocates disagree in their interpretations of the First Amendment, specifically the Establishment Clause and the Free Exercise clause. Finally, I will show how people disagree on which types of prayer should be allowed in public schools. By the end of my speech, I hope you will have a better understanding of this complicated and often divisive issue.

Conclusions are somewhat less rigid than introductions and have fewer functions to fulfill. Still, as chapter 10 showed, you want to make sure that you perform at least two functions: reinforce your central ideal, and indicate the end of your speech. Consider the needs of your speech to see whether you need additional points. For example, continuing with the example of the speech on religion in public schools, the conclusion might look like this:

CONCLUSION

Reinforce central idea.

I. In my speech, I intended to explain to you some of the key areas of disagreement regarding prayer in public school. Some disagreements focus on the different types of prayer that are or should be allowed in public schools, such as student-led prayer groups and "moments of silence." These disputes are grounded in disagreements over the meaning of the Establishment and Free Exercise clauses of the First Amendment.

Indicate end of speech.

II. You will hear about these ideas again next month, when the Supreme Court is expected to rule on an important prayer case that hinges on the meaning of the Free Exercise clause. I hope that the knowledge you gained about school prayer today will help you grasp the significance of that case.

At this point, your working outline is nearly complete. It should display all the content that you intend to include in your speech. Review your outline to ensure that it contains everything you want to say and that it is organized to follow the organizational pattern you have chosen.

Produce Organizational Markers

Once the content of your speech is in place, you can add **organizational markers**, phrases and sentences that connect points and signal organizational shifts in a speech. These markers help the audience to see how the main points or sections in a speech are related to one another. These markers are commonly called *transitions*, but transitions actually are just one of several types of organizational markers that you might use in your speeches. This section describes four types: signposts, internal previews, internal summaries, and transitions.

Signposts A **signpost** in a speech signals an order or sequence. These are easy markers to incorporate in a speech, but they serve a crucial function. They remind both you and your audience where you are in your speech. For example, you have probably heard many speeches that include signposts that enumerate a series of points:

> The <u>first</u> type of home loan we'll examine is a fixed-rate loan.
>
> An ARM, or adjustable-rate mortgage, is the <u>second</u> type of loan to consider.
>
> <u>Third</u>, let's discuss an interest-only home loan.

If the points are complex, you can use parallel structure along with signposts to make this sequence of points even clearer:

> The first type of home mortgage is a fixed-rate loan.
>
> The second type of home mortgage is an adjustable-rate loan.
>
> The third type of home mortgage is an interest-only loan.

In addition to these numerical signposts, you can vary your wording by using other words and short phrases to serve as signposts to guide your audience through a series of subpoints or pieces of supporting material:

> The typical adjustable-rate mortgage has several important advantages. The <u>primary</u> advantage is that the first few years of payments are low. <u>In addition</u>, it is often easier to qualify for an ARM than for other types of mortgages. <u>Also</u>, if you are able to make extra payments during the initial period, you build equity more quickly.

Speeches using chronological or causal order might rely on other words to place events in sequence:

> <u>At first</u>, Felicia was satisfied with her home loan. . . .
>
> <u>But then</u> the interest rate increased. . . .
>
> <u>Consequently</u>, she had difficulty making her payments. . . .
>
> <u>Finally</u>, Felicia had to work with a collection agency to arrange a new payment schedule.

Another type of signpost will reinforce a point. If you want to emphasize something or restate it in simpler terms, you can start a sentence with a signpost to get your audience's attention:

> <u>In other words</u>, you are essentially gambling on future interest rates.
>
> <u>The most important point</u> is that you are not actually paying down your principal.
>
> <u>It bears repeating</u>: You can pay off your loan several years early by making an extra monthly payment each year.

One final note: It is easy to overdo it with signposts. Think about signposts on a highway. Most highways have a signpost marking every mile, but it would be overkill if they marked every foot. In a speech, if every single sentence on your outline starts with "First" or "Second" or "Third," your audience probably will get more confused than anything. They might not be able to keep track of whether "Second" refers to your main points, a subpoint, or an additional piece of supporting material. As you incorporate these kinds of markers into your outlines, then, use signposts only as needed to guide your audience.

Internal Previews   An **internal preview** states what will be discussed in a subsequent part of the speech. For example, in chapter 10, you learned that effective introductions typically include a preview statement about the entire speech. But you also might use a preview in the body of a speech to forecast subpoints within a section. In a speech about controls over Internet access for children, for example, you might devote a section to filtering and blocking:

> Filters and blocking software are another source of controversy surrounding Internet access. <u>As you will see, parents, public libraries, and schools all have taken different approaches to controlling Internet access for children.</u>

In this instance, the speaker states a main point and then follows with an internal preview of the subpoints that will be used to illustrate it. With this type of preview, the speaker could then use "First," "Second," and "Third" to enumerate the subpoints, or just use phrases such as "Many schools also use software . . ." or "In addition, public libraries have gotten into the practice of filtering." Internal previews also can be structured according the types of supporting material that you will use to establish a point:

> To examine the issue of cyberstalking, I will first look at some of the statistics about this problem, share the views of scholars who have studied the issue, and then tell you about a shocking case involving two students on our campus.

Like signposts, internal previews give audiences a "heads-up" about what comes next in a speech. As you build your outlines, look particularly for areas of complexity or detail. In these spots, an internal preview can help your audience to anticipate a series of points or moves in your speech. Preparing your audience for these passages ahead of time can minimize the chances that audience members will get lost.

Internal Summaries   An **internal summary** recaps the main ideas or highlights in a specific section of a speech. As an organizational tool, it signals to an audience that one section is concluding and that another will begin soon. But it also helps your audience to grasp the content of your speech by highlighting and repeating key ideas.

An internal summary often pulls together the key ideas within a section of a speech. For example, this summary covers the three subpoints of a section as well as examples of each subpoint:

> Let's review some of the signs and symptoms of methamphetamine use. We saw physical symptoms such as weight loss, abnormal sweating, and burn marks. Behavioral signs included social withdraw, repetitive behaviors, and

significant changes in sleep patterns. And mentally, meth users may exhibit paranoia, anxiety, and agitation (Partnership for a Drug-Free America).

This internal summary restates the main point and the two subpoints:

Methamphetamine production, then, has significant effects on our community beyond users. Children face the risk of burns and toxic exposure, and the byproducts of meth production are a threat to our community's water resources (Partnership for a Drug-Free America).

Internal summaries also can conclude a section by emphasizing one idea rather than hitting all the key ideas:

As this overview shows, health professionals have developed several strategies to combat meth. For young adults in particular, peer intervention is an increasingly popular strategy.

Thus, while the short-term effects of meth use may be disturbing, a growing body of evidence is beginning to reveal significant long-term impacts to the central nervous system.

Among the many volunteer opportunities I've described, giving presentations about meth to community groups is one that allows you to put your public speaking skills to good use.

As always, think about your audience's needs and your overall purpose as you develop internal summaries for your outline. No matter how much or how little you include in an internal summary, it should crystallize and reinforce those points you want your audience to remember.

Transitions A **transition** is a statement that explicitly connects the previous idea to the next idea in your speech. Transitions look backward and forward in the same sentence. In some cases, a transition will connect these ideas by combining a summary and a preview in a single statement. In fact, some people refer to all these organizational markers as transitions, but here the term refers to this more complex type of connecting marker. When stated well, a transition effortlessly moves your speech from one section to the next:

Now that I've given you some background on the rise of the mobile phone industry, let's move on to the challenges that the industry faces.

To illustrate these ideas about innovation in the mobile phone industry, we can look at the specific instance of how the iPhone challenged its rivals.

In the latter example, the transition not only signals movement from one section to the next. It also is worded to reinforce the logical relationship of your points or the organizational pattern you are using; in this instance, it shows a deductive pattern. Other patterns can be reinforced through transitions, too:

Spatial order: Now that we have discussed overfishing in the Atlantic, let's move south to explore similar problems along the Gulf Coast.

Causal order: Given this knowledge of the problem of overfishing, it makes sense to explore some of the underlying causes.

<u>As a result</u> of overfishing, the rest of the ecosystem has experienced many negative effects.

Compare and contrast: <u>Even though there are important similarities</u> between the Atlantic and Pacific fish stocks, <u>there are significant differences</u>, too.

<u>While many people</u> share these perceptions about the availability of tuna, <u>the actual situation</u> described by commercial fishermen is more complicated.

Key issues: <u>In addition to the question</u> of whether the commercial fish catch should be limited, <u>another important issue</u> is whether bottom trawling should be banned.

As you incorporate organizational markers into your outline, keep the following tips in mind:

- Signposts can be written directly into the statements on your outline. As you get more experienced, including signposts will become a natural part of phrasing your main points and subpoints, rather than a separate step in the outlining process.

- Internal previews, summaries, and transitions should be labeled and set apart from the rest of the outline. You do not need to include them in the system of letters and numbers that you use. Visually, you can set them off by placing them in parentheses or italicizing them.

Constructing your organizational markers is an excellent way to help you see the big picture of your speech. By dwelling on the important points in your speech and the connections between those points, you get another opportunity to ensure that this picture is clear, vivid, and coherent.

Provide a Title

After your outline is complete, consider adding a title. For classroom purposes, a title can give your instructor a quick sense of your speech. A title is especially important in public settings, if your speech is going to be publicized ahead of time, or if it will be published afterward. Titles should convey your topic clearly while also highlighting the unique focus or approach of your speech. For example, "Home Mortgage Loans" would be a standard title for a speech on that topic. But you might make it more specific with a title such as "Comparing Your Mortgage Options" or "The Advantages of ARM Loans." In some situations, you might try to pique your audience's interest with a creative title instead of directly stating your topic. "Home Sweet Loan" or "The Five-Year Gamble" might do a better job of attracting your audience's attention than a generic title.

Generate Your Reference List

The last part of your outline should list the sources you used in preparing your speech. Check with your instructor about the format you should use. Some instructors will ask you to list the "Works Cited," which are only those sources you actually mention in your speech. Others will ask for a list of "Works Consulted," which are all the sources you reviewed during your research. In addition, check with your instructor about the preferred citation style. Most college-level public speaking instructors will expect you to use either the format of the Modern Language Association (MLA) or that of the American Psychological Association (APA). See Figures 11.1 and 11.2 for examples.

FIGURE 11.1   Citation Examples: MLA Style

Book

    Neumann, Mark. *On the Rim: Looking for the Grand Canyon.* Minneapolis: University of Minnesota Press, 1999.

Magazine or Newspaper Article

    Shaddox, Colleen. "Juvenile Justice and the Theater of the Absurd." *Miller-McCune.* November/December 2008: 30–35.

Unsigned Magazine or Newspaper Article.

    "The Pakistan Connection." *The New York Times.* 6 Dec. 2008: A20.

Journal Article

    Santelli, John S., Laura Duberstein Lindberg, Lawrence B. Finer, and Susheela Singh. "Explaining Declines in Adolescent Pregnancy in the United States: The Contribution of Abstinence and Improved Contraceptive Use." *The American Journal of Public Health* 97.1 (2007): 150–156.

Government Publication

    National Council on Disability. *Quarterly Meeting: People with Disabilities and Emergency Management.* Washington: GPO, January 29, 2008.

Website

    Cheetham, Nicole, Debra Hauser, and Naina Dhingra. "Improving U.S. Global HIV Prevention for Youth." *Advocates for Youth.* August 2006. Accessed July 15, 2007. Available at http://www.advocatesforyouth.org/PUBLICATIONS/policybrief/pbabc.htm

Personal Interview

    Bach, Betsy. Personal Interview. 10 Sept. 2008.

Correspondence

    Revkin, Andrew. "Meeting on Thursday." E-mail to the author. 4 Dec. 2008.

FIGURE 11.2   Citation Examples: APA Style

Book

> Neumann, M. (1999). *On the rim: Looking for the Grand Canyon.* Minneapolis:
>   University of Minnesota Press.

Magazine or Newspaper Article

> Shaddox, C. (November/December 2008). Juvenile justice and the theater of
>   the absurd. *Miller-McCune*, 30–35.

Unsigned Magazine or Newspaper Article.

> The Pakistan connection. (2008, December 6). *The New York Times*, A20.

Journal Article

> Santelli, J. S., Lindberg, L.D., Finer, L.B. & Singh, S. (2007). Explaining recent
>   declines in adolescent pregnancy in the United States: the contribution of
>   abstinence and improved contraceptive use. *The American Journal of Public
>   Health* 97(1), 150–156.

Government Publication

> National Council on Disability. (January 29, 2008). *Quarterly meeting: People
>   with disabilities and emergency management.* Washington, DC: Government
>   Printing Office.

Website

> Cheetham, N., Hauser, D. & Dhingra, N. (August 2006). *Improving U.S. global
>   HIV prevention for youth.* Retrieved from
>   http://www.advocatesforyouth.org/PUBLICATIONS/policybrief/pbabc.htm

APA reference lists do not include interviews or personal correspondence.
Instead, they can be cited where the material appears in your outline in the
following format: A. Revkin (personal communication), December 4, 2008.

Developing Your Speaking Outline

A **speaking outline** is a short outline that is intended to serve as an aid to
your performance. As described at the beginning of this chapter, your speaking outline condenses the material in your working outline. Condensing your

material encourages you to sustain eye contact with your audience while also recalling the content and structure of your speech. Rather than having a full sentence for each point, most of your speaking outline should be limited to key words and phrases that remind you of what you plan to say. The only full statements in the speaking outline should be items for which exact wording is necessary: your central idea, quotations, and transitions (Millen).

A speaking outline also can include cues for delivery. Especially for beginning speakers, these cues can remind you about aspects of your delivery that you might forget during the excitement of your performance. It is easy to get so focused on the content of your speech that you forget about effective delivery techniques. Think of the speaking outline as a guide for both the verbal and nonverbal dimensions of your speech.

Plan to generate your speaking outline *after* you have completed your working outline and *before* you produce any note cards. A working outline ensures that you have included everything you need for the speech in one document and have placed it in the order in which you intend it to occur. Then the speaking outline can be based on that complete document. A speaking outline can be useful even if you prefer to use note cards when you present your speech. A speaking outline will give you an idea of how much space you will need for notes. Then you can create cards that are coordinated with the various units of your speech. For example, you might need only one card for everything under your first main point, but a single quotation might require a full card by itself.

Although speaking outlines tend to be more personalized and informal than a working outline, there are some basic guidelines that will make your outline more effective. For starters, remember the three guidelines from chapter 3: be brief, make your outline legible, and use it to enhance your delivery. The rest of this section expands on these guidelines, giving detailed tips for each.

Be Brief

Creating an effective speaking outline is a balancing act. Your speaking outline needs to preserve key elements from your working outline so that your speech is clear to you, but it should not include so much detail that you are lured into reading your notes rather than giving a speech. This balance between clarity and brevity should guide your construction of the speaking outline.

First, try to *condense sentences to their bare minimum*—a few words that capture the overall idea. You might look at the subject and verb of the sentence, the subject and object, and the key descriptive words. Compare how these elements from a working outline could be condensed for a speaking outline.

Working Outline	**Speaking Outline**
Franklin College was the first coeducational college in the United States.	Franklin: 1st coed college in U.S.
Many alumnae of women's colleges have challenged their schools' decisions to become a coeducational school (Powers).	Alumnae challenged coed decisions.

Where possible, *use abbreviations and symbols* that make sense to you in order to condense your outline. This also preserves space on note cards.

Working Outline	**Speaking Outline**
Declining enrollments have led many single-sex schools to switch to coeducational schools.	↓ enroll. → single-sex schools coed
One issue is whether the academic experience at women's colleges is better than that at coed schools.	Issue: Acad exp. women's coll > than coed?

At first, you might not want to use a great many symbols. They can be confusing if they are not readily familiar to you. Be sure to rehearse with your outline multiple times so that you can immediately recognize those abbreviations and symbols as you present your speech.

In balancing brevity and clarity, err on the side of clarity when the exact wording of a sentence is important. Your central idea, certain types of supporting material, and transitions are parts of your speech that typically require precise wording. You may want to italicize or highlight these items so you can see that you need to give close attention to the wording. Statistics are one good instance of this.

    A. The switch to coed has ↑ applications and class size

        1. Wells College

            a. *From 2000-2004, Wells averaged 396 applications annually.*

            b. 2005: 1,012 apps (Jaschik).

        2. Immaculata College

            a. 1st Catholic coll for women, in Philly

            b. *The # of men making tuition deposits for Immaculata's first year of coed was > the total freshman class two years prior* (Jaschik).

Direct quotations also need exact wording as well as an attribution statement or lead-in to the quotation itself. This ensures that you share the relevant citation material with your audience. The next chapter, on delivery, will explain how to include this information easily during your speech.

Make Your Outline Legible

Look back to the example note cards on page 47 in Chapter 2. If you plan to use your speaking outline when you present your speech, it needs to be just as legible as note cards. Your outline should be easily readable from a distance, it should use a large point size for your font, and it should have plenty of spacing between lines.

For a speech that has several subpoints and lots of supporting material, it is important to follow the indentation pattern from your working outline. Besides helping you to maintain logical relationships in your working outline, the indentation pattern serves an important practical purpose in your speaking outline: *It helps you to find your place in the speech as quickly as possible.* The indentation pattern does this by keeping main points to the left and supporting material to the right. So if you have finished discussing some supporting material and cannot remember the next main point, you will know where to look on the page.

LEGIBILITY
Whether you use an outline, note cards, or a teleprompter, large print is necessary for your speaking outline.

Use the Outline to Enhance Your Delivery

Keeping your speaking outline brief and legible while preserving the key elements of the speech will maximize the positive use of an outline. Brevity and legibility will keep you from reading your speech or stumbling over writing that you cannot decipher. In addition, these tips can help you to prepare a speaking outline that enhances your delivery:

- *Include previews, summaries, and transitions* in your speaking outline. By setting these off from the rest of the speech and writing them out as full sentences, you can avoid the awkward pauses that often interrupt the flow of a speech.

- *Add delivery cues* to your speaking outline. While the other guidelines for speaking outlines focus mostly on phrasing your speech's content, cues bring attention to the nonverbal aspects of your delivery. All the elements of delivery that were described in chapter 2 can be flagged by delivery cues on your outline. Volume, rate, and pauses are among the most common delivery elements for beginning speakers to identify on speaking outlines and note cards. For example, if you are concerned that your voice might not be heard easily in the room, you could add a cue of [LOUDER] or [SPEAK UP!] at the top of each page of your outline. If you tend to speak at a fast rate, you could insert the cue [SLOW DOWN] throughout the outline. You can also use cues to remind you of delivery changes at a specific point. For example, many speakers will cue a [PAUSE] at the end of a section or will <u>underline</u>, *italicize,* or CAPITALIZE a very important word or phrase.

- *Avoid using the outline as a prop.* It can be extremely distracting when speakers make gestures while holding the outline. The paper inevitably makes noise, and especially if there are multiple sheets, there is the risk of dropping the sheets. When you produce your speaking outline, then, limit the number of sheets you have, staple them together in sequential order, number the pages, and keep them on the lectern or steady in front of you as you are delivering the speech.

CASE CONCLUSION

Cole's Speech on Alternative Fuels

During the research phase, Cole learned that there are significant differences between the various alternative fuels. It was difficult to compare them directly, and since his assignment was to give an informative speech, he wanted to be sure that he avoided making one sound better than the other. As he thought more about his organizational strategy, he decided that his audience probably would benefit most from hearing about the advantages and disadvantages of each type of fuel. So he kept the topical order for his main points and then adapted the key issues pattern to create three subpoints under each. The main points would be supported by (A) a description of the fuel, (B) evidence about its advantages, and (C) evidence about its disadvantages. With these points figured out, Cole was ready to outline his entire speech.

SAMPLE OUTLINE

Cole's Working Outline

FUELING OUR FUTURE

Cole first states his specific purpose and central idea. Then he can refer back to these as he develops his outline.

Specific purpose: To share information with my audience about the advantages and disadvantages of alternative fuels.

Central idea: Three major alternative vehicle fuels—ethanol, natural gas, and hydrogen—each have important advantages and disadvantages.

INTRODUCTION

Cole's introduction starts with a familiar symbol that is related to his topic.

I. (Arousing Audience Attention)
   Remember that shiny Prius you parked next to this morning? They seem to be everywhere today. The popularity of the Prius is the first sign of things to come.

II. (Demonstrating Public Significance/Personal Relevance)

As oil supplies dwindle and awareness of climate change grows, more and more people are looking for alternative fuel sources for their cars. As a society, we are struggling to figure out the best path for our energy future. And the decisions we make about fuels today will have a direct impact on the kind of cars you will be able to buy in a few years.

This part of the intro-duction shows how an issue with public significance has rel-evance on a personal level, too.

III. (Enhancing Your Ethos)

Cars have been a hobby of mine for as long as I can remember. So the growth in alternative fuel sources has been very interesting to me, and I have been reading and researching this topic for several months. While I'm interested in how these alternative fuel sources will affect the design of cars, all of us should be interested in how these fuels might affect our transportation choices, our pocketbooks, and our environment.

Cole highlights his own interest in the topic as well as his efforts to learn more about it.

Here, Cole suggests that he is speaking to address the audience's concerns, not just his own interests.

IV. (Stating Your Central Idea)

Today, then, I want to discuss three potential fuel sources for cars and in-form you about the advantages and disadvantages of each.

The central idea hints at the organizational pattern of Cole's speech.

V. (Preparing Your Audience for the Rest of the Speech)

In the rest of my speech, I will focus on three major alternative fuels: ethanol, which can be used as a direct substitute for gasoline; natural gas, one of the cleanest fossil fuels available; and hydrogen, the most abundant element in the universe.

His preview identifies the three main points and an important idea about each that he will reinforce later.

BODY

I. The first alternative fuel is ethanol.

A. Ethanol is essentially alcohol.

1. Ethanol is produced by fermenting sugars with yeast.

2. For fuel purposes, corn and sugar cane are the two primary sources of sugar for ethanol production.

3. Ethanol can be blended with standard gasoline or used directly as fuel.

Cole sets off his first main point in bold.

B. Ethanol blends have several benefits.

1. First, ethanol is compatible with existing car engines.

2. Second, ethanol blends reduce the amount of gasoline used.

3. Third, ethanol blends also reduce emissions of pollutants, especially the greenhouse gasses that contribute to climate change

Cole uses signposts to number the benefits of ethanol.

C. However, there are some disadvantages to ethanol, too.

1. In the United States, ethanol production has diverted a significant por-tion of the corn crop, affecting food production.

a. Marianne Lavelle and Bret Schulte write in the Feb. 12, 2007, *US News & World Report* that in 2006, ethanol production required 20% of the nation's corn crop, more than all the corn Americans consumed as food

b. This has had a significant impact on food prices.

The benefits and disadvantages are coordinate points on his outline.

The opening phrases of supporting statements a and b show relationships between the ideas under subpoint 2.

2. More important, the energy balance of corn ethanol is poor.

    a. In other words, the amount of energy we get from ethanol is not much more than the amount of energy needed to produce it.

    b. As a result, many researchers are looking to produce ethanol from sources other than corn to improve on the energy balance.

The transition is set off from the rest of the outline and reinforces his overall organizational pattern.

(Transition: Since ethanol has strengths as well as weaknesses, it is worth exploring other alternative fuels, such as natural gas.)

II. Natural gas is a second alternative fuel.

    A. Natural gas is a mixture of hydrocarbons.

       1. Natural gas is primarily composed of methane.

       2. Most natural gas is extracted from underground wells, although it can also be saved from landfills and sewage plants.

       3. Natural gas can be distributed in either liquid or gaseous form.

    B. Natural gas has two important benefits.

       1. It burns extremely cleanly.

Subpoints B and C show how additional supporting points are subordinate in the outline.

          a. Among light-duty vehicles, natural gas reduces carbon monoxide emissions at least 90%.

          b. In fact, the EPA calls the natural gas Honda Civic GX the cleanest internal-combustion vehicle on Earth.

       2. Most natural gas is available domestically.

       3. Because of these two benefits, some experts see natural gas as the best "transition" to hydrogen-powered fuel cell vehicles.

Note how Cole uses "However" to signal the shift from advantages to disadvantages. He did this in the ethanol section, too.

    C. However, natural gas also has some key drawbacks.

       1. Storage efficiency is one of the primary challenges related to natural gas vehicles.

          a. Storage cylinders are large, which means less space for passengers.

          b. Even with large cylinders, the driving range of the Civic GX is only 220–250 miles, according to Honda.com.

       2. The driving range problem is made worse by the fact that natural gas refueling stations are few and far between.

       3. Finally, like gasoline, natural gas is still a nonrenewable resource.

(Transition: Now that we have examined two gasoline substitutes, let's turn our attention to a fuel that would move us into an era of electric cars.)

III. Hydrogen is a third major alternative fuel.

    A. Hydrogen is one of the basic building blocks of the universe.

       1. It is rarely found alone but is present in many compounds.

       2. These compounds must be broken apart to get hydrogen.

          a. Energy from other sources is used to break hydrogen off from compounds such as water and methane.

b. The hydrogen then serves as a carrier of this energy.

c. In cars, fuel cells use the hydrogen to create an electrical current that propels your car.

B. Several benefits follow from hydrogen use.

   1. First, hydrogen is abundant. Unlike gas, we are not going to run out.

   2. Second, it is efficient. According to the DOE, hydrogen vehicles have the potential to be 2–3 times more efficient than gasoline-powered vehicles.

   3. Third, it is clean. The only emission would be water, as hydrogen interacts with oxygen in the atmosphere.

C. In spite of these benefits, hydrogen is far from a perfect solution.

   1. The National Research Council reported four major challenges as of 2004.

   2. In terms of technology, fuel cells are not yet small enough to be feasible in regular cars.

   3. In terms of infrastructure, there is no distribution system in place.

   4. In terms of production, the process is extremely inefficient.

      a. The NRC report highlights costs and wasted energy in the current methods of producing hydrogen.

      b. "These technology pathways for hydrogen production make electricity, which is converted to hydrogen, which is later converted by a fuel cell back to electricity. These steps add costs and energy losses that are particularly significant" (p. 2).

   5. In terms of the environment, the coal needed to produce hydrogen would create massive amounts of greenhouse gases.

Cole uses organizational markers and parallel structure to clearly identify each of the benefits.

Cole has incorporated specific pieces of supporting material from external sources under each of his main points.

CONCLUSION

I. (Reinforce Your Central Idea)

In these few minutes, I have tried to show you that many alternatives are being explored for powering our vehicles. Current vehicles can use ethanol blends, reducing gasoline use and noxious emissions in the process. Natural gas burns even more cleanly and could facilitate the transition to the third alternative I discussed, hydrogen.

Cole reinforces his main idea and also reminds his audience of the relationship between the three fuels.

II. (Indicate the End of the Speech)

No doubt you will hear more and more about these options in the coming years. I hope this brief introduction to alternative fuels will encourage you to seek more information about them. While each fuel has drawbacks and challenges, they all present ways to wean us from our "addiction to oil."

Cole ends by calling for further engagement from his audience.

WORKS CITED

"2008 Honda Civic GX Natural Gas Vehicle." *Honda.* Accessed February 1, 2008. Available at http://automobiles.honda.com/civic-gx/refueling.aspx

Here, Cole lists only the sources that were actually cited in the speech. In some instances, you may want to provide a list of all works consulted, especially if your audience is likely to want more information about your topic.

Lavelle, Marianne, and Bret Schulte. "Is Ethanol the Answer?" *U.S. News & World Report* 4 Feb. 2007: 30–9.

National Research Council and National Academy of Engineering. *The Hydrogen Economy: Opportunities, Costs, Barriers, and R&D Needs*. Washington: National Academies Press, 2004.

U.S. Department of Energy. "Hydrogen as an Alternative Fuel." *US DOE Energy Efficiency and Renewable Energy*. Accessed February 1, 2008. Available at http://www.eere.energy.gov/afdc/fuels/hydrogen_alternative.html

SAMPLE OUTLINE

Cole's Speaking Outline

FUELING OUR FUTURE

[Keep it SLOW, and full of ENERGY]

INTRODUCTION

Cole gives himself a reminder of goals for his delivery of the speech.

I. Remember that shiny Prius . . . Everywhere today. Sign of things to come.

The introduction condenses this portion of the working outline while still keeping many key words.

II. As oil supplies ↓, awareness of climate Δ↑, people look for alt. fuel.

    Society struggling to figure out best path for energy future

    Fuel decisions today have direct impact on cars you'll buy.

He eliminates the functions from his working outline and includes only actual content or delivery cues.

III. Cars a hobby of mine

    Growth in alt fuel interesting; read, rsch for months

    While I'm interested how alt fuel sources affect car design, all of us . . . transp. choices, $, environ.

The central idea is still included as a complete sentence.

IV. Today, then, I want to discuss three potential fuel sources for cars and inform you about the advantages and disadvantages of each.

Visually, the spacing here reminds him to emphasize each point and to pause between them.

V. Rest of speech: three major alt fuels:

    ethanol, used as direct sub for gas

    natural gas, one of cleanest foss-fuels

    hydrogen, most abundant element in universe.

    [PAUSE]

BODY

I. The first alternative fuel is ethanol.

    A. E = alcohol.

        1. Produced by fermenting sugars with yeast.

        2. For fuel, corn & sugar cane sources

        3. E blended w/gas or used directly.

B. E blends benefits.

    1st, Compatible w/existing engines.

    2nd, ↓ gas used.

    3rd: ↓ emissions of pollutants, esp. GHG → climate Δ

C. However, E disadvantages.

    E production has diverted signif portion of corn crop, affecting prod.

        a. *Marianne Lavelle and Bret Schulte write in the Feb. 12, 2007* US News & World Report *that in 2006, ethanol production required 20% of the nation's corn crop, more than all the corn Americans consumed as food.*

        b. Significant ↑ food $

    More important, energy balance poor.

        a. In other words, the amount of energy we get from ethanol is not much more than the amount of energy needed to produce it.

        b. rschers looking to other sources to improve energy bal.

[SLOW!!!! PAUSE here before transition]

(Transition: Since ethanol has strengths as well as weaknesses, it is worth exploring other alternative fuels, such as natural gas.)

II. Natural gas is a second alternative fuel.

A. Natural gas is a mixture of hydrocarbons.

    NG primarily methane.

    Most NG extracted from underground wells; also from landfills, sewage

    NG distributed liquid or gas.

B. NG 2 benefits.

    It burns extremely cleanly.

        a. Among light-duty vehicles, ↓ CO 90%.

        b. EPA calls the natural gas Honda Civic GX the cleanest internal-combustion vehicle on earth.

    Most NG domestic.

    Because of these two benefits, some experts see natural gas as the best "transition" to hydrogen-powered fuel cell vehicles.

C. NG drawbacks.

    Storage efficiency primary challenge.

        a. Storage cyl's large—less space for passengers.

        b. Even w/large, driving range Civic only 220-250 (Honda.com).

    Range worse b/c few refueling stations.

    Like gas, NG nonrenewable.

[PAUSE . . .]

(Transition: Now that we have examined two gasoline substitutes, let's turn our attention to a fuel that would move us into an era of electric cars.)

This speaking outline uses symbols and shorthand notation that is familiar to this speaker.

Cole italicizes material from outside sources to remind him about exact wording and citations.

He writes out spots where precise wording is important.

Cole continues to give himself delivery directions and full sentences for transitions.

III. Hydrogen is a third major alternative fuel.

A. H basic building blocks

Rarely found alone, present in compounds.

Compounds must be broken to get H.

   a. Energy from other sources is used to break H from H_2O, methane.

   b. H as carrier of energy.

   c. In cars, fuel cells create elec, propels your car.

B. H benefits.

   1st: H abundant. Unlike gasoline.

   2nd: efficient. DOE: hydrogen fuel cell vehicles have the potential to be 2–3 times more efficient than gasoline-powered vehicles.

   3rd: clean. Only emission H2O.

C. In spite of bens, H imperfect.

   NRC 4 major challenges as of 2004.

   6. Tech: fuel cells not small enough for regular cars.

   7. Infra: no distribution system.

   8. Prod: process inefficient.

      a. NRC report highlights $, wasted energy in current method.

      b. *"These technology pathways for hydrogen production make electricity, which is converted to hydrogen, which is later converted by a fuel cell back to electricity. These steps add costs and energy losses that are particularly significant"* (p. 2).

   9. Env: coal to produce H → massive GHG.

CONCLUSION

I. In these few minutes, tried to show alternatives.

Current vehicles can use E blends, ↓ gas & nox emissions.

NG burns more cleanly, could facilitate trans. to 3rd alt: H.

II. You will hear more about options.

Hope brief intro will encourage you to seek more info.

Each has +/−, they all present ways to wean us from our addiction to oil.

[SMILE — *"Thank you!"*]

Summary

DEVELOPING YOUR WORKING OUTLINE

- A working outline assembles all the details of your speech in one document.

- The working outline is written in full sentences and includes all the substantive content and organizational markers of your speech as well as a title, statement of the specific purpose and central idea, and a reference list.

- A crucial aspect of assembling a good working outline is applying a consistent outline form that follows the principles of coordination, subordination, adequacy, and consistency.

DEVELOPING YOUR SPEAKING OUTLINE

- A speaking outline condenses the content of the working outline into notes that aid your memory and allow you to maintain eye contact with your audience.

- The speaking outline should be constructed directly from your working outline so that you are sure to preserve all the key elements of your speech. Brevity and legibility should guide your construction of the speaking outline.

- Speaking outlines can include delivery cues to help you attend to the nonverbal dimensions of your presentation. Be sure to rehearse with your speaking outline so that you can test its adequacy for your actual presentation.

Key Terms

working outline, p. 268
coordination, p. 271
subordination, p. 272
adequacy, p. 272
consistency, p. 272
organizational marker, p. 274

signpost, p. 275
internal preview, p. 276
internal summary, p. 276
transition, p. 277
speaking outline, p. 280

Comprehension

1. How is a working outline different from a speaking outline?

2. What is the difference between coordination and subordination?

3. If you divide any point in your speech, how many subpoints should it have?

4. What are some examples of signposts?

5. How might a transition combine an internal preview and an internal summary?

6. Why should you generate your speaking outline after your working outline?

7. What types of material should be written out word-for-word in speaking outlines?

Application

1. In groups of four classmates, share your working outlines, and examine them using the principles of good outline form. Have one person focus on a single principle for each outline: coordination, subordination, adequacy, and consistency.

2. Examine a recent high point of political speech making, such as an inaugural address or State of the Union Address. In the speech, try to identify examples of the organizational markers described in this chapter: signposts, internal previews, internal summaries, and transitions.

3. After creating your working and speaking outlines for an upcoming speech, trade your working outline with one of your classmates. Create a speaking outline for your classmate's speech, and then compare it to your speaking outlines. You may get some good ideas by observing how others try to condense key ideas.

Presenting Your Speech

This chapter is intended to help you:

- Understand different methods of delivering a speech
- Incorporate external sources effectively in your speech
- Avoid plagiarism
- Construct and present visuals in ways that enhance your speech
- Handle the question-and-answer period that follows your speech

By now, you recognize that preparing an effective speech involves many steps before you actually present your speech. The final step of rehearsal is crucial to your success. Especially for beginning speakers, practicing your speech ahead of time and focusing on unique elements of oral presentation can make the difference between a speech that is good on paper and a speech that has a positive impact on an audience.

You encountered some of the fundamentals of good delivery in chapter 2. Look back to the tips on building confidence, constructing your notes, and using your voice and body effectively. This chapter builds on those fundamentals by taking a broader look at presentation and adding new delivery skills to your

CASE SCENARIO

Julie's Speech on the Central Asia Institute

Julie had been assigned Greg Mortenson's book *Three Cups of Tea* during freshman orientation and found it fascinating. She had the opportunity to hear Mortenson speak about the Central Asia Institute's school-building program in Afghanistan and Pakistan, and she thought that she should share this information with her classmates. Some of them had read the book, but she wanted to provide them with more context about what was happening in those countries and show them what this work looked like on the ground. She knew that she would need additional sources and some visuals to make this work.

repertoire. The chapter begins by discussing presentation techniques appropriate for different public speaking situations. Then it focuses on three specific skills needed for longer classroom speeches and speeches in the public sphere: incorporating sources, using visual aids, and handling questions. ■

Delivery Methods

As with every other aspect of public speaking, your choice of delivery methods depends on the rhetorical situation. Some situations require a level of preparation that allows you speak in a conversational style with your audience. Other situations demand that you speak with virtually no advance preparation. Yet others encourage careful attention to every word of your speech. Familiarity with four delivery methods can help you to adapt appropriately to various speaking situations: extemporaneous speaking, impromptu speaking, manuscript speaking, and memorized speaking.

Extemporaneous Speaking

In most public speaking situations, audiences appreciate listening to a speech that is focused and easy to follow, but they also appreciate speakers who are truly present in the situation and not just reading or reciting a canned speech. The challenge for you as a speaker, then, is to achieve a level of familiarity with your speech that gives you the confidence to speak conversationally with your audience. This is the challenge of **extemporaneous speaking**, a delivery style that involves advance preparation and rehearsal of a speech that is neither fully written nor fully memorized.

Extemporaneous speaking will be the best delivery style for most speeches on public issues. If you are trying to inform fellow students about financial aid, you will need to prepare ahead of time so that you can explain complex financial issues simply and appear knowledgeable on the topic. Likewise, if you are trying to persuade university officials or legislators on this issue, they might not be moved if you merely read a speech. Engaging these decision makers confidently, in a more interactive way, is more likely build a sense of connection and concern about the issue.

How can you develop the skill of extemporaneous speaking? Several tips and techniques deserve attention:

- *Anticipate adjustments to your speech.* Extemporaneous speaking gives you flexibility to respond to audience feedback immediately. So think ahead about how you might adjust your speech in light of typical reactions. For example, if you are explaining a complex idea, you might want to identify a few extra ways of describing that idea in advance in case your audience appears confused. A definition, a metaphor, or additional examples all can help to clarify complex ideas.

- *Rehearse small portions of your speech.* Start rehearsal by working on a single section that develops just one main point, and then add sections to build up to rehearsing the entire speech. This technique reminds you that your goal is to reinforce main ideas in language that comes naturally rather than to memorize an exact wording of your speech. It also gives you the opportunity to experiment with some of the adjustments that were mentioned above.

- *Rehearse with an audience.* This key idea from chapter 2 bears repeating. The real way to gauge whether your speaking strikes the balance between structure and spontaneity is by getting feedback from listeners. Only listeners can tell you whether your eye contact and body movement establish **immediacy**, a perception of physical and psychological closeness between you and your audience.

- *Seek opportunities for practice.* Extemporaneous speaking occurs in many informal settings. For example, in your classes, you might be asked to initiate discussion, summarize readings or other materials, or make a position statement. These brief speaking opportunities are served well by some advance preparation, but they would come off as a little stilted if you memorized them. Use such opportunities to work on an extemporaneous speaking style.

Impromptu Speaking

Suppose it is time for a toast at your friend's wedding. Or suppose one of your instructors unexpectedly asks you to comment on how the reading assignment relates to a current issue in the news. Or suppose you are at a public lecture or business workshop and the speaker says something so outrageous that you feel compelled to respond. All of these situations call for **impromptu speaking**, which is a delivery style that relies on little or no advance preparation.

PREPARATION
Steve Jobs, the CEO of Apple, spends weeks reviewing products and takes two full days to rehearse his product launch presentations and keynote speeches at the annual MacWorld conference.

Although impromptu speeches are usually short, the basic principles and concerns of public speaking are still relevant. Consider how these principles can be adapted to impromptu speaking situations.

- *Audience.* Because you do not have time for thorough analysis, look for the most obvious connections between your audience, the topic, and the occasion. For example, in a class or a public meeting, that link might be something that a previous speaker has said.

- *Purpose and central idea.* In impromptu speaking situations, audiences expect a short speech with a single purpose and a simple central idea. You might have observed someone at a public talk who gets up to ask a question but then rambles on about all sorts of ideas for several minutes. Instead, speakers should take a few seconds to reflect on the single idea that they wish to address and limit their remarks to that idea.

- *Organization.* You also can avoid a stream-of-consciousness delivery by recalling a few simple organizational patterns. The standard introduction–body–conclusion pattern described in chapter 2 is always a good starting point. Sequential strategies for the body of the speech—chronological and spatial order, discussed in chapter 9—match natural patterns in the world that make it easy for you to stay on track. Cause-and-effect and problem–solution strategies also provide simple patterns for organizing a short speech into two main sections.

- *Supporting materials.* Even though you do not have time to conduct external research, your audience will still expect to hear material that supports your central idea. Common knowledge, your own existing knowledge of the topic, and personal experience typically serve as supporting materials for impromptu speeches. The standard toast at a wedding or other celebration comes alive with vivid personal narratives.

Finally, a few specific delivery tips can help make the experience of impromptu speaking less daunting:

- *Jot down a few notes.* If you have time to make a few notes, they can help to keep you on track. Do not be afraid to use the notes; again, audiences recognize that you are speaking off the cuff and will not mind if you check your notes occasionally.

- *Use techniques for dealing with anxiety.* Attend to your breathing, interpret your nervousness as positive energy, and carry yourself with confidence to deal with anticipatory anxiety.

- *Keep it brief.* This tip can help you to alleviate the fear that you will forget something or go blank; during your speech, it can keep you from rambling. A short impromptu speech that makes one point in a compelling way is far more effective than a longer, unfocused speech.

Manuscript Speaking

Another form of delivery merits discussion, although the situations for it are less common than situations for extemporaneous and impromptu speaking. **Manuscript speaking** involves giving a speech from a written text that has been prepared in advance. Speakers use manuscripts to ensure precision and accuracy when the consequences of vagueness or misunderstanding are high. A judge's instructions to jurors, for example, must clearly explain how to apply the law correctly to a particular case.

However, while it is appropriate for certain situations, *manuscript speaking should not be used as the default mode of public speaking.* Unfortunately, many beginning speakers do just that. They might be unfamiliar with how to produce effective notes, or they might be anxious about speaking extemporaneously. It might seem reasonable to have all the words written down. But inevitably, the script becomes a security blanket, and the speaker's delivery actually gets worse—face buried in the script, reading words rather than communicating with an audience.

The challenge of manuscript speaking, then, is to embody the spontaneity of extemporaneous speaking even though your words are right in front of you. This can take as much practice as extemporaneous speaking, if not more! Consequently, manuscript speaking takes a special set of techniques:

- *Make sure your manuscript is easy to read.* Use a large font, including both uppercase and lowercase letters, and use margins, indentation, and spacing that makes it easy to identify transitions and changes in thought.

- *Identify natural breaks.* Look for points where you can move smoothly between checking your script and making eye contact with your audience.

- *Give special attention to eye contact during rehearsal.* Your listeners can help you to identify when your eye contact is strong and when your movement between script and audience gets distracting.

- *Be mindful of vocal variety and body movements to enliven your speech.* Even if you have good eye contact, remember that effective speeches are fully embodied—given by real people whose energy and feelings are displayed through their voices and bodies. Focusing on these aspects will keep your speech from being merely words on a page.

PUBLIC SPOTLIGHT

Jon Favreau

Even if you are not regularly in the public spotlight, there are other ways in which you can put your public speaking skills to good work in the public sphere. Imagine getting an internship in Congress and suddenly finding yourself writing speeches for a U.S. Senator. Then within a few years, at the age of 27, you are writing speeches for the President of the United States. That is the unexpected career path of Jon Favreau, the chief speechwriter for President Barack Obama.

While he was in college, Favreau was involved with community service projects and landed an internship with Senator John Kerry (Pierce). When Kerry ran unsuccessfully for President in 2004, Favreau stepped in as deputy speechwriter after some of his fellow staffers read the speech he had given at his college commencement (Saslow). After that election, Obama recruited Favreau as a speechwriter, and they have worked together since then.

Many speakers in the public spotlight rely on a **ghostwriter**, or professional speech writer, as a way to manage their time. For example, for a major speech, Obama and Favreau have a conversation about the main themes and direction of the speech, and then Favreau works with his team and Obama to craft and revise the speech.

"What I do is to sit with him for half an hour," Favreau explains. "He talks and I type everything he says. I reshape it, I write. He writes, he reshapes it. That's how we get a finished product. It's a great way to write speeches. A lot of times, you write something, you hand it in, it gets hacked by advisers, it gets to the candidate and then it gets sent back to you. This is a much more intimate way to work" (Wolffe).

In professional and political settings, the use of ghostwriters is widely accepted. Audiences are well aware that prominent figures have staff members who write speeches for them. In the classroom, however, where the purpose is to learn the basic techniques of public speaking, having someone else write your speeches would be a clear-cut instance of plagiarism. Take the opportunity to learn and practice the techniques in this book—it just might land you a job as a ghostwriter.

Memorized Speaking

A fourth delivery method is **memorized speaking**, or giving a speech word for word without any notes. Presenting memorized speeches has been a part of speech instruction and competition since the earliest days of rhetorical training in ancient Greece. Certainly, memorized speaking has some advantages: It gives you the opportunity for maximum eye contact, and it allows you to devote the most attention to the performance aspects of speaking. Memorized delivery of a speech can be an impressive feat.

However, like manuscript speaking, memorized speeches can lack spontaneity. With such an emphasis on performance, they can seem more like acting than an attempt to communicate with an audience. And you always run the risk of forgetting your words. Consequently, even if you have memorized your speech, you might do well to treat it more like an extemporaneous speech to give you a little more flexibility.

The advantages of this can be seen in situations in which a memorized speech is used. Perhaps you are making a fund-raising pitch for a campus organization or trying to raise awareness about a public issue, and you need to give an informative speech on these topics to several different audiences. In these situations, it is necessary to follow your script to get the details right and to present a consistent message about your organization or topic. As long as you can do that, then a bit of improvisation and adaptation to particular audiences can help to make that memorized portion of your speech even more effective.

Incorporating Sources

The rest of this chapter looks at three skills that often pose challenges in presenting a speech. The first skill, incorporating sources, is especially important in classroom speeches, which often require support from multiple external sources. But speakers in the public sphere benefit from using external sources, too. Consider this excerpt from a speech by Barack Obama during the 2008 presidential campaign:

> If we want to keep up with China or Europe, we can't settle for crumbling roads and bridges, aging water and sewer pipes, and faltering electrical grids that cost us billions to blackouts, repairs and travel delays. It's gotten so bad that the American Society of Civil Engineers gave our national infrastructure a "D" (Obama).

Even a brief mention of an external source can strengthen your speech. If you are informing a community group about human rights conditions in a foreign country, for example, they will want to know whether that information comes from personal experience, the report of a human rights organization, or the statement of a government official.

In the classroom, most instructors will probably expect more citation information than what is in the excerpt from Obama's speech. But by learning how to cite sources thoroughly during your classroom speaking experience, you will be prepared to include whatever amount of detail is appropriate for the varied situations of the public sphere.

Avoiding Plagiarism

Incorporating and citing sources effectively will help you to avoid plagiarism. In the context of public speaking, **plagiarism** is the use of another person's words or ideas in a speech without citing the source. You should check your college's student conduct code to find out how it defines and determines plagiarism. But one common distinction is the difference between wholesale plagiarism and partial plagiarism.

Wholesale Plagiarism **Wholesale plagiarism** occurs when a speaker reproduces someone else's words as his or her entire speech. Many scenarios can count as wholesale plagiarism; the following true examples are just a few possibilities:

- A student is scheduled to give a speech in a few days and finds out that her topic is the same one that a friend of hers used when he took the class last semester. She gets her friend's outline, makes a copy, and then gives a speech based on that outline.

- A student is scheduled to speak in class the next day and has done little work on his speech. He goes online and buys a research paper and then rearranges it into a speech outline.

- A student and her roommate are interested in the same topic. They run out of time when it comes to putting together their speeches, so they stay up late one night to create a single speech. Both present the exact same speech in their respective public speaking classes the next day.

Each of these scenarios illustrates wholesale plagiarism. Rather than coming up with distinctive ideas that are based on careful audience analysis and topic research, these speakers passed off the work of others as if it were entirely their own.

You might notice that each of these students appears to have procrastinated. Instead of developing their speech over time, some speakers will scramble at the last minute for anything that they can pass off as their own speech. Therefore, the best strategy for avoiding plagiarism is to start working on your speech as soon as possible so that you can truly invent a speech that is your own.

Partial Plagiarism **Partial plagiarism** is the use of a specific piece of supporting material without citation. Although it is more limited than wholesale plagiarism, partial plagiarism is still a serious concern in the classroom, especially if it is intentional. There are several common situations that fall under the heading of partial plagiarism:

- A speaker fails to identify the author or source of a piece of supporting material.

- A speaker fails to designate someone else's exact words as a quotation.

- A speaker gives a **paraphrase**, a restatement of someone else's ideas or opinions, but passes it off as the speaker's own viewpoint.

In all of these situations, the original source is not getting the credit. Pieces of supporting material and the exact words of someone else need to be linked to their original author. And even though paraphrases are your own words, the original thinking is really the work of someone else, so that person needs to be credited, too.

How do you avoid partial plagiarism? If you followed the suggestions in chapter 6 and have compiled thorough notes about your research, full citation information and exact wording of quotations will give you what you need to cite your sources. At this point, you are ready to apply specific techniques for incorporating source citations smoothly in your presentation.

Citing Sources in Your Speech

Citing sources in a speech is far different from citing sources in a research paper. Readers of a paper can go to the footnotes or reference list to check sources. But in a speech, listeners do not have that luxury. Therefore, it is your responsibility to provide that information in the speech itself, and it is your challenge to do it clearly.

Speakers cite a source by crafting an **attribution statement**, a phrase or sentence that orally designates a source of information in your speech. As with other aspects of public speaking, attribution statements are necessary on the grounds of ethics and effectiveness. Ethically, it is imperative to give credit for the work that others have done; failure to do so is plagiarism. Pragmatically, attribution enhances your ethos. It shows your audience that you have done your homework and that you are not just making up things to suit your purpose. It also allows the audience to retrieve the information if they are interested in your topic. So don't think of attribution as a chore; it's an easy way to improve the audience's perception of you and your speech.

Use ADP: Author, Date, Publication No matter how you actually phrase the attribution statement, a full citation must include three key pieces of information: author (who said it), date (when it was said), and publication (where it is located). You can remember the elements of an attribution statement by the acronym "ADP" and call it the ADP method.

AUTHOR	**DATE**	**PUBLICATION**
(who said it/wrote it)	(when it was said or published)	(where it is located)

As Condoleezza Rice stated in the July/August 2008 issue of *Foreign Affairs* . . .
    (author)   (date)   (publication)

On June 26, George Will wrote in the *Washington Post* that . . .
  (date)   (author)   (publication)

As these examples show, the order of these elements does not matter. Use them in a different order for variety in your speech, or arrange them strategically to emphasize or compare certain features of your sources:

A senior lawyer for the privacy group Electronic Frontier Foundation, Kurt Opsahl, was quoted in the July 4 *New York Times* as saying . . .

But Viacom issued a statement on their company website on July 7 that read . . .

This example places the author or organization first in each attribution as a way to highlight the two contending organizations. You might place the date first if the chronology is an important aspect of your speech.

Highlight Exact Words When you are quoting someone's exact words, the most explicit way to signal those words is to say "quote" and "end quote" (not "unquote") at the beginning and end of the quotation. This distinguishes the source's words from your own words. Maintaining this distinction is important for setting off your own interpretation of the source's words (as you will see below), and it is especially important if you are criticizing or disagree with the source's words.

In addition, consider using special formatting to remind you to treat these words somewhat differently from the rest of your speech. A speaking outline or manuscript with direct quotations might look like this:

> On June 30 Noah Garrison, an attorney for the Natural Resources Defense Council, was quoted in the *Los Angeles Times* stating that:
>
> QUOTE, "The problems that we have in this country with beach water contamination in general are not getting better." ENDQUOTE

Some instructors may ask you to use extended pauses or vocal changes to signal quoted material, rather than constantly saying quote and end quote. (Check with your instructor about which techniques you should use.) If you are required to do this, be aware that it takes some practice to use these techniques to clearly distinguish your own words from others' words.

Use Creative Lead-Ins As you become comfortable with the elements of attribution statements, you can try out more creative ways of giving credit than the typical "according to . . ." lead-ins. For example, consider how the name of the author could be incorporated into an attribution statement:

> This point is verified by _____, who claimed _____ put it well when she said . . .
>
> What causes this situation? One answer to that question is provided by _____ when he writes that . . .

A well-developed lead-in will weave together all the relevant attribution information seamlessly so that the attribution statement feels like an organic part of the speech and not an abrupt shift:

> The latest Gallup poll, cited in the February 10 issue of *Newsweek*, reveals . . .
>
> How did this issue come to the public's attention? Let's look back to Ms. Gerberding's October 2007 testimony before the Senate Environment and Public Works Committee, when she asserted . . .
>
> The broader picture about housing can be found by consulting the 2009 Statistical Abstract of the United States, which shows . . .

Interpreting Sources

After you cite your sources, it is important to interpret those sources for your audience. In this context, interpreting your source simply means *explaining* the meaning of a piece of supporting material and *connecting* that material to the main point that it supports.

Explain Supporting Material Explaining your supporting material involves summarizing or paraphrasing it so that your audience has an additional, alternative way of understanding that information. Even if your supporting material seems straightforward, remember that your audience will be hearing these words for the first and only time. Following up with an explanation is a helpful form of redundancy. Some categories of supporting material are especially in need of explanation.

Statistics Numbers often need explanation to be meaningful to an audience. For example, you might explain statistics with a statement that *clarifies the broader trend* that they represent. Take a look at this extended excerpt from testimony by Dr. Martha Cantu, Director for the University of Texas–Pan American GEAR UP Project, which provides educational services to middle school students. Dr. Cantu is interpreting the results of a survey for Congressional representatives:

> Of the 7800 students surveyed, 94% reported that they would like to obtain a college degree. I remind you that these are 8th grade students that have already formed an aspiration to graduate from college. Of parents surveyed, 99% of them indicated that they want their children to obtain a college degree.
>
> These are compelling numbers. They show the passion for education shared by Hispanic parents and children that are traditionally underrepresented in colleges and universities in our nation (Cantu).

In the first paragraph, Cantu provides two statistics as supporting material. In the second paragraph, she explains their meaning by saying that they are indicative of an underlying passion for education. Her explanation reinforces the idea that there is a widespread desire for college education among Hispanic parents and children.

Another common way to explain a statistic as supporting material is to *translate or compare it* to something that is more familiar to your audience. Sukhinder S. Cassidy, Vice President of Asia-Pacific & Latin America Operations for Google translated a statistic about cost efficiency in computer disk prices by showing what that level of efficiency would look like in relation to gas mileage:

> So disk prices have come down some 3.6 million times since 1982. To give you some context, if gas mileage improved that much, one gallon could take you two thousand times around the earth as it sits here today if you saw the same improvements in gasoline pricing as we do in the cost of disk space (Cassidy).

Here, Cassidy states the 3.6 million statistic and then translates that into the realm of gas mileage. In her next few sentences, she uses a similar strategy to speculate about the future:

By another interesting measure, think about your iPod or for many of you whatever that MP3 Player may be, that sits in the palm of your hand today. Today it holds something around ten thousand songs—the average iPod. If we continue at the cost of storage decreasing at the rate it has historically done since the early or mid Eighties, by 2014 that same device will store a full year of video. Fast-forward to 2016, it will be able to store all commercial music ever produced. So that point, you know, less than ten years from now you may be able to sit there and literally every song you could conceive of is in the palm of your hand and you simply have to choose what you would listen to (Cassidy).

Instead of providing raw statistics about gigabytes or rates of change, Cassidy goes straight to the numbers that will matter to his audience: how much video, how many songs. Those statistics are far more meaningful for a general audience.

Quotation Occasionally, speakers will use quotations not because they are particularly eloquent, but because they come from a respected expert or provide a unique perspective on a topic. Then it is the speaker's job to *rephrase and simplify* the quotation so that it is easier to understand. For example, at a conference on media reform, Bill Moyers rephrased a quotation from a scholar in a simpler way:

> The patriarch of your movement warned a generation ago of what was coming. In his magisterial book *Media Monopoly* Ben Bagdikian wrote: "The result of the overwhelming power of relatively narrow corporate ideologies has been the creation of widely established political and economic illusions with little visible contradictions in the media to which a majority of the population is exclusively exposed." In other words, what we need to know to make democracy work for all Americans is compromised by media institutions deeply embedded in the power structures of society (Moyers).

Moyers summarizes this quotation in about half the length of the original and phrases it in a way that emphasizes its importance for the audience ("what we need to know").

Explaining your supporting material is an especially important skill to master for effective extemporaneous speaking. If your listeners appear confused, you might need to restate or rephrase evidence in your own words to ensure that they understand that material.

Connect Supporting Material to Your Main Point It is critical to connect that material to the larger point that you are trying to make. Even if your supporting material does not need much explanation, listeners always want to know how supporting material is relevant to your main point. Certain types of material often need this connection.

Statistics Earlier in the chapter, you read an excerpt of Dr. Cantu's speech that explained survey results. She went on to introduce additional evidence and then connected all of this supporting material to her larger point:

> Clearly aspirations are high, but now I would like to share additional information collected in the same survey that shows that our parents lack knowledge on the processes involved in college enrollment and degree attainment. . . . Only thirty-four percent of parents accurately reported the cost of college, and only 43% report knowing college admissions requirements. This is why GEAR UP is critical; there is a perilous disparity between aspirations and the knowledge necessary to make those aspirations a reality (Cantu).

In her last sentence, she connects statistical evidence to a clear conclusion about a disparity between aspirations and knowledge, which demonstrates a clear need for her programs.

Personal experience The importance of your experience may be obvious to you, but it needs to be made explicit to your audience. In a commencement speech at Georgetown University, Wendy Kopp, the founder and CEO of Teach For America, used a personal story to illustrate the novel idea that inexperience can be a positive contributor to solving problems:

People want to know how I started Teach For America straight out of college, and honestly my greatest asset was my inexperience. It proved critical at many junctures. When I declared in my thesis that I would try to create such a corps myself, my thesis adviser pronounced me "deranged". When he looked at my thesis, which included a budget for the first year of $2.5 million, he asked me if I knew how hard it was to raise $2,500, let alone two and a half million dollars. But aided by my inexperience, I was unfazed by these reactions. When school district officials literally laughed at the notion that the Me Generation would jump at the chance to teach in urban and rural communities, their concerns too went unheard. My very greatest asset in reaching this point was that I simply did not understand what was impossible (Kopp).

Without these connections back to the main point, Kopp's story still would have been interesting, but listeners might have perceived it differently. They might have seen it as evidence that she was naïve or not very thoughtful rather than understanding it as a story about what it takes to address issues that seem impossible to solve.

Quotations An eloquent or provocative quotation may not always have an obvious connection to your point, so you might need to state it directly for your audience. Here, former Senator Sam Nunn makes his main point first and then uses a clever quotation to reinforce the logic of his position:

Nuclear weapons nations must visibly and steadily reduce their reliance on nuclear weapons. Today the world believes they are not—and that belief has a clear and increasingly negative impact on our efforts to prevent the spread and use of nuclear weapons. As IAEA Director El Baradei has said: "It's hard to tell people not to smoke when you have a cigarette dangling from your mouth" (Nunn).

Later chapters will return to examine this important skill of connecting evidence to your main points.

Using Visuals

You already know from chapter 2 that the visual dimension (your appearance, body movement, gestures) is an important aspect of public speaking. This holds true for other visual elements that you might incorporate into your speeches. You probably have attended presentations that were going along smoothly, but then the speaker fumbled around with a chart that was impossible to read. Or you might have suffered "death by PowerPoint" as the repetitive use of presentation technology sucked the life out of the speaker's presentation. These examples show that constructing and presenting visuals effectively is critical for public speaking.

Visual Aids and Visual Rhetoric

Whether you are using a chart, a model, an image, an object, or presentation software such as PowerPoint, your primary goal should be the seamless integration of visuals with other parts of your message. This is not an abstract goal, but a necessary response to how audiences have been shaped by contemporary culture. The dominant means of communication in the last century—television, film, and the Internet—have led audiences to expect that memorable images will accompany almost any verbal message.

Visual Aids Visuals can play two basic roles in public speaking. One role is the supporting role that is played by a **visual aid**, a tangible object that displays some aspect of your message to your audience. Visual aids support by *clarifying and reinforcing the verbal part of your message*. In this role, visual aids can serve many instrumental purposes:

- *Attracting attention.* Like the cover of a book or a photo in a newspaper, visuals can aid a speech by getting your audience's attention and adding interest beyond the verbal message. For example, after describing the procedures involved in getting a travel visa, you might show your own visa to the audience.

- *Providing support.* Visuals can present supporting material that cannot be conveyed adequately through words alone. A picture of ramshackle houses may be the best way to demonstrate poverty. A graph or chart may be more effective than statistics to show the declining state support for higher education.

- *Illustrating processes.* If your speech narrates events across time, visuals can help your audience to see that process. For example, a series of photographs or a time-lapse image can help audiences to see how development has occurred in your community.

- *Increasing retention.* A growing body of research shows how visuals have a positive effect on audience members' memory of a presentation (Mayer). Consequently, you might choose to use a visual to reinforce your most important point or encourage your audience to connect your speech to an especially powerful image.

Visual Rhetoric Presentation tools such as PowerPoint, Keynote, and Prezi have transformed the role of visuals in public speaking. Rather than just adding a few visual aids after a speech has been composed, some speakers begin their speech preparation with the goal of crafting a **visual rhetoric**, a mode of communication in which images, graphics, video, and other visual elements play a central role in the construction of public discourse.

Communication scholar Dale Cyphert has found that contemporary advice on presentations tells speakers to think about visuals not simply "as an aid to verbal argument" nor as just another type of supporting material. Instead, speakers are encouraged to consider how a focus on visuals can influence basic steps in the construction of a speech:

- *Invention.* A speech that is composed around visuals typically focuses on the *scenes, characters, and conflicts* that are at the heart of any public issue. These focal points easily fit with the ideas about invention that were discussed in chapter 8. For example, you might use visuals if you are trying to draw a comparison or explain a conflict. You could show pictures from the Depression era to make a comparison to more recent economic downturns, or you might show the faces of people who are affected in various ways by a change in immigration policy.

- *Organization.* Cyphert suggests that an increasing reliance on visuals tends to generate speeches that are structured as narratives and organized in chronological order. But visuals can serve the other organizational patterns that you learned in chapter 9 equally well. A speech that focuses on different scenes would have a spatial order; a speech that is intended to visualize conflicts would use a key issues strategy. Also, visual elements such as repeated colors or graphics can serve as effective organizational markers.

- *Style.* When used well, visuals can enable a personal, conversational style of speaking and can help a speaker to build rapport with an audience. For example, political speakers who are anticipating media coverage will stage "photo opportunities" to show their attachment to and concern for particular places, such as national parks or military institutions. In more mundane settings, visuals can promote interaction about a shared image—say, engaging an audience's response to a powerful video clip about successful student activism.

Use this distinction between visual aids and visual rhetoric to help you think about how to approach your rhetorical situation. In situations that call for a short, simple speech, you might compose the speech first and then add a few visual aids for illustration or attention. But if audiences need or expect plenty of visuals—especially if you are using presentation software—you will want to think about visuals much earlier in the process of composing your speech.

Types of Visuals

Most visuals fall into one of a few basic types. Each type tends to be useful for accomplishing certain purposes in your speech.

Objects and Models Showing your audience the actual thing you are talking about can often be the perfect visual aid to make an abstract idea tangible.

In a speech about energy, you might use a compact fluorescent light bulb or a lump of coal. Activist Diane Wilson set up a vendor stand on Wall Street that attempted to sell bottles of cloudy water in order to publicize water pollution by chemical companies.

It might not be feasible to use actual objects in every instance. Especially in classroom settings, illegal substances, weapons, and other objects that may be perceived as dangerous are typically considered inappropriate by most instructors.

Other limiting factors on the use of objects are size and availability. In these cases, consider using a model that accurately represents the object you want to display. For example, it is probably impractical to bring an actual human muscle that has been affected by steroids or an organ that has been decimated by cancer, but you might be able to locate a model to help you illustrate these effects. Using models also helps you to scale things to your audience. You might use a model to display how new construction will affect your campus.

Photographs and Drawings Alternatives to objects and models are photographs and drawings. Although they provide only two dimensions, photographs and drawings are usually simpler to create than models and easier to handle during a speech. In some settings, it also may be easier for your audience to see a drawing or photo than a model. That model of your campus might work in a small meeting where listeners can move around, but a larger audience might respond better to an artist's rendition that is easily visible from a distance.

While photos and drawings can be used as visual aids to attract attention and provide support, be aware of how they can work as visual rhetoric. Many scholars have shown how images such as famous photographs and political cartoons can have persuasive effects, such as evoking emotions or encouraging identification with a particular point of view (Edwards and Winkler). Consequently, it is important that you choose photographs and drawings that are appropriate to the general purpose of your speech, and use words to establish the context for using these images.

Charts and Graphs When asked to use a visual aid, many beginning speakers immediately think of charts and graphs. Generally, a **chart** provides a visual display of supporting material, while a **graph** refers specifically to a visual representation of statistics. Both can help you to summarize and simplify information for your audience.

Charts are especially useful for ranking items, showing relationships, and showing processes. You might use a chart to rank the five best beaches or the ten least livable metropolitan areas. An organizational chart might be used to help an audience to understand relationships within a company or between related organizations. Processes—the steps to follow in applying for a grant or how milk gets

THE ETHICAL DIMENSION

The Ethics of Using Photographic Images

Ethics comes into play with all types of visuals. You have already read about how inappropriate objects, and charts and graphs can be used to distort audience perceptions of supporting material. But one type of visual—photographs—especially deserves ethical reflection. If you plan to use photographs in your presentation, think about the following questions:

How does the photograph create a reality for viewers? Photographs deserve careful ethical scrutiny because they appear to be an objective, neutral reflection of reality. But in fact, every photograph is taken at a particular time, from a specific point of view, with a unique focus. Many aspects of reality are left out of the frame of the photograph. Therefore, photographs do not just capture reality; they *create* a reality for viewers.

For example, imagine that before taking your public speaking course, you saw a photograph of your instructor giving a lecture. That photo might have shaped your perception of your instructor—but a photo of your instructor playing with his or her children or working out at the gym might have given you a very different perception. As you consider photographs for your presentation, think about how they highlight or downplay certain aspects of reality that might be relevant to the reality contained in the photograph.

How does the photograph position viewers? Photographs implicitly put viewers in a position relative to the photo. This is an especially important issue when a photograph depicts the lives of others. Such photographs can easily objectify the people who are depicted and put viewers in the position of a voyeur or passive onlooker (Twigg).

Ethically, speakers can counteract this by allowing the people who are depicted in the photograph to express themselves, perhaps through a quotation. For example, instead of just showing a photo of a homeless person, you might include a statement from the homeless person that allows him to describe his living conditions in his own words. Including this kind of statement is another way of affirming the ethical principle of reciprocity that you learned about in chapter 3.

To what extent does the photograph evoke emotional responses? Photographs have the

Photographs and televisual images such as this one played an important role in shaping public opinion about the Vietnam War. What ethical issues might arise in deciding to use graphic images of war in a speech?

capacity to evoke strong emotions (Hariman and Lucaites). Fear, anger, joy, and pity all can be triggered by powerful images. The ethical challenge lies in determining when and for what purposes the use of these photos is appropriate.

For example, emotionally powerful images can be useful for raising awareness in informative speeches. But be wary of using those images to encourage value-laden judgments in informative speaking. Photographs that are used to evoke strong emotional responses and encourage your audience to take sides in an informative situation would be ethically inappropriate—and pragmatically, they may create distrust among your audience members.

In persuasive speaking, the potential emotional response to photographs should remind you of another principle from chapter 1: Are my emotional appeals consistent with reasonable arguments, or do they undermine reasonable thinking? If a photograph distorts the reality of a situation or positions viewers so that they are unable to fully grasp that situation, then the use of that photograph might be considered manipulative. Make sure that the visual as well as the verbal parts of your message give an accurate depiction of your topic.

FIGURE 12.1 Sample Line Graph

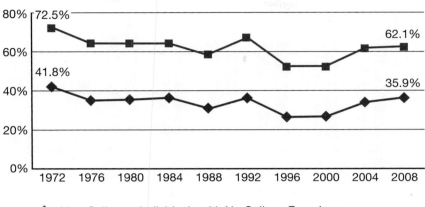

18-to 29-Year-Old Citizen Turnout by Educational Level, Presidential Years

◆ Non-College—Individuals with No College Experience
■ College—Individuals with Some College Experience

Center for Information and Research on Civic Learning and Engagement, "Youth Voting."

from the farm to your table—also can be illustrated with charts. Consequently, charts can come in handy for supporting speeches that are organized in sequential order, causal order, or the problem–solution order used in persuasive speaking.

Graphs allow you to make comparisons and show trends based on statistical data. Three types of graphs are especially common in basic public speeches:

- A **line graph** connects data points to show a trend over time. See how the line graph in Figure 12.1 tracks voter turnout according to educational level over time. The lines make it easy to see that turnout spiked in 1992, went down in 1996, and then rose again in recent years. This graph also emphasizes that turnout for both groups has followed a roughly similar trend.

- A **bar graph** shows the magnitude of data points and is useful for displaying comparisons. In Figure 12.2, the bar graph compares voter turnout for various groups depending on whether they had access to Election Day registration.

- A **pie graph** displays the distribution of data in percentages or shares. The pie graph in Figure 12.3 focuses on one population (15- to 25-year-olds) and shows the percentages of that group that are light, moderate, or heavy television viewers. The speaker should orally explain what those categories mean; in this study, a heavy viewer is defined as someone who watches four or more hours per day.

FIGURE 12.2 Sample Bar Graph

Effect of EDR on Youth Voter Turnout

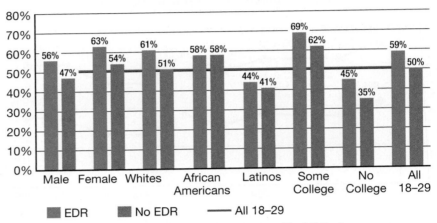

EDR   No EDR   —— All 18–29

Center for Information and Research on Civic Learning and Engagement, "Youth Voting."

FIGURE 12.3 Sample Pie Graph

Television Consumption per Day Among 15- to 25- Year Olds

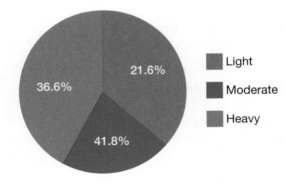

Light
Moderate
Heavy

Center for Information and Research on Civic Learning and Engagement, "Television Consumption."

Visual Technologies In addition to these specific types of visual aids, other technologies can help you to generate or display visuals for your audience. Classrooms and business settings often have *flipcharts or drawing boards* for writing text or images. *Videoplayers and projectors* are standard technologies for moving images. *Presentation software* can be understood as the most recent visual technology connected to public speaking, one that incorporates the functions of these other media.

Be sure to plan ahead when considering your use of visual technologies. While it is easy to bring a chart, not all public speaking situations will have a videoplayer or a computer and projector for presentation software. Identify the available technologies ahead of time, learn how to operate them, and be prepared with alternatives in case the technology does not work.

Preparing Visuals

After you have determined the role visuals will play in your speech, you can begin to prepare your visuals. Their effectiveness depends as much on smart development ahead of time, based on a few simple principles, as it does on smooth presentation during your speech.

Simplicity Keeping your audience's attention requires keeping your visuals simple. If your chart lists the fifteen best beaches rather than just five, your audience will spend more time reading the list and less time focusing on your explanation of the list. Similarly, detailed drawings or models with lots of parts can be more distracting than informative. *Use visuals to capture a single, simple idea*; use oral messages to fill in the context and to connect that idea to other ideas in your speech.

Simplicity should not be a substitute for professionalism, however. Especially in the classroom, students can be tempted to use the chalkboard or whiteboard as a simple, easy visual aid. But for a formal presentation, the use of these technologies never appears as professional or as neat as an aid that was prepared in advance.

Visibility It is not unusual for beginning speakers to use whatever visual aid is convenient without considering whether the audience will be able to see important features. For example, a map from an atlas or a website illustrates things at such a small scale that it will probably be useless for a public speech. Instead, resize the map on a computer or copy machine so that your audience can immediately recognize the features that are relevant to your speech.

Color and light also can affect the visibility of visuals. Use bold, contrasting colors when preparing drawings, charts, or graphs so that your audience can easily see your material and observe important comparisons. Light matters when you are creating or identifying photos and video clips; the quality of these images can vary widely, so be sure to use visuals that have been lit well and have clear images. In addition, determine the lighting options in the room, since some technologies may not be visible if you are unable to dim the lights.

Readability Any display of written text must pass the readability test. Titles, identifying words and phrases, and verbal charts all need to be large enough that the people at the back of your audience can see them. Also, use just one or two bold, plain fonts to make your visuals consistent and readable. Unusual or decorative lettering styles should be used only when there are very few words and your primary purpose is to attract attention.

Following the principle of simplicity will usually improve readability. For example, one student's speech on the Bowl Championship Series used a chart showing a dizzying amount of statistics for the top twenty football teams that year. It had far more information than he could explain, and it was impossible for the audience to read the relevant portions. A more readable and less distracting visual would have compared two teams with just a few statistics for each.

Rehearsal The only way to truly tell whether your visuals put these principles into practice is to practice! As was recommended in chapter 2, rehearse with an audience in a setting that is similar to the one where you will give your actual performance. After all, the ultimate judge of a successful visual aid is not you at your desk, but an audience that may be sitting some distance from you.

Presenting Visuals

Rehearsals also give you practice in presenting your visuals. Keep in mind the overall goal of a seamless *integration* of your visual and verbal messages as you rehearse. To achieve this goal, you will want to think carefully about the placement, timing, and explanation of your visuals.

Placement For starters, *place visuals where everyone can see them.* In the classroom, it is tempting to set visuals where it is convenient for you—by the lectern, on the tray of a chalkboard or whiteboard, or attached to the wall behind you. But any public speaking instructor can give you examples of how these places failed a student speaker: A visual next to the lectern is usually visible only to a few folks in front, posters inevitably fall off the eraser trays, and wall hangings get blocked by the speaker. No matter what type of visual you use, place it in a conspicuous, unobstructed area that makes it easy for everyone to see.

In addition, *keep your body from blocking the visual during presentation.* Stand well to one side of your visual, and use your arm or a pointer to direct the audience's attention to specific parts. Alternatively, you might hold an object or model directly in front of you if you do not have a stand to support it.

Timing Imagine that someone recorded the first few lines of your speech and played them back continuously as you gave the rest of your speech. It would be distracting! Just as a competing verbal message would hurt your effectiveness, a visual that remains visible for too long can become a distraction, too. You need to control the audience's span of attention to visuals in your speech. Several practical guidelines are useful here.

First, *plan the timing of handouts to your audience.* Inevitably, audience members will start reading upon receiving a handout rather than listening to you, and they will start reading again if they get bored. Instead, provide a summary handout at the conclusion of your speech.

Second, *be wary of passing visuals among your audience.* Speeches are intended to be a group experience; passing around a visual interrupts that experience and works against your attempts to unify the audience. It also works against the integration of the visual and verbal parts of your message. The first few people may see the visual while you are talking about it, but most of your audience will receive it much later. For the latter group, the speech loses its coherence twice: first when they hear the message but cannot see the visual and later when you are speaking about something else but they are looking at the visual.

Third, it follows that you should *display visuals only with the corresponding verbal message.* Rather than having it visible throughout your speech, reveal the visual only when you begin discussing it, and remove it from sight when you have made the relevant point. You can make finer adjustments to timing depending on your purpose for using the visual aid:

- To attract attention and arouse interest, display your visual aid for a few seconds and then begin speaking about it.

- To provide support, state your main point *before* revealing the supporting visual. Otherwise, your audience might miss the main point as they turn attention to the visual. For example, using the line graph in Figure 12.1, you might start with a sentence such as "Historically, young people without college experience have lagged behind their peers in voter turnout" and then display the graph, leading in with a phrase such as "As this graph shows . . . ."

- To illustrate a process, reveal each part of the process as you talk about it rather than displaying all the parts. This can help to keep you on track and prevents your audience from getting distracted by other parts of the visual.

Explanation Displaying visuals in the right place and at the right time does not guarantee that your audience will grasp the meaning and relevance of your visuals. Providing an oral explanation is critical for successful integration of the verbal and visual elements of your speech.

The most basic element of your explanation is an **oral caption**, a spoken sentence that states the main idea of a visual. Just like a caption for a newspaper photo, an oral caption introduces the visual to the audience and attaches words to it:

In this photograph, we can see why feedlots are unhealthy.

Let's examine this graph, which illustrates the income distribution of students in three state universities.

Oral captions are especially important if you are trying to develop a visual rhetoric. For example, if you are using several visual images to structure a speech about feedlots, the first caption above signals a turn to health issues and directs audience members to focus on those rather than on other aspects of the visual.

Beyond an oral caption, you might want to engage in an *analysis* or *dissection* of the visual. This means indicating or describing specific parts of the visual one by one. For photos or drawings, analysis is important to focus attention on those aspects that you want to highlight. For charts and graphs, be sure to define categories, state what the x- and y-axes represent, and talk about specific items in addition to the purpose of chart as a whole. Look at two ways of explaining the pie graph in Figure 12.3 about television consumption.

Less effective: This is a graph about how much TV people watch. As you can see, the biggest chunk is the moderate viewers.

More effective: Here, we see a breakdown of 15- to 25-year-olds as light, moderate, or heavy viewers according to their television consumption. About 22% in this group are considered light viewers, defined as watching fewer than 2 hours per day. More than one third are heavy viewers of more than 4 hours per day. The largest proportion, almost 42%, watch 2 to 4 hours per day.

In this example, notice the precision of the more effective analysis. It makes it clear that the graph is about 15- to 25-year-olds, not just "people," and it defines what is meant by light, moderate, and heavy viewers.

Finally, provide a *connection* between the visual and your larger point. When you have finished analyzing your visual aid, try to show how it reinforces your current main point or develop a transition into the next point:

Overall, these data make it clear that different universities in our system attract a very different socioeconomic mix of students.

Now that you have seen inside a nuclear reactor, you will better understand some of the safety concerns involved with their operation.

One final point about presenting visuals: *Always talk to your audience, not to your visuals.* This can be a difficult guideline to follow, especially if you are using PowerPoint or have lots of text on your visuals. But remember from chapter 1: You are engaged in *public* speaking, not just speaking. No matter how important or powerful your visuals are, your effectiveness will be diminished if you do not establish a connection with your audience.

Using PowerPoint to Create Visual Rhetoric

The popularity of PowerPoint and the many bad presentations that have resulted from it have led to hundreds of books, articles, and websites that discuss how to create effective presentations. An entire trade journal, *Presentations*, is devoted to discussion of presentation software technologies. However, many of the principles about visual aids that were discussed above also apply to PowerPoint. This section will focus on a few of the most important principles.

Simplicity Moving text! Sounds! Internet links! Slide transitions! Embedded video! PowerPoint has endless possibilities, but they are often abused by people who are more excited about playing with the "bells and whistles" than about giving an effective presentation. When used indiscriminately, these features can be extremely distracting. On the flip side, other speakers use PowerPoint simply to display their speech outline. Not only can this bore an audience, but it also can lead to slides packed with words.

Both the flashy presentation and the wordy one forget the principle of simplicity. When building a presentation, keep your slides simple by following these guidelines:

- *Limit the number of slides.* There is no absolute rule for the right number of slides per minute (or per speech). Instead, ask yourself, "How many images do I need to tell the story?" (Cyphert). Err on the side of fewer slides.

- *Limit the number of points on each slide.* Remember that each slide should focus on just one idea, so you should not need more than a few subpoints. Some users suggest eliminating words altogether on some slides in favor of an image slide while speaking about related points.

- *Use a few words or short phrases rather than sentences.* Again, think about how verbal and visual cues can work together. Use your slide to convey the core of your idea, and use your speech to explain that idea. Likewise, a long quotation may be more powerful if you speak it instead of having your audience read it from a slide.

- *Use only special effects that are specific to your topic.* The sounds, clip art, animation, and transitions that are built into PowerPoint are generic. They serve no substantive purpose other than to call attention to themselves. Your presentation will look far more professional if you intentionally seek out images, video, and other visuals that are specifically relevant to your speech.

See Figures 12.4 and 12.5 to compare two slides that vary in their level of simplicity. While the slide in Figure 12.5 contains more information, that is not necessarily the best for your audience. The slide in Figure 12.4 contains the core ideas, allowing the speaker to discuss the details orally or provide them on later slides.

FIGURE 12.4 Effective PowerPoint Slide

This simple slide reflects several key principles of effective slide design: a few points, short phrases, and no unnecessary or confusing special effects.

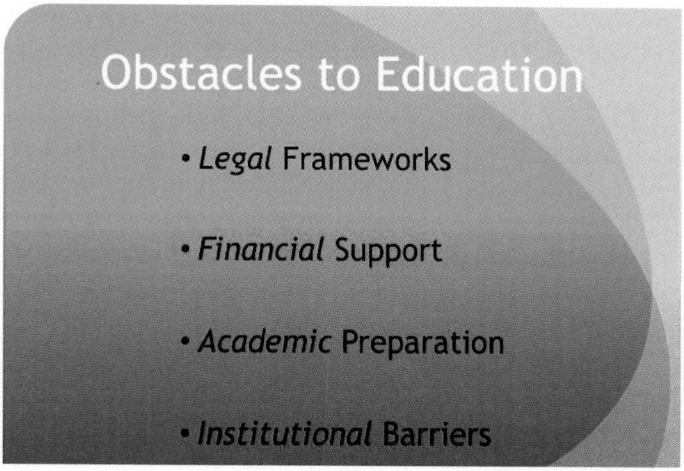

FIGURE 12.5 Ineffective PowerPoint Slide

This slide suffers from information overload, poor font choices, and an image that adds nothing to the verbal message.

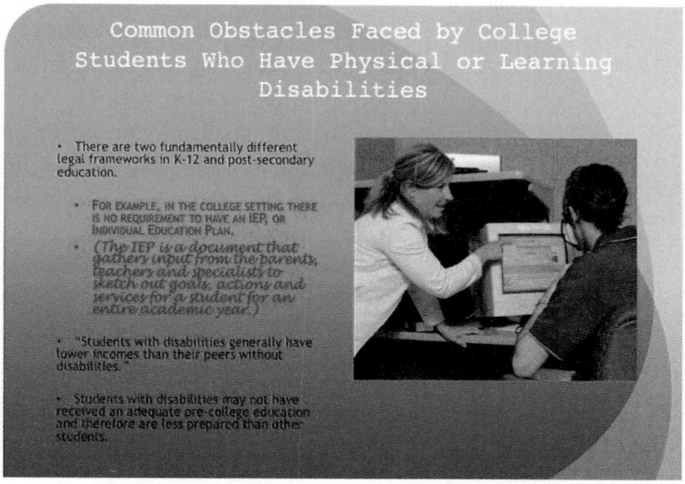

Visibility and Readability The earlier suggestions about visibility and readability are directly applicable to PowerPoint. Size, color, lighting, font size, and font style all must be considered in developing an effective presentation. In particular, most advice on using PowerPoint suggests using fonts that are at least 30 points in size and no more than two font styles in a single presentation.

A related issue with computer-generated presentations is selecting a font style that is easily readable in a large size. Rather than spending a lot of time experimenting with exotic fonts, rely on standard fonts such as Arial or Helvetica. These are **sans-serif fonts**, typefaces without flared edges. **Serif fonts**, or typefaces with flared letter edges (such as Times New Roman), are preferred for a longer stretch of text.

The slides in Figures 12.4 and 12.5 show how readability can be compromised in several ways. The less effective slide shows poor color and font choices. In addition, because too much information is crammed onto one slide, the font size had to be reduced considerably. Finally, it includes a photo that is not clearly linked to the verbal content, wasting space and potentially confusing the audience. The simpler slide shows the sans-serif font Trebuchet MS, which is automatically used in some PowerPoint slide themes.

Placement In many instances, you will have little choice about where your presentation is projected. Well-designed rooms will make the screen visible to everyone, but be sure to check visibility before your speech, and check with the audience at the beginning of your speech. If your equipment is portable, plan to arrive well ahead of time so that you can arrange the room to ensure good visibility.

The placement of your body is an equally important issue. Some users nearly disappear from the audience, either by dimming the lights or by speaking far off to the side or back of the room. PowerPoint becomes the speech itself rather than a tool that a speaker uses to enhance his or her speech. Other speakers allow themselves to be stuck behind a desk with a stationary computer, reading every slide from the monitor or the screen. None of these options build rapport with an audience.

Instead, position yourself at the front of the room as you would for any speech, making sure that your audience can still easily see the screen. A laptop computer or a remote control can allow you to advance your slides without feeling trapped. If a particular slide requires special attention from your audience, such as a video clip, you might move off to the side while the audience views that slide. Afterward, move back to continue your speech. Above all, rehearse your speech enough that you are not merely reading all your slides off the screen. If your body and eye contact are constantly oriented toward the screen or a computer monitor, you may be speaking—but you are not engaged in *public* speaking.

Timing and Rehearsal The rhythm of an effective performance should be guided by the principle of displaying visuals only with the corresponding verbal message. Consequently, *avoid making your slide show automatic.* If it is automatic, this completely takes the control away from you and prevents you from being responsive to your audience. Second, *use a blank slide or blank screen when appropriate.* If you are going to spend additional time on a particular idea or need to redirect the focus to you as a speaker, this tactic is necessary. Third, *use rehearsal to get feedback* about where the presentation drags or moves too quickly. Just as with other visual aids, the real test for timing is not you but your audience.

Handling Questions

For many speakers, handling questions is even more anxiety-producing than giving a speech. You can prepare and rehearse your speech thoroughly to gain confidence, but the question–and–answer (Q&A) period creates uncertainty. Who will ask questions? What will they ask? Will they try to trip me up? What if I don't know the answer to their questions?

You may feel this anxiety especially in public settings. If you speak at an event or meeting that is open to the public, you might not know many people in your audience. If important issues are at stake, listeners might ask difficult questions or use the Q&A period to challenge your views. So take advantage of the experience you will gain by handling questions in the classroom. As you get to know your classmates and instructor, you will feel more and more at ease with them; this will give you more of a chance to focus on the following strategies for handling questions.

Anticipate Questions as You Prepare Your Speech

If you want to see experts handling questions, watch a White House press secretary during a press conference. You will be amazed at this person's ability to respond to tough questions immediately, often with detailed answers. While skill, practice, and natural ability all play a role, the press secretary's talent is also due to intense preparation based on ongoing discussions with the President and advisers.

This shows yet another reason why thorough research is so crucial for effective public speaking: It exposes you to additional ideas and viewpoints that can be useful for anticipating questions. For example, if you are giving a speech on population control, you might come across some articles that discuss alternatives to population control. Even if you do not discuss these in your speech, your reading might spur you to think about potential questions:

What are alternatives to population control?

What are the objections to population control?

What countries have rejected certain population control measures?

On of the most practical things you can do, then, is to *make a list of potential questions and short answers before you give your speech.* This can do wonders for your confidence, reminding you that you probably know a lot more about your topic than most of your audience members do.

Signal the Q&A Period

Once a speech has concluded and the applause has died down, there often is an awkward silence in the room. Listeners might not know whether asking questions is allowed or expected, and some listeners might be hesitant to ask questions. Therefore, take control of the situation, and let your audience know that you are ready to take questions. You can do this in a general way, or you might inform the audience how you would like to proceed with questions.

> Thank you. I'm happy to answer any questions you might have.
>
> Let's start with questions about the proposal and then talk about any concerns or criticisms.
>
> We have about fifteen minutes for questions; please step to the microphone if you wish to ask a question.

The latter two statements not only shape your audience's expectations; they also help you to reduce some of the uncertainty in the situation.

Listen Attentively and Courteously

Put your listening skills from chapter 3 to work during the Q&A period. It is especially important to listen attentively so that you hear the entire question and understand the perspective of the person who is asking the question. For example, if a questioner mentions that she is a single mother, that fact may be an important clue to her concerns or to why she is asking the question. Or a questioner might start out by saying that he agrees with most of your speech but then asks a question about the one part he disagrees with. If you missed his agreement, you might end up giving an answer that rehashes what you both agree on rather than answering his actual question.

Restate the Question

It is usually a good idea to restate a listener's question. It benefits the questioner, who knows that you have heard and understood the question. It also benefits the audience; if they could not hear or understand the questioner, they get another opportunity to hear the question. It also benefits you as a speaker; it gives you an opportunity to check with the questioner that you heard it correctly. It also gives you a "running start" to answering the question. It will feel more like a normal conversation and less like you are producing a set speech on command.

Respond to the Entire Audience

Even though the Q&A may feel like a conversation at times, it is important not to lose sight of the rest of your audience when answering questions. After all, the period is an extension of your speech, and other people in your audience might have the same questions as the ones that get asked. Therefore, after you restate the question and confirm it with the questioner, be sure to present your answer to the entire audience. You may continue to make extra eye contact with the questioner, but others should be included, too.

Refer Back to Your Speech

It is impossible to generate tips for every possible type of question that you may be asked. However, a general technique is to connect your answer back to some part of your speech. This can function as a kind of supporting material for your answer. Your answer should not be solely material from your speech; otherwise, listeners might think that you are evading the question. Instead, simply refer back to the speech as part of a larger answer.

Acknowledge a Lack of Knowledge

When you do not know the answer, do not try to fake it. It is far better to gain the trust of your audience by saying when you don't know something than to pretend having knowledge and risk being proved wrong. For example, a speaker might be asked to speculate beyond what was discussed in a speech:

Question: Does advertising affect the body images of young boys, too?

Answer: That's an important question. The studies in my speech looked only at pre-teen girls, and I have not seen any research that explores your question. If I find some, I would be happy to share it.

Rather than speculating, the speaker both refers back to what is known and acknowledges what she does not know in response to the factual question.

Practice Inclusiveness

Occasionally, a single questioner will want to engage you in a long line of questioning. While it is important to listen courteously, it is also important to remember the ethical principle of inclusiveness. Having one person dominate the Q&A period not only can be annoying to you, but also excludes the rest of the audience members and can leave them with a negative memory of your presentation.

In such instances, you need to provide a transition that moves firmly but politely from one questioner to another. For example, if a questioner seems to want to ask a series questions, you might allow one follow-up question but give a brief answer to it. Then say something like "I'd like to hear what others think about this" or "I appreciate your questions; perhaps we can talk more about this afterward." Similarly, to questioners who ramble, you might calmly and politely say, "Excuse me, I'd like to hear from others too; is there something specific you'd like me to comment on?"

CASE CONCLUSION

Julie's Speech on the Central Asia Institute

By preparing her speech early and having plenty of rehearsal time, Julie was able to have an effective extemporaneous speech. She practiced a couple of sections each night and then rehearsed the entire speech with her roommate to get feedback. One thing she learned during the process was that it helped to have both narrative and expert testimony to show the significance of the underlying issue. Julie's roommate said that this helped Julie's credibility while also maintaining interest via Greg Mortenson's story. The same was true for Julie's visuals; her use of a chart and a photo allowed her to incorporate factual information and make the issue even more immediate to her listeners.

WORKING OUTLINE

Julie's Speech on the Central Asia Institute

Specific purpose: To inform my audience about the development, mission, and accomplishments of the Central Asia Institute.

Central idea: The Central Asia Institute is a program dedicated to building schools in Pakistan and Afghanistan and thus promoting peace.

INTRODUCTION

Julie starts her speech with a hypothetical example.

1. Imagine that this building crumbled. Your pencils and pens disappeared. Our professor didn't come today. Would you still come to class?

2. Many children in Pakistan would.

    A. Unfortunately, such an atmosphere isn't very conducive to learning, even if the motivation is there.

    B. This is where the Central Asia Institute (CAI), an institute dedicated to building schools in Pakistan and Afghanistan, comes in.

Even though she is not an expert on the topic, Julie has done research and can offer a credibility statement to her audience.

3. I have read a book about this institute, listened to a lecture by the founder, written essays on it, and continued to research it.

4. Today, I would like to inform you about the beginning, mission, and accomplishments of the Central Asia Institute.

(*Transition:* I'll start by explaining the origins of the CAI.)

BODY

1. The Central Asia Institute started with one man, Greg Mortenson.

   A. Mortenson traveled in Pakistan in the early 1990s.
      i. While there has been some question about the exact sequence of events, his experiences there showed him the poor state of education in the region.
      ii. Greg made a promise to come build a school after spending time in the village of Korphe.
   B. Greg returned to the United States determined to fulfill his promise.
      i. Searched for donors, as he didn't have the necessary funds.
      ii. Gained enough support to create the Central Asia Institute.

> Julie's speech uses a narrative about Mortenson to sustain audience attention.

(*Transition:* Of course the creation of this institute was driven by a specific purpose, so I will now tell you about the CAI's mission.)

2. As I already mentioned, the CAI is dedicated to building schools in Pakistan, particularly for girls.

   A. There is a lack of education in this region.
      i. According to a 2004 Congressional research report on education in Pakistan, the country's literacy rate is just 40%.
      ii. That report also states that only one third of children will complete fifth grade (the average girl completes only 2.5 years of education).
      iii. Education is supposed to be funded by the government, but according to a foreign affairs report to Congress, only 2% of the GNP of Pakistan goes to education.
      iv. As you can see by this chart comparing education spending across countries, most countries spend 4–8% of their GNP on education.
   B. This scarcity of schools is dangerous for Pakistanis and for us in the United States.
      i. As both Greg's book and the CRS report pointed out, madrassas, or religious schools, replace general schools.
      ii. About 10% of madrassas preach extremism, and many terrorists are trained in such schools, according to Greg and the report.

> This is a smooth way of providing an attribution statement for one of her sources.

> Julie brings in her first visual aid here, a chart that compares education spending. This allows her audience to understand the Pakistani situation relative to something that is more familiar.

> Here, Julie paraphrases the two sources without directly quoting them.

(*Transition:* Now that you know the background and the mission of the CAI, I will discuss some of its accomplishments.)

3. In its relatively short time in existence, the CAI has accomplished a great deal.

   A. Many schools have been built, and many children have been educated.
      i. As listed on the CAI's website, more than 170 schools have been fully or partially supported, and there are currently 24,000 students (including 14,300 girls) enrolled.

Julie brings in another visual here, a photo of one of the schools to help her audience see what the outcome of CAI's work looks like.

    ii. This photo shows one of these schools. Compared to what they had before, it is a tremendous improvement in the lives of these students.

B. The organization has taken on terrorism and discrimination in an innovative way.

    i. After Sept. 11, Greg got hate mail, but now he is widely supported.

    ii. Since there are more options besides extremist schools and women are better educated, terrorism is being fought at its roots.

CONCLUSION

1. I have told you about the development, mission, and accomplishments of the CAI.

2. The CAI is important to know about because it exemplifies another way to fight terrorism and improve not only one nation, but multiple nations, the United States included.

3. I have been very inspired by the CAI and the people and foundations that run it, so I hope that I have instilled enough interest in you that you will look deeper into, if not the CAI, then an organization or idea similar to it.

BIBLIOGRAPHY

Kronstadt, Alan K. *CRS Report for Congress: Education Reform in Pakistan.* 23 Dec. 2004. U.S. Foreign Affairs and Defense Division. 30 Sept. 2007 http://www .fas.org/man/crs/RS22009.pdf

Mortenson, Greg, and David Oliver Relin. *Three Cups of Tea: One Man's Mission to Promote Peace, One School at a Time.* New York: Penguin Books, 2006.

Mortenson, Greg. Guest Lecture. Lecture on the Central Asia Institute and Education in Pakistan. University Theater, University of Montana, Missoula, MT. 21 Sept. 2007.

Central Asia Institute. *The CentralAsia Institute.* 01 Oct. 2007 http://www.ikat .org/about.html

Summary

DELIVERY METHODS

- Extemporaneous speaking, involving advance preparation but not complete memorization, is the preferred delivery method for classroom speeches.

- Impromptu speaking focuses on a single point in a brief speech with little or no advance preparation, while manuscript speaking and memorized speaking require extensive preparation and rehearsal.

INCORPORATING SOURCES

- To avoid plagiarism, speakers need to include a complete attribution statement that states the author, date, and publication for both paraphrased and quoted material.

- Direct quotations should be signaled by saying "quote" and "end quote," using extended pauses, or making vocal changes.
- After including your supporting material, interpret that material by explaining it in your own words and connecting it to your main point.

USING VISUALS

- Visuals can play two roles in public speaking. Visual aids play a supporting role and are typically generated after a speech has been fully drafted. In other instances, speakers can craft a visual rhetoric by composing main points around visuals.
- Your choice of objects, models, photographs, drawings, charts, graphs, and other visual technologies will depend on the kind of supporting material you need in your speech.
- Keep in mind the principles of simplicity, visibility, and readability when constructing visuals and the guidelines for placement, timing, and explanation when presenting visuals. These principles and guidelines are equally relevant for PowerPoint presentations.

HANDLING QUESTIONS

- Before your speech, try to anticipate a few of the most likely questions.
- After you have concluded your speech, clearly signal your expectations for the question-and-answer period, and listen attentively and courteously to questions.
- When answering questions, start by restating the question. Feel free to refer back to your speech, and acknowledge when you do not know the answer.

Key Terms

extemporaneous speaking p. 294
immediacy p. 295
impromptu speaking p. 295
manuscript speaking p. 297
ghostwriter p. 298
memorized speaking p. 298
plagiarism p. 299
wholesale plagiarism p. 299
partial plagiarism p. 300
paraphrase p. 300
attribution statement p. 301

visual aid p. 307
visual rhetoric p. 307
chart p. 309
graph p. 309
line graph p. 311
bar graph p. 311
pie graph p. 311
oral caption p. 315
sans-serif fonts p. 318
serif fonts p. 318

Comprehension

1. What is the difference between extemporaneous speaking and impromptu speaking?

2. Describe three general situations that would qualify as partial plagiarism.

3. What three elements need to be in a complete attribution of a source?

4. After you present supporting material, what two things can you do to interpret your source?

5. What are four purposes that can be served by visual aids?

6. How can the goal of crafting a visual rhetoric influence the invention stage of speech development?

7. What are three practical guidelines for the appropriate timing of visuals?

8. What are four ways in which the principle of simplicity can be applied to the creation of PowerPoint presentations?

9. Why is it important to restate a listener's question?

Application

1. Find a video of a recent commencement address from your college or another college, and view it with classmates. After determining the speaker's delivery method, discuss how well the speaker used that method. Consider issues such as evidence of preparation, credibility, eye contact, vocal variety, body movements, and overall coherence of the speech.

2. Find a recent magazine or newspaper article that is related to your speech topic. Identify a good quotation that could be used to support a point in your speech, and then craft a short passage of your speech that uses the quotation. Your passage should include a lead-in, a complete attribution statement, a signal of the quotation, and an explanation or connection of the quotation to your main point.

3. Create an ineffective visual aid for your speech that violates two of the construction and presentation guidelines in this chapter. Present it to your classmates, and see whether they can identify which principles are being violated.

4. Hold a practice Q&A period with a few of your classmates before your assigned speaking day. Practice restating the question and referring back to your speech as you answer the question.

Inventing and Organizing Your Persuasive Speech

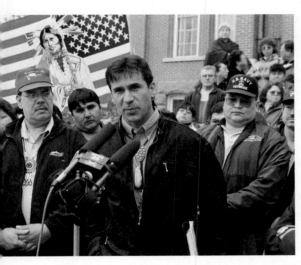

This chapter is intended to help you:

- Identify the purposes of persuasive speaking
- Explore and generate ideas for your persuasive speech
- Use organizational patterns that are adapted to your audience and purpose

Persuasion has always been at the heart of public speaking. One traditional definition of rhetoric describes the primary skill of public speaking as the speaker's ability to identify the "available means of persuasion" in a situation (Aristotle). But persuasive speaking can be especially challenging today. One of the main challenges is your competition in the public sphere. Considering only commercial messages, the average American has approximately 3,000 exposures each day (Jacobson and Masur). The numbers might be even higher among younger people; one study of youth in the United States showed an average of eight hours of daily media exposure (Roberts).

As a result, listeners have developed some defense mechanisms against this onslaught of persuasion. Some communication scholars have referred

CASE SCENARIO

Anne's Speech on Disability Access

Earlier in the semester, Anne had given an informative speech about access to campus buildings for disabled people. In that speech, she shared a memorable story about a class project that required her to move around campus for a few hours in a wheelchair. Her vivid story captured her audience's attention, but she was not sure how motivated they might be to act on this issue. She decided to revisit this issue for her persuasive speech. Would her audience be willing to do something outside of class about disability access? It would be a challenge to identify the right purpose and set of persuasive strategies that fit her classmates' level of concern.

to a general state of **distraction**, or fleeting attention to a single message, among contemporary audiences (DeLuca and Peeples). Because traditional and social media are saturated with messages, we give little attention to any one message. The next time you walk past a bulletin board of flyers and announcements on your campus, note how many you notice and how few you bother to read. Audiences also may develop **cynicism**, a distrustful and largely negative attitude, when it comes to persuasive messages. When everyone is trying to persuade—and when many people appear to be untrustworthy—it can be difficult to treat every persuasive message seriously (Hart and Hartelius; Hariman).

The challenges of distraction and cynicism are just two of the prominent obstacles in contemporary public speaking. This chapter will help you to confront these obstacles by guiding you through the invention process for persuasive speaking. Like chapter 8 on invention in informative speaking, this chapter will begin by looking at the primary purposes of persuasive speaking and the resources for invention that are available. The last section of the chapter will focus on the organizational strategies that are standard ways of engaging the typical challenges of persuasive speaking. ■

Purposes of Persuasive Speaking

As you learned in chapter 4, speaking to persuade means that your primary aim is to influence the attitudes and actions of your audience. In some situations, this may mean reinforcing the beliefs and feelings that your audience members already hold. In others, it may mean challenging their beliefs or weakening their commitments to open the way for other views. Or it may mean encouraging the audience to act on the attitudes they already hold. As a result, the general purpose of persuading your audience can take many specific forms depending on the situation and your audience.

Civic and Political Purposes of Persuasive Speech

Persuading audiences is a vital part of civic and political engagement. If you are working on a community project such as a new park or playground, you might need to persuade local residents of the importance of public space or convince them to donate time or money to the project. If you are trying to improve relationships between your campus and the surrounding community, you might need to persuade your fellow students that their weekend parties are having a negative impact on the community

Often, these civic activities can set the groundwork for political persuasion. If audiences see the importance of public space, it might be easier to persuade them to support a local bond initiative. Students with greater sensitivity to campus–community relationships might be more willing to participate in discussions of your campus's building plans or engage in advocacy about transportation and development near campus. In all of these scenarios, persuasion is necessary for promoting certain courses of action, as well as for electing and supporting leaders who will make the ultimate decisions.

In these contexts, persuasive speaking typically focuses on one of three purposes: strengthening commitments, moderating opposition, and advocating action. The first two purposes are concerned primarily with influencing the audience's attitudes; the third is concerned with translating audience attitudes into action.

Strengthening Commitments Back in chapter 5, you learned that an *attitude* could be thought of as a preference—a favorable or unfavorable disposition toward some idea or practice or some judgment of that idea or practice as either desirable or undesirable. Much persuasive speaking has the purpose of strengthening a favorable or neutral audience's commitments, making those attitudes or preferences more pronounced. You are trying to strengthen an audience's commitment to an attitude when you speak to a sympathetic audience about an important civic or political issue, when you encourage a neutral audience to see certain ideas as desirable, or when you encourage any audience to see one option as better than another.

Civic and political speech often attempts to strengthen an audience's commitment by heightening their concern about some issue. Chapter 8 suggested that this type of persuasive speech often flows naturally from an informative speech that intends to raise awareness of an issue. The persuasive speech differs because you are going beyond raising awareness in an attempt to influence the audience's feelings and responses to that new awareness. For example, if you are speaking about cancer treatments, your speaking goal might be to persuade your audience to favor reducing restrictions on experimental drugs. In this way, you are trying to clarify the audience's preference.

You also learned in chapter 5 that attitudes are based on both beliefs and values. Therefore, strengthening an audience's commitments often requires

THE ETHICAL DIMENSION

Preaching to the Choir

Speaking to people who already agree with you is sometimes called "preaching to the choir." As was mentioned earlier in the chapter, this might seem like the easiest type of public speaking, but it raises challenges all its own. Some of these challenges are explicitly ethical and worth considering before you engage in persuasive speaking.

Your choices of supporting material and language have significant ethical implications when you are speaking to a sympathetic audience. Using only the most outrageous examples or appealing primarily to emotion certainly can excite an audience—you have probably heard this kind of "red meat" rhetoric in political campaigns—but also can distort the audience's judgment.

However, there is a larger ethical issue about preaching to the choir: Should you do it in the first place? In some situations, you might not have a choice. If you are asked to give a presentation to your organization and most of its members see things the same way, then you need to be careful with the tactics and appeals mentioned above. But in other situations, you might have more flexibility in how you constitute your audience. Imagine that you are a student leader who is speaking to students about a proposed tuition increase. Even if a majority of the student body opposes the increase, is it ethically sound to give a speech that speaks only to the majority with the purpose of strengthening their commitment?

In such situations, think about the range of possible short-term effects as well as potential long-term consequences of your rhetoric. In the short term, you might get the majority on board and riled up, but ignoring other viewpoints could create a backlash where none existed before. In the long term, this kind of rhetoric can lead to **polarization**, in which one group in a society perceives itself as absolutely opposed to another group. Many observ-

Political campaign speeches can often involve "preaching to the choir." How can speakers invigorate their supporters without demonizing their opponents?

ers believe that polarization is detrimental to effective democratic decision making. Finally, it might not serve you well to constitute audiences that are unwilling or unable to engage in critical thinking about important public issues. Even if preaching to the choir seems easy, its ethical dimensions should make you think carefully about how you constitute your audience and about the most appropriate ways to persuade them.

WHAT DO YOU THINK?

1. If you are speaking to a sympathetic or like-minded audience, what sort of language should you use to refer to your opponents? What types of language would be inappropriate?

2. Think of a public issue about which you are undecided or uncertain of your position. How would you respond to a speaker who seems to be preaching to the choir? What lessons does this suggest about your own choices as a speaker?

that you engage audiences on both of those levels. For example, if you want to persuade your classmates that the amount of money that is allotted to student groups is undesirable, then you might need to address factual issues about the size of the budget and which groups get funding, as well as the value of extracurricular groups and ideals such as fairness and financial responsibility. All of these points could affect whether your audience sees the current budget as desirable or not or whether they might prefer an alternative budget.

Moderating Opposition When an audience does not favor your position, an appropriate persuasive purpose is to moderate their opposition to your position. For instance, imagine that you are trying to extend the library hours on campus but the library staff is opposed to that change. If you are going to speak to the staff, your initial task should be to determine the basis for their opposition. If you can address some of their reasons and therefore weaken some of their commitments, you might be able to moderate that opposition to make them more open to your viewpoint.

Moderating opposition is a staple of civic and political engagement. Because democratic principles require us to respectfully engage people with opposing points of view, the skill of being able to moderate that opposition is necessary if one want to be an effective agent in the civic and political arena. For example, an advocate of abstinence-only sex education is likely to face opposition from people who prefer sex education that directly discusses sexual activity. Opponents might not ever support abstinence-only education, but they might be persuaded to moderate their opposition if abstinence is taught as one of many options for promoting sexual safety. Moderating opposition, then, is not about getting opponents to completely switch their position but instead about encouraging them to see your position in a somewhat more favorable light.

Advocating Action The other major purpose of persuasive speech is *advocating action*. Persuading people to vote in a certain way, encouraging elected officials to make certain decisions, and simply motivating other citizens to get up and do something are all examples of how persuasive speech can advocate action. All of these examples may involve influencing people's attitudes in some way, but in some situations, simply generating a favorable attitude is not enough from the viewpoint of the persuasive speaker. For that speaker, the real goal is getting a favorably disposed audience to move from attitude to action.

Advocating action takes a variety of forms. In terms of civic engagement, the challenge might be getting co-workers to volunteer for a Saturday charity event or soliciting contributions from individual or institutional donors. In terms of political engagement, advocacy might involve encouraging other students to vote for a student government candidate. Once a candidate is in office, you might attempt to persuade

MODERATING OPPOSITION
A classic example of a speech designed to moderate opposition is John F. Kennedy's speech to the Houston Ministerial Association during his campaign for President. His speech was intended not to shift votes, but to moderate opposition that was based on prejudice against his religion.

him or her to address certain issues or to vote a certain way on legislation. In all of these situations, persuasive speech is designed to direct the action of others in consequential ways.

Aligning Your Purpose and Your Subject

The persuasive purposes described above are ultimately shaped by your consideration of audience. But the *subject* of your speech also shapes your persuasive purpose. Persuasive speaking in the public sphere tends to address one of four subject areas: facts, attitudes, policies, and direct action. Once you have clarified both the subject area of your speech and the desired movement that you seek from your audience, your invention process will be much more focused.

Addressing Questions of Fact It might seem odd that persuasive speeches would focus on facts. Aren't facts just true statements? Why would we need to waste our time speaking about facts?

Certainly, some facts are beyond dispute and do not require much discussion. For example, there are many facts about the September 11, 2001, attacks that can be stated conclusively. We know the precise times when the World Trade Center buildings were hit. We know which people hijacked which planes. And we know that a network called al-Qaeda orchestrated the attacks.

But many questions remain about the facts surrounding those attacks. A key question is why the attacks were not stopped ahead of time. Did government officials downplay or ignore the signs of a threat? Was there a failure of communication among intelligence agencies? Was there inadequate monitoring of sites where the attackers trained? The 9/11 Commission Report stands as one attempt to assemble the available evidence and offer a persuasive answer to these and other questions about the facts surrounding 9/11.

Whenever there is a dispute about the facts, a difference in interpretation, or a lack of conclusive evidence, there is an opportunity for persuasive speech to play an important role in the public sphere. Some disputes involve *questions about the past:*

> Did our university ever have discriminatory admission policies?
> What caused the recession that started in 2008?

Others are *questions about the present:*

> How does participation in extracurricular activities affect academic performance?
> Is organic food healthier than conventional food?

Still other factual disputes involve predictions, or *questions about the future:*

> What are the prospects for the nuclear energy industry in the next decade?
> Will the Social Security system be available when my audience retires?

Each of these questions could have a conclusive answer. But because there is likely to be disagreement about the answer, persuasive speaking can help us to figure out the answer. A persuasive speech that tries to answer questions of facts does not simply inform an audience about what is already known. It attempts to persuade the audience that this explanation of the available evidence is the correct or most plausible one. Consequently, speeches about facts involve strengthening commitment or moderating opposition to a particular explanation.

Addressing Attitudes Speeches that focus on attitudes also attempt to strengthen an audience's commitment or moderate its opposition to an idea or practice. This focus can be a smart choice depending on your rhetorical situation. For example, if you are involved in a campaign to increase your college's support for the arts, you might need to heighten concern among the student body—in other words, strengthen students' commitments—before trying to get them to support a policy or take action. If you are speaking in support of gay marriage to an audience that has diverse viewpoints, you might decide that it is more important to moderate opposition and seek common ground than to promote a policy that is supported by only a portion of your audience.

Inventing and organizing a speech that focuses on attitudes will depend on the specifics of your topic and whether you want to strengthen or moderate your audience's existing commitments. In some instances, speakers will start by offering a coherent account of the evidence and then connecting that evidence to shared values. In other situations, speakers will start by amplifying shared values, offering criteria for evaluating an idea or practice, and then applying the criteria to the specific idea or practice under consideration.

Addressing Policies Policy speeches attempt to persuade audiences about the decisions that some group should make. It might be a decision that is made jointly by you and your audience, as when you are trying to persuade other people on your residence hall floor to agree on a policy about quiet hours. Or it might be a decision that you want other people to make, such as encouraging the city council to pass an ordinance that restricts panhandling.

Speeches focusing on policies might pursue any of the three audience-oriented purposes discussed above. However, the typical policy speech advocates action; the entire speech is designed to explain why some group should take a particular action or resist taking action. Depending on your audience, though, your speech may involve the other purposes. For example, advocating less regulation of industry in front of a liberal audience would mean moderating opposition, while discussing it with a group of students who are interested in joining Young Republicans might lead to a speech that is primarily about strengthening commitments.

PUBLIC SPOTLIGHT

Eboo Patel

Eboo Patel has emerged as one of today's leading voices for religious pluralism and interfaith dialogue. After nearly dropping out of college, he founded and now directs the Chicago-based Interfaith Youth Core (IFYC), which brings together high school students from diverse religious backgrounds to engage in service projects in their communities. A key part of Patel's vision for IFYC is that it encourages young people to "identify values they share with one another and then articulate how their religious traditions speak to those shared values" ("Eboo Patel"). Patel was named one of "thirty social visionaries under thirty changing the world" by *Utne Reader* in 2002 and was selected to be on the President's Faith Advisory Council in 2009.

Patel is a compelling speaker, both for his organization and for the broader importance of interfaith dialogue and bridging cultural divides based on shared values. His speech to the Nobel Peace Forum in 2004, for example, suggests that the religious mix of the contemporary United States is reflective of America's historical cultural diversity:

> America is a grand gathering of souls, the vast majority from elsewhere. A century ago it was Jews and Catholics from Southern and Eastern Europe who came, adding new texture to the American tradition. A century ago, it was Jane Addams who imagined and created a new America. Her conviction was that America needed to invite its new Catholic and Jewish immigrants to sit at its table. Her creation, Hull House, succeeded in deepening American democracy. More recently it has been Buddhists, Hindus, Muslims and a range of new Christians from Asia, Africa, the Middle East and the Latin world that have come. America is now the most religiously diverse nation on the planet (Patel).

Throughout his work, Eboo Patel persistently challenges his audiences to observe the overlap between different religions—not only to enrich their understanding of their own religious tradition, but also to create more favorable attitudes toward different religious perspectives.

 Social Media Spotlight

The Interfaith Youth Core has an active social media presence. In addition to Facebook and Twitter sites, its website includes a blog and podcasts that feature the voices of IYC alumni as well as staff members describing ongoing projects and issues. Their YouTube channel catalogs videos of participants and highlights media coverage of the organization.

Facebook: http://www.facebook.com/pages/Interfaith-Youth-Core/29924369552

Twitter: http://twitter.com/IFYC

Blog: http://www.ifyc.org/category/topics/blog

YouTube: http://www.youtube.com/user/InterfaithYouthCore

Discussions of policy have always been a part of public discourse. Over time, theorists of rhetoric and public speaking have identified the recurring issues in policy speeches and have developed organizational strategies that address these issues. The most fundamental strategy, as you will learn, is the problem–solution strategy, which provides evidence of a problem, outlines a solution, and justifies the solution in relation to its effects.

Addressing Direct Action When you want your audience to act directly rather than merely to support the actions of others, you are developing a speech that truly addresses action. The action may be individual-level behavior change, as in a speech encouraging students to be a designated driver. Or it may be collective action, as in a speech that asks students to join in a rally at the state capitol.

Speeches that attempt to motivate direct action often look similar to policy speeches, since both offer good reasons in support of some position on a significant issue. But direct action speeches ask for something more from an audience. It is one thing to solicit an audience's support for building a new gym on campus. It is quite another to persuade audience members to write a letter to the college president or donate some of their hard-earned money. Therefore, speakers who are focusing on action need to consider what would move the audience beyond passive agreement to direct action.

One tried-and-true format for speeches that promote action is known as Monroe's motivated sequence. It follows a pattern that is similar to a problem–solution strategy, with each step leading audiences toward a call to action that comes at the end of the speech.

Clarifying Your Persuasive Purpose

The above material suggests a variety of ways in which you can tailor your persuasive purpose for a more effective speech. Let's look at further examples to see how you might clarify your purpose.

Narrow Your Purpose At first, the most important way of narrowing your topic is to decide whether you are trying to influence your audience's attitude, either by strengthening a commitment or by weakening opposition, or whether your primary purpose is to promote action.

> *Topic:* Puppy mills
>
> *General purpose:* To persuade
>
> *Specific purpose:* To influence my audience to have a less favorable attitude toward puppy mills.

> *Topic:* Music with explicit lyrics
>
> *General purpose:* To persuade
>
> *Specific purpose:* To persuade my audience to boycott stores that refuse to sell music with explicit lyrics.

If your speech is attempting to influence attitudes, narrowing also can help you to identify whether your speech will focus on questions of fact or on values.

> *Specific purpose:* To influence my audience that puppy mills are unhealthy for both puppies and humans.
>
> *Specific purpose:* To influence my audience that limiting the sale of music is a threat to our freedoms.

In the first example, the specific purpose clearly intends to shape *attitudes* by casting puppy mills as a problem. But the focus on health suggests that the speech will answer factual questions about the impacts of puppy mills. The second example intends to influence attitudes about limitations on music sales by linking those limits to the value of freedom.

Identify Specific Audience Attitudes Reflecting on the specific attitudes of your audience is another means for clarifying your persuasive purpose. For example, a persuasive speech on nuclear energy might have a slightly different specific purpose depending on the audience.

> *Topic:* Nuclear energy
>
> *General purpose:* To persuade
>
> *Specific purpose* (sympathetic audience): To intensify my audience's attitude that nuclear energy is superior to coal as a fuel for electricity.
>
> *Specific purpose* (neutral audience): To influence my audience that nuclear energy is a desirable energy source for the twenty-first century.
>
> *Specific purpose* (hostile audience): To influence my audience to have a more favorable attitude toward nuclear energy.

Notice how the wording of the specific purpose does not change the general purpose of the speech: to persuade the audience by influencing their attitudes. But the wording does show how the speaker's purpose changes depending on the existing attitude of the audience. Unlike the first two audiences, a hostile audience is not likely to believe that nuclear energy is "a desirable energy source" after a single speech. But trying to moderate that audience's opposition by influencing them to have a slightly more favorable attitude might be a realistic goal.

Purpose statements for speeches that advocate action also can benefit from careful tailoring in light of audience attitudes. For example, if you are advocating that your college should build a new activities center, an effective specific purpose statement for a speech to administrators might look like this:

> *Topic:* Building a new student activities center
>
> *General purpose:* To persuade
>
> *Specific purpose:* To advocate that our college should build a new student activities center.

Different audiences and different obstacles could lead to more focused statements:

> *Specific purpose:* To persuade my audience that they should contribute to the fund for a new student activities center.
>
> *Specific purpose:* To persuade my audience that building a new activities center is a better use of resources than building a new residence hall.

Check with your instructor about how specific your purpose statement needs to be. The point is not to achieve a "perfect" statement, but to allow the process of writing your specific purpose statement to help you invent your persuasive speech as a whole.

Inventing Your Persuasive Speech

Several of the invention cues from chapter 8 are useful for identifying potential main points and supporting material in your persuasive speech. However, the rhetorical situations of persuasive speaking raise additional constraints and opportunities for you to consider.

Using Audience Feedback

In the classroom, you can use feedback that you received on previous speeches to help you prepare later speeches. What were your audience's questions? What ideas generated a lot of interest? Did your audience give you new information or share how your speech was relevant to them? Especially if you are continuing with the same topic in your persuasive speech, audience feedback can suggest a starting point for inventing a persuasive speech.

Audience questions provide an easy entry point into a subsequent speech. For example, after Kim's informative speech on credit cards, her audience was left wondering what rules their college had for allowing credit card companies to promote products on campus. Even though this was not the initial focus of Kim's interests, she learned that her audience wanted to know how this issue affected their campus and what they might do. As a result, Kim decided to explore her university's policies and determine how students might influence those policies.

Flashpoints of *audience interest* also can stimulate thinking about later speeches. Calvin's informative speech on genetically modified foods, for example, touched off a discussion about the high price of organic and natural food. His audience had a generally favorable attitude toward organic food, but they were convinced that it was too expensive for the average college student. Calvin knew that if he wanted to persuade people to eat more organic food, he would have to address the price issue in a compelling way.

Information provided by the audience also can help a speaker to find new possibilities for speeches. Aziz gave a speech about the tenets of Islam for his informative assignment, and during the feedback period, one of his classmates mentioned that she had seen a report about unfair and inaccurate media representations of Muslims. Aziz looked up the report and found several examples from U.S. media and popular culture that would provide a familiar point of reference for his audience in his persuasive speech.

Incorporating this kind of feedback into your next speech can help you to boost your ethos. By referring back to earlier speeches or mentioning specific statements from your audience, you will show that you have listened to their comments and taken them seriously enough to address. For example, Calvin decided to begin his persuasive speeches by acknowledging the strong opinions of his audience about food prices:

> "Organic food is so expensive!"
>
> "On my budget, I can hardly afford to pay for regular groceries, much less organics."
>
> "I don't call it Whole Foods—it's Whole Paycheck!"
>
> Have you ever found yourself thinking or saying any of these things? Some of you mentioned them after my last speech, and I have thought these same things when I make my weekly food run. But after doing a little investigating, I'm having a change of heart about organic food.

Here, Calvin is attempting to moderate his audience's opposition with regard to the price of organic food. He directly acknowledges his audience's beliefs and attitudes based on prior feedback and states that he shares some of those opinions. This helps him to establish common ground with his audience before posing challenges to their opinions.

Using Audience Research

Researching audience opinions is absolutely necessary for inventing an effective persuasive speech. This process can be broken down into two phases: identifying the crucial audience obstacles to persuasion and potential adaptation strategies and developing questions that help you to see which obstacles and strategies have relevance for your topic.

Identify Obstacles Each of the three persuasive purposes raises specific obstacles to persuasion that invite different adaptation strategies. At first, it might seem that there would be few obstacles for a speaker who is trying to strengthen a commitment. This purpose is typically appropriate for a sympathetic or neutral audience—in other words, people who are already open to the speaker's ideas if not outright supportive. But even these audiences might not be especially concerned about the issue. Therefore, a primary adaptation strategy is to *heighten the public significance of the issue* so that audience members perceive it as worthy of exploration. This is a necessary first step if you want the audience to make an informed judgment about whether something is favorable or desirable. In addition, speakers can adapt by *emphasizing the personal connection of the issue to the audience* so that the audience members' abstract concern for the issue becomes concrete. Finally, if an audience's support is based on limited awareness of alternatives, then you might decide to *inoculate the audience members against counterarguments* so that they can resist opposing messages.

For oppositional audiences, the primary obstacle is a difference of opinion with the speaker in terms of *values*. Audience members might simply have a different set of value priorities that lead them to see very different things as desirable. With such an audience, a speaker should focus on *establishing common ground* and *identifying shared values*, a topic that will be discussed in more detail later in this chapter. In other instances, opposition may come from incomplete or incorrect knowledge; in this case, a speaker should focus on *connecting new facts to strongly held audience values* or possibly *shifting to an informative speech*.

As with other types of persuasive speaking, advocates of policy and action may confront audiences that perceive a lack of urgency and importance. But these purposes raise additional obstacles. Taking then, action has costs as well as benefits, so the perceived costs—both to the individual and to the society as a whole—are always a primary obstacle for this type of persuasive speaking. In turn, speakers need to *minimize the costs of action, highlight the benefits,* and *show the audience members how they can act effectively*. When speaking to a hostile audience, an additional obstacle is the audience's attraction to alternatives, whether that is the current state of affairs or a different course of action. For these situations, speakers need to *highlight the flaws or limitations of possible alternatives*. Because oppositional audience members are not likely to completely change their mind, this strategy focuses instead on weakening their commitment to alternatives. You might even decide that influencing the attitudes of a hostile audience is a more appropriate purpose than trying to get the audience to act.

Table 13.1 shows how each of the persuasive purposes faces particular obstacles and suggests possible adaptation strategies.

TABLE 13.1 Persuasive Purposes, Obstacles, and Adaptation Strategies

Persuasive Purpose	Potential Obstacles	Adaptation Strategies
To strengthen commitments	Lack of commitment	Intensify commitment Heighten significance
	Awareness of other points of view	Inoculate, address objections
	Lack of coherent viewpoint	Provide a perspective
To moderate opposition	Incomplete/incorrect knowledge	(*Try informative speech*)
	Value conflicts	Establish common ground, shared values
To advocate action	Costs and barriers	Minimize costs, show efficacy
	Lack of urgency	Emphasize timeliness, costs of inaction
	Lack of importance	Heighten significance, emphasize outcomes
	Commitment to status quo/ other options	Show limits/flaws of other options

Develop Questions Once you have considered the typical obstacles to persuasion and the potential adaptation strategies, develop questions that you can ask your audience directly or determine indirectly. Your goal is to find opportunities for overcoming key obstacles or pursuing adaptation strategies that might resonate with their existing attitudes. Consider the following categories for developing questions:

- *Beliefs.* Incorrect, incomplete, or inadequate knowledge of your topic is often a critical obstacle in speaking to a general audience. Without adequate information, an audience may lack strong commitments on an issue, may not perceive the issue as urgent, and may not understand the practicality or desirability of certain courses of action. Therefore, it is important to identify whether your audience shares beliefs that are supportive of your point of view.

  As you saw in chapter 5, true/false questions and carefully crafted multiple-choice questions can reveal areas of belief that may deserve elaboration in your speech. For example, Cameron found out that his audience had a wide range of strong opinions about delisting wolves as an endangered species, but hardly anyone knew how many wolves were needed to maintain a viable population. Consequently, he spent more of his speech talking about the latest ecological research on wolf populations.

- *Values.* Taking stock of your audience's values can give you a sense of why audience members perceive the topic the way they do. Values can affect their perception of the problem and its importance, the coherence of their viewpoint, and the desirability of certain actions. For example, an audience that values material well-being over intellectual stimulation is likely to have different attitudes about what your college's academic requirements should look like.

  In addition, values point to opportunities for motivating your audience. Classmates who value material well-being may be persuaded to take more communication classes when they find out that employers rank strong communication skills as one of the highest criteria for making hiring decisions. As this example suggests, effective persuasion is often a matter of sharing important information to shape beliefs and then attaching those beliefs to key values.

- *Relevance and perceived significance.* Does your audience see the topic as personally relevant or important on a public level? In the context of persuasive speaking, relevance and significance are directly related to whether your audience will have strong commitments on your topic, whether audience members have become aware of alternative viewpoints, and whether they see the issue as urgent.

- *Resistance to action.* Listeners have all sorts of reasons for not taking action on some issue: It's too difficult; it costs too much; they don't know where to start; it's inconvenient; they don't have time; it won't make a difference; it might not work. By finding out what is really stopping your audience from acting, you can give special attention to minimizing or eliminating those barriers to action. For example, Amber's audience was sensitive to the plight of restaurant servers and supported the idea of tipping. But they also thought that tipping restaurant servers really had no effect on the quality of service. So Amber spent a fair amount of time in her speech describing how servers talk about and react to getting a poor tip and a great tip.

Ultimately, using audience research as well as audience feedback is a matter of honest, patient, and respectful listening as described in chapter 3. If you really listen to what your audience knows about your topic and what really concerns and motivates the audience members, then you are in a much better position to engage their viewpoints directly with effective, ethical persuasion.

Using Topic Research

As with audience research, your first step with topic research should be to revisit the invention cues from chapter 8. The common topics—existence, definition, comparison, causality, correlation, and time and space—are just as pertinent to persuasive speeches, and several are absolutely necessary to examine, depending on the organizational pattern you use.

On civic and political matters, topical analysis also takes the form of identifying the stock issues that are related to a proposed policy. **Stock issues** are similar to common topics because they apply regardless of the subject matter. However, stock issues are specific to questions of policy or action; when a change is being proposed, stock issues are the typical issues on which people are likely to disagree or resist change. If you are considering a speech that proposes some policy, consider the following stock issues:

- *Need for change.* Does the current state of affairs need to be changed? If the audience does not see a need for change, then a persuasive speech should focus on shifting audience attitudes or advocating a very limited course of action. For example, Thomas believed that there was a need to repeal the Patriot Act, but his audience did not see the Act as a relevant issue in their lives. As a result, he stepped back from advocating a repeal of the Act; instead, he attempted to persuade his audience to have unfavorable attitude toward it.

- *Barriers to change.* What is standing in the way of change? If the current situation is framed as a problem, then the barrier is often an underlying cause of that problem. If the situation is framed as "OK but needs improvement," then the barrier is some obstacle that is preventing things from being ideal. For Amy, the barrier that related to her speech on healthy food options on campus was the college's contracts with outside vendors. If those contracts could be changed, then more nutritious foods would be available. Her speech would need to spend a fair amount of time explaining those contracts before advocating a change.

- *Proposal for change.* What should be done? Thinking about alternative proposals for change is absolutely necessary for speeches that advocate action. If there are several proposals for change circulating in public discourse, then a persuasive speech might need to spend time comparing those proposals. Kira's speech on repurposing a nearby mall, for example, compared three different proposals before advocating her preferred choice. If the only alternative is doing nothing, then speakers might need to explore why doing nothing is still appealing. Eric's speech proposing a city ordinance mandating helmets for bicyclists focused on people's strong resistance to wearing helmets.

- *Practicality of change.* Is the change feasible? It is one thing to have a great idea for change but quite another to plan how that change will actually happen. Therefore, a key issue for any proposed change is whether it can be implemented practically. Tanner's speech on "greening the campus" had a lot of great ideas about sustainability, but without a clear idea of the steps that would make that change real and the funding and staffing that would be needed to implement the changes, his audience thought his speech seemed too idealistic. Additional research on how other campuses have put similar ideas into practice would have been a great addition to his speech.

- *Advantages of change.* Will the change create benefits? If your audience is trying to decide between different courses of action or is uncertain about the benefits of adopting your proposed action, then you might spend time discussing the many ways in which your proposed action will be better than the current state of affairs or other actions. In Eric's speech on bicycle helmets, he vividly compared the effects of bike accidents on helmet wearers and nonwearers.

Using stock issues for analysis also can help you to reflect further on the purpose of your speech. A speech that advocates policy or action may spend a fair amount of time trying to shift attitudes about the feasibility of that proposal. For example, a speech that advocates boycotting of a product or company might need to overcome resistance to the idea of boycotts in general by showing audiences how a boycott can be a practical and effective strategy for pursuing change.

Organizing Your Persuasive Speech

As with invention, the organizational strategies that you learned for informative speaking also can be applied to persuasive speaking situations. Sequential and analytical strategies can be useful for developing specific sections of a persuasive speech. For example, a speech might track the progression of a public issue such as AIDS or illustrate a shift over time in social attitudes about interracial relationships. The compare-and-contrast strategy and the key issues strategy both can be useful for showing how one position—whether on facts, attitudes, policy, or action—is superior to another.

In most situations, though, you will be best served by employing organizational patterns that serve particular persuasive purposes. This section identifies some of these patterns and provides concrete suggestions for when and how to use those patterns.

Criteria–Application Pattern

The **criteria–application pattern** offers audiences a set of standards or criteria and then applies those standards to a specific situation. This pattern is especially useful when you want to make a clear-cut judgment about factual issues or when you want to use shared values or goals to evaluate a specific practice or policy. In relation to your audience, the criteria help you to establish common ground by stating broad, general ideas before getting into the details of a particular situation.

The criteria–application pattern works well to focus attention on the most relevant criteria for establishing facts. Often, a speech like this will define key terms in the process of developing the criteria in the first part of the speech (Inch and Warnick). Consider this basic outline for a speech about standardized tests:

Specific purpose: To persuade my audience that standardized tests do not accurately measure a student's capabilities.

Central idea: Standardized tests fail to measure important student capabilities.

Main points:

    I. Definitions

        A. Standardized tests are examinations of general intellectual skills that are scored in a consistent way for all students.

        B. In this context, capabilities are the behaviors, attitudes, and skills needed to succeed in school and in the workplace.

    II. Criteria

        A. Tests need to measure writing skills.

        B. Tests need to measure speaking skills.

        C. Tests need to measure one's ability to adapt to new situations.

        D. Tests need to measure skills fairly, without cultural bias.

III. Application
    A. Most standardized tests explicitly measure writing skills.
    B. However, no standardized tests measure speaking skills.
    C. Standardized tests are not designed to measure or evaluate intangible capabilities.
    D. There is some evidence that standardized tests are culturally biased.

After defining the key terms, this speech provides criteria for considering the supporting material. Think of these criteria as providing ground rules for the rest of the speech: What should count as evidence? What conditions need to be met to support the central idea? The application section of the speech then presents supporting material that addresses each of those points. In this speech, for example, the subpoints under "Application" might include examples of specific standardized tests or testimony from educational experts.

The criteria–application pattern also can be used in speeches that attempt to influence attitudes or advocate policies. For example, the criteria may be broad goals or values that are intended to shape the audience's attitudes about a specific practice or policy:

Specific purpose: To moderate my audience's opposition to new graduation requirements.

Central idea: Our new graduation requirements are better than the current requirements.

Main points:

I. Definitions
II. Criteria
    A. In general, requirements should ensure that students understand and appreciate different cultures.
    B. Requirements also should ensure that students have basic competency in writing, speaking, and mathematics.
    C. Requirements should also be focused and straightforward so that students can complete them efficiently.
III. Application.
    A. The new Global Cultures requirement will better prepare graduates for our multicultural world.
    B. The new Public Speaking requirement will give students practical skills that employers desire most.
    C. The new distribution requirements have fewer categories, and each category requires exactly one course.

Here, the speaker uses criteria to put specific requirements in a positive light. If the audience is resistant to the idea of having new requirements, the criteria encourage them to see that these requirements may in fact have some benefit for them.

Problem–Solution Pattern

The **problem–solution pattern** offers audiences a policy that will contribute to fixing some damaging conditions. This pattern is a standard option for most policy speeches. Beyond an explanation of the problem that motivates the policy, this pattern invites speakers to spend roughly half of the speech discussing how the policy will be implemented and what the likely consequences will be. The stock issues that you learned about earlier in the chapter should be used to flesh out this basic organizational pattern.

For problem–solution speeches, the stock issues are generally addressed in the following order:

I. Problem
   A. Need for change
   B. Barriers to change

II. Solution
   A. Proposal for change
   B. Practicality of change
   C. Advantages of change

In this pattern, the first half of the speech is devoted to demonstrating the existence of the problem and identifying causes or factors that perpetuate it. The second half of the speech proposes a solution and provides support for it in two main ways: by showing that the proposal can be implemented practically and by showing that it will have advantages over the current state of affairs or rival plans. Examine this working outline:

Specific purpose: To persuade my audience to support "take-back" laws for consumer electronics.

Central idea: Congress should pass a law requiring producers of consumer electronics to sponsor collection and recycling programs for computers and televisions.

Main points:
   I. Electronic waste is a growing problem in the United States.
      A. Millions of tons of e-waste are dumped in U.S. landfills annually. This waste presents clear risks to human health and the environment.
      B. There is little incentive for producers to take responsibility for this unique type of garbage.
   II. This problem can be solved with a national "take-back" law.
      A. Congress should pass a take-back law requiring electronics companies to collect and recycle computers and televisions.
      B. This law would direct environmental agencies to work with companies to coordinate the collection of used consumer electronics.

      C. Funds for the program would be generated by a surtax on new
computers and televisions.

      D. Take-back laws would have several advantages over our current
situation.

        1. They would increase the rate of recycling.

        2. They would direct e-waste into safe recycling programs,
thereby protecting workers' health.

        3. They would keep toxic metals from leaching into ground water,
thereby keeping our drinking water safe.

        4. By forcing companies to deal with their own waste, these laws
would encourage companies to produce more environmentally
friendly products.

Notice how the solutions section is organized to address each of the stock issues. First, it states the specific proposal for change; then it explains how that
change would be put into practice. Finally, the advantages section starts by
describing how the proposal solves the problem and then adds an additional
benefit of the proposal. In a more developed outline, these portions of the
speech should be carefully tailored to the knowledge level of the audience.

Comparative Patterns

Two types of comparative patterns work well for persuasive speaking. The
comparative advantages pattern pits two competing solutions against one
another to highlight the advantages of one solution. This pattern is essentially
a version of the compare/contrast pattern for informative speeches, and it can
be used in conjunction with the key issues pattern.

    For example, suppose that your campus is considering where to build a
new residence hall and has narrowed down the available areas to two choices.
A persuasive speech could advocate for one location over the other:

Specific purpose: To persuade my audience that North Campus is the best
location for the new residence hall.

Central idea: North Campus is a better location for the new residence hall than
South Campus.

Main points*:*

    I. North Campus has better automobile access than South Campus.

    II. North Campus is closer to most academic buildings.

    III. North Campus would have less impact on wildlife.

Because the need for change is usually well established, a comparative advantages approach like this one begins by presenting the proposal for change.
Then the bulk of the speech focuses on the key issues for decision makers,
showing how, on each issue, the proposal is superior to alternatives.

The **elimination of alternatives pattern** offers audience a series of proposals and shows the flaws of each one before settling on the speaker's preferred alternative. This pattern can be useful when you are trying to help your audience work through competing factual explanations or several potential policies or actions. Thus, it works well when the audience is already aware that alternatives exist but is uninformed about their strengths and weaknesses or perhaps committed to a different alternative than the one you are proposing. The following example identifies alternative policies, eliminating two ideas before advocating the third.

> *Specific purpose:* To persuade my audience that the best way to improve the state's financial situation is to lower taxes on businesses.
>
> *Central idea:* Our state should reduce business taxes by 2%.
>
> *Main points:*
>
> I. There is widespread agreement that the state's financial situation is shaky. In recent months, legislators, the governor, and advocacy groups have been debating how to improve the state's financial situation.
>
> II. Increasing government spending may stimulate the economy in the short term, but it will significantly increase the state's budget deficit.
>
> III. Implementing a statewide lottery could yield a significant amount of money, but it is essentially a regressive tax.
>
> IV. Reducing business taxes is the option most likely to spur long-term economic growth in our state.

In this example, the speaker begins by establishing common ground by discussing the public controversy. The speech then proceeds to explain the various alternatives that have emerged in that controversy. It saves the preferred alternative for the final point, showing how it has the greatest strengths compared to the others.

Motivated Sequence Pattern

The **motivated sequence pattern** is the primary strategy for speeches that ask audiences to take action. As the title suggests, this organizational pattern takes an audience through a sequence of steps that are designed to increase listeners' motivation to act. The specific action is the central idea of the speech.

The motivated sequence shares some characteristics of the problem–solution and elimination patterns. Like the elimination pattern, the motivated sequence delays statement of the central idea. But instead of examining alternatives, the motivated sequence focuses on the speaker's preferred alternative—an action that the speaker wants the audience to take. The speaker sets up the desirability of this action by evoking a need in the audience that can be satisfied by the action.

The sequence of steps moves as follows:

I. *Attention:* Arouse the audience's interest in your topic.

II. *Need:* Evoke a need or unmet goal.

III. *Satisfaction:* Offer a course of action that satisfies the need.

IV. *Visualization:* Depict how life will be better if the audience acts.

V. *Action:* Direct the audience to take specific action.

Notice that these steps are similar to the problem–solution pattern. Both patterns attempt to show some need in the first half of a speech. The satisfaction and visualization steps show the fulfillment of that need, in much the way that the solution section shows how a public problem can be solved. Both patterns have the same underlying logic; they simply apply that logic differently depending on whether the purpose is passive agreement with a policy proposal or a direct action by listeners.

For example, consider how you could make minor adjustments to shift between a motivated sequence speech and a problem–solution speech:

Motivated Sequence Pattern	**Problem–Solution Pattern**
I. Attention	I. Introduction
Think about the majesty of our national parks.	Think about the majesty of our national parks.
II. Need	II. Problem
National parks have big staffing shortages.	National parks have big staffing shortages.
	This problem results from dwindling public funding and limited training opportunities.
III. Satisfaction	III. Solution
This summer, volunteer at a national park.	Congress should increase funding for staff and volunteers in the National Park Service.
	This increase could be achieved with a small increase in user fees.
IV. Visualization	
Imagine the people you will meet and the positive experiences you will create.	Better staffing would enhance visitor experiences and strengthen public support for the National Park Service.
V. Call to Action	IV. Conclusion
In early spring, contact a park to get involved with their Volunteers-In-Parks program.	Congress can sustain the majesty of our national parks by increasing funding for staff and volunteers.

As you can see, the main points of the motivated sequence correspond with the problem–solution pattern. If you are still wrestling with the specific purpose of your speech, experiment with the different patterns to see how they can help you to generate different possibilities for your purpose as well as your central idea.

MOTIVATING AUDIENCES
Individuals may resist taking action if they believe that their input will not make a difference. Persuasive speakers can remind them that their individual voices are amplified when they are part of a larger collective effort.

CASE CONCLUSION

Anne's Speech on Disability Access

Anne considered advocating for institutional changes to improve handicapped accessibility, but the solution would have been long and difficult to explain, and her classmates were not much interested in campus politics. Instead, she decided to ask for direct action on a personal level. She crafted her specific purpose as follows:

Specific purpose: To persuade my audience that they have the power to alleviate handicap inaccessibility on our campus.

Another round of audience questionnaires showed that Anne had convinced listeners of the problem. The main resistance to action was that they simply did not know what to do and whether any action would be feasible. This made the motivated sequence an appropriate pattern for her speech. She gained attention with a clever quotation and statistic about wheelchair use and picked up on this appeal in the need step by describing all the challenges she experienced when she was put in the position of a disabled student for an afternoon. Anne also made an explicit connection to how this problem had personal relevance for her listeners.

Her satisfaction step then offered an acronym that identified simple, personal actions that her audience could take on a daily basis. She took advantage of her audience's feeling of disempowerment about influencing bigger changes to explain that these personal actions were something they could do right away that would help other students immediately. Then her visualization step envisioned a ripple effect: a campus where the spirit of helpfulness was pervasive. Finally, her call to action reinforced the acronym and reminded the audience of what they could do as soon as they left the classroom that day.

WORKING OUTLINE

Anne's Speech on Disability Access

Specific purpose: To persuade my audience that they have the power to alleviate handicap inaccessibility on our campus.

Central idea: Overcoming architectural and attitudinal barriers to accessibility starts with every individual becoming "A.W.A.R.E."

I. Introduction

Anne starts with a quotation that has a twist at the end to gain the audience's attention.

A. "From sea to shining sea, like Lady Liberty. She reigns over all she sees. She's beauty and she is grace, she is queen of 50 states. She is elegance and taste, she's Miss <u>wheelchair</u> United States."

B. According to researchers at the University of California in San Francisco, 1.6 million people use wheelchairs in the United States to get around. With a number like this, this also means that more people in wheelchairs are becoming active in wheelchair beauty pageants, but more important, we are going to be increasingly more likely to encounter these individuals on our campus.

Her brief reference to personal experience enhances her ethos and gets developed in the body of the speech.

The central idea introduces the acronym that she returns to in the satisfaction step.

C. I may not be in a wheelchair today, but I have been, and every day I am one of many people on this campus who see handicap inaccessibility and feel that they can do nothing about it.

D. Overcoming the architectural and attitudinal barriers to accessibility on our campus starts with every individual becoming "aware." A-W-A-R-E: Attitude for Willingness to Act, and Reinforcement Everywhere.

E. Today in my speech, I will illustrate everyday problems with accessibility and how becoming AWARE will empower these individuals and make our campus fit for a "Miss wheelchair United States."

(*Transition: First let's take a look at some common problems on our campus that cause wheelchair inaccessibility.*)

II. Problem/Need

A. One fall day in my freshman year of college, my classmates and I decided to sit down for what we believed in and spend a day in the life of someone who spends all the days of their life in a wheelchair. Having never been handicapped before, much like many of you, I must say that this experience opened my eyes to the way the world sees, or doesn't see, people in wheelchairs on this campus.

B. I experienced several architectural barriers when I was in a wheelchair.
   1. Doors
      a. Even though many buildings on campus have automatic doors, several do not.
      b. Classroom doors also present accessibility barriers.

2. Bathrooms
   a. A handicap bathroom is not just a bathroom with more room for people who do not live in a wheelchair.
   b. Story about my experience in waiting for bathroom.

C. Now if I were Miss Wheelchair Montana and the announcer asked me what I'd like to change about the world, I'd have to say, "I'd like to be able to open a door."

D. This accessibility problem is relevant to students who are not handicapped.
   1. Blocking ramps with bikes.
   2. Using handicap bathrooms.
   3. Blocking doorways.

(Transition: Now that we understand some common accessibility issues, I want to show you how you can help.)

III. Plan/Satisfaction

Many of you may think that handicap accessibility is an important issue but feel that there is nothing that you personally can do about it. Overcoming architectural and attitudinal barriers to accessibility starts with a simple step: Every individual needs to become "A.W.A.R.E." A-W-A-R-E.

A. A is for attitude. Attitudes can promote or preempt action. What are your attitudes about your ability to foster change? What are your attitudes toward people in wheelchairs? Having the right attitude is the first stage in becoming AWARE.

B. W is for willingness. You must be willing to take a moment out of your day to open the door for someone who is struggling. You must be willing to wait for an open stall in the bathroom that is not the handicap one. You must be willing to see these people for who they are, not how they get from point A to B.

C. A is for action. Join or simply support ADSUM or measures on campus that make accessibility more achievable. Advocate for a change in the way those around you see people in wheelchairs.

D. R is for reinforcement. Reinforcement among your group of friends or your classmates, reinforcement of the attitudes and willingness to change. Talk to your peers, and look for opportunities to raise awareness.

E. E is for everywhere. Here in this building, here on campus, here around town. Everywhere all the time, for everyone.

(Transition: Now that you know what to do, I'd like you to imagine yourself doing it and the cascading consequences of your actions.)

Tangible, concrete examples give listeners a clear sense of the existence of this problem.

This portion of the speech heightens personal relevance and identifies a cause of the problem without directly blaming listeners.

This section states the central idea and gives students a concrete guide for action.

These five elements incorporate both individual-level change and larger policy-level change, but the emphasis is on individual action in this speech. The motivated sequence is thus an appropriate organizational pattern.

IV. Practicality/Visualization

A. Awareness is knowledge, and knowledge is power. You have the power to change this campus for the better and change the lives of your fellow classmates in the process.

The visualization step makes an appeal to sympathy here.

B. Think about how you appreciate it when someone opens a door for you. It may be a small thing for you, but it makes a real difference for students with disabilities.

C. When you reinforce these ideas among your friends, it is like a ripple in a lake. People all across campus can benefit just from a few words you say.

V. Conclusion/Call to Action

The simile used here gives listeners a visual representation of the effects of their action.

A. Sometimes people need a ramp to create a level playing field. You have the power to make yourself and our campus more AWARE of accessibility issues on campus.

B. Albert Einstein once said, "A mind that has been stretched will never return to its original dimension." I dare you to stretch your mind and attitudes through this plan of awareness, and I promise you it is an attitude you will never regret.

Summary

PURPOSES OF PERSUASIVE SPEAKING

- The purpose of a persuasive speech is determined by aligning the audience response you desire with the general subject of the speech.

- Persuasive speeches usually seek to strengthen an audience's commitment, moderate their opposition, or advocate some form of action. Their subject may be a question of fact, an attitude, a policy, or direct action.

INVENTING YOUR PERSUASIVE SPEECH

- Audience research for persuasive speeches should focus on beliefs, values, perceptions of significance and relevance, and sources of resistance.

- Topical analysis can highlight the stock issues that speakers are expected to address, especially for speeches about policy or action.

- Linguistic analysis can direct attention to key values as resources for persuasion.

ORGANIZING YOUR PERSUASIVE SPEECH

- The criteria–application pattern establishes clear standards or guidelines for answering questions of fact, shaping attitudes, or evaluating policies.

- The problem–solution and motivated sequence patterns share the logic of identifying a need or problem and then proposing an action or solution to address it.

- Comparative patterns can be used to evaluate the strengths and weaknesses of competing solutions systematically. Finally, the motivated sequence relies on a psychological pattern of need arousal and fulfillment to encourage listeners to take action.

Key Terms

distraction, p. 328
cynicism, p. 328
polarization, p. 330
stock issues, p. 341
criteria–application pattern, p. 343

problem–solution pattern, p. 345
comparative advantages pattern, p. 346
elimination of alternatives pattern, p. 347
motivated sequence pattern, p. 347

Comprehension

1. What are two obstacles that speakers face in a public sphere that is overloaded with persuasive messages?

2. What are two primary adaptation strategies for trying to strengthen an audience's commitment to their current point of view?

3. When speaking to an audience that is opposed to your point of view, should your goal be to get audience members to switch their position? Why or why not?

4. How can speeches on questions of fact be persuasive, not just informative?

5. What is the difference between a speech that addresses policy and a speech that addresses direct action?

6. What are three ways in which audience feedback on prior speeches can help you invent a persuasive speech?

7. What are the stock issues in persuasive speeches?

8. Which organizational patterns would be appropriate for a speech addressing a question of fact?

9. What are the five steps of the motivated sequence?

Application

1. Take an informal survey of your classmates' attitudes about a current campus issue. Then come up with central ideas for three speeches: one that strengthens their commitments, one that moderates opposition, and one that advocates action.

2. Look at a national newspaper or magazine that discusses current events, and identify two articles: one that appears to be *informative* and another that seeks persuasion on a question of fact. How can you tell the difference between the two?

3. Find the website of your Congressional representative or Senator, and locate a page that describes this person's position on a particular issue. Which of the stock issues does he or she address, and what sort of language does he or she use to describe the issue?

4. Using the same issue that you chose for question 1, develop a simple outline for a problem–solution speech. Then, with a small group of classmates, play the roles of different people or groups on campus that might disagree with that speech. Have these people raise disagreements on the stock issues.

5. Develop a motivated sequence speech that encourages students to take this course next semester. Feel free to tailor different speeches to different groups of students who provide ready-made audiences for you.

Supporting Your Persuasive Speech

This chapter is intended to help you:

- Craft emotional appeals and use them ethically
- Establish credibility and trust with your audience
- Develop sound patterns of reasoning to support your main points
- Avoid fallacies that are often used to advocate policies

In chapter 1, you learned that speakers appeal to audiences in three main ways. These three appeals—ethos, logos, and pathos—are all crucial forms of support in persuasive speaking. Think of them as three legs of a stool. A speech that offers a lot of good evidence (logos) and reveals the speaker as a knowledgeable person (ethos) may not be persuasive if it fails to stir the emotions of the audience (pathos). Likewise, a speech with strong reasons and emotional appeals may not be persuasive if the audience doesn't trust the speaker.

The challenge of persuasive speaking is determining the mix of appeals that will work best for your audience and your situation. If you are speaking to a hostile audience, for example, establishing your ethos may matter more than the specific evidence or reasons you provide. As you learn more about rhetorical

Lindsey's Speech on Adderall

For many reasons, Lindsey felt that it was important to do her persuasive speech on the topic of Adderall. She wanted to persuade her classmates to have a more negative perception of the drug so that they might think twice about using it as a "study drug." She knew that the drug was prevalent on campus, yet she observed that many of her peers did not seem to know much about it. So Lindsey knew that she would have to establish a unique perspective on the topic. She would have to use supporting material that would make her appear credible, and she would need to do something to connect with her audience emotionally to challenge their carefree attitude about the drug.

appeals in this chapter, you should develop a better sense of *what* these appeals look like as well as *when and how* they can be used most effectively in persuasive speaking. ■

Pathos: The Appeal of Emotion

Perhaps no part of public speaking is more misunderstood than pathos, or the appeal to the audience's emotions. The conventional wisdom since the time of the Sophists in ancient Greece is that emotion gets in the way of reason and interferes with a listener's ability to make good decisions. During the Enlightenment, with the rise of science as the privileged way of knowing the world, "*reason* was widely taken to be the most valuable and most important human faculty" (Brummett). Even today, it is not surprising to see a headline that reads, "Jury verdict a triumph of reason over emotion."

But the rhetorical tradition has often resisted the privileging of reason over emotion, instead seeing the two as closely intertwined. Aristotle saw that thoughts and beliefs—the stuff of rational thinking—contribute to our emotional responses. For example, feeling joy after successfully tutoring someone is based on a rational belief that you actually helped to improve the person's performance. More recently, the political consultant and neuroscientist Drew Westen has argued that voters do not make decisions with cold logic alone; instead, their emotional attachments play a key role in how they evaluate political candidates and policies.

Effective—and ethical—use of emotional appeals demands that speakers give careful attention to how pathos and logos fit together. As you will see, both the purposes of pathos and the emotional appeals themselves reveal the complex mixture of reason and emotion in our lives.

The Purposes of Pathos

It might seem obvious that you should use emotional appeals in persuasive speaking, but why? What are the reasons for or purposes of incorporating pathos in your speeches? Scholars have pointed to several ways in which emotional appeals provide support for speeches.

Gaining Attention A tear-jerking movie, an elated friend, and even a hopeful politician all can attract people's attention through their emotional appeal. Sadness, joy, hope, and anger all can jostle people out of their ordinary routine, moving them from a state of distraction or apathy to one of engagement. Drew Westen makes this point eloquently with regard to the discussion of public issues:

> We do not pay attention to arguments unless they engender our interest, enthusiasm, fear, anger, or contempt. We are not *moved* by leaders with whom we do not feel an emotional resonance. We do not find policies worth debating if they don't touch on the emotional implications for ourselves, our families, or things we hold dear (16).

His point is not limited to political leaders. Even in the classroom or on campus, you are speaking in a world that is overloaded with messages, as we saw in chapters 1 and 13. As a result, contemporary speakers need to consider how they might break through the noise of the public sphere without sacrificing credibility or ethical standing with their listeners.

Focusing Perception Scholars who take a cognitive approach to emotions have shown how our emotional responses are not just knee-jerk, thoughtless reactions. Instead, emotions can serve us by guiding us to what is most relevant and meaningful about a particular situation. Emotion can help us to perceive "a situation or event as a moral problem" (Koziak 16); emotions give us a sense of which things are right or wrong.

This way of thinking about emotions should remind us that good decision making does not mean suppressing or ignoring emotions. For example, getting angry when a fellow student has been assaulted is an appropriate response, and having a feeling of kindness toward others is arguably better than being completely emotionless. Feeling these emotions and allowing them to play a part in our thought processes are not the sign of irrationality; they are the sign of humanity.

Connecting Us to Others The kinds of emotions that are relevant to rhetoric are what we might call "social emotions." They orient us in the world and shape our relationships with others. As rhetorical theorist Thomas Farrell argues, "Emotions are themselves relational, allowing the recognition we require whenever we are taken outside our own immediacy: from the neighborhood to the moral community" (71). In other words, emotions are not simply the way we feel "inside" ourselves. Our internal feelings are always connecting us to other people in certain ways.

This reason explains more broadly why pathos is so important to public speaking and the public sphere. When you appeal to emotions, you are not only trying to motivate your audience; you are also encouraging them to have a certain kind of relationship with other people. The rest of this section will identify some of these "social emotions" and discuss how to use them ethically in your speeches.

Identifying and Using Appeals to Pathos

Speakers can call on a wide range of emotions. Anger, fear, sympathy, and friendliness are some of the key emotions to which you might appeal regularly in persuasive speaking.

Anger The classic definition of anger is the impulse for revenge when you observe an unfair attack on something you cherish. Today, it would probably be considered unethical for speakers to encourage or provoke revenge. But we can think of **anger** as that sense of being upset about an injustice and wanting to rectify it. From this perspective, an appeal to anger is a rhetorical strategy connecting some supporting material about an injustice or unfair situation to a broader attitude, policy, or action.

These definitions suggest that an effective and ethical appeal to anger needs to meet several criteria. It needs to *identify a specific action or situation,* depict it as *unfair or unwarranted,* and *encourage identification* with the person or group that has been wronged. For example, trying to generate anger about a large institution such as "our university" or "the government" is ethically questionable, since it prevents your audience from accurately understanding who took a particular action and determining whether that person's action was fair or warranted. Instead, be specific and give details that suggest why the action is unfair.

> Vice President Jones's decision to cut funding for the Student Health Center is unconscionable! With the rise in attempted suicides and assaults reports on our campus, student health deserves more support, not less. These cuts mean that the Suicide Prevention Hotline and the Peers Against Sexual Assault group will be less equipped to help our fellow students when they need it the most.

Fear **Fear** involves feeling upset about some dangerous or destructive event in the future. As with anger, you can see that an appeal to fear needs to be based on adequate evidence about the event in question. An effective, ethical fear appeal requires that you not only *display the dangers* of the event, but also *provide an honest assessment of the probability* of those dangers actually happening.

For example, during discussions of health care reform, some advocates appealed to fear by claiming that certain proposals would force people to face "death panels" to judge whether individuals were worthy of getting medical treatment. This claim was deemed the 2009 "Lie of the Year" by the staff of the website Politifact.com; no such panels were proposed, showing that this appeal failed to honestly state the probability of danger (Holan). A better fear appeal might show specific examples of how treatment costs negatively affect health care decisions.

In other words, fear appeals that are effective and ethical do not exaggerate the threat. Outlandish or extreme claims may get people's attention, but critical listeners will want to know whether some event is likely to happen to them. In addition, if you hype fears now, you are likely to be less credible with audiences over time.

Sympathy **Sympathy** is the feeling of compassion or sorrow that emerges when we see others suffering. For example, you might sympathize with a person who falls gravely ill, especially if the person is not responsible for his or her illness. Sympathy also is connected to perception of our own circumstances and anticipation of our future. We may be more likely to feel sympathy for another person when we sense our own vulnerability to a similar situation.

Consider this example of an appeal to sympathy in testimony from Texas resident Robin Beaton on health insurance reform:

> In May 2008, I went to the dermatologist for acne. A word was written on my chart and interpreted incorrectly as meaning pre-cancerous. Shortly thereafter, I was diagnosed with Invasive HER-2 Genetic Breast Cancer, a very aggressive form of breast cancer. I was told I needed a double mastectomy. When the surgeons scheduled my surgery I was pre-certified for my two days hospitalization. The Friday before the Monday I was scheduled to have my double mastectomy, Blue Cross red flagged my chart due to the dermatologist report. The dermatologist called Blue Cross directly to report that I only had acne and please not hold up my coming surgery. Blue Cross called me to inform me that they were launching a 5 year medical investigation into my medical history and that this would take approximately 3 months.

This passage shows how even a plain description can evoke sympathy. An ordinary citizen is suffering through no fault of her own, and listeners may sense that a similar fate could happen to themselves. This reveals two important criteria for a sympathy appeal: It should involve characters who are *relatively blameless* for their situation, and it should *provide an honest assessment of the probability* of that situation occurring in their own lives. A statistic earlier in the speech about the number of people who lose coverage each day helps this appeal to meet that latter criterion.

Kindness and Friendship Finally, the emotions of kindness and friendship are very similar in their underlying feeling. **Kindness** is the generous feeling of wanting to help others for their own sake, not for the sake of one's own personal gain or the possibility of getting something in return. **Friendship** is the ongoing connection you feel to others when you want them to have a good life for their own sake, not because you may perceive a benefit for yourself as a result. You feel both emotions when you respect the needs and wants of others.

The difference between kindness and friendship is mostly a matter of scope. Kindness moves people to act directly and so is important for speeches that motivate direct action. If you are advocating involvement in a local blood drive, an appeal to kindness might describe situations in which blood donations saved lives. Thus, an effective appeal to kindness *shows people in great need* and *connects the audience's action to the fulfillment of that need.*

Appeals to friendship are typical in speeches that attempt to shape an audience's commitments or need to establish common ground. You can do this by *identifying the things that you and your audience agree are good or bad* or *displaying your own acts of generosity or kindness* as a concrete way of articulating shared values. For example, imagine that your local hospital wishes to expand onto city property. If residents are skeptical of the hospital directors and their motives, a hospital administrator might remind the audience of shared commitments as well as acts of generosity to the community:

> One thing that is great about our community is that we care about one another. We all want one another to live happy and healthy lives. We volunteer at the homeless shelter, we contribute to charities, and we do important work through our communities of worship. We at the hospital do our share, too, most directly by providing hundreds of thousands of dollars of care to those who are unable to pay for emergency care.

The appeal to friendship in public speaking, then, should not be thought of as a speaker's attempt to "make friends" with the audience as one might do in a context of interpersonal communication. Instead, the goal is to reveal the values that we share as members of a community.

Pathos and Delivery

Using the guidelines for emotional appeals in the previous section will help you to generate the content of those appeals in your speeches. But one other issue often comes up for beginning speakers who are trying to use emotion effectively: What is the most effective way to deliver an emotional appeal?

Much of rhetorical theory follows the ancient teachers of rhetoric, who emphasized that speakers need to display their emotions through their delivery. One scholar identifies a clear rule from the ancient teacher Quintilian: "The advocate must imagine and feel the emotion himself. Sincerity counts" (Katula 9). This rule says much more about effective delivery than a "how-to" list of gestures, vocal changes, or facial expressions can. The key to delivering an effective emotional appeal is that you, as a speaker and a citizen, actually feel the emotion that you have on display. After all, emotions are social; they are ways of relating to your audience, not just feelings that you attempt to manipulate.

Consequently, emotional appeals need to be delivered in a way that is authentic to your own feelings if you wish to maintain an ongoing relationship with your audience. Listeners will not trust you if they perceive that you are acting out a role. If you try to fake emotion, you will likely come off as a fake—which is neither effective nor ethical. Deliver emotional appeals authentically to develop a durable bond with your audience.

Ethos: The Appeal of Character and Credibility

When you were deciding where to attend college, whose voices were most persuasive? Perhaps it was an admissions counselor who put all the basic facts together in a compelling way. Perhaps it was a trusted friend who was already attending the school and knew what you might like about it. Or maybe it was the enthusiastic tour guide who was the best proof of how the college turned out confident, articulate students.

These examples show that persuasive appeal comes from who is speaking just as much as it does from the words that are said. The counselor might have high credibility with you regarding academic programs but less credibility when talking about the student culture. Ethos will vary according to audience, too. Each of these speakers might have a very different ethos for your parents than for you.

As you can see, your ethos as a speaker is a dynamic construct, not a fixed part of who you are. It must be renewed every time you speak. Chapter 10 focused on establishing ethos in your introduction; this section examines the dimensions of ethos in more detail so that you can enhance your ethos throughout your speech.

Demonstrating Knowledge

As you learned in chapter 10, your introduction is an important time to tell your audience about your education, training, or experience related to the speech topic. During the rest of the speech, you need to *show* them how these factors have made you a knowledgeable, intelligent person. Several techniques can heighten this dimension of ethos.

Offer a Comprehensive Picture Audiences will appreciate speakers who can show how the topic fits into a broader context. If you are trying to persuade a campus committee to give your organization funding, you might show that you understand the overall budget for student groups:

> We realize that by asking for $5,000, we are asking for an increase in our funding from last year. However, we have looked at the student organization budget from the past three years, and our request this year is actually a smaller percentage of your overall budget. That means that you will actually have a greater share of money for other groups this year.

If you are trying to persuade local residents to support a farmers' market, you might discuss how markets have worked in other cities or how markets are part of broader shifts in the food system. Showing your audience the big picture can suggest that you are thoroughly engaged with your topic and have a broad understanding of how it connects with other public issues.

Give Attention to History and Recency Well-informed speakers will use recent supporting material on their topic, but they will also display an understanding of the history of the issue. Historians Richard Neustadt and Ernest May state that while most decision makers jump right to the question "What should we do?," they would do better to ask "What's the story?" (Neustadt and May). Audiences will appreciate understanding how a current issue has emerged over time and will respect your knowledge of that history.

For example, if you are trying to influence decision makers to raise wages for student workers on campus, you might share how such an increase has been put off for years. For people who may be focused on the immediate issue, your information can show that you have done your research and are able to bring an important perspective to the discussion. You can enhance your credibility by showing how past events are relevant to present circumstances.

Explain Key Concepts Clearly and Simply With complex or technical topics, it can be tempting to dive right into the details. But consider your audience. If they have a similar level of expertise on the issue, jargon may be appropriate. But for a general audience, you may lose credibility if you try to impress them with a lot of complex ideas. Instead, take time to define key concepts and clarify complex ideas using ordinary language.

The student who spoke about coal-bed methane in chapter 10, for example, needed to explain several technical concepts for an audience that knew nothing about the topic. Here is how she described one process:

> Hydro-fracking is somewhat like taking an axe to a piece of wood. Just like you use an axe to pry apart the wood, hydro-fracking uses high-pressure liquid to pry apart rocks. A few bugs may crawl out of the wood when you're done with an axe, but with hydro-fracking the treasure is much more valuable. Inside those rocks is methane gas.

This clear, simple analogy boosts the speaker's credibility far more than a complex lecture on petroleum geology would.

Use Diverse, Authoritative Sources You also can strengthen your ethos by citing multiple, diverse sources throughout the body of your speech. This not only demonstrates broad knowledge, but also can help your ethos by showing that you are attentive to multiple perspectives.

Sources enhance your ethos when your audience perceives them as authoritative on your topic. For example, consider this approach:

> I found that I am not alone in thinking that medication labels are confusing. The Institute of Medicine, a branch of the National Academy of Sciences and our nation's top independent advisory group on health matters, convened a workshop on this very issue in 2007. They identified some of the same problems I have discussed so far.

The ethos of knowledgeable sources can rub off on you as a speaker, showing that your opinions have been informed by intelligent participants in the public sphere.

Show Instances of Practical Knowledge When you have practical knowledge or have learned from experience, this can be another powerful source of appeal in a persuasive speech. Stories and examples from your experience can provide vivid proof that you know what you are talking about. In addition, examples can show how your knowledge "works" in the real world and that your knowledge leads you to make good decisions:

> If you are still skeptical about conservation efforts, then it's time to hit the showers—literally! Last year, our group worked with the Residential Life office to find efficiency opportunities in the dorms. Through our research, we discovered that a big cost for the dorms was hot water, so for our first project we decided to install water-saving showerheads. The payoff was huge. According to the Campus Facilities Office, the energy savings for the year was more than three times the cost of the showerheads, and it cut our water usage in half. It's hard to dispute that this was a smart investment.

In this example, the speaker's credibility gets a boost by having a personal connection to the topic. Instead of talking about hypothetical savings, he can take advantage of an actual project in which his knowledge was the basis for an action that had a positive outcome.

Building Trust

If someone is trying to persuade you, issues of trust should arise almost immediately. Why should I believe the speaker? Is she really telling me the whole story? Is he the kind of person I should respect? Your audience needs to have confidence that you are telling the truth about your topic and that you possess some of the qualities of character that they respect. When building your speech, then, think about the implicit messages you can develop that build trust around facts as well as values.

PRACTICAL KNOWLEDGE
Bill and Melinda Gates often give examples of success stories that show "what works" in speeches about agricultural development and poverty reduction.

"I'm Consistent" Showing your audience that you have held a consistent position over time or that your speech is consistent with your actions addresses the concern that you are pandering to your audience as described in chapter 5. Imagine that two administrators at your college are discussing support for a new international student center on campus. Which of the following are you more likely to trust?

> We have every intention of adding an international student center on campus. As you know, international students are very important to our university. Our entire campus is enriched by a diverse student body.

> We have every intention of adding an international student center on campus. I personally have been committed to strengthening support for international students for the past five years by adding two new advisors for international students and supporting the establishment of an international student association. I have also started a reserve fund for a center that, along with some grants, could help to make the center a reality.

The first speaker offers vague clichés that do little to suggest a genuine personal commitment. The second speaker offers specific actions, in both the past and the present, that display an ongoing attention to the needs of international students.

"I Have a Track Record of Good Judgment" Showing that you have made good decisions in the past can encourage listeners to trust your judgment.

For example, if you have been involved in pedestrian safety initiatives near your campus, you might say the following:

> Back when we were debating whether to add a warning light at Main Street and University Drive, I felt strongly that student safety should be our top priority. Fortunately, we haven't had any accidents at that intersection since installing the light. I'm convinced that we should add lights at the other crossings on University Drive, too.

This strategy is easier to use when you have strong initial credibility prior to your speech. If you have been part of a community or organization for some time, your reputation and track record may precede you—for better or worse. Rhetorical theorists have long recognized this, leading some to claim that the best speakers will try to sustain a positive reputation at all times and not merely create the appearance of goodness during a speech.

"I Share Your Experiences and Values" In some situations, your audience may know little about your background or reputation. As a result, highlighting shared experiences and values—creating identification—is a crucial aspect of building trust. Shared experience builds trust by affirming listeners' perceptions of the world and showing that you can relate to their concerns and challenges. Displaying shared values can lead audience members to trust your judgment.

For example, in a persuasive speech you might identify a specific action or decision and have a particular value judgment about it. Then you can highlight that value and use it as the basis of persuasion regarding some other issue:

> Like many of you, I was upset with the recent cuts to the university budget. Some were arbitrary and not made with much foresight. Talented people were let go, and some of the best programs were hurt the most. Unfortunately, arbitrary and short-sighted thinking seems to be the norm in our state these days. A look at our state's economic development office reveals a similar pattern—one that should worry you as future workers and residents in our state.

Notice that showing your audience shared values is not just a matter of stating that you adhere to those values. As we saw with the college administrator examples above, it is better to offer specific instances and put values into a context to *show* your audience what you mean.

Creating Goodwill

Even if your audience trusts your facts and shares your values, listeners still may wonder whether you intend to help them, not just yourself. You need to demonstrate goodwill, a perceived caring and genuine concern for the needs and desires of your audience.

PUBLIC SPOTLIGHT

Yaicha Bookhout

Around the world, college students have demonstrated civic and political engagement on a variety of issues related to energy and climate change. Persuasive speaking is a necessary skill for effective engagement, and college student Yaicha Bookhout has recognized the importance of creating identification and selecting the right supporting material in her own persuasive speaking.

Yaicha has spoken to a variety of groups about the impacts of climate change and the need for action and has organized students locally and nationally to pressure decision makers on climate-related policies. "To reach students, I can't just give a bunch of statistics about climate change. I have to show them how climate change is going to affect their recreation year-round. I have also tried to inspire them with examples of how young people in past generations have changed the course of history."

Yaicha also was selected to run a workshop at the national Powershift climate summit to help youth climate leaders speak more effectively to oppositional audiences who are skeptical of the need for climate action. She emphasized the need to understand audience concerns and identify their goals and values in order to make effective persuasive appeals.

 Social Media Spotlight

Advocates have taken advantage of social media to address global issues such as climate change. College students have been a central part of climate movements worldwide, using online tools to organize events and circulate information. For example, 350.org has used social media to raise awareness of the safe upper limit for CO_2 in the atmosphere and to coordinate thousands of simultaneous climate actions worldwide. The Energy Action Coalition coordinates youth-led climate organizations and convenes the Powershift climate summits in Washington, DC.

- 350.org produced a wordless video to depict the significance of the number 350: http://www.350.org/en/videos.
- They also use a Flickr photostream for participants to share examples of events and demonstrations: http://www.flickr.com/photos/350org/.
- Social media connections related to Powershift can be found at: http://www.wearepowershift.org/organize/spread-the-word.

Communication researcher James McCroskey describes three dimensions that contribute to the perception of goodwill: understanding, empathy, and responsiveness (McCroskey and Teven). From the speaker's perspective, these translate into three things you want to show your audience: that you understand what they think and feel, that you care about what they think and feel, and that you are willing to engage and address the audience's needs and desires.

Barack Obama's "A More Perfect Union" speech in 2008 contains several attempts to show understanding and empathy. Given at a time of intensified racial discussion during the Presidential campaign, Obama's speech made these attempts not only to build his own ethos, but also to improve understanding and empathy among his diverse audiences. For example, Obama tried to show understanding of the history and reasons for frustration among some African-Americans:

> Segregated schools were, and are, inferior schools; we still haven't fixed them, fifty years after Brown v. Board of Education, and the inferior education they provided, then and now, helps explain the pervasive achievement gap between today's black and white students.
>
> Legalized discrimination—where blacks were prevented, often through violence, from owning property, or loans were not granted to African-American business owners, or black homeowners could not access FHA mortgages, or blacks were excluded from unions, or the police force, or fire departments—meant that black families could not amass any meaningful wealth to bequeath to future generations. That history helps explain the wealth and income gap between black and white, and the concentrated pockets of poverty that persists in so many of today's urban and rural communities.

Notice how these passages are not so much about channeling the anger felt by the audience or agreeing with that anger. Instead, they explain its basis, illustrating how relatively neutral and informative language can show understanding of an audience's point of view.

Later in the speech, Obama shows empathy with the feelings of some white Americans relative to race:

> In fact, a similar anger exists within segments of the white community. Most working- and middle-class white Americans don't feel that they have been particularly privileged by their race. Their experience is the immigrant experience—as far as they're concerned, no one's handed them anything, they've built it from scratch. They've worked hard all their lives, many times only to see their jobs shipped overseas or their pension dumped after a lifetime of labor. They are anxious about their futures, and feel their dreams slipping away; in an era of stagnant wages and global competition, opportunity comes to be seen as a zero sum game, in which your dreams come at my expense. So when they are told to bus their children to a school across town; when they hear that an African American is getting an advantage in landing a good job or a spot in a good college because of an injustice that they themselves never committed; when they're told that their fears about crime in urban neighborhoods are somehow prejudiced, resentment builds over time.

Here, the more personalized language, especially in the last sentences, shows an empathy with the experience and feelings of some of his audience members.

The concluding sections of Obama's speech also show responsiveness to the needs of his audiences. In contrast to focusing on divisive racial politics, Obama suggests that the public discourse surrounding the election should focus on the real concerns that cross racial lines:

Or, at this moment, in this election, we can come together and say, "Not this time." This time we want to talk about the crumbling schools that are stealing the future of black children and white children and Asian children and Hispanic children and Native American children. This time we want to reject the cynicism that tells us that these kids can't learn; that those kids who don't look like us are somebody else's problem. The children of America are not those kids, they are our kids, and we will not let them fall behind in a 21st century economy. Not this time.

This time we want to talk about how the lines in the Emergency Room are filled with whites and blacks and Hispanics who do not have health care; who don't have the power on their own to overcome the special interests in Washington, but who can take them on if we do it together.

Ultimately, creating goodwill hinges less on clever rhetorical tactics than on careful listening to your audience's needs and concerns. By listening with an ear for what your audience really thinks, feels, and desires, you will be in a much better position to understand and empathize with their concerns and to respond to them accordingly.

Logos: The Appeal of Evidence and Reasoning

"Why do you think that?" This simple question, one that should be asked of any persuasive speaker, gets at the heart of the appeal to logos. When listeners ask why you hold a certain belief or advocate a particular position, they are asking for the evidence and reasoning that supports your point of view. This is what make your position *reasonable*, rather than just a whim, a gut reaction, or a personal prejudice.

Logos versus Logic

Although logos is related to the word "logic," the rhetorical appeal to logos is different from the kind of formal logic that you may learn about in a philosophy course. Formal logic draws conclusions that necessarily follow from true **premises**, or starting points for an argument. But this ignores the audience and social context for arguments. In contrast, public speaking addresses issues in which premises are disputed and audiences respond differently according to their concerns and values. As a result, the rhetorical appeal to logos is not simply the application of logic, but the use of evidence and reasoning to influence a particular audience to adhere to the strongest possible conclusion.

Let's look at a highly controversial public issue to better understand this difference between rigid logic and the rhetorical appeal to logos. This example attempts to draw a logical conclusion from a set of premises:

> Statistics show that handguns are involved in a significant number of accidental deaths. And obviously, it is important to prevent accidental deaths. Therefore, it follows that we should ban handguns.

Under the rules of logic, if you accept the first two statements, then you should accept the final statement. But it is easy to imagine audience members raising all kinds of questions about this pattern of reasoning. They might question your premises: Exactly how many deaths? Why is that a "significant" number? Even if they agree that preventing accidental deaths is important, they might not accept your conclusion. Perhaps there are other actions that could help to prevent accidental deaths from handguns.

In public speaking, then, strictly formal logic is not necessarily the best strategy for persuading an audience. It would be impossible to come up with a "perfect" example of a better pattern of reasoning, since different audiences would have different questions and objections to that argument. Instead, you want to learn a variety of patterns of reasoning and then use the ones that are best suited to your topic, purpose, and audience.

Patterns of Reasoning

The scholar Stephen Toulmin describes a general pattern of reasoning that is useful for developing appeals to logos. This pattern, usually called the **Toulmin model**, identifies the component parts of any argument and their relationships to one another. This model can help you to develop more specific patterns of reasoning, which we will discuss later, and can help you to identify potential areas of audience disagreement.

The Toulmin Model

Main Parts of the Model. The basic parts of an argument as identified by the Toulmin model include a **claim**, a disputable statement that you want your audience to accept; **grounds**, specific statements about observable conditions that offer support for the claim; and a **warrant**, a general statement that justifies or explains how the grounds support the claim. An audience should be able to recognize or infer each of these parts from your speech. Typically, the model diagrams these parts as in Figure 14.1.

Let's look back at the handgun argument to see how this model works. Start by identifying the claim—the idea that the speaker ultimately wants the audience to accept. In this case, the claim is that we should ban handguns.

Once you have identified the claim, two simple questions will help you to understand the relationship between these parts. The first question to pose in response to the claim is: *Why do you think that?* The answer to this question is the ground of the argument. Remember that the grounds are typically statements about things that are specific, observable, or concrete. In this case, the statement that handguns are involved in a significant number of deaths

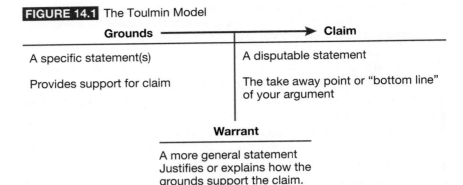

FIGURE 14.1 The Toulmin Model

Grounds ──────────► Claim

Grounds	Claim
A specific statement(s)	A disputable statement
Provides support for claim	The take away point or "bottom line" of your argument

Warrant

A more general statement
Justifies or explains how the
grounds support the claim.

is the most specific answer to the question "Why do you think we should ban handguns?"

The second question is posed in response to the grounds: *So what?* This question asks what *relevance* the grounds have to support the claim, or why the grounds are a reasonable basis for supporting the claim. The answer to this question is the warrant of the argument. In this example, the warrant says that because we believe that it is important to prevent accidental deaths, the fact that handguns lead to accidental deaths is a reasonable basis for considering a handgun ban. A model of this argument would look like Figure 14.2.

Putting arguments into the Toulmin model helps you to diagnose the quality of arguments. It does not necessarily make the argument sound or persuasive. It helps you to see whether you have all the necessary parts, and it can help you to think about the process of audience adaptation. For example, if you think that your audience will not accept the warrant, then developing a new warrant may require you to also bring in new grounds.

Secondary Parts of the Model. Other parts of the model can help you to develop more complex or extended arguments. Many arguments include

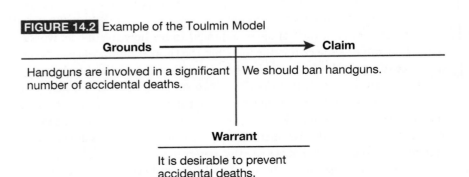

FIGURE 14.2 Example of the Toulmin Model

Grounds ──────────► Claim

Grounds	Claim
Handguns are involved in a significant number of accidental deaths.	We should ban handguns.

Warrant

It is desirable to prevent
accidental deaths.

FIGURE 14.3 Extended Example of the Toulmin Model

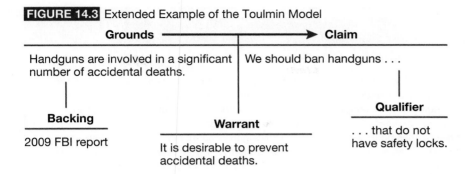

backing, or additional support for the grounds or warrant. The example above might add a couple of studies or testimony that backs up the idea that handguns are involved in a "significant number" of deaths. Some arguments attach a **qualifier** to the claim, which clarifies the force of the argument with words such as "certainly" or "generally" or defines the scope of the argument with words such as "in the next decade" or "on our campus." Figure 14.3 shows one way in which these parts might work in the handgun example.

Finally, some analysts of argument will include a **rebuttal**, the primary objection that could be made against the claim, and a **reservation**, a response to the rebuttal that often identifies exceptions to the claim. These do not affect the basic structure of the argument but are useful for brainstorming extensions of your argument. Your instructor may give you additional guidance about using these to develop your persuasive speech.

The Role of Warrants in the Model. Before looking at how this model can help you to produce more specific patterns of reasoning, two important points must be mentioned about the warrant. First, *in many arguments, the grounds are explicitly stated but the warrant is left unstated.* This style of argument is called an **enthymeme**, a pattern of reasoning in which the audience supplies one of the premises. Especially in public speaking, it can be excessive to spell out premises that are obvious. Do audiences really need to be told that it is important to prevent accidental deaths? By leaving warrants unstated, audience members supply them mentally and thus participate in their own persuasion—a powerful persuasive tactic.

However, "unstated" does not mean unimportant. This raises the second key point: *Warrants make arguments reasonable.* Without a warrant, there is nothing that connects your grounds to your claim, nothing that allows your audience to understand why the grounds are a legitimate basis for accepting your claim. Whether stated or not, warrants are the linchpin of good arguments. The Ethical Dimension feature can help you to decide whether to include or omit warrants in your speeches.

THE ETHICAL DIMENSION

Omitting Warrants in Persuasive Speaking

Ancient teachers of rhetoric believed that the enthymeme was one of the most persuasive ways to construct an oral argument. For example, your friend tries to persuade you to vote for a state legislator because that legislator has promised to freeze college tuition. That may be an appealing reason, but should it persuade you? What is your friend assuming about your interests and values that makes freezing tuition a good reason?

These questions point toward the ethical issues that are involved in omitting a warrant from an oral argument. By omitting the warrant, your friend is assuming that you believe certain things: that freezing tuition is obviously a good thing and that it is a sufficient reason by itself to vote for a legislator. It is one thing to omit these ideas if your friend knows you very well and fully understands your opinions.

But in public speaking, the situation generally is different. The primary ethical question is: *Should the warrant be omitted if some listeners would dispute it?* In this example, not everyone would agree that freezing tuition is obviously a good thing. While it may save students some money, it also may harm certain programs at your college.

In addition, most people are not one-issue voters; focusing only on the tuition issue can deflect your audience's attention from other matters of even greater importance.

Omitting the warrant may help you to make an eloquent shortcut to your claim, but that shortcut will be unethical if it glosses over weaknesses in your argument and issues that would create real disagreement if they were stated. As a speaker, you have an obligation to identify warrants during invention to be sure that you are making a reasonable argument. If the warrant is weak or a source of potential disagreement, then omitting it harms your audience's ability to make rational choices.

WHAT DO YOU THINK?

1. How would your classmates respond to the tuition freeze argument? Could you ethically omit the warrant if they were your audience?

2. What other concepts have you learned in this book that would help you to develop warrants that have broad agreement and thus ethically could be omitted?

Reasoning by Generalization In **reasoning by generalization**, a speaker uses a set of examples or specific instances as grounds for inferring a broader principle or a statement about a larger group of examples. The grounds suggest some sort of general pattern that the speaker wants the audience to accept.

Arguments by generalization are used when it is impossible to examine every single instance, but a few instances can provide a good overall picture. For example, consider the generalization about mining towns in Figure 14.4. The claim makes a general assertion about mining towns based on three specific instances. The warrant explains the conditions under which these instances would be reasonable support for that claim. When you are reasoning by generalization, your audience must accept that there are a *sufficient number of examples* to support the claim and that those examples are *representative or typical instances*. If the audience members think that your examples are extreme or unusual instances, they will be less likely to accept the generalization.

In addition, while doing research, be attentive for a **counterexample**, an instance that is an exception to a generalization. Counterexamples do not

FIGURE 14.4 Reasoning by Generalization

Grounds ——————→	Claim
The examples of Keystone, WV; Butte, MT; and Uravan, CO show how the boom and bust cycle works.	Mining towns are prone to economic booms and busts.

Warrant

These examples are representative and sufficient. (What is true of them is generally true of mining towns.)

necessarily disprove generalizations; in fact, they can help you to qualify and complicate your argument. In this case, a counterexample of a successful mining town might reveal proactive measures that communities can take to provide economic stability, feeding into your overall persuasive purpose. In addition, if those measures were absent in the other towns, they would actually strengthen your generalization.

Reasoning by Analogy The overall pattern in much persuasive speaking is to start with ideas that are familiar to or accepted by your audience before moving on to less familiar or more controversial ideas. This pattern is also reflected in **reasoning by analogy**, in which a speaker refers to the known characteristics of one instance as grounds for inferring unknown or uncertain characteristics of a similar instance.

In persuasive speeches, analogies are especially useful for advancing a new practice or policy based on our knowledge of how that practice or policy has worked in a different place or time. The analogy gets its strength from the similarities of the compared items. For example, an analogy might be used to argue for adopting another college's program on your campus, as in Figure 14.5.

FIGURE 14.5 Reasoning by Analogy

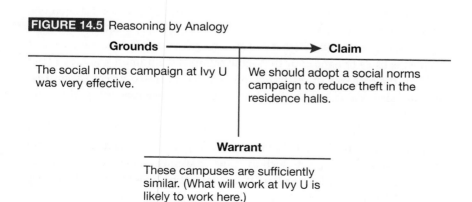

Grounds ——————→	Claim
The social norms campaign at Ivy U was very effective.	We should adopt a social norms campaign to reduce theft in the residence halls.

Warrant

These campuses are sufficiently similar. (What will work at Ivy U is likely to work here.)

REASONING BY ANALOGY
Persuasive speaking about foreign policy and international relations often relies on reasoning by analogy that compares past situations to present circumstances.

The warrant in this example shows that analogies are reasonable when the compared instances are more similar than different. As a speaker, then, you want to *highlight similarities* and *account for any differences* between the situations that have relevance for your claim. In this example, it might be important to address similarities and differences between the two campuses regarding campus population or overall crime rates on campus and community.

Reasoning by Cause Persuasive speeches also rely heavily on **reasoning by cause**, in which a speaker infers a direct, substantive connection between one action or event and a subsequent effect. Reasoning by cause can take two different forms, depending on whether you are trying to persuade your audience that an effect is likely to happen or that some action is the primary cause of a later effect. In the first type of reasoning, often called **cause-to-effect reasoning**, the claim asserts an effect; in the latter, **effect-to-cause reasoning**, the claim asserts the cause.

Cause-to-effect reasoning occurs when speakers argue about the likely effects of a policy or action: "If we do X, then Y is likely to happen as a result." You can see this pattern in statements such as "If we implement a new science curriculum, test scores will likely go up" or "If we raise tuition, enrollment will probably go down." A full-blown causal argument might look like Figure 14.6.

FIGURE 14.6 Reasoning by Cause

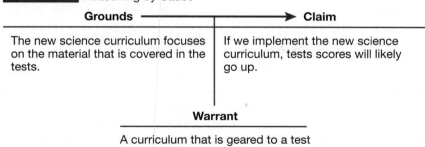

Grounds	⟶	Claim
The new science curriculum focuses on the material that is covered in the tests.		If we implement the new science curriculum, tests scores will likely go up.

Warrant

A curriculum that is geared to a test generally leads to better student performance.

This example shows how grounds and warrants sometimes look very similar. Both are factual statements that could get backing from additional evidence. But remember that grounds are more specific than warrants are. Here, the grounds describe *this particular curriculum,* while the warrant describes how curriculum generally affects performance. Both the specific statements and the more general warrant need to be accepted by your audience members for them to see the causal link as reasonable.

As a speaker, then, you face two key challenges with cause-to-effect reasoning. First, you need to *make a direct, material connection* between the cause and the effect. If you advocated for a new science curriculum but did not explain how it was related to the tests, you would not have very strong grounds for a claim about test scores. Second, you need to *think about intervening factors* that might prevent the effect from occurring. Perhaps students might have a difficult time adjusting to a new curriculum. Familiarity with the social and political context surrounding your topic can help you to anticipate these intervening factors.

In contrast, effect-to-cause reasoning pinpoints a cause or set of causes that led to a later situation or event. Typically, this type of reasoning is used to identify a causal factor that the speaker wants either to promote or to eliminate in order to achieve goals beyond the speech. For example, consider the following claims about the factors leading to divorce:

> Our state's high divorce rate is the direct result of a lack of moral commitment.
>
> Our state's high divorce rate is the direct result of economic pressure on families.
>
> Our state's high divorce rate is the direct result of no-fault divorce laws.

Here, each claim directs audience attention to a single causal factor that the speaker might want to eliminate in order to lower the divorce rate. For example, the last claim might be a part of a speech that is intended to persuade the audience to change divorce laws. But the other two claims offer alternative causes that may be plausible. Because many public issues like this one are socially complex, it may be important to *examine and acknowledge multiple causes* in your speech before trying to argue that one is particularly important.

Reasoning by Sign Causal reasoning is sometimes confused with **reasoning by sign**, in which the speaker infers that some unobservable condition exists on the basis of observed features or conditions. In this type of reasoning, the observed features or conditions are the grounds, and the warrant is the general assumption that those grounds typically or reliably serve as a sign of the unobserved condition. For example, the phrase "Where there is smoke, there's fire" is a warrant that connects the observation of smoke to the claim that a fire must exist, even though the fire itself is not directly observable.

Sign reasoning and causal reasoning often are confused because both types of reasoning attempt to establish a relationship between two things. The key distinction is that causal reasoning tries to explain *why* something occurs, but sign reasoning simply tries to prove *that* something occurs. For example, in Figure 14.7, the grounds are not the *cause* of success; instead, it is simply a marker or indicator of success. The question remains as to what caused the increase in major—perhaps a popular introductory course or an influx of new faculty members.

In everyday life, sign reasoning is used to make sense of situations even if we do not know the cause. Diagnosing disease exemplifies sign reasoning: A runny nose and a cough are signs of a cold; an X-ray or MRI can exhibit signs that lead doctors to infer a particular disease. But none of these signs tell us what caused the diseases. Similarly, on public issues, sign reasoning helps us to infer broader conditions even when we do not have direct evidence of what caused those conditions. A successful military operation may be a sign of a well-trained military, but since the operation happened *after* the training, it could not have a causal impact on the training.

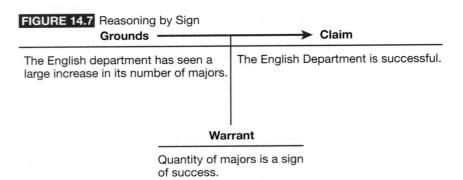

FIGURE 14.7 Reasoning by Sign

Grounds ——————→	Claim
The English department has seen a large increase in its number of majors.	The English Department is successful.

Warrant

Quantity of majors is a sign of success.

In addition to this challenge of *distinguishing sign from cause,* another key to effective sign reasoning is *asking whether the sign is fallible.* In other words, how reliable is the sign as an indicator of the underlying condition? For example, imagine that after spring break, attendance in your courses is down 40%. These grounds could be the sign of many different things; perhaps students have "spring fever" or instructors assign most of the work early in the semester. Because multiple conclusions could reasonably be inferred from the observed attendance, that sign is fallible; it does not simply stand for one thing. Like the practice of acknowledging alternative causes, asking whether the sign is fallible can help you to think about the limits of your reasoning and the potential objections of your audience.

Fallacies in Reasoning

As you have seen, each pattern of reasoning has inherent limitations and typical problems. When a speaker's argument falls prey to one of these problems, they have generated a **fallacy**, or pattern of flawed reasoning. Although some scholars have cataloged hundreds of fallacies (Damer), this section will focus on the fallacies that are directly related to the patterns of reasoning described above and are especially common in persuasive arguments on public issues.

Because reasoning on public issues can be very context-specific, it is useful to think of fallacies as starting points for closer inspection rather than as absolute judgments that you might make about a speaker's pattern of reasoning. What makes a generalization "hasty" or a dilemma "false" cannot be determined strictly by a textbook definition; it needs close analysis that is sensitive to the particular topic.

Hasty Generalization The charge of **hasty generalization** occurs when a speaker has chosen examples that audience members find to be unrepresentative or insufficient. If you claimed that efforts to stop panhandling in your community will not work because a previous campaign failed, it's easy to see how such a generalization might be hasty or premature.

Unfortunately, there is no "magic number" of examples that are needed to make a generalization absolutely valid. However, you can bolster the strength of generalizations in several ways. First, use multiple examples rather than just one that is easier to challenge. Second, explain how your examples are representative by showing their similarities or contrasting them with more extreme examples. Finally, bring in other forms of evidence to support the generalization. For example, if you are discussing how unnecessary medical procedures drive up health costs, you might first discuss some particular procedures and then bring in statistics about the average amount of extra costs, allowing you to compare the individual cases to a norm.

False Analogy A **false analogy** compares things that are fundamentally dissimilar or that have critical differences that undermine their comparison. One of the most common false analogies in U.S. public discourse is the comparison of any political adversary to Nazis or any proposal to fascism. Such comparisons are rarely if ever reasonable; speakers would have to demonstrate the existence of an organized political system based on explicit racial prejudice and direct attacks on democratic practices, backed up by state-sanctioned violence.

False analogies also emerge when the number of relevant differences begins to outweigh similarities. In the previous section, you saw an analogy between two college campuses used to develop support for a theft reduction program. This analogy is likely more reasonable than one that tries to draw an analogy between a private business's theft program and a campus program. The structural, age, and role differences between a campus and a business create entirely different cultures and populations, making the comparison a relatively weak one.

Post Hoc **Fallacy** Our desire to figure out why things happen can sometimes lead us astray. When one event follows another, it can be tempting to see the earlier event as the cause:

> No wonder I flunked the exam; that breakfast burrito made me sick.
>
> After the Democrats got into office, the economy improved. They sure know how to turn things around.
>
> Applications went up 15% this year. Clearly, it's because of those glossy new brochures.

But a critical thinker should be on the lookout for the ***post hoc* fallacy**, which occurs when a speaker inaccurately presumes that an earlier event caused a later event simply because of their sequence in time. This label is shorthand for the Latin phrase "*post hoc, ergo propter hoc*," which means "after this, therefore because of this."

Especially for persuasive speaking, the *post hoc* fallacy can be attractive because it seems to offer plausible explanations for events and often reinforces one's own biases. Take the example about Democrats above. If you prefer that party, then selective perception can lead you to see their policies as the cause of good effects. But also ask: Are there other possible causes? What evidence shows that their policies were the primary cause of those effects? Perhaps a much earlier decision about interest rates or factors outside of government policy had a greater impact. You can avoid the *post hoc* fallacy by considering alternative causes and remembering to draw a direct material connection between cause and effect.

False Dilemma At the beginning of this course, you read and probably heard about many of the benefits of taking public speaking. These benefits provide good reasons to take the course. But imagine if the argument about the benefits of public speaking were posed like this:

> Either you take public speaking, or you will never be a success.

It seems a little far-fetched, doesn't it? The alternative to taking public speaking is not necessarily a mediocre life. Those are not the only two paths you might take. This phrasing of two options, known as a **false dilemma**, poses a choice between only two alternatives when others may exist. This fallacy is often referred to as the either/or fallacy for an obvious reason.

False dilemmas can be hard to resist if one option is contrasted with an obviously undesirable alternative, which makes the first option seem more appealing. "Look, either you can have a gun in your house, or you can be robbed on a regular basis." No one wants to be robbed regularly, but that does not mean that one *must* have a gun in one's house. The false dilemma distracts from the good reasons why one may or may not choose to possess a gun.

As these example show, persuasive speaking is especially prone to the false dilemma fallacy when questions of policy are being addressed. In the desire to make a specific policy seem like the best choice, it can be tempting to make it appear as if it is the *only* choice. This is an ethical problem because it fails to empower your audience to make a sound decision among alternatives. But it is also a problem if it blinds you to the problems of your own position and the potential strengths of other alternatives. Consequently, if you find yourself turning to a dilemma to encourage a particular choice, take a step back and find stronger arguments for your position.

CASE CONCLUSION

Lindsey's Speech on Adderall

Lindsey recognized that her audience had been exposed to a lot of fear appeals from antidrug campaigns, and she figured that they would be skeptical of such appeals. So she decided instead to develop an ongoing appeal to sympathy. In her introduction, she shared her own story, describing how occasional and recreational use of Adderall quickly turned into addiction and drug dealing. Her purpose in appealing to sympathy was not to make her audience feel sorry for her, but to demonstrate how drug abuse could easily happen to any of them.

Lindsey's introduction established her ethos and personal connection to the topic in a powerful way. But she realized that establishing ethos on this topic would require more than just a description of her personal experiences. So Lindsey went the extra mile to find testimony from university researchers and federal agencies that could speak with authority about Adderall, its relationship to other narcotics, and its health impacts.

Lindsey developed an important enthymeme in her speech that was grounded in an extended example of a student who became a heavy user of Adderall in college. She thought that her audience would easily infer from this example that Adderall should be avoided. From audience research, she knew that her classmates valued their health and were not so motivated by high grades that they would see the student's choice as sound. As a result, she did not have to explicitly state all of her premises—she just needed to develop the example and provide additional evidence about health effects. The audience's own values would lead them to see Lindsey's conclusion as reasonable.

SAMPLE OUTLINE

Lindsey's Speech about Adderall

Specific purpose: To strengthen my audience's negative attitude toward Adderall.

Central idea: Adderall should be a major public health concern, especially among college students.

I. Introduction

Lindsey establishes ethos with her personal connection to the topic, without making the speech all about herself.

    A. You've got an exam or a paper due the next day, and it looks like it could be another all-nighter. You might grab an energy drink, have a few extra cups of coffee, or maybe even try a little Adderall from one of your friends.

    B. I've been there myself. During my first semester, it seemed like I was always waiting until the last minute to study. Some friends of mine gave me some Adderall in a pinch. But it didn't take too long before this study drug became a party drug for me. Within a few months, I had fallen into addiction, and drugs became a way not just to have fun, but to make money.

    C. Most people don't end up as addicts and drug-runners, but that doesn't mean we shouldn't be concerned about Adderall, Ritalin, and other prescription amphetamines. The widespread use of these drugs, even for legitimate purposes, is an important public issue.

She has a clear and concise central idea.

    D. In my speech, I want to convince you that Adderall should be a major public health concern, especially for students of our generation.

    E. My speech has three parts. After providing some basic facts, I want to explain why Adderall is a growing problem on college campuses and then discuss some of the negative health impacts that can result from this so-called study drug.

(Transition: To understand why Adderall is so popular, we first need to look at what it really is.)

II. Adderall is a prescription methamphetamine.

    A. In other words, Adderall is a stimulant. It produces a short-term increase in cognitive and physical functions.

The first part of the body uses several different definitions and comparisons as supporting material to shape the audience's perspective on Adderall.

    B. A 2006 article by Harry Jaffe on Washingtonian.com described it through a comparison to drug that may be more familiar in our part of the country. "In street terms, Adderall is 'speed' in a very low dose. Methamphetamine, the drug made in clandestine labs that is tearing up families and communities across the country, is speed in high doses" (Jaffe).

    C. Like other stimulants, such as caffeine, nicotine, or meth, Adderall creates feelings of increased awareness and concentration.

D. As a result, Adderall can be an appealing drug for several reasons.

    1. First, according to the National Center for Biotechnology Information, it can be used to treat symptoms of ADHD, or attention deficit hyperactivity disorder (NCBI). This is the main reason why Adderall is legitimately prescribed.

    2. Second, Adderall is also used for "off-label" purposes, which are not approved by the manufacturer or federal regulators.

       a. For example, in March 2008, ABC News reported that Adderall was a popular weight loss drug among some female celebrities (Childs).

       b. Treating depression is also another common off-label use of Adderall.

(Transition: But these uses have not received nearly as much attention as the use of Adderall as a study and recreational drug on college campuses, which I will cover next.)

III. Adderall is a significant problem on college campuses.

A. The real problem with Adderall lies in its use as a cognitive aid or "neuroenhancer." It can be used to sharpen thinking and sustain attention for long periods of time. This is exactly what college students often need to do—but at what cost?

B. The Washingtonian.com article I mentioned earlier reports the stories of several students at universities who use Adderall to maintain a high-intensity life.

    1. For example, Kirk struggled to keep up with his classmates at Duke during his freshman year.

    2. The following year, he took Adderall that was offered by a fraternity brother, studied for fourteen hours, and got an A on his chemistry exam.

    3. But that was not the end. "One Tuesday night before winter break, Kirk crushed more than 40 milligrams of Adderall. He had knocked off a physics exam that afternoon. He was determined to drink all night. He snorted the Adderall and reached into the refrigerator for a beer. His legs buckled, and he passed out. Kirk awoke in the morning in a pool of vomit with the worst hangover of his life. He swore off Adderall as a recreational stimulant. He figured if he limited the drug to schoolwork, he could control it."

    4. But he couldn't. During finals week, he downed 200 milligrams in five days and was taken to the hospital with a 103.5 degree fever before his last exam. You would think that a pre-med major would know better.

The speech acknowledges that there is a legitimate reason why someone may use Adderall, before getting into its illicit uses.

Lindsey adapts to her audience by acknowledging why the drug may appear beneficial at first glance.

This extended example vividly depicts the experience of a college student.

C. But many students seem to view Adderall as an appealing drug.

> Lindsey brings in multiple scholarly studies here to boost her ethos.

   1. One prominent study by researchers at the University of Michigan Substance Abuse Research Center published in 2005 reported that just over 4% of U.S. college undergraduates sampled had used prescription stimulants for off-label use (Talbot).

   2. However, at individual colleges, rates varied from 0% to 25%.

   3. More recently, a 2008 study by University of Kentucky researchers found that 34% of their respondents had used ADHD drugs illegally (DeSantis, Webb, and Noar). Other recent studies also suggest that the use of Adderall and similar prescription stimulants is on the rise.

> This passage shows that Lindsey has dug into the study's details.

   4. These studies generally show that most students are using it as a study drug. In the Kentucky study, the top three reasons for using Adderall were "to stay awake to study, to concentrate on your work, and to help memorize" information. But many others also reported using it to sustain their energy during "marathon party sessions."

> These statements connect the evidence back to her main point in this section.

   5. This is what makes Adderall a potentially big problem on college campuses. The pressure to succeed, both in the classroom and socially, makes college students especially susceptible to the continued use—and abuse—of drugs like Adderall.

> This supporting material anticipates potential objections, showing that even skeptics recognize some aspects of this problem.

D. Even those who do not see it as a serious problem still recognize the potential for abuse.

   1. Gretchen Feussner, a pharmacologist with the DEA, does not see Adderall as a major problem compared to other drugs.

   2. However, she does say that "If the use is continued and the dose escalates . . . they're setting themselves up for a real problem, especially if there's a history of addiction in the family" (Jaffee).

   3. Indeed, the FDA warning label on Adderall says that "amphetamines have a high potential for abuse" and that when administered over a long time, "can lead to drug dependence."

   4. As my story and Kirk's story show, this is the real problem with Adderall: how easily it can lead to addiction and real health problems.

(Transition: Let's now turn to look at some of these side effects in more detail.)

IV. Adderall has many negative side effects.

A. Like any drug, Adderall can have minor side effects that result from the "crash" of the drug wearing off. For example, Talbot states that "Drugs such as Adderall can cause nervousness, headaches, sleeplessness, and decreased appetite, among other side effects."

> Like the other sections, this section relies on a variety of supporting materials to illustrate a range of side effects.

B. However, more severe side effects also can result from the drug.

   1. Canadian regulators pulled Adderall off the market in 2005 after learning of twenty deaths and a dozen strokes that were linked to prescribed use of the drug.

2. Fourteen of the deaths were in children, and none of these reactions were associated with overdose or misuse of the drug, according to the Associated Press ("Canadian Regulators").

C. The possibility of unanticipated side effects is heightened if users are taking other drugs or have other medical conditions that might lead to bad interactions.

1. This is a real issue on college campuses, where students who previously had an ADHD diagnosis bring their Adderall prescription to college and distribute pills to friends.

2. Maryland psychiatrist David Zwerdling says, "There are side effects and toxicity when Adderall is taken in an unregulated way." While parents can keep better tabs on their children's pills in high school, "In college that breaks down," Zwerdling says. "Who's going to control this medication?" (Jaffe).

Lindsey shows how the issues are connected to the specific context of college campuses.

V. Conclusion

A. After researching my topic, I am even more convinced that Adderall should be a major public health concern for college students. The pressures of college and the easy availability make this drug a perfect fit for the college scene, but its side effects and potential for dependence and abuse should lead you to avoid it.

B. It's true that Adderall can give you a mental boost. But is it worth it? Not just for you personally, but for us as a society. We need to resist the possibility that performing on drugs will become the norm.

Lindsey poses a rhetorical question and then offers a quotation that summarizes her own position.

C. Margaret Talbot in the *New Yorker* captures my feelings best: "All this may be leading to a kind of society I'm not sure I want to live in: a society where we're even more overworked and driven by technology than we already are, and where we have to take drugs to keep up; a society where we give children academic steroids along with their daily vitamins." Avoiding Adderall can help us to avoid this kind of society.

REFERENCES

"Canadian Regulators Order ADD Drug Withdrawn." Alliance for Human Research Protection website. Available at http://www.ahrp.org/infomail/05/02/10a.php

Childs, Dan. "Adderall: Weight Loss Fix of the Stars?" ABC News website. Available at http://abcnews.go.com/Health/Diet/story?id=4515712&page=1

DeSantis, Alan D., Elizabeth M. Webb, and Seth M. Noar. "Illicit Use of Prescription ADHD Medications on a College Campus: A Multimethodological Approach." *Journal of American College Health* 57.3 (2008): 315–24.

Jaffe, Harry. "ADD & Abusing Adderall." Washingtonian.com website. Available at http://www.washingtonian.com/articles/education/1729.html

National Center for Biotechnology Information. "Dextroamphetamine and Amphetamine." PubMedHealth website. Available at http://www.ncbi.nlm.nih.gov/pubmedhealth/PMH0000166/.

Talbot, Margaret. "Brain Gain: The Underground World of Neuroenhancing Drugs." *The New Yorker* 27 April 2009.

Summary

PATHOS: THE APPEAL OF EMOTION

- Pathos focuses your audience's perception on what is most important about a situation and encourages relationships with others within the public sphere.

- To use pathos ethically, a speaker needs to avoid exaggerating the scenarios that are used to evoke emotions.

ETHOS: THE APPEAL OF CHARACTER AND CREDIBILITY

- Speakers need to demonstrate clear and comprehensive knowledge of their topic, use diverse and authoritative sources, and demonstrate practical knowledge.

- Speakers can build trust by demonstrating consistency and a record of good judgment and highlighting experiences and values that they share with their listeners.

- Speakers can evince goodwill by showing understanding, empathy, and responsiveness toward listeners' needs and desires.

LOGOS: THE APPEAL OF EVIDENCE AND REASONING

- Reasoning in public speaking involves using the strongest forms of evidence and reasoning that resonate with the premises already accepted by your particular audience. The Toulmin model can help you to identify these premises and the relationships between grounds, warrants, and claims.

- Specific patterns of reasoning include generalization, analogy, cause, and sign. Each of these patterns has an inherent limitation that can generate a fallacy.

Key Terms

anger p. 358
fear p. 358
sympathy p. 359
kindness p. 359

friendship p. 360
premises p. 368
Toulmin model p. 369
claim p. 369

Comprehension

1. In what ways does emotion contribute to sound reasoning?

2. What three rhetorical purposes are served by appeals to emotion?

3. What are two requirements for an effective and ethical fear appeal?

4. Who determines the ethos of a speaker: the speaker or the audience?

5. Name four ways in which you demonstrate knowledge about your topic.

6. What are the three dimensions of goodwill?

7. What is the difference between the grounds of an argument and the warrant?

8. Under what conditions is it ethical to omit the warrant in a speech?

9. As a speaker, what can you do to avoid making a false analogy?

Application

1. Create two appeals to anger that relate to some aspect of college life: one that is ethical and another that is ethically questionable. Compare the two appeals among your colleagues, and see whether they can explain which appeal is ethically questionable.

2. Identify a charitable or service organization in your community. Obtain some of the organization's promotional materials, and see whether you can identify appeals to kindness and friendship.

3. Talk to a professor, a staff member, and a student about your upcoming speech, and ask them who they would find to be an authoritative source on your topic. Then discuss with your colleagues whether any of those sources should *not* be used, regardless of audience.

4. Examine the letters to the editor in your school newspaper, and see how many fallacies you can identify. Rewrite one letter by fixing the fallacy in it.

Developing Your Ceremonial Speech

This chapter is intended to help you:

- Identify the various purposes of ceremonial speaking
- Apply skills of invention and organization to ceremonial speaking situations
- Use appropriate supporting material in ceremonial speeches

For many of you, the first speech that you will give after leaving this class will be some sort of **ceremonial speech**, a speech that recognizes and helps to create a special moment in the life of a community. It could be making a toast at your best friend's wedding or presenting an award to one of your co-workers. It might involve inspiring your organization's members at a banquet, honoring the memory of a family member with a eulogy, or celebrating life in your community.

In spite of the diversity of these situations, each of them marks a unique moment in the lives of those who are involved. While their purpose is different from the informative and persuasive speeches that are central to addressing public issues, ceremonial speeches nonetheless serve an important public purpose. When done well, ceremonial speeches engage the principles, values, and goals that connect people to one another. In the words of rhetorical scholar

---

CASE SCENARIO

Treva's Speech on the Neuro Networking Club

Treva started an organization in her community called the Neuro Networking Club. Focused on young adults who are on the autism spectrum, the club is a way to offer social support for these young adults as well as to provide support and information to their families. Treva felt very comfortable speaking about the topic; she had given lots of speeches about autism and the joys and challenges of her son's Asperger syndrome. But she wasn't quite sure how she might adapt this information for the purposes of her ceremonial speech assignment.

James Jasinski, they "generate, sustain, or modify a community's existence" (Jasinski 211; Condit).

Thus, ceremonial speaking is an important type of speaking in the public sphere. No matter what the size of the community, people need occasions to reflect on their life together. They need to be reminded of what "the good life" means in their community and what it looks like to live that good life. This chapter will explore how different kinds of speeches respond to ceremonial situations and will give you practical guidance in developing ceremonial speeches of your own. ■

Purposes of Ceremonial Speech

Like informative and persuasive speech, ceremonial speech is significantly influenced by the demands of the rhetorical situation. For example, the situation makes it fairly clear when a wedding toast, a eulogy, or a Memorial Day speech is the appropriate type of speech. But developing an effective ceremonial speech requires you to understand the more fundamental purpose that underlies each of these speech types. Once again, we can consider how a broad category of speeches can serve civic and political purposes as well as other purposes in your personal and professional life.

Civic and Political Purposes of Ceremonial Speech

Ceremonial speeches have a long tradition of serving key civic and political purposes. Aristotle referred to these types of speeches as **epideictic rhetoric**, a type of public discourse that engages in praise or blame in ceremonial contexts. In Aristotle's time, civic rituals such as festivals and public funerals were occasions for this type of rhetoric, when speakers would make great efforts to celebrate the values of the community. For example, the funeral oration by the Athenian leader Pericles is considered a classic example of a speech that reinforces communal values.

Contemporary scholars have explained that the purposes of epideictic rhetoric can be united under the heading of *display* (Poulakos and Poulakos). How does ceremonial speech engage in display?

- *It puts the people, practices, and ideals of a community on display.* Ceremonial speech uncovers the aspects of life that are not seen and highlights what is overshadowed in day-to-day life.

- *It puts language itself on display.* Ceremonial speech especially invites speakers to use artistic language to heighten an audience's appreciation of the topic.

- *It puts speakers on display.* As Jasinski says, "Through the display of eloquence, an advocate positions himself of herself as someone to whom the community should listen."

Through display, ceremonial speech takes us out of our normal, everyday existence and illuminates those things that matter most to a community. Let's take a look at some of the ways in which this display serves civic and political purposes.

Commemorating Leaders and Role Models One purpose of ceremonial speaking is to recognize individuals who have accomplished great things or acted in ways that deserve praise. A speech that pursues this purpose is called a **commemorative speech**, or a speech of tribute. By commemorating a leader or role model, a speaker displays characteristics of that person that the audience should imitate.

Speeches that commemorate occur at award ceremonies, banquets, or other special events at which unique or excellent achievements are recognized. For example, an end-of-the-year banquet might feature a commemorative speech about a student government leader who has been an especially strong advocate for the interests of the student body. Or it might highlight a classmate who has overcome a physical disability to receive his or her college degree.

Recognizing leaders and role models is useful for identifying the *characteristics, actions, and values* that make your community flourish. Although these types of speeches focus on individuals, the person is being commemorated not just for who he or she is but for this person's commitments, traits, and efforts. What did she do that was so amazing? How did he persevere under such difficult circumstances? What actions show this person's commitment to excellence? Commemoration depends on how vivid and clear you can make this person's life to your audience.

Inspiring Enthusiasm A closely related purpose of ceremonial speech is inspiring enthusiasm. The **inspirational speech** attempts to stir an audience's passion and commitment toward some topic, goal, or purpose. As you might imagine, a speech of inspiration may involve commemorating a person, but its purpose goes beyond celebrating an individual to celebrating a broader goal or purpose. This purpose also overlaps with the persuasive purpose of influencing attitudes; essentially, your task is to create a highly positive attitude toward the subject of your speech. But again, ceremonial speeches generally seek to shape a broader or more general attitude than that in a persuasive speech.

For example, a persuasive speech on freedom of expression might seek to strengthen an audience's attitude against a particular piece of legislation that threatens freedom of expression. And a commemorative speech might celebrate the efforts of someone who has defended freedom of speech. An inspirational speech, however, would seek to reinforce the importance of free expression in general and inspire listeners to continue to resist threats to free speech.

An inspirational speech is common at gatherings of political or civic organizations. In many ways, this type of speech builds the moral support and emotional energy that are needed to carry out long-term political and civic projects. If you are involved with a group that is fighting discrimination in your community, for example, it might not be enough to inform and persuade your members about the importance of a specific ordinance. To motivate people in your organization and to keep them engaged over the long run, you need to inspire enthusiasm.

Renewing Civic Identity As was mentioned at the beginning of this section, some ceremonial speeches are more narrowly defined by the demands of the occasion. In the United States, for example, events on Memorial Day, Independence Day, and Veterans Day are clear opportunities for renewing civic identities. These holidays, as well as moments such as presidential inaugurations and State of the Union addresses, are generally observed as a time to reflect on the values of the nation as well as the actions and sacrifices that other people have made on our behalf (Beasley; Vivian).

Renewal of civic identity occurs on local levels, too. Your hometown, for example, might have a festival that involves some formal events at which local leaders extol the virtues of living in your community. College campuses might have a Founder's Day or Charter Day, as do many campus organizations such as fraternities and sororities. Civic identity does not necessarily have to be limited to a specific place, either. Events ranging from Black Awareness Month to Universal Women's Week to Earth Day all offer a chance to unite people around identities that are meaningful to them.

Like commemorative and inspirational purposes, the purpose of renewing civic identity is crucial to the public sphere, as it strengthens the bonds of community. By reminding people of the identities that they share with others, speeches that renew civic identity can empower people to work together to fulfill common needs and goals.

Other Purposes of Ceremonial Speech

You may be familiar with other ceremonial speech types that are more common in your personal and professional life. Like the purposes of the speeches described above, these purposes also are largely about establishing common ground and a sense of identification among speakers, audience members, and the subject of the speech.

Introducing Speakers The **speech of introduction** prepares an audience for a featured or keynote speaker. If a prolific scholar, an inspiring leader, or prominent alumnus is going to speak on your campus, you might be asked to introduce that person to the audience. Or you might need to introduce a keynote speaker at an organization meeting or professional convention. Your role is to act as a liaison between the speaker and your colleagues in the audience but in a more formal way.

Like the introduction you invent for your own speeches, a speech of introduction sets the stage for what comes next. However, when giving a speech of introduction, you should not draw attention to yourself with a bold attention-grabber or comments that enhance your own credibility. Instead, you need to put the speaker on display and keep yourself in the background. Generally, a speech of introduction will do the following things:

- *Identify the speaker's name and occupation.* Be sure to confirm the accuracy and pronunciation with the speaker before the speech.
- *Enhance the credibility of the speaker.* Highlight the speaker's experience and achievements that are relevant to the speech and your audience.
- *Note the significance and relevance of the speaker's topic.* Try to evoke the audience's interest in and excitement about the speech.
- *State the title of the speech.* This is all you need to do by way of offering a main idea or preview of the speech.
- *Ask the audience to join you in welcoming the speaker.* Showing appreciation helps to establish a positive mood right off the bat.

Displaying the speaker in a positive light is your ultimate goal with this type of ceremonial speech. Potentially embarrassing anecdotes and excessive praise can be awkward, as can an introduction that is too short or that drags on too long. Depending on the length of the featured speech, your introduction might run anywhere from two to five minutes. Err on the side of brevity.

Presenting and Accepting Awards Your familiarity with an award presentation speech and an award acceptance speech might come from the creative and often quirky speeches that are given during award ceremonies for television, film, and music performances. Like clockwork, the MTV Video Music Awards ceremonies generate odd award speeches and supposedly "spontaneous" events that are usually more about self-promotion than about celebrating excellent performance. While entertaining, these instances reveal much about what *not* to do when you want to truly give credit for accomplishments.

The **award presentation speech** is essentially a tribute for a specific action or the quality of performance over a limited time frame—the top essay in your composition class, for example, or the most improved speaker during the season. As a result, award presentation speeches should focus on the performance that is being honored and leave out extraneous details that are not related to the award.

Also, consider explaining the award to your audience. Think about the criteria–application organizational pattern that you read about in chapter 14. Describing the criteria for the award can help the audience to better understand the awardee's accomplishments and direct you to talk about specific details. In addition, many awards on campus or in your community are named in honor of the award's sponsor. Recognizing that person adds meaning to the award and is a great way of keeping local history alive.

If you have the honor of receiving an award, a few key guidelines are necessary for the **award acceptance speech**, a speech that acknowledges an award and those who made it possible:

- *Express your gratitude for the award.* Humility is absolutely necessary for a successful acceptance speech.

- *Thank those who are bestowing the award.* It takes time and energy for organizations to give awards. Let them know that you appreciate it.

- *Thank those who aided your accomplishment.* The community angle on this speech is the reality that family, friends, and colleagues made your accomplishment possible. Mention them so that all of you can celebrate the moment.

Celebrating Milestones Different cultures, religions, and social groups have ceremonies that celebrate milestones that members of the group have reached. It could be a first communion, a bar or bat mitzvah, or a wedding. It could be a commencement ceremony at a school or college. It could be a work-related milestone, such as a promotion or a retirement party. Whether these ceremonies are formal or informal, they often include opportunities for speaking that recognizes the people who are reaching the milestone.

The most common speech in these situations is the **toast**, a brief speech that celebrates a milestone by amplifying feelings of goodwill. The specifics of the toast will depend on the particular milestone that is being celebrated. For example, a toast that celebrates a confirmation or other religious milestone will praise a person's religious development rather than other aspects of his or her identity. Also, toasts give speakers latitude to talk about the relationship between

PUBLIC SPOTLIGHT

Marisol Becerra

Marisol Becerra has been an active member of the Little Village community in Chicago since her early teens. Shocked by the pollution from coal-fired power plants in her community, Becerra worked with the Little Village Environmental Justice Organization (LVEJO) to map and inventory the toxins near these plants and to draw attention to related health problems, such as increased rates of asthma and premature births. She developed an interactive online map called OurMap of Environmental Justice that incorporates youth videos and displays toxic sites and gang territory.

For her work on these issues, Becerra has been honored with the Brower Youth Award from Earth Island Institute and has given inspirational speeches at the Clinton Global Initiative and PowerShift 2009. Her speech of acceptance at the Brower Youth Awards is a great example of a ceremonial speech that addresses a significant public issue. In it, she gave credit to her family, community members, and professors who mentored her; used statistics and testimony to raise awareness of the environmental injustice challenges in Little Village; and

inspired her audience members to raise their voices for a safe and healthy environment.

 Social Media Spotlight

Marisol Becerra's speeches are able to circulate far beyond their initial performance, as the organizations that support her take advantage of websites and social media to connect activists on related issues.

- Marisol Becerra's Brower Youth Award acceptance speech: http://www.broweryouthawards.org/userdata_display.php?modin=50&uid=3678
- Marisol Becerra's Power-Shift 2009 speech: http://www.youtube.com/watch?v=LITrHkVwtxA
- OurMap of Environmental Justice: http://www.elcilantro.org/?page_id=6
- LVEJO Facebook page: http://www.facebook.com/pages/Little-Village-Environmental-Justice-Organization-LVEJO/92669819450

Marisol Becerra has used ceremonial speaking to draw attention to the need for sustainable natural and social systems.

the speaker and the person who has reached the milestone. A toast at a wedding, for example, often will involve a speaker sharing a brief expression of friendship for the couple or a short anecdote that encapsulates their relationship.

The social expectations for toasts are much like those of other ceremonial speeches. Be brief, focus on the subject rather than yourself, and avoid potentially embarrassing stories. Films with wedding scenes are filled with examples of toasts, most of which are either extremely effective or extremely inappropriate. Take a look at a few, and try to determine what distinguishes the successful ones from the bombs.

As a college student, you should also reflect on the possibility of giving a **commencement speech**, a speech that occurs during celebration of the successful completion of an educational program. The interesting thing about the speech is that "commencement" means beginning, so the speech also marks a transition to a new phase of life. Consequently, a commencement speech both should celebrate accomplishment and inspire enthusiasm for what lies ahead. Because these speeches are so ritualized, speakers can easily fall into clichés and vague or sappy language. The rest of this chapter should give you some concrete ideas for making your commencement speech lively, instructive, and inspiring.

Memorializing Loved Ones A milestone that deserves its own section is the funeral, in which a **eulogy** serves the purpose of memorializing someone who has died. It can be a difficult speech to develop and deliver if you are close to the person you are memorializing, which is the case for most eulogies. The emotional intensity and grief can add to the normal challenges involved with public speaking.

But it can also be therapeutic for you. In many ways, a eulogy is a form of **auto-communication**, or communication in which the speaker is an important part of the audience. In other words, by thinking about what you would want to hear as a grieving audience member, you can develop a message that will be meaningful to the rest of your audience, too.

Traditionally, eulogies have contained three basic parts that are crucial for helping an audience to process their loss and move forward (Poulakos):

- *Praise of the deceased.* A good eulogy is as much a celebration as it is an expression of sorrow. Show the audience all of the positive things that came from the person's life: his or her character, actions, relationships, and accomplishments.

- *Lament of our loss.* Expressing grief is an important and necessary part of any eulogy. It can be cathartic for the audience members, and it shows that you recognize and share their feelings.

- *Consolation of the audience.* **Consolation** is the act of comforting the audience members and lessening their grief. Although words cannot eliminate grief, they can help an audience to see a world beyond their time of sorrow.

Often, the consolation of the audience will draw on those aspects of the person's life that were praised. The way to honor the memory of the person is to cherish the person's values and follow his or her model.

Clarifying Your Purpose and Central Idea

Compared to an informative or persuasive speech on a public issue, a ceremonial speech usually has a fairly clear purpose. The descriptions above should give you a clear sense of what you are trying to accomplish. However, especially for some of the longer ceremonial speeches, such as a commemorative

PRAISE IN EULOGIES
Oprah Winfrey's eulogy of Rosa Parks praised Parks' courageous actions during the civil rights movement.

speech or a speech of inspiration, it may be useful to sharpen your purpose to keep your speech on track.

For example, a speech that intends to pay tribute to an individual can start meandering if the speaker does not have a clear sense of the characteristics, actions, or values that she wishes to praise:

Purpose: To pay tribute to Nathan Miller, student body president.

Better purpose: To pay tribute to Nathan Miller's devotion to the needs of disabled students on campus.

Better purpose: To pay tribute to Nathan Miller's commitment to equal treatment of all students.

The better purpose statements clarify which aspects of Nathan's experience and character will be on display. Likewise, a more focused purpose statement could help to focus a speech intended to inspire or renew civic identity:

Purpose: To inspire appreciation for veterans.

Better purpose: To inspire appreciation of other students who are veterans.

The success of a traditional commencement speech can hinge on whether a speaker has a coherent purpose. One of the most fascinating commencement speeches came from novelist David Foster Wallace, who spoke at Kenyon College in 2005 ("David Foster Wallace"). His speech did not sound like a typical commencement speech, but it was driven by a fairly specific purpose: to inspire students to reflect on the idea that a liberal arts education teaches you how to think. Wallace used jokes, philosophy, and examples, in order to illustrate that idea and explore its meaning in everyday life. In contrast, many commencement speeches have a purpose that is little more than a few platitudes about the graduating class with some self-centered stories thrown in as filler. Having a more specific purpose than "celebrating the graduates" likely will make your commencement speech more memorable than the average speech.

Even short speeches can benefit from some careful thinking about your precise purpose. A speech of introduction, as we saw above, should dwell on the aspects of the speaker that are most relevant to the topic of his or her speech:

> *Purpose:* To introduce David Orr to my audience.
>
> *Better purpose:* To introduce David Orr as a knowledgeable and experienced speaker about "post-carbon" cities.

The same principle holds for award speeches. These are not times to say whatever you like about the award recipient or to elaborate on your personal opinion about a topic that is unrelated to your award. Focus instead on the reasons the ceremony is being held in the first place.

Finally, not all ceremonial speeches will have a central idea that is as clear and direct as those in informative and persuasive speeches. For example, it would probably sound a little stiff to start a toast by saying, "Today I want to show that Sharice and Alan are a great couple for three reasons." Likewise, an award acceptance speech makes several acknowledgements rather than establishing a core idea.

However, commemorative speeches, eulogies, milestone speeches, and inspirational speeches often will have an overarching theme that can be encapsulated in a sentence early in the speech:

> *Eulogy central idea:* No matter how you knew Jennifer, her saucy humor made her loved by everyone.
>
> *Commemorative central idea:* Barb's commitment to our entire association, not just a few certain groups, has established a model for leadership that we should all try to follow.
>
> *Inspirational central idea:* With your hard work, we can restore conservative values as the bedrock principles guiding our legislature.

For these somewhat longer ceremonial speeches, the central idea is not so much a claim that needs to be established as a theme on which you can develop variations throughout your speech. Your entire speech, then, involves amplifying and magnifying that theme to develop a rich and satisfying depiction of your subject.

THE ETHICAL DIMENSION

Using Ceremonial Speech to Engage Differences

At the beginning of this chapter, you learned that effective ceremonial speaking should engage the audience's principles, goals, and values. But *how* should it engage? Is it preferable to reinforce the meanings that audiences give to goals and values, or can ceremonial speech engage differences and offer meanings that raise disagreement?

Chris Hedges's commencement speech at Rockford College in 2003 offers a provocative case for examining this ethical dimension of ceremonial speaking. Hedges, a war correspondent and author of the book *War Is a Force That Gives Us Meaning,* delivered a speech that was largely about war and comradeship. Coming shortly after the U.S. invasion of Iraq, his speech drew national attention after a few members of the audience booed and tried to get onto the stage and the sound system was cut off twice during the speech. The public sphere buzzed with discussion about the appropriateness of Hedges's speech as well as the behavior of audience members who disagreed with his message.

Rhetorical scholar Lois Agnew analyzed the tumult over Hedges's speech and explains that the speaker and the audience share the blame. On one hand, Hedges's speech appears to violate the usual norms of commencement speaking. He did not acknowledge the accomplishments of the graduates, and he did little to develop identification with his audience. On the other hand, critical responses to the speech generally refused to see the moment as "an educational moment that appropriately culminates the students' academic experiences" (160).

For Agnew, the case shows the challenge of making ceremonial speech something more than just empty platitudes. Agnew frames her conclusion for a new vision of epideictic rhetoric in relation to the ethical principle of reciprocity that has been discussed throughout this book: "Audiences and speakers who enter into epideictic moments with a genuine commitment to learn from each other, even as they respectfully acknowledge their differences, will be uniquely prepared to respond to a world in which difference is often seen as a divisive force" (161).

WHAT DO YOU THINK?

1. Read the text of the speech at http://www .commondreams.org/headlines03/0520-13.htm, or watch the video (the first of four clips) at http:// www.youtube.com/watch?v=SAWMgYyAtHU. If you were in the audience, how would you have responded to the speech?

2. What adaptations to the immediate audience or occasion might have softened the response to the speech?

3. Who do you think was Hedges's primary audience for the speech? How might this have influenced his rhetorical strategies?

Inventing Your Ceremonial Speech

The topical system that you have been using for informative and persuasive speeches also can be applied in ceremonial situations. After all, your audience and the topic of your speech remain the central constraints for rhetorical invention regardless of the type of speech you are giving. The topic of language analysis, however, needs to be adapted for ceremonial situations.

Using Audience Research

Demographic factors can be surprisingly useful for ceremonial speaking. If you need to make an impromptu toast or are struggling with the challenge of developing a eulogy in a short time, a simple demographic analysis can help you to make some basic choices and steer clear of important hazards.

For example, a successful impromptu wedding toast can benefit greatly from examining age, religion, race, and class. A toast that might be fine when you are out with friends of the couple the night before the wedding might not be acceptable at a wedding reception with older family members and children. Similarly, be wary of making assumptions about shared experiences when making a toast to an audience of mixed religious backgrounds or an audience that is racially or economically diverse.

Likewise, a eulogy often brings together people of diverse backgrounds who might have known the deceased person at different ages or stages in life. If you are familiar with the range of people who are likely to attend a memorial, you can consider adapting your speech to address events and memories that will resonate with different groups.

In other ceremonial situations, demographics can give you hints about whether your audience has deficient or abundant knowledge about the topic of your speech. Age is again an important factor. A younger audience might not know much about a particular award or milestone, requiring you to go into greater depth and make your speech somewhat more informative. If you are trying to inspire a young audience about civil rights, they might need to know more about the history of civil rights struggles than an older audience would.

Consider how race and ethnicity can influence your invention. On the topic of civil rights, an audience that is dominated by one ethnic group might need to know more about the struggles of other groups. Conversely, a speech that is attempting to renew civic identity might focus specifically on celebrating the contributions that one ethnic or racial group has made to the community.

Overall, audience research is critical for determining your audience's disposition and knowledge base about the topic of your speech. As with every other type of speech, these factors should shape how you approach your topic. Just because the focus of ceremonial speaking often is a person does not mean that you can ignore the other people—the audience—who are ultimately the ones you are trying to reach with your speech.

Using Topic Research

Nevertheless, the subject of your speech is typically much richer than you might know. A bit of research can often yield an interesting anecdote or new perspective that changes a ceremonial speech from a boring ritual to a moment of real audience engagement. Come back to the common topics discussed in chapter 8 to brainstorm possibilities for your speech.

Existence Paying tribute to collective groups such as organizations or communities requires you to make them come alive for your audience. Use concrete and active language to show where the spirit of your community exists or how your organization plays an important role on campus. Likewise, you can do a better job of inspiring enthusiasm for an abstract idea or value by showing where it already exists or specific obstacles to its achievement.

Definition You could develop an entire speech around the definition of a key term or idea. A commemorative speech might show how a lawyer or victim's advocate exhibits a commitment to "justice," or a eulogy could show that the definition of a "patriot" fits a the person you are memorializing. Definitional strategies also can come into play for award presentations, when you might explain the denotative meaning of the award criteria or some of the connotative meanings that are embodied by the award recipient.

Comparison When used carefully, comparison can be an excellent strategy for developing the accomplishments of a person. Comparing the achievements of your subject to other respected people will magnify the importance of your subject. Think, for example, of how an award-winning athlete will be compared to others stars or hall of fame players.

However, be sure that your comparison does not overshadow the primary subject of your speech. In a milestone speech, it would be embarrassing to spend more time talking about past presidents of your organization than about the president whose efforts are being celebrated. Also, avoid contrasting your subject to "average" people, many of whom may be your audience members. Your purpose, after all, is to celebrate and inspire audience members, not make them feel bad.

Causality Remember that causal strategies involve both effect-to-cause and cause-to-effect thinking. For example, when you accept an award, your recognition of the people who have supported you is essentially a movement from effect (award-winning achievement) to cause (the support of others). Conversely, speeches that pay tribute or inspire might narrate how certain actions, initiatives, or commitments have caused positive results. In either direction, though, ceremonial speeches tend to dwell on the causes or actions that bring about positive effects

Correlation Correlation also can show how a person's presence is associated with positive things. Eulogies use this when they show how a person "lights up a room" or brings joy to people's lives. A milestone speech might use correlation when it is difficult to demonstrate causation. For example, you might celebrate someone's involvement with the committee that organizes your campus blood drive, since it may be a challenge to specify individual actions.

Time and Place Ceremonial speeches often show how an individual has made a long-term commitment to a cause or activity. Or they may focus on specific moments in time that highlight unusual or extraordinary efforts.

specific moments in time that highlight unusual or extraordinary efforts. Place also offers a way to think about the diversity of instances in which an individual or group had made an impact on the world. And of course, renewing civic identity often will incorporate celebration of a specific locale. You might include references to the natural world or recognizable landmarks to unite people through a shared sense of place.

Using Effective Language

The purpose of many ceremonial speeches is not only to celebrate but also to inspire and motivate, so choices of language and style are central to the development of an effective speech. Think about the strategies for effective language that you learned about in chapter 7. It is not enough to merely talk about the subject of your speech; instead, the goal is to *depict* or *paint a picture* of the subject that captures the audience's attention and moves the audience to appreciate, celebrate, or identify with that subject. Consequently, for ceremonial speeches, think about how different types of language can help you to extend or elaborate your ideas.

A metaphor can provide a great unifying theme for your speech. For example, Dr. Beryl Brubaker developed her commencement speech at Eastern Mennonite University around the metaphor of "bridge builders," highlighting examples of people who enabled reconciliation and peaceful relationships among individuals and groups in conflict (Groff). Commencement and other inspirational speeches often rely on metaphors for depicting future challenges and obstacles: climbing a mountain, walking a path, swimming against the current, or taking a test. Well-chosen metaphors give listeners a vivid image as well as a connection to something that resonates with their everyday experience.

Alliteration is another common way of elaborating a series of ideas. In a baccalaureate address, the Rev. Dr. Kirk Byron Jones used alliteration to link pieces of advice to his overarching theme that graduates need to "pause" in their lives.

> Here are "four Ps" for you to remember should you so dare:
>
> 1. *Permission.* If you don't value your rest, no one else will. . . .
> 2. *Planning.* Schedule daily and weekly times of rest and leisure, and be open to the unscheduled graces of free time to simply be. . . .
> 3. *Practice.* Don't just plan your rest and leisure, but live it. . . .
> 4. *Personhood.* Know that having regular periods of rest and relaxation helps you to remember that you are infinitely more than what you do. . . . (Jones).

Similarly, anaphora encourages thinking about how you might expand on an idea to develop a set of related or parallel instances. For example, in his

LANGUAGE IN CEREMONIAL SPEECHES

Ceremonial speeches do not need ornate language; concrete details and vivid language like that in Conan O'Brien's Harvard Class Day speech are the keys to a memorable speech.

Harvard Class Day speech in 2000, comedian Conan O'Brien used anaphora and metaphor together to emphasize his larger message about the importance of risk-taking and resilience. In a series of sentences, he repeated the notion of leaving a cocoon and shared how he left a string of comfortable and successful jobs at Saturday Night Live and The Simpsons. This repetition underscored the necessity of taking chances and not resting on one's past successes.

These techniques can make for memorable ways of developing main points or elaborating on a central idea. More broadly, though, do your best to use concrete, familiar, and active language that sustains audience attention throughout your speech. Read aloud these words from Paul Hawken to hear how carefully chosen language can evoke powerful images and feelings:

> There is invisible writing on the back of the diploma you will receive, and in case you didn't bring lemon juice to decode it, I can tell you what it says: You are Brilliant, and the Earth is Hiring. The earth couldn't afford to send recruiters or limos to your school. It sent you rain, sunsets, ripe cherries, night blooming jasmine, and that unbelievably cute person you are dating. Take the hint. And here's the deal: Forget that this task of planet-saving is not possible in the time required. Don't be put off by people who know what is not possible. Do what needs to be done, and check to see if it was impossible only after you are done.

Organizing Your Ceremonial Speech

The basic strategies that you learned earlier in the semester can be adapted easily to ceremonial speaking. As with informative and persuasive speaking, some of the topics for invention lead directly to specific organizational patterns. Especially prominent in ceremonial speaking are chronological, causal, and topical order.

Chronological Order

Chronological order makes sense for those ceremonial speeches that attempt to capture the life or career of a person being commemorated or memorialized. Eulogies, for example, often touch on the significant moments in one's life, such as significant work or volunteer accomplishments, marriage, and the birth of children. Speeches of introduction and award presentations also will often use a chronological order to build a list of achievements that culminates with one's current work.

Speeches that attempt to renew civic identity may review historical events in chronological order, too. For example, Deborah Parker's Memorial Day Speech in 1997 used chronological order—moving from World War II to Vietnam to Somalia—to show how the U.S. military has long been a melting pot of Americans from diverse backgrounds. Similarly, President Bill Clinton used chronological order at the beginning of his first inaugural address to develop the theme of American renewal:

> Though our challenges are fearsome, so are our strengths. Americans have ever been a restless, questing, hopeful people. And we must bring to our task today the vision and will of those who came before us. From our Revolution to the Civil War, to the Great Depression, to the civil rights movement, our people have always mustered the determination to construct from these crises the pillars of our history. Thomas Jefferson believed that to preserve the very foundations of our Nation, we would need dramatic change from time to time. Well, my fellow Americans, this is our time. Let us embrace it.

Chronological order also can work well for speeches of inspiration. Like the motivational sequence order for persuasive speeches, a chronological speech intended to inspire can be effective if it narrates a history that inspires an audience to support some value or idea in the future.

Causal Order

Causal order makes sense when you are trying to highlight the actions and accomplishments of your subject. This type of speech might place those actions as the causal factor that led to praiseworthy outcomes. For example, a speech celebrating World War II veterans might focus on specific battles or decisions that were especially important in bringing about the Allies' victory. Or in an inspirational speech, you might use cause-and-effect order if you provide a series of examples that show how commitment to a principle caused people to act in heroic or admirable ways.

Topical Order

Topical order is a standard organizational strategy for assembling a list of virtues or qualities of a person whom you want to praise. Consequently, this strategy comes in handy for commemorative and inspirational speeches as well as eulogies. Speeches that attempt to renew civic identity may also be organized a series of values or ideals that citizens should strive to live by as members of a community.

An interesting speech that blends chronology with topical order is Blaine McCormick's "Benjamin Franklin and the Real 'National Treasure.'" In it,

McCormick develops a set of "financial and entrepreneurial virtues" that emerge from a narrative about the early part of Benjamin Franklin's life. The speech weaves these virtues into the narrative, stopping at times to offer an internal summary:

> His early experiments with vegetarian diets led to a lifetime of curiosity and—given the other patterns that have emerged—it's no wonder he ended up being one of the top scientists of his age. So industry and self-education are two of the early virtues that we want to highlight as we seek to find the real national treasure.

Here, McCormick identifies two of the key topics that he has developed before moving on with his narrative. This is a creative way of developing a series of topics that blends different organizational patterns together.

Again, the diversity of situations that call for ceremonial speech means that there is no easy guide for the most appropriate organizational strategy for your speech. But recalling the basic patterns that you have learned throughout this book can give you some creative options for developing a unique and memorable ceremonial speech.

Supporting Your Ceremonial Speech

Regardless of the topic of your ceremonial speech, supporting material is absolutely necessary if you want your speech to be more than a series of clichés and platitudes. You audience members will want details about the person who is being commemorated. They will be fascinated by new stories that are part of their civic identity. They will want to be reminded of the distinctive characteristics and events that shaped the life of the person you are eulogizing.

Most ceremonial speeches, then, have a significant component of informative speaking at their core. But as much as your audience members want to learn more about the topic of your speech, you ultimately want them to be moved by your speech. You want to stir their emotions, enhance their appreciation, and potentially encourage them to imitate the subject of your speech. For example, if you wish to pay tribute to your college football team, you cannot simply describe the team and its accomplishments. You must use vivid depictions and concrete examples that convey the meaning of the actions, and you must make their meaning available to those listeners who are not football fans.

All of this points to the importance of selecting supporting material for your ceremonial speech. As you return to the types of supporting material that we have learned about so far, think about how these materials can best serve the various purposes of ceremonial speaking.

Narratives

As you have seen, narratives are at the heart of much ceremonial speaking. Whether it is a lengthy tribute or a short toast, a narrative can help a speaker to achieve the purposes of most types of ceremonial speaking.

The keys to selecting a good narrative for a ceremonial speech come down to its vividness and ability to encapsulate a core idea. First, vivid narratives make a ceremonial speech truly a speech of display. They evoke images that an audience will not soon forget. Elie Wiesel's Nobel Prize acceptance speech uses narrative, not to provide detailed description of specific events of the Holocaust, but to create an image of his personal experience and to set a mood:

> I remember: it happened yesterday or eternities ago. A young Jewish boy discovering the kingdom of night. I remember his bewilderment, I remember his anguish. It all happened so fast. The ghetto. The deportation. The sealed cattle car. The fiery altar upon which the history of our people and the future of mankind were meant to be sacrificed.
>
> I remember: he asked his father: "Can this be true?" This is the 20th century, not the Middle Ages. Who would allow such crimes to be committed? How could the world remain silent?"
>
> And now the boy is turning to me. "Tell me," he asks. "What have you done with your life?" And I tell him that I have tried. That I have tried to keep memory alive, that I have tried to fight those who would forget. Because if we forget, we are guilty, we are accomplices" (Wiesel).

Narrative also works powerfully when it can capture a key idea. Ceremonial speeches often use narratives and parables to frame ideas in a novel way. For example, Booker T. Washington's Atlanta Exposition Address of 1895 used a short narrative to define his perspective on race relations and advancement among blacks in the South.

> A ship lost at sea for many days suddenly sighted a friendly vessel. From the mast of the unfortunate vessel was seen a signal, "Water, water; we die of thirst!" The answer from the friendly vessel at once came back, "Cast down your bucket where you are." And a third and fourth signal for water was answered, "Cast down your bucket where you are." The captain of the distressed vessel, at last heeding the injunction, cast down his bucket, and it came up full of fresh, sparkling water from the mouth of the Amazon River. To those of my race who depend on bettering their condition in a foreign land or who underestimate the importance of cultivating friendly relations with the southern white man, who is their next-door neighbor, I would say; "Cast down your bucket where you are"—cast it down in making friends in every manly way of the people of all races by whom we are surrounded.

Washington's perspective was not uncontroversial; critics such as W.E.B. DuBois found it insufficient for pursuing civil rights. Yet in this speech, his narrative was an effective way to address his ideas with a mixed-race audience.

The story said more about diversity and its importance than could have been said in an extended discussion of the topic. When chosen and told carefully, narratives can make your point with eloquence.

Examples

Examples are a staple of all types of speeches, and ceremonial speeches are no exception. The primary importance of examples is for making ideas concrete and tangible to your audience, much in the way that narratives make action vivid for your audience. In his eulogy of President Kennedy, Lyndon Johnson mentioned several examples of Kennedy's goals as a way to give people tangible ways for Kennedy's legacy to live on:

> The dream of conquering the vastness of space, the dream of partnership across the Atlantic—and across the Pacific as well—the dream of a Peace Corps in less developed nations, the dream of education for all of our children, the dream of jobs for all who seek them and need them, the dream of care for our elderly, the dream of an all-out attack on mental illness, and above all, the dream of equal rights for all Americans, whatever their race or color. These and other American dreams have been vitalized by his drive and by his dedication. And now the ideas and the ideals which he so nobly represented must and will be translated into effective action (Johnson).

Notice how these examples provide specific details about what could otherwise be a broad or vague idea. Instead of saying, "Kennedy was a man with a lot of dreams about what America could be like," Johnson gave life to those dreams, helping different parts of the audience to connect with different aspects of the Kennedy legacy.

Testimony

Testimony can be powerful in certain kinds of ceremonial speech and somewhat awkward in others. To understand this, think about how testimony functions in informative and persuasive speaking. Primarily, it lends credibility to the speaker by drawing on other people's experience or expertise about the topic.

Thus, testimony is likely to work well in those situations in which communal recognition of outstanding achievement is the overarching goal. Award presentation speeches, for example, might draw on quotations from other people in the field who have praised the recipient's work. Other speeches that pay tribute to a person or an organization can benefit from testimony, too. If the point is to praise your subject, then the praising words of other people can be appropriate.

In contrast, the testimony of others may be more difficult or awkward to use if your speech mostly emphasizes your personal connection to the subject. Toasts and some eulogies might fit into this category. For example, it would seem odd if you began a toast by sharing a personal experience that has led you to admire the person you are toasting but then launched into a discussion of how other people are filled with admiration too.

Likewise, a eulogy that is primarily about your personal relationship with the deceased probably does not need the testimony of others to convey the spirit of that relationship. Such testimony might be relevant if your eulogy focuses on the respect and high regard that the person had. The choice of whether to include testimony, then, should be shaped by whether you intend to take a personal or a more public perspective in your speech.

Statistics

Like testimony, statistics vary in their usefulness as supporting material for ceremonial speeches. In general, statistics are seen as a rather dry form of supporting material; they often lack the emotional appeal of a narrative or a concrete example. But when used strategically, they certainly can magnify the importance of your subject and his or her accomplishments. A speech of introduction might mention the number of books a speaker has written on the subject, or an award presentation speech might offer a statistic that was used to determine who would receive the award.

Inspirational speeches can use statistics strategically to show accomplishment. If an organization tells its members that last year's walkathon had 100 participants, that number can inspire them to work on getting more participants this year. Or if you show that donations to a charity improved the lives of 500 families in your community, that can let people know that their efforts are having a real impact. These kinds of statistics can be crucial in inspiring people to see their individual action as meaningful, contributing to a much bigger collective action.

CASE CONCLUSION

Treva's Speech on the Neuro Networking Club

Treva decided that her speech should attempt to inspire enthusiasm about the club. In doing so, she would also be raising awareness about autism and encouraging people to come to the club's annual Spring Hullabaloo. Her main hope was to increase the buzz on campus about the group in the hopes that more people would hear about and participate in the club.

From audience research, it was clear that her classmates knew little about autism in general, so Treva knew that they would need some information before she talked about the specifics of this club. She chose to develop her speech around the common topics of existence (both the existence of autism and the existence of the club) and comparison (to show that autism is far more common than many other prominent health issues). Statistics and testimony would be important pieces of supporting material for developing the latter point. In addition, Treva recognized that to inspire enthusiasm, she needed to include narratives that conveyed the fun and lively spirit of the club. Relying on both her personal experience and the testimony of other people in the group, she was able to paint an inspiring picture of the group.

WORKING OUTLINE

Treva's Speech on the Neuro Networking Club

Specific purpose: To inspire enthusiasm in my audience about the Neuro Networking Club

Central idea: The Neuro Networking Club is changing the face of autism on campus and in our community.

I. Introduction

Treva starts her speech with shared goals to build common ground.

    A. Acceptance. Encouragement. Support. Every one of us needs these things. For many of us, they come easily. But for people with autism, they do not come so easily.

A simple statistic conveys the significance of the public issue connected to her speech.

    B. It's increasingly likely that someone you know is facing this challenge. The Autism Society of America reports that "autism is the fastest growing developmental disability with a 10 to 17% annual growth rate" (Autism Society).

    C. I know what these challenges are like. My son has autism, and during the past few years, I have developed a group here in town called the Neuro Networking Club, which helps young adults with autism to overcome obstacles, find a sense of belonging, and meet their goals.

The central idea conveys Treva's purpose of inspiration.

    D. In the next few minutes, I want to share with you how the Neuro Networking Club is changing the face of autism on campus and in our community. I think you'll find that the club is a wonderful part of our community, and I hope that you will be inspired to get involved with us.

    E. Most of all, I want to share with you some stories about our club—both from people with autism and from "neurotypical" members—that will show you what we're all about. I also want to give you an idea of some of the things we're doing so that you might see where you could connect with us.

(Transition: Before getting to these details, though, I'd like to give you some background on autism.)

II. Background on Autism

    A. There is good reason why you have been hearing more about autism. It is a very prevalent problem.

On the basis of audience research, Treva recognizes that some basic information is necessary to share with the audience early in the speech.

        1. In 2009, the CDC reported that "1 in every 110 children in the United States has an Autism Spectrum Disorder (ASD)" and "considers it an urgent public health concern" (Centers for Disease Control).

        2. In the words of a 2003 study by the California Department of Developmental Services, autism is now "more prevalent than childhood cancer, diabetes and Down Syndrome" (California Department of Developmental Services).

B. But you might not know exactly what autism is. The National Autism Association defines it as "a bio-neurological developmental disability that generally appears before the age of 3" (National Autism Association).

C. This disability shows up differently in different people.

    1. The National Institute for Mental Health says that the defining characteristics of autism are "deficits in social interaction, verbal and nonverbal communication, and repetitive behaviors and interests" (NIMH).

    2. For example, children with autism often have speech delays, and they may react intensely or completely withdraw from regular social interaction.

    3. Some people with autism may also experience physical problems, such as allergies, epilepsy, or frequent infections.

    4. This range of disabilities and behavioral responses is often referred to as the autism spectrum.

(Transition: While the focus of much autism research is on diagnosing young children, there is less attention to the needs of young adults with autism. That's where the Neuro Networking Club comes in.)

III. Neuro Networking Club Serves the Autistic Community

A. Young adults with autism have unique needs.

    1. They are no longer looking for "early intervention" or "behavior modification programs."

    2. Instead, they are looking for acceptance and support. This especially applies to the desire be a part of the community and attend college.

    3. A college student with autism has many challenges that neurotypical students do not face. While students with autism struggle with acute sensitivities to sounds, odors, lights, and human interactions, they also want to be recognized for their intelligence, talents, and contributions.

B. The Neuro Networking Club helps to serve those needs.

    1. We meet regularly to socialize and help one another understand the many faces of autism.

    2. We also share our challenges and success stories with one another in order to provide support and encouragement.

    3. For example, at a meeting, we might gather at someone's house to watch a movie, celebrate a birthday, or have a holiday party.

C. Our club members' stories provide the best evidence of what we do.

    1. Allison Pak, an Honors Student in Geography, is a great example. She not only has autism to overcome, she also has rheumatoid arthritis, which makes every step and movement an energy-draining and painful endeavor. But through the club, Allison has found reasons to celebrate life and appreciate neurodiversity.

While not all ceremonial speeches use external sources, they are appropriate in this situation.

The speech divides its main points by the different groups served by the club.

Comparative statements throughout the speech help with audience adaptation.

Narratives about personal experience show the impact of the group on people's lives.

2. Allison says, "I hated myself for being different and for not being able to do the things everyone else seemed to have no problems with, like having a simple conversation with someone, going into a coffee shop or making phone calls."

3. The club, she said, is "the ultimate reward for all those years of torment, anxiety and pain. Everything we talk about and do has a positive outlook. Nobody criticizes anyone for their difference. It's great to be around people like that—who understand and are 100 percent supportive. I am much happier since joining. I realize that when I am with all of these amazing individuals, the diagnoses become irrelevant. Everyone just belongs."

(Transition: But the club is not just about serving the needs of people with autism.)

Multiple examples in this section amplify the positive qualities of the group.

IV. Neuro Networking Club Also Serves the Rest of Community

A. Members of the club have been interviewed and featured multiple times in local newspaper and television. This has raised awareness about autism throughout the region.

B. We also organized a one-day conference on autism that brought more than 200 professionals, students, and families dealing with autism together to learn more about it.

C. We've raised funds for people with autism who need medical help. For example, we raised $12,000 for Heather Stone's dental surgery.

D. More important than these accomplishments is that we are shattering stereotypes.

1. People often believe the erroneous stereotype that people with autism have no feelings, are not creative, do not have a sense of humor, and do not want to engage with people. You only have to attend one Neuro Networking Club meeting to break all of these stereotypes.

2. As Laura Olsonoski (a neurotypical member of our club) said, "They're the coolest individuals I've ever met. They just have different ways of thinking. They are just such amazing people."

The conclusion reinforces the central idea and provides an outlet for this inspiration.

V. Conclusion

A. I hope you can now see how the Neuro Networking Club is changing the face of autism.

B. It is changing the way people with autism are being perceived and treated. It is giving people with autism a feeling of belonging. It is giving them a voice and the chance to have a place and influence in their community.

C. You can see what this great group is all about next month. We are holding our annual Spring Hullaballoo on the afternoon of April 23 at the University

Center, where we will have entertainment and information for everyone. Come join us and celebrate neurodiversity!

REFERENCES

Autism Society of America. "Facts and Statistics." Autism Society website. Available at http://www.autism-society.org/about-autism/facts-and-statistics.html

California Department of Developmental Services. "Autism Spectrum Disorders: Changes in the California Caseload 1999-2002." April 2003. Available at http://www.dds.ca.gov/Autism/docs/AutismReport2003.pdf

Centers for Disease Control and Prevention. "Prevalence of Autism Spectrum Disorders—Autism and Developmental Disabilities Monitoring Network, United States, 2006." CDC website. 18 Dec. 2009. Available at http://www.cdc.gov/mmwr/preview/mmwrhtml/ss5810a1.htm

National Autism Association. "Definitions." NAA website. Available at http://www.nationalautismassociation.org/definitions.php

National Institute of Mental Health. "Autism Spectrum Disorders." NIMH website. Available at http://nimh.nih.gov/health/publications/autism/complete-index.shtml

Pak, Allison. Personal interview. 23 March 2011.

Summary

PURPOSES OF CEREMONIAL SPEECH

- Ceremonial speaking in civic and political contexts often involves commemorating notable individuals, inspiring civic action, or renewing civic identity.

- Other purposes of ceremonial speech include introducing speakers, presenting and accepting awards, celebrating milestones, and eulogizing loved ones.

INVENTING YOUR CEREMONIAL SPEECH

- Demographic categories and the common topics can help you to generate ideas for your speech.

ORGANIZING YOUR CEREMONIAL SPEECH

- Topical order is often used to assemble a list of virtues or qualities of a person that you want to praise.

- Chronological order is useful for recounting a person's life and accomplishments that are relevant to a particular ceremonial speaking situation.

SUPPORTING YOUR CEREMONIAL SPEECH

- Narratives, examples, and testimony are useful for moving beyond common knowledge and clichés as the basis for ceremonial speaking.

- Statistics can be used strategically to show individual or collective accomplishments.

Key Terms

ceremonial speech, p. 386
epideictic rhetoric, p. 387
commemorative speech, p. 388
inspirational speech, p. 388
speech of introduction, p. 390
award presentation speech, p. 391

award acceptance speech, p. 391
toast, p. 391
commencement speech, p. 392
eulogy, p. 393
auto-communication, p. 393
consolation, p. 393

Comprehension

1. How does ceremonial speaking serve an important public purpose?

2. Identify three occasions that might call for a commemorative speech.

3. What are the three basic parts of a eulogy?

4. Explain how the main points of commemorative speech would look different depending on whether the speech was organized in chronological, topical, or causal order.

5. In what situations would it make sense to include testimony in a ceremonial speech?

Application

1. Produce a short commemorative speech about your college with alumni as the intended audience. Think carefully about which characteristics, actions, and values would be best to commemorate.

2. Consider arranging an awards ceremony for you and your classmates, complete with speeches of award presentation and acceptance.

3. Use three of the common topics to invent an inspirational speech about a topic that is important to you.

4. Imagine that the public figure who is most inspiring to you has been invited to your campus and you have been asked to give a speech of introduction. Do some research to find a piece of testimony that could be incorporated in your speech.

Understanding Public Discourse

This appendix is intended to help you:

- Identify the typical patterns of language use for various public voices
- Determine the values and goals that motivate different voices
- Observe informational biases in news reports about public issues
- Become a more critical analyst of other people's messages and a more reflective language user in your own speeches

The power and importance of language have not receded with the rise of a highly visual culture. No matter what one's political viewpoint, participants across the public sphere recognize that language is still one of the most powerful influences on how we think about public issues. From a conservative viewpoint, the pollster and campaign consultant Frank Luntz has collected insights from the numerous campaigns he has advised in a book titled *Words That Work.* From a liberal perspective, the cognitive linguist George Lakoff explains that the language used to frame issues helps speakers to clarify their values in ways that resonate with diverse audiences.

The popularity of Luntz's and Lakoff's work shows that language matters to those who want to have an effective voice in the public sphere. It also shows that the language that we hear in the public sphere is often designed strategically to persuade. Therefore, it is crucial that public speakers understand the range of public voices and the typical language strategies of these voices that circulate in the public sphere. This will help you to become a more critical consumer of other people's messages and will help you to become a more savvy user of language yourself. Read this chapter in conjunction with chapters 6 and 7 to maximize your ability to engage with the language of public issues. ■

Understanding Public Voices

Your understanding of public discourse will be strengthened as you recognize how language choices are influenced by an advocate's interests and values. Political campaign consultants like Luntz and Lakoff try to identify language that resonates with wide audiences while also reflecting the goals and commitments of a candidate or party. For example, in the United States, conservatives are more likely to praise free markets in order to expand opportunity, while liberals are more likely to speak about regulating markets in the pursuit of justice and equity.

In other words, public voices have language patterns. Communication critic Bernard Brock and his colleagues capture this relationship clearly when they say, "Proponents of the different political positions call upon strategies typical of their position to connect their underlying political philosophy with the action they advocate" (Brock et al. 67). In other words, *there are typical ways of using language that signal an advocate's overall political stance.* Brock and his colleagues categorize the four positions in terms of their general attitude toward existing political institutions and the drift of cultural and policy change:

- *Reactionary:* a position that rejects the political structure and resists cultural change
- *Conservative:* a position that accepts the political structure but generally resists cultural change
- *Liberal:* a position that accepts the political structure and generally accepts cultural change
- *Radical:* a position that rejects the political structure and accepts cultural change

It is important to note that these are not the only four positions on public issues. The positions have some overlap, and individuals may embrace different positions on different topics. Also, these voices were identified in U.S. public discourse and might not apply perfectly to other political contexts. But knowing these differences and recognizing language that signals these positions is a good first step toward understanding other voices in the public sphere.

Reactionary Voices

A **reactionary voice**, according to Brock and colleagues, discusses public issues by connecting them to essential truths and higher purposes. These principles should guide our decision making. Because the world rarely conforms to these idealized principles, the reactionary voice tends to see rampant disorder and moral decline. Believing that the culture is in decline and that the political system is corrupt, the reactionary voice often calls for a restoration of order and traditional values among ordinary citizens.

Many examples of reactionary voices can be found in times of economic distress, when they often gain a greater hearing. In the 1930s, Father Charles Coughlin spoke vehemently against both capitalism and communism and railed against the New Deal efforts of President Roosevelt. More recently, speakers at "Tea Party" rallies in 2009 and beyond did not simply disagree with policies but were highly critical of political institutions. In their view, order needed to be restored to these institutions by getting back to fundamental principles:

> If you believe as I do, if you want America to remain a free society governed by the rule of law and not by the whims of men, then you <u>must</u> stand up, take action and make your voices heard. . . . We're all living in what's left of a seriously weakened Constitutional republic in which the collapse of the *ideas* underlying individual liberty is very far advanced (Dorrity).

The driving force behind the reactionary voice, then, is deviation from traditional principles and values. Their rhetoric will focus more on restoring those principles than on compromising to solve problems within the current system of governance.

Conservative Voices

A **conservative voice** generally has fewer problems with existing political institutions than a reactionary voice does, but a conservative voice is nevertheless resistant to significant changes in policy or the culture as a whole. Rather than using political institutions to advocate for broad social change, conservative voices tend to propose more modest changes that help individuals to overcome obstacles and exercise maximum control over their lives. As a result, the conservative voice places a premium on "freedom" and "individualism" as ideographs and characterizes broader proposals for change as "big government."

Among contemporary speakers, U.S. Representative Paul Ryan from Wisconsin has been a prominent conservative voice. His remarks on federal health care reform show the conservative preference for market-driven solutions to public problems and an emphasis on individual freedom.

> Do we want a system that is command and controlled, price controlled, formulaically controlled by government, or do we want a system where the patient is the center, where the patient is sovereign, where they get to decide, where providers—doctors, hospitals, insurers—compete against each other for our business or do we want them competing for favoritism from a shrinking pool of government resources? While I am opposed to the President's health care law, I want to find solutions to these problems.

Although both reactionary and conservative voices highlight freedom, traditionally conservative voices in the United States acknowledge that governing institutions play a beneficial role in protecting freedoms and establishing national security. However, Ryan's quotation shows how conservatives often disagree with liberals about the appropriate scope of that role, especially regarding taxes and regulation.

Again, while both the reactionary and conservative voices highlight freedom and liberty, the conservative voice in the United States acknowledges some of the ways in which government plays a beneficial role in protecting freedoms and establishing national security. However, the conservative voice tends to disagree with liberals about the appropriate extent of the government's role, especially regarding taxes and regulation of business.

Liberal Voices

A **liberal voice** generally accepts the drift of cultural change and sees the existing political system as a means for creating change. In other words, both liberals and conservatives seek to work within the political system rather rejecting the system as a whole. But liberals differ from conservatives in supporting a more active role for government institutions. Liberals tend to focus more on the contexts and circumstances that influence individual behavior and the concerns of disempowered groups in society. The liberal voice often examines these contexts and circumstances in terms of "fairness" and "equality," some of the key liberal ideographs.

Barbara Boxer, U.S. Senator from California, exemplifies the liberal voice on many public issues. Her Senate web page highlights many laws and programs she has championed, such as protecting children from dangerous toys and increasing financial support for programs to limit the spread of HIV/AIDS and tuberculosis. In the following passage about the federal budget, Boxer makes standard liberal appeals:

> Why would we cut a program [child support enforcement] that has the sole purpose of helping to ensure that our children's basic financial needs are being met? Irresponsible deadbeat parents are getting off, and this must change. If delinquent parents fully paid their child support, thousands of women and children could be taken off welfare. . . . This budget bill fails the American people, and it fails the test of fairness.

Boxer's concerns for the circumstances surrounding child support and the idea of fairness mark her position as a liberal one. A conservative position might focus more attention on lowering taxes or creating greater economic opportunity so that there is less need for public welfare and child support enforcement.

It is important to note that the liberal and conservative positions often can be couched in very similar rhetoric. For example, Boxer goes on to suggest that there is common ground between her and her political opponent:

> The challenges we face are as great as the differences between our parties, but American values transcend politics. We must find a way to unite behind those values for the common goal of protecting and strengthening America's families.

Boxer's statement suggests that liberal and conservative voices may share some common ideographs, such as "family," while differing on how best to serve those values. This makes it all the more important to inspect specific language and proposals and not only the broad values used to justify their positions.

Radical Voices

Finally, a **radical voice** supports cultural change but finds existing political institutions to be an obstacle to change. Like the reactionary voice, the radical voice finds institutions fundamentally flawed. But the flaw is not disorder or rejection of tradition; on the contrary, the radical voice finds institutions to be too traditional, too committed to the status quo, and unresponsive to what is happening in the culture. Consequently, the radical voice tends to support positions that are more liberal than conservative, but the radical voice also pushes for more far-reaching and fundamental changes in politics and society.

Noam Chomsky is one of the more prominent radical voices in the United States today. Chomsky is highly critical of existing political institutions and the ways in which they work to advance the interests of those who are economically powerful rather than the population as a whole. In Chomsky's view, institutions work to "manufacture" popular consent for policies that help the powerful at the expense of others:

> As history shows, it is all too easy for unscrupulous leaders to terrify the public, with consequences that have not been attractive. That is the natural method to divert attention from the fact that tax cuts for the rich and other devices are undermining prospects for a decent life for a large majority of the population, and for future generations.

Radicals like Chomsky and reactionaries share some similarities in that they see fundamental problems with the current state of affairs. But radicals tend to be suspicious of the reactionary's calls for order and tradition, which are seen as obstacles to positive change. Instead, the radical voice calls for fundamental changes in political institutions that would serve the goal of equality.

While the differences between these public voices are especially clear on national issues, these stances can be seen in public discourse that is used to discuss issues on campus or in your community. Consider how different voices might engage issues surrounding the funding of public higher education in your state. Reactionaries might say that the state has no business funding higher education. Conservatives might argue that the state should give vouchers that can be used at any college, thereby promoting choice. Liberals might advocate for increased state funding of higher education, while radicals might charge that the education system has become subservient to the demands of the global economy and needs a complete overhaul.

Why Public Voices Matter

Why does identifying these voices matter? How can it help your public speaking? As was noted above, understanding public voices can help you to figure out the motives that are at work in discussions of public issues. Now that you have a better understanding of some of the most prominent voices, we can explore these questions more fully.

First, you can better evaluate the *soundness* of an advocate's typical language strategies for a particular situation. One of the biggest points of this section is that these voices are enduring; these rhetorical stances are used to address a variety of situations. Table A.1 summarizes how different voices tend to rely on particular myths and ideographs. It is up to you to think about when one of these "typical" responses best fits the particular situation.

Second, you can better assess the *values and goals* that matter to these voices. Giving attention to ideographs can help you to think about whether you support the goals of different advocates and whether you think other values should be emphasized. In addition, observing differences in values and

TABLE A.1   Understanding Public Voices in the United States

	General Stance	**Key Ideographs**	**Supporting Myths**
Reactionary	Rejects structure Resists change	"Order"	"Mob at the gates"
Conservative	Supports structure Resists change	"Freedom" "Individualism"	"Triumphant individual"
Liberal	Supports structure Supports change	"Equality" "Civil rights"	"Benevolent community"
Radical	Rejects structure Supports change	"Revolution"	"Rot at the top"

Source: Adapted from Brock, Bernard L., Mark E. Huglen, James F. Klumpp, and Sharon Howell. *Making Sense of Political Ideology: The Power of Language in Democracy.* Lanham: Rowman & Littlefield, 2005, pp. 77 and 94.

goals can also help you to see whether advocates are ignoring or omitting supporting materials that might be damaging to their position. A radical, for example, might not want to include evidence about some of the advantages or benefits of existing institutions.

Third, you can better observe when you need to find a *wider range of voices* on your issue. If your research has turned up only liberal voices, then it's important to seek out conservative voices that bring a different perspective. Moreover, if you get too caught up in the debates between conservative and liberal voices, it might be worth your time to identify more fundamental analyses and criticisms of those voices that come from radical and reactionary voices.

Understanding the News

Just as there are typical ways in which speakers talk about public issues, there are typical ways in which journalists describe and depict those issues. As you are reading news sources about your public issue, then, it is important for you to understand how those descriptions might shape your perception of the issue. Think of the articles you find in a newspaper or a website that focuses on public issues:

- Do they focus more on recent developments or on past history?

- Do they highlight conflicts and change, or do they look at things that have stayed the same over time?

- Do they focus on people or on abstract ideas?

These questions about news coverage point us to identifying problems with **information bias**, or preferences in news coverage that "hinder the efforts of citizens, whatever their ideology, to take part in political life" (Bennett 44). This type of bias distorts or constrains the information that citizens receive from news outlets. Observable across all kinds of mainstream news content, this bias is different from the claim of **ideological bias**, or preferences in news coverage that tend to favor a particular public voice or political viewpoint over others. While there is concern about ideological bias, media scholars tend to be more concerned about information bias—specifically, the ways in which mainstream news coverage highlights certain kinds of information about public issues and downplays other ways of examining those issues.

Because of information biases, the language of news reports can significantly influence the information that we receive about public issues and, consequently, our perception of those issues. Therefore, critical analysis of the news is vital for effective research, invention, and audience adaptation in the process of developing a speech.

Personalization

First, news reports tend toward the **personalization** of issues, focusing more on the individuals who are debating the issue than on the issue itself. Or they will focus more on people who represent the issue—those who put the "human face" on an issue—and downplay the structural or systemic aspects of the issue. These human interest stories may capture reader's attention, but they often provide a limited way of understanding the big picture related to the issue.

For example, personalized media reports on legislation focus on elected officials themselves. In these kinds of stories, the "news" often becomes the latest developments on how certain officials are likely to vote. So, a story might dwell on how a particular legislator is considered a "swing" vote who could tip the outcome in one direction. Or, it might discuss how an official's vote is related to his or her political standing. A story might explain how a legislator is trying to please a certain interest group or is attempting to move to the center to in order to position herself for an upcoming election. Or, a story might suggest that political disagreements are driven by a personality clash between various officials and advocates.

While these types of stories can help you to observe different public voices and place them on the political spectrum, they do not tell you much about the substance of the issue, the strengths and weaknesses of particular proposals, or the competing interests and systemic forces that are influencing the legislation. Ultimately, personalized news covers public voices as if they were celebrities, and obscures citizens' understanding of the underlying issues.

Personalization also occurs through human interest stories that are emotionally compelling. Like stories that focus on political leaders jockeying for position, these stories do little to empower audiences to engage the issues. Scholars have referred to this process as **spectator politics**, a mode of politics that encourages ordinary citizens to be passive audience members rather than active participants.

As you interpret the news, be wary of getting caught up in personalization. While some stories can provide useful supporting material for your speech—through examples or citizen testimony—you also should try to find other sources that explain the broader issues.

Dramatization

Dramatization refers to the way in which news stories tend to focus on conflict rather than on issues that do not involve any no clear conflict. Without that conflict, journalists find it more difficult to develop a compelling story about the issue that will hold audience attention. Dramatization also reinforces personalization, because these dramas rely on distinctive characters who represent opposing sides in the conflict.

Dramatization creates bias by influencing *what you don't see in the news.* The tendency toward dramatization makes it less likely that you will see stories on chronic, enduring problems in which there is little immediate or emerging conflict. It also means that you are less likely to see the complexities and details of an issue, since dramatization relies on simple story lines of actors in conflict. Media scholar Lance Bennett captures the bias of dramatization best:

> News dramas emphasize crisis over continuity, the present over the past or future, conflicts and relationship problems between the personalities at their center, and the impact of scandals on personal political careers. News dramas downplay complex policy information, the workings of government institutions, and the bases of power behind the central characters (46).

In other words, the crisis of the moment is more likely to get covered than the complicated, behind-the-scenes details that have been in motion for some time.

Consider the issue of poverty, a chronic problem that gets little day-to-day coverage. The issue can be difficult to dramatize because it is a systemic problem; it does not lend itself to clear characters that are in conflict. But poverty can get on the public agenda when someone prominent makes a concerted effort to demonstrate that some leader or organization could be doing more to address poverty. At that point, a conflict emerges, and sides to the conflict can be seen.

For example, the Chinese Vice Foreign Minister He Yafei raised the issue of poverty in the context of UN negotiations over climate change:

> Developed countries should, in line with the principles of common but different responsibility, undertake substantial mid-term reduction commitments or targets. They have to fulfill their obligation . . . to provide funds to the developing countries, to provide technologies to the developing countries, to help developing countries in capacity building. The priority for developing countries is still the reduction of poverty ("Excerpts").

By stating the issue as one of a conflict between the needs of developing countries and the responsibility of developed countries, this speaker begins to dramatize the poverty issue in ways that journalists might see it as a story worth covering. A few days later, a *Wall Street Journal* article that reported on this speaker led with these sentences:

> The political script for a big climate-change conference in this Danish city has U.S. President Barack Obama and other world leaders flying in later this week to christen a new era of global environmental cooperation. In reality, the summit is shaping up as a pivotal economic showdown between the U.S. and China (Ball).

The important point to draw from this example is how the issue changes as it gets dramatized in news coverage. What is newsworthy is not the conditions or experience of poverty itself, but the economic conflict between two countries. As with personalization, then, be attentive to how dramatization can shape your perspective on issues and how it can screen out topics that do not seem urgent or controversial.

Authority–Disorder

The **authority–disorder bias** describes the way in which news coverage tends to focus on how authorities are addressing disorder in the world. This informational bias can be seen in the most mundane "breaking news" story on local televisions as well as in stories about urgent national issues. The authority–disorder bias leads to stories that highlight the words and actions of authorities and develop a plotline about how those actions are restoring order or contributing to disorder. Both of these dimensions contribute to the bias.

First, the focus on authorities means that stories will tend to focus the voices of those in positions of power. There is good reason for this, since part of the function of journalism is to hold decision makers accountable. But it also means that stories might not represent the diverse perspectives that are relevant to a particular issue. Even a story that is critical of some authorities will often rely on other authorities.

Second, images of disorder will tend to drive news coverage and shape our perception of issues. Stories on crime, terrorism, public health threats, or other threats to the smooth functioning of society are likely to get covered. But scholars are growing increasingly concerned that disorder bias can exaggerate the extent of some problems. In the 1990s, for example, news coverage of violent crime in the United States skyrocketed, even though the actual rates of violent crime dropped significantly (Bennett). As with dramatization, then, the authority–disorder bias shapes perception by using predictable storylines that resonate with audiences but also can cultivate a misleading or inaccurate understanding of events.

Balance

A fourth type of bias stems from **balance**, the tendency for news coverage to give roughly equal attention to two sides in a dispute. It might seem odd to think of balance as a form of bias. Doesn't giving both sides the same amount of coverage ensure fairness and objectivity? It can do that, but it also can create informational biases that can distort an accurate understanding of the issue and its complexities.

Balance can create bias in several ways. One way occurs when an inaccurate statement or a noncredible voice is offered as a "balance" to a more accurate or credible position. For example, if your campus newspaper published an article about the latest research on quantum mechanics, would it make sense to balance the explanation of an award-winning physics professor with the opinions of a freshman physics major? Probably not.

The tendency for mainstream news sources to seek conflict or dramatization often leads to that sort of inaccurate balance. Scholars have demonstrated this bias in coverage of climate change science, in which the untested ideas of scientists affiliated with the fossil fuel industry were "balanced" against well-established conclusions among climate scientists (Boykoff and Boykoff). In this case, the false balance heightened uncertainty and confusion about the actual state of climate science.

Balance also can create bias by oversimplifying issues within a two-sided, pro–con framework. This bias can prevent audiences from seeing potential areas of agreement between the two positions. It also can prevent audiences from additional perspectives. Political news coverage in the United States is especially vulnerable to this form of bias because it typically balances Democratic and Republican voices, leaves out third party voices, and reinforces the marginalized status of reactionaries and radicals. Not only does this make narrow our thinking about issues, but it also may limit the ability of third parties and other critics of the system to have meaningful influence in the public sphere.

Summary

UNDERSTANDING PUBLIC VOICES

- There are typical ways of using language that signal an advocate's overall stance toward political institutions and cultural change. Understanding these patterns can help you to assess the values and goals of other participants in the public sphere and to recognize the limits of the existing range of public voices.

- A starting point for understanding public voices is to distinguish among reactionary, conservative, liberal, and radical voices.

UNDERSTANDING THE NEWS

- The typical ways in which journalists describe and depict public issues often lead to information bias. Therefore, critical analysis of these patterns is vital for effectively research, invention, and audience adaptation in public speaking.

- Personalization, dramatization, authority-disorder bias, and balance are common rhetorical features of news stories that can shape perception of public issues.

Key Terms

reactionary voice, p. 413
conservative voice, p. 413
liberal voice, p. 414
radical voice, p. 415
information bias, p. 417
ideological bias, p. 417

personalization, p. 418
spectator politics, p. 418
dramatization, p. 418
authority–disorder bias, p. 420
balance, p. 420

Comprehension

1. Why is it important for public speakers to understand the range of voices and typical language strategies that circulate in the public sphere?

2. What distinguishes the reactionary voice from a conservative voice, according to Brock's definition of these terms?

3. How do conservatives and liberals differ on the proper role of government institutions?

4. What is the difference between information bias and ideological bias?

5. How can dramatization affect what you do not see in the news?

6. How might journalistic balance fail to produce fairness and objectivity?

Application

1. Locate a speech or debate transcript from a recent candidate for national office (President, Senator, Representative). Identify which of the four voices this candidate's rhetoric fits best, and compare it to the voices of other candidates identified by your classmates. See whether you can place them on a spectrum of voices.

2. Work with a librarian to identify sources that are likely to contain examples of reactionary or radical voices. Share your results with your classmates, and find out whether these sources are familiar to them.

3. Watch a half-hour of television news, and see how many examples of information bias you can identify. Which information biases seem to be most prominent?

4. Find a short newspaper or magazine article on your speech topic that exhibits an information bias. On the basis of research for your speech, revise that article to reduce or eliminate the bias.

Glossary

abstract language Words that refer to general ideas or concepts.

active language (or active voice) The use of active verbs and a subject–verb sentence structure.

adequacy A principle of outline construction requiring that if you want to divide any point of your speech, that point should have at least two subordinate subpoints.

alliteration The repetition of initial sounds to connect related words and phrases.

amplification Giving extra emphasis to an idea through supporting materials and artistic language.

analytical strategies Organizational strategies that break down a topic into its related parts or components.

anaphora The repetition of entire words and phrases to connect related ideas.

anger A feeling of being upset about an injustice and wanting to rectify it.

anticipatory anxiety Anxiety that is felt before speech performance.

antithesis The use of parallel structure to heighten the movement or contrast between ideas.

appreciative listening Listening that helps you to enjoy a speaker's abilities or participate in the world of politics.

arrangement The process of organizing your ideas and appeals strategically to help you accomplish your purpose.

articulation The clear utterance of syllables.

attention-getter A tactic to draw in the audience during the initial sentences of a speech.

attentive listening Listening that focuses attention and minimizes distractions.

attitude An expression of an individual's preferences that is based on both beliefs and values.

attribution statement A phrase or sentence that orally designates a source of information in your speech.

audience adaptation The process of modifying both your message and your audience's identity to achieve a message that resonates with your audience.

audience demographics Information about relatively stable characteristics of audience members.

audience opinions The beliefs, attitudes, and values an audience holds in relation to your topic.

audience-centered Considering the needs of the audience throughout speech preparation and delivery.

authority–disorder bias The tendency for news stories to focus on how authorities are addressing disorder in the world.

auto-communication Communication in which the speaker is an important part of the audience.

award acceptance speech A speech that acknowledges an award and those who made it possible.

award presentation speech A tribute for a specific action or the quality of performance during a limited time frame.

backing Additional support for the grounds or warrant of an argument.

balance The tendency for news stories to give roughly equal attention to two sides in a dispute.

bar graph A representation that shows the magnitude of data points.

belief A statement that expresses what an individual thinks is true, probable, or factually correct about the past, present, or future.

body The middle and largest portion of the speech; the heart of the speech where you present your information or persuasive argument.

boilerplate language Standardized language that could be used in different contexts without significant changes.

brainstorming Generating many ideas rapidly without criticizing, analyzing, or discarding any of them,

call for action A statement that advocates for a specific policy or change in behavior and encourages listeners to act in ways that are consistent with that advocacy.

call for engagement An explicit statement of how an audience can continue involvement after the speech.

call for learning A statement that shows an audience what they can do to become more informed and knowledgeable about the speech topic.

causal order A strategy of organizing a series of points according to cause-and-effect relationships.

causality A common topic that explores relationships between cause and effect.

cause-to-effect reasoning A pattern of reasoning in which the claim asserts an effect of some cause.

central idea The one-sentence statement that you want your audience to accept by the end of the speech.

central tendency Statistics that characterize some set of data by looking toward the middle of the data.

ceremonial speech A speech that recognizes and helps to create a special moment in the life of a community.

characterization Common descriptions of people, actions, or things that reinforce particular meanings and associations.

chart A visual display of supporting material.

chronological order A pattern of speech organization that presents ideas and events in the order in which they actually happened.

circulation The constant and unpredictable flow of messages among diverse speakers and audiences.

citizen testimony Words that get rhetorical power from the person's firsthand experience.

civic engagement Hands-on work with others that seeks to achieve a public good.

claim A disputable statement that you want your audience to accept.

closed question A question that yields definite answers within a predetermined set of choices; a forced-choice question.

clutter Excess wording that does not aid audience understanding.

cognitive engagement Participation in public life by paying attention to politics and public issues.

cognitive restructuring Mentally reframing your thoughts and perceptions, often through positive self-talk.

commemorative speech A speech that pays tribute to individuals who have accomplished great things or acted in ways that deserve praise.

commencement speech A speech that occurs during celebration of the successful completion of an educational program.

common knowledge Widely shared beliefs and values in a society; what everyone "knows" and does not need citation as a formal piece of evidence.

common topics General themes and relationships that are common to all types of public speaking.

communication Interaction that creates meaning through symbols.

comparative advantages pattern An organizational strategy that pits two competing solutions against one another to highlight the advantages of one solution.

comparative order A strategy of organizing a series of points by drawing direct connections—usually similarities and differences—between two or more things.

comparison A common topic of identifying similarities and differences to enhance understanding of a subject.

comprehensive listening Listening that helps you to understand the speaker's primary messages.

conclusion The last section of a speech that reinforces the central idea and indicates the end of the speech.

concrete language Words that refer to tangible, specific things.

connotative meaning The range of meanings and associations related to a word that easily evoke attitudes in listeners.

conservative voice A public voice that typically accepts the political structure and resists cultural change.

consistency A principle of outline construction requiring that you use the same system of numbering and lettering during the entire outline.

consolation The act of comforting the audience and lessening their grief.

constraint A factor that might influence the audience's receptiveness to the speech.

coordination A principle of outline construction requiring that elements of equal importance should occur at the same level of the outline.

correlation A common topic that explores the relationship between two coexisting events or phenomena.

counterexample An instance that is an exception to a generalization.

criteria–application pattern An organizational strategy that offers audiences a set of standards or criteria and then applies those standards to a specific situation.

critical listening Listening that helps you to evaluate the speaker's arguments and appeals.

cynicism A distrustful and largely negative attitude.

deductive order A sequence of supporting material that starts with general statements and then provides specifics to back up those statements.

definition A common topic that encourages a speaker to clarify the meaning of a term.

denotative meaning The literal meaning of a word.

descriptive feedback A response that shares an individual's reaction to a speech; it is especially useful in the classroom and other venues where participants are focused on the speaking process itself.

direct address A tactic of explicitly hailing the audience with the words you, we, or us.

discriminative listening Listening that helps you to pay attention to aspects of delivery that shape the speaker's intended meaning.

distraction Fleeting attention to a single message.

domain The last three letters in a website address, such as .com or .gov.

double-barreled question A question that forces two ideas into the same question when they should be treated separately.

dramatization The tendency for news stories to focus on conflict rather than on issues that do not involve any clear conflict.

effect-to-cause reasoning A pattern of reasoning in which the claim asserts the cause of some phenomenon.

egocentrism The habit of privileging one's own knowledge and interests above others.

elimination of alternatives pattern An organizational strategy that offers audience a series of proposals and shows the flaws of each one before settling on the speaker's preferred alternative.

empathic listening Listening that provides emotional support for the speaker.

enthymeme A general pattern of reasoning in which the audience supplies one of the premises.

epideictic rhetoric A type of public discourse that engages in praise or blame in ceremonial contexts.

ethics Guides for personal conduct in relation to one's community.

ethnocentrism The habit of assuming that one's own cultural standards are, or ought to be, shared by others.

ethos The character and credibility of the speaker.

eulogy A speech that memorializes someone who has died.

euphemism A mild or vague description of something that is troubling or unpleasant.

examples Support for a speech in the form of specific instances.

exigence The aspect of the rhetorical situation that motivates a speaker to speak; typically, it is the issue that is timely for the audience.

existence A common topic that explores the most basic features of a particular subject.

expert testimony Words that get rhetorical power from the person's specialized knowledge or training.

extemporaneous speaking A delivery style that involves advance preparation and rehearsal of a speech that is neither fully written nor memorized.

external distractions Obstacles to listening that are outside the listener's control.

fallacy A pattern of flawed reasoning.

false analogy A comparison of things that are fundamentally dissimilar or that have critical differences that undermine their comparisons.

false dilemma The construction of a choice between only two alternatives when other choices may exist.

fear A feeling of concern about some dangerous or destructive event in the future.

figurative language Language that alters or turns the usual meanings of words to create new perceptions and associations among listeners.

friendship A feeling of connection to others when you want them to have a good life for their own sake, not because you may perceive a benefit for yourself as a result.

gender A person's enactment of his or her sex in relation to cultural norms and expectations, often described with words such as "masculine" or "feminine."

general purpose The overall goal or desired effect of your speech.

ghostwriter a professional speech writer

graph A visual representation of statistics.

grounds Specific statements about observable conditions that offer support for the claim of an argument.

group communication Interaction among multiple people for purposes such as mutual understanding, exploration of ideas, or coordination of action.

habitual association Reinforcement of certain attitudes as a result of persistent exposure to the same beliefs and values without thoughtful and critical reflection.

hasty generalization A generalization based on examples that listeners find to be unrepresentative or insufficient.

heteronormative language Words and phrases that assume that everyone's romantic partner is of the opposite sex.

heterosexism The assumption that all people desire an opposite-sex romantic partner.

hourglass order A sequence of supporting material that places the most significant pieces of evidence at the beginning and end of a series and puts the least important material in the middle.

hypothetical examples Examples that ask an audience to imagine a scenario to illustrate a point.

ideograph An important cultural value term that is regularly used to justify public decisions and actions.

ideological bias Preferences in news coverage that tend to favor a particular public voice or political viewpoint over others.

I-language Wording that phrases your feedback so that it describes your individual response, not an assumption about the response of others.

immediacy A perception of physical and psychological closeness between you and your audience.

immediate audience The people who gather to hear the initial presentation of a speech.

impromptu speaking A delivery style that relies on little or no advance preparation.

inclusiveness An ethical principle of openness to diverse viewpoints and a willingness to listen to others.

inductive order A sequence of supporting material that starts with specific instances or examples and uses them to build a more general or abstract point.

information bias Preferences in news coverage that hinder citizens from participating in public life; these preferences distort or constrain the information that citizens receive from news outlets.

informed analysis Thoughtful and critical reasoning about a topic based on sound evidence.

inspirational speech A commemorative speech that attempts to stir an audience's passion and commitment toward some topic, goal, or purpose.

internal distractions Obstacles to listening that emerge primarily from the listener.

internal preview A statement of what will be discussed in a subsequent part of the speech.

internal summary A statement that recaps the main ideas or highlights in a specific section of a speech.

interpersonal communication One-on-one conversation that is primarily about negotiating relationships.

introduction The first section of a speech that arouses the audience's attention and prepares them for the rest of the speech.

invention The generation of ideas, strategies, and appeals for a speech; the creative process of topic development, audience analysis, and research to build the content of your speech.

jargon Language that is specific to a profession or field and rarely understood outside that field.

key issues A strategy of organizing a series of points around a set of questions that are relevant to decision making.

kindness A feeling of wanting to help others for their own sake, not for the sake of one's own personal gain or the possibility of getting something in return.

leading question A question that assumes a shared perspective and encourages the answer that is desired by the questioner rather than an honest response.

liberal voice A public voice that typically accepts the political structure and accepts cultural change.

line graph A representation of data points that show a trend over time.

loaded question A question that uses descriptive language in ways that could influence how a respondent perceives available choices.

logos The reasoning that is offered in the speech.

manuscript speaking A delivery style that involves giving a speech from a written text prepared in advance.

mass communication Interaction between a source and a large, impersonal audience via messages circulated by media.

mean A measure of central tendency; the average of a data set, calculated by adding all the items and dividing by the number of items in the set.

median A measure of central tendency that refers to the middle item in the set when the items are ordered numerically.

memorized speaking A delivery style that involves giving a speech word for word without any notes.

metaphor Figurative language that compares two objects or ideas generally perceived as dissimilar.

motivated sequence pattern An organizational strategy that takes an audience through a sequence of steps designed to increase their motivation to act.

myth A common cultural story or parable that reinforces values or political lessons.

neutral A person who neither supports nor opposes your position; he or she might be uninformed, apathetic, or well informed but undecided about your topic.

nominalization Turning verbs into nouns, which often leads to complicated and passive sentence structure.

open question A question that permits respondents to answer in their own words.

opponent A person who disagrees with your position or has an unfavorable attitude about your topic.

oral caption A spoken sentence that states the main idea of a visual aid.

organizational markers Phrases and sentences that connect your main points and signal organizational shifts in your speech.

pandering Agreeing with one's audience on all issues or merely telling them what they want to hear.

parallel structure Phrasing a series of ideas with the same grammatical pattern.

paraphrase A restatement of someone else's ideas or opinions in one's own words.

partial plagiarism The use of a specific piece of supporting material without citation.

participation An ethical principle of ensuring that all people have the opportunity to voice their opinions, to be heard by others, and to have their opinions count.

partisan A person who supports your position or has a favorable attitude toward your topic.

pathos The emotions that can be evoked in the audience.

pause A brief period of silence in a speech

percentage A statistic that explains a relationship between an entire population and some subset of that population.

personal experience Support for a speech in the form of events that have happened to you.

personal narratives Stories about yourself or others.

personalization The tendency for news stories to focus more on the individuals debating an issue than the issue itself.

pie graph A representation that displays the distribution of data in percentages or shares.

pitch Designates where a sound lies on the musical spectrum.

plagiarism The use of another person's words or ideas without citing the source; a significant violation of ethical codes at colleges and universities.

polarization A state in which one group in a society perceives itself as absolutely opposed to another group.

political engagement Engagement that focuses on government and aims to influence policy or the election of public officials.

post hoc fallacy The inaccurate presumption that an earlier event caused a later event simply because of their sequence in time.

premises Starting points for an argument.

pretentious language Wording that is pompous and not part of someone's everyday vocabulary.

preview A statement that tells your audience how you will proceed through your speech.

primacy effect The effect of being most influenced by the first message heard about a topic.

primary audience The portion of an audience that most want to engage with your speech; sometimes called a target audience.

private question A question that might elicit information or provoke emotions that people would prefer to leave undisturbed.

problem–solution pattern An organizational strategy that offers audiences a policy that will contribute to fixing some damaging conditions.

processing gap The difference between a normal speaking rate and the rate at which listeners process words.

pronunciation How a speaker speaks individual words and syllables.

public A group of people who are engaged in addressing issues of common interest.

public discourse Messages that are already circulating in the public sphere, including conversations, news reports, and public advocacy.

public sphere model A model of communication that focuses on the role of public speaking in a democratic society and its connection to political and civic engagement.

public voice the expression of opinions about significant issues.

qualifier A word or phrase that clarifies the force or scope of an argument.

questionnaire The tool that is used in demographic and opinion surveys.

radical voice A public voice that typically rejects the political structure and accepts cultural change.

rate The speed at which a person speaks.

ratio The measure of relative sizes of two populations.

rationalization Taking a position before examining the evidence and seeking only sources that support that position.

raw numbers Numbers that add up specific instances.

reactionary voice A public voice that typically rejects the political structure and resists cultural change.

reasoning by analogy A pattern of reasoning in which a speaker refers to the known characteristics of one instance as grounds for inferring unknown or uncertain characteristics of a similar instance.

reasoning by cause A pattern of reasoning in which a speaker infers a direct, substantive connection between one action or event and a subsequent effect.

reasoning by generalization A pattern of reasoning in which a set of examples or specific instances as grounds for inferring a broader principle or a statement about a larger group of examples.

reasoning by sign A pattern of reasoning in which the speaker infers that some unobservable condition exists based on observed features or conditions.

rebuttal The primary objection that could be made against the claim of an argument.

recency effect The effect of being most influenced by the last message heard about a topic.

reciprocity An ethical principle of equality among participants, indicating that everyone has the opportunity to speak and to listen in a particular communication situation.

research plan A systematic process of locating sources that is manageable and efficient.

research tool A database, catalog, search engine, or other aid that collects, organizes, or directs you to source material.

reservation A response to the rebuttal that often identifies exceptions to the claim of an argument.

rhetorical audience Listeners who are open-minded and see themselves as empowered to do something about a speaker's topic.

rhetorical listening A type of listening that pays attention to the rhetorical forms and language patterns that shape our perception of a situation.

rhetorical situation A situation that emerges when speakers perceive some significant issue that needs to be addressed through political participation or civic engagement.

rhythmic language Language that uses the sounds of words and phrases to create a pleasing or memorable effect.

sans-serif fonts Typefaces with straight edges on the letters.

scapegoating An unethical rhetorical tactic that involves blaming some individual or group as the source of problems that are actually shared by a larger group or society as a whole.

selective attention The tendency to focus on simple or reassuring ideas and ignore complexity or troubling ideas.

selective exposure The tendency to seek out messages that reinforce existing attitudes and avoid messages that conflict with those attitudes.

sequential strategies Organizational strategies based on natural patterns in the world.

serif fonts Typefaces with flared letter edges.

sex One's identity as male, female, or intersexed based on biological and physical characteristics.

sexual orientation A person's romantic and erotic desires, often as heterosexual, gay or lesbian, or bisexual.

shock/startle A tactic that gets an audience out of its comfort zone.

signpost A simple word used at the beginning of a sentence to mark a series of related points. Also, an organizational marker signaling order or sequence.

simile Figurative language that draws a comparison using the words *like* or *as*.

source The actual material that you will use in your speech, such as an article, chart, or photograph.

spatial order A strategy of organizing a series of points according to location or direction.

speaking outline A short outline that is intended to serve as an aid to your performance.

specific purpose The desired effect on a particular audience; it connects the general purpose to the particular speaking event.

spectator politics A mode of politics that encourages citizens to be passive audience members rather than active participants.

speech anxiety The unpleasant physical and psychological responses to public speaking situations.

speech communication model A model of communication that emphasizes the ongoing transaction between speaker and audience.

speech of introduction A short speech that prepares an audience for a featured or keynote speaker.

statistics Support for a speech in the form of numbers that summarize specific instances or express relationships.

stereotyping The habit of overgeneralizing about the characteristics of a group.

stock issues Typical issues related to policy or action on which people are likely to disagree or resist change.

style The rules and practices of composing effective discourse.

subordination A principle of outline construction requiring that within any point, your subpoints and supporting material should descend in order of importance.

survey A systematic attempt to gather information about a particular population.

sympathy A feeling of compassion or sorrow that emerges when one sees others suffering.

testimony The words of others used to support a point; includes quotations and paraphrases.

toast A brief speech that celebrates a milestone by amplifying feelings of goodwill.

topical order A pattern of speech organization that presents material as a series of topics or main points.

Toulmin model A general pattern of reasoning that identifies the component parts of any argument and their relationships to one another.

transition A statement that explicitly connects the previous idea to the next idea in a speech.

transmission model A model of communication that is intended to study how messages are transmitted and where various problems could emerge.

URL Abbreviation for Uniform Resource Locator, or website address.

value A relatively stable commitment about the quality or merit of objects, actions, or ultimate goals.

value hierarchy The relative importance of different values within an individual or group's value system.

visual aid A tangible object that displays some aspect of your message to your audience.

visual rhetoric A mode of communication in which images, graphics, video, and other visual elements play a central role in the construction of public discourse.

volume The relative loudness of the speaker's voice.

warrant A general statement that justifies or explains how the grounds support the main claim of an argument.

wholesale plagiarism The use of another person's words or ideas as one's entire speech.

working outline A complete, full-sentence outline that includes all the material you plan to have in your speech.

References

Chapter 1

Asen, Robert, and Daniel C. Brouwer. *Counterpublics and the State*. Albany: SUNY Press, 2001.

Billig, Michael. *Arguing and Thinking*. New York: Cambridge UP, 1996.

Buffett and Gates go Back to School. PBS Home Video. Lincoln: Net Foundation for Television, 2006.

Campbell, Karlyn Kohrs. *Man Cannot Speak for Her*. Vols. I and II. Westport: Praeger, 1989.

Ceccarelli, Leah. "Polysemy: Multiple Meanings in Rhetorical Criticism." *Quarterly Journal of Speech* 84 (1998): 394–414.

CIRCLE *The 2006 Civic and Political Health of the Nation*. College Park: Center for Information and Research on Civic Learning and Engagement, 2006.

"Cooling Our Future: Young Evangelicals Take Powerful Message to U.S. Congress." *Creation Care Magazine* (Winter 2007). Accessed May 25, 2008. Available at http://www.creationcare.org/magazine/winter07.php#congress

Diamond, Robert M. "Curriculum Reform Needed If Students Are to Master Core Skills." *The Chronicle of Higher Education,* August 1, 1997: B7.

Evangelical Youth Climate Initiative. "Cooling Our Future: A Declaration by Young Evangelicals on Climate Change." May 2006. Accessed May 25, 2008. Available at http://www.christiansandclimate.org/pub/eyci.pdf

Fiske, John. *Understanding Popular Culture*. London: Unwin Hyman, 1989.

Fortis, Bianca. "Students, Workers Protest Burger King." *Central Florida Future*. April 25, 2008. Accessed May 27, 2008. Available at http://www.centralfloridafuture.com/home/index.cfm?event=displayArticlePrint erFriendly&uStory_id=0db5dba1-c856-47af-85fe-73ed4d9f10de

Habermas, Jurgen. "The Public Sphere." *Rethinking Popular Culture: Contemporary Perspectives in Cultural Studies*. Ed. Chandra Mukerji and Michael Schudson. Berkeley: U of California P, 1991. 398–404.

Hauser, Gerard. *Vernacular Voices: The Rhetoric of Publics and Public Spheres*. Columbia: U of South Carolina P, 1999.

Herrick, James A. *The History and Theory of Rhetoric: An Introduction*. 3rd ed. Boston: Pearson Allyn & Bacon, 2005.

Hove, Thomas. "The Filter, the Alarm System, and the Sounding Board: Critical and Warning Functions of the Public Sphere." *Communication and Critical/Cultural Studies* 6.1 (2009): 19–38.

Jamieson, Kathleen Hall. *Eloquence in an Electronic Age: The Transformation of Political Speechmaking*. New York: Oxford UP, 1990.

Lake, Randall A. "Between Myth and History: Enacting Time in Native American Protest Rhetoric." *Quarterly Journal of Speech* 77 (1991): 123–51.

Loehwing, Melanie, and Jeff Motter. "Publics, Counterpublics, and the Promise of Democracy." *Philosophy and Rhetoric* 42.3 (2009): 220–41.

Long, Sarah E. *The New Student Politics: The Wingspread Statement on Student Civic Engagement,* 2nd ed. Providence, RI: Campus Compact, 2002.

McPherson, Bill. "Student Perceptions about Business Communication in Their Careers." *Business Communication Quarterly* 61.2 (1998): 68–79

Morreale, Sherwyn P., Michael M. Osborn, and Judy C. Pearson. "Why Communication Is Important: A Rationale for the Centrality of the Study of Communication." *Journal of the Association for Communication Administration* 29 (1998): 1–25.

Pittenger, Khushwant K. S., Mary C. Miller, and Joshua Mot. "Using Real-World Standards to Enhance Students' Presentation Skills." *Business Communication Quarterly* 67 (September 2004): 327–36.

Potkay, Adam S. "Theorizing Civic Eloquence in the Early Republic: The Road from David Hume to John Quincy Adams." *Early American Literature* 34 (1999): 147–70.

Shannon, Claude. "A Mathematical Theory of Communication." *Bell System Technical Journal* 27 (1948): 379–423.

Student/Farmworker Alliance. "Dine with Dignity Campaign Headquarters." Accessed December 23, 2010. Available at http://www.sfalliance.org/foodservice.html

Warner, Michael. *Publics and Counterpublics*. Cambridge: Zone Books, 2002.

World Commission on Environment and Development. *Our Common Future*. Oxford: Oxford University Press, 1987.

Zukin, Cliff, Scott Keeter, Molly Andolina, Krista Jenkins, and Michael X. Delli Carpini. *A New Engagement?: Political Participation, Civic Life, and the Changing American Citizen*. New York: Oxford UP, 2006.

Chapter 2

Behnke, Ralph R., and Chris R. Sawyer. "Conceptualizing Speech Anxiety as a Dynamic Trait." *Southern Communication Journal* 63 (1998): 160–68.

Bowker, Michael. *Fatal Deception: The Untold Story of Asbestos and Why It Is Still Legal and Still Killing Us*. Emmaus: Rodale, 2003.

Christenfeld, Nicholas, and Beth Creager. "Anxiety, Alcohol, Aphasia, and Ums." *Journal of Personality and Social Psychology* 70 (1996): 451–60.

DeLuca, Kevin Michael. "Unruly Arguments: The Body Rhetoric of Earth First!, Act Up, and Queer Nation." *Argumentation and Advocacy* 36 (1999): 9–21.

Gallup, George, Jr. *The Gallup Poll: Public Opinion 2001.* Lanham: Rowman and Littlefield, 2002: 70.

"Family, Political Luminaries Honor Kennedy." CBSNews.com, August 28, 2009. Accessed December 23, 2010. Available at http://www.cbsnews.com/stories/2009/08/28/politics/main5272094.shtml

Hawhee, Debra. *Bodily Arts: Rhetoric and Athletics in Ancient Greece.* Austin: U of Texas P, 2005.

Hawhee. Debra. *Moving Bodies: Kenneth Burke at the Edges of Language.* Columbia: U of South Carolina P, 2009.

MacIntyre, Peter D., Kimly A. Thivierge, and J. Renee MacDonald, "The Effects of Audience Interest, Responsiveness, and Evaluation on Public Speaking Anxiety and Related Variables." *Communication Research Reports* 14.2 (1997): 157–68.

McCallum, Laura. "Wellstone Colleagues Join Thousands for Minnesota Memorial." October 30, 2002. Accessed May 19, 2008. Available at http://news.minnesota.publicradio.org/features/200210/28_ap_memorialservice/

Pezzullo, Phaedra. "Resisting 'National Breast Cancer Awareness Month': The Rhetoric of Counterpublics and their Cultural Performances." *Quarterly Journal of Speech* 89.4 (2003): 345–65.

Reynolds, Rodney, and J. Lynn Reynolds. "Evidence." *The Persuasion Handbook.* Ed. James Price Dillard and Michael Pfau. Thousand Oaks: Sage, 2002: 427–44.

Stein, M. B., J. R. Walker, and D. R Forde. "Public-Speaking Fears in a Community Sample: Prevalence, Impact on Functioning, and Diagnostic Classification." *Archives of General Psychiatry* 53.2 (1996): 169–74.

Chapter 3

Browne, M. Neil, and Stuart M. Keeley. *Asking the Right Questions: A Guide to Critical Thinking.* 8th ed. Upper Saddle River: Prentice Hall, 2006.

Carr, Nicholas. *The Shallows: What the Internet Is Doing to Our Brains.* New York: Norton, 2010.

Clark, Thomas. "Sharing the Importance of Attentive Listening Skills." *Journal of Management Education* 23.2 (1999): 216–23.

Daly, Brian. "Blair Honoured for Peace Commitment." *Sky News.* April 14, 2008. Accessed June 1, 2008. Available at http://news.sky.com/skynews/article/0,,91211-1312673,00.html

Jackson, Maggie. *Distracted: The Erosion of Attention and the Coming Dark Age.* Amherst: Prometheus Books, 2008.

Kopecky, Courtney C., Chris R. Sawyer, and Ralph R. Behnke. "Sensitivity to Punishment and Explanatory Style as Predictors of Public Speaking State Anxiety."

Communication Education 53.3 (2004): 281–85.

McKay, Matthew, Martha Davis, and Patrick Fanning. *Messages: The Communication Skills Book.* Oakland: New Harbinger Publications, 1995.

Nichols, Ralph. "Listening Is a 10 Part Skill." Accessed May 20, 2008. Available at http://www.listen.org/Templates/Nichols10Part Skill.pdf

Rakow, Lana. "The Future of the Field: Finding Our Mission." The Ohio State University. 13 May 1994.

Ritzhaupt, Albert D., Neil D. Gomes, and Ann B. Barron. "The Effects of Time-Compressed Audio and Verbal Redundancy on Learner Performance and Satisfaction." *Computers in Human Behavior* (2008). doi:10.1016/j.chb.2008.02.017.

Smith, Camille D., and Paul E. King. "Student Feedback Sensitivity and the Efficacy of Feedback Interventions in Public Speaking Performance Improvement." *Communication Education* 53.3 (2004): 203–16.

Stephens, Philip. "Blair's Remarkable Record." *The Financial Times.* May 10, 2007. Accessed June 1, 2008. Available at http://www.ft.com/cms/s/0/36fa51da-fe30-11db-bdc7-000b5df10621.html?nclick_check=1

Tompkins, Paula S. "Rhetorical Listening and Moral Sensitivity." *International Journal of Listening* 23.1 (2009): 60–79.

Wolvin, Andrew D., and Carolyn G. Coakley. *Listening.* 5th ed. Dubuque: Brown & Benchmark, 1995.

Chapter 4

Asen, Robert. "Reflections on the Role of Rhetoric in Public Policy." *Rhetoric & Public Affairs* 13.1 (2010): 121–43.

Bitzer, Lloyd F. "The Rhetorical Situation." *Philosophy and Rhetoric* 1.1 (1968): 1–14.

Bryant, Donald C. "Rhetoric: Its Function and Its Scope." *Quarterly Journal of Speech* 39 (1953): 401–24.

Bryant, Donald C., and Karl R. Wallace. *Fundamentals of Public Speaking.* 2nd ed. New York: Appleton-Century-Crofts, 1953.

Edelman, Murray. *Constructing the Political Spectacle.* Chicago: University of Chicago Press, 1988.

Hauser, Gerald. *Introduction to Rhetorical Theory.* Long Grove: Waveland Press, 2002.

Hove, Thomas. "The Filter, the Alarm System, and the Sounding Board: Critical and Warning Functions of the Public Sphere." *Communication and Critical/Cultural Studies* 6.1 (2009): 19–38.

McCroskey, James C. *An Introduction to Rhetorical Communication.* 8th ed. Boston: Allyn & Bacon, 2001.

Redmond, Mark V., and Denise Vrchota. *Everyday Public Speaking.* Boston: Allyn & Bacon, 2007.

Simons, Herbert W. *Persuasion in Society.* Thousand Oaks: Sage, 2001.

Smith, Craig R., and Scott Lybarger. "Bitzer's Model Reconstructed," *Communication Quarterly* 44.2 (1996): 197–213.

Vatz, Richard. "The Myth of the Rhetorical Situation." *Philosophy and Rhetoric* 6 (1973): 154–61.

Walter, Otis M., and Robert L. Scott. *Thinking and Speaking: A Guide to Intelligent Oral Communication*. 5th ed. New York: Macmillan, 1984.

Chapter 5

Butler, Judith. *Gender Trouble: Feminism and the Subversion of Identity*. London: Routledge, 1990.

Cooper, Brenda. "Boys Don't Cry and Female Masculinity: Reclaiming a Life and Dismantling the Politics of Normative Heterosexuality." *Critical Studies in Media Communication* 19.1 (2002): 44–63.

Inch, Edward S., Barbara Warnick, and Danielle Endres. *Critical Thinking and Communication: The Use of Reason in Argument*. 5th ed. Boston: Allyn & Bacon, 2006.

Kemmis, Daniel. *Community and the Politics of Place*. Norman: U of Oklahoma P, 1990.

Maathai, Wangari. "Nobel Lecture." Accessed November 10, 2007. Available at http://nobelprize .org/nobel_prizes/peace/laureates/2004/maathai-lecture-text.html

Maibach, Edward, Connie Roser-Renouf, and Anthony Leiserowitz. *Global Warming's Six Americas 2009: An Audience Segmentation Analysis*. Yale Project on Climate Change and the George Mason University Center for Climate Change Communication, May 2009. Available at environment.yale.edu/uploads/6Americas2009.pdf

Morey, Peter, and Amina Yaqin. *Framing Muslims: Stereotyping and Representation after 9/11*. Cambridge: Harvard UP, 2011.

Rieke, Richard D., Malcolm O. Sillars, and Tarla Rai Peterson. *Argumentation and Critical Decision Making*. 6th ed. Boston: Allyn & Bacon, 2005.

Snyder, Gary. "The Place, the Region, and the Commons." In *The Practice of the Wild*. New York: North Point Press, 1990. 25–47.

Chapter 6

Bean, Hamilton. "'A Complicated and Frustrating Dance': National Security Reform, the Limits of Parrhesia, and the Case of the 9/11 Families. *Rhetoric & Public Affairs* 12.3 (2009): 429–59.

Condit, Celeste Michelle, and John Louis Lucaites. *Crafting Equality: America's Anglo-African Word*. Chicago: U of Chicago P, 1993.

Fox, Michael J. *Always Looking Up: The Adventures of an Incurable Optimist*. New York: Random House, 2008.

Fox, Michael J. *Lucky Man: A Memoir*. New York: Hyperion, 2002.

Gayle, Barbara Mae. "Transformations in a Civil Discourse Public Speaking Class: Speakers' and Listeners' Attitude Change." *Communication Education* 53.2 (2004): 174–84.

Jamieson, Kathleen Hall. *Dirty Politics*. New York: Oxford UP, 1992.

McGee, Michael Calvin. "The 'Ideograph:' A Link Between Rhetoric and Ideology." *Quarterly Journal of Speech* 66.1 (1980): 1–16.

Purdue University Online Writing Lab. "Conducting Online Research." PowerPoint slides. Created July 29, 2009. Accessed December 26, 2010. Available at http://owl.english.purdue.edu/media/ppt/20090729115320_558.ppt

Stewart, Charles J., and William B. Cash, Jr. *Interviewing: Principles and Practices*. 11th ed. New York: McGraw-Hill, 2006.

Tesh, Sylvia Noble. *Uncertain Hazards: Environmental Activists and Scientific Proof*. Ithaca: Cornell UP, 2000.

Walter, Otis M., and Robert L. Scott. *Thinking and Speaking: A Guide to Intelligent Oral Communication*. 5th ed. New York: Macmillan, 1984.

Wikipedia: Researching with Wikipedia." Accessed March 4, 2011. Available at http://en.wikipedia.org/wiki/Wikipedia:Researching_with_Wikipedia

Chapter 7

Brock, Bernard L., Mark E. Huglen, James F. Klumpp, and Sharon Howell. *Making Sense of Politicial Ideology: The Power of Language in Democracy*. Lanham, MD: Rowman & Littlefield, 2005.

Burke, Kenneth. *The Philosophy of Literary Form*. Berkeley: U of California P, 1941.

Bush, George W. "State of the Union Speech." Washington, DC. 21 Jan. 2006. Available at http://www.americanrhetoric.com/speeches/stateoftheunion2006.htm

Clinton, Bill. "State of the Union Speech." Washington, DC. 25 Jan. 1994. Available at http://www .presidency.ucsb.edu/ws/index.php?pid=50409

Cloud, Dana L. "Hegemony or Concordance? The Rhetoric of Tokenism in Oprah Winfrey's Rags-to-Riches Biography." *Critical Studies in Mass Communication* 13 (June 1996): 115-37.

Dudley, Meela. "Political Activism and Free Expression Take Over the Fence." *The Tartan*. 2 Dec. 2009. Available at http://www.thetartan.org/2009/9/28/pillbox/art_fence

Kennedy, John F. "Inaugural Address." Washington, DC, 20 Jan. 1961. Available at http://www .americanrhetoric.com/speeches/jfkinaugural .htm

Makau, Josina M., and Debian L. Marty. *Cooperative Argumentation*. Waveland Press, 2001.

McGee, Michael Calvin. "The 'Ideograph': A Link between Rhetoric and Ideology." *Quarterly Journal of Speech* 66 (1980): 1–16.

Reich, Robert. *Tales of a New America: The Anxious Liberal's Guide to the Future*. New York: Vintage Books, 1988.

Solis, Hilda. "JFK Profile in Courage Award Acceptance Speech." Boston. 22 May 2000. Available at http://www.jfklibrary.org/Education+and+Public+Programs/Profile+in+Courage+Award/Award+Recipients/Hilda+Solis/Acceptance+Speech+by+Hilda+Solis.htm

Steven Barclay Agency. "Terry Tempest Williams." Accessed December 22, 2010. Available at http://www.barclayagency.com/williams.html

"V for Vendetta." Internet Movie Database Website. Accessed December 20, 2010. Available at http://www.imdb.com/title/tt0434409/quotes

Williams, Terry Tempest. "Commencement: The Open Space of Democracy." *Orion Magazine* March/April 2004. Available at http://www.orionmagazine.org/index.php/articles/article/136/

Chapter 8

Ahlfeldt, Stephanie L. "Serving Our Communities with Public Speaking." *Communication Teacher* 23.4 (2009): 158–61.

Aristotle. *On Rhetoric.* Trans. George A. Kennedy. New York: Oxford UP, 1991.

Gring, Mark. "Epistemic and Pedagogical Assumptions for Informative and Persuasive Speaking: Disinterring the Dichotomy." *Argumentation and Advocacy* 43 (2006): 41–50.

Herrick, James A. *The History and Theory of Rhetoric.* 3rd ed. Boston: Allyn & Bacon, 2005: 98–101.

Johnson, John R., and Nancy Szczupakiewicz. "The Public Speaking Course: Is It Preparing Students with Work Related Public Speaking Skills?" *Communication Education* 36 (1987): 131–36.

Rowan, Katherine. "A New Pedagogy for Explanatory Speaking: Why Arrangement Should Not Substitute for Invention." *Communication Education* 44 (1995): 236–50.

Rowley, Coleen. "Testimony to the Senate Judiciary Committee." Oversight Hearing on Counterterrorism. June 6, 2002. Available at http://judiciary.senate.gov/hearings/testimony.cfm?id=279&wit_id=628

Chapter 9

American Lung Association. "Cold and Flu Guidelines: Myths and Facts." Accessed January 10, 2008. Available at http://www.lungusa.org/site/pp.asp?c=dvLUK9O0E&b=35869

Break Away. "Misty Romero Active Citizen of the Year Award." Accessed January 10, 2008. Available at www.alternativebreaks.org/active_citizen.pdf

Common Cause. "The Fallout from the Telecommunications Act of 1996: Unintended Consequences and Lessons Learned." 9 May 2005. Accessed January 10, 2008. Available at: www.commoncause.org

ConsumerAffairs.com. "Credit Cards Ensnare, Victimize Working Families, Report Finds." 12 October 2005.

Accessed January 17, 2008. Available at http://www.consumeraffairs.com/news04/2005/plastic_safety_net.html

Dworkin, Ronald D. "The Cultural Revolution in Health Care." *Public Interest* (Spring 2000): 35–50.

Gee, Constance Bumgarner. "Valuing the Arts on Their Own Terms? (Ceci n'est pas une pipe)." *Arts Education Policy Review* 108.3 (2007): 3–12.

Manning, Robert D., and Ray Kirshak. "Credit Cards on Campus: Academic Inquiry, Objective Empiricism, or Advocacy Research." *NASFAA Journal of Student Financial Aid* 35.1 (2005): 40.

Murphy, Jamie, Charles Hofacker, and Richard Mizerski. "Primacy and Recency Effects on Clicking Behavior." *Journal of Computer-Mediated Communication* 11.2. (2006), article 7. Available at http://jcmc.indiana.edu/vol11/issue2/murphy.html

National Education Association. "NCLB Timeline." Accessed January 15, 2008. Available at http://www.nea.org/neatoday/0604/nclbtimeline.html

Oregon Department of Human Services. "Gambling and College Students: Literature Review." Accessed January 15, 2008. Available at www.oregon.gov/DHS/addiction/gambling/collegestudents-gambling.pdf

Prevention Research Center. "Facts and Myths about College Drinking: A Serious Problem with Serious Solutions." Berkeley: Pacific Institute for Research and Evaluation. Accessed January 10, 2008. Available at http://resources.prev.org/documents/FactsMyths-CollegeDrinking.pdf

Riedl, Brian M. "Halving Student Loan Interest Rates Is Unaffordable and Ineffective." Washington: Heritage Foundation. 16 January 2007. Accessed January 17, 2008. Available at http://www.heritage.org/Research/Education/wm1308.cfm

Rowan, Katherine. "A New Pedagogy for Explanatory Speaking: Why Arrangement Should Not Substitute for Invention." *Communication Education* 44 (1995): 236–50.

Rubinstein, Alvin Z. "The Case against Puerto Rican Statehood." *Orbis* 45.3 (2001): 415–31.

Sadler, Roger L. *Electronic Media Law.* Thousand Oaks: Sage, 2005.

U.S. Department of Energy. "Annual Energy Review 2007." Report No. DOE/EIA-0384, Washington, GPO, 2007.

U.S. Department of Health and Human Services. "Is It a Cold or the Flu?" Bethesda: National Institute of Allergy and Infectious Diseases, 2008. Accessed April 10, 2011. Available at http://www.niaid.nih.gov/topics/Flu/Documents/sick.pdf

U.S. General Accounting Office. "Consumer Finance: College Students and Credit Cards." GAO-01-773. Washington, GPO, 2001.

Williams, Mike. "Puerto Rico Resumes Debate on Statehood." *Austin American-Statesman* 25 December 2007, A21.

Chapter 10

Beins, Agatha. "Sisterly Solidarity: Politics and Rhetoric of the Direct Address in US Feminism in the 1970s." *Women: A Cultural Review*, 21.3 (2010): 292–308.

Berry, Wendell. *What Are People For?* New York: North Point Press, 1990.

Callahan, Sean. "Delivering International Food Aid and Providing Foreign Agricultural Development Assistance." Testimony before the House Agriculture Subcommittee on Specialty Crops, Rural Development, and Foreign Agriculture. 16 July 2008. Available at http://crs.org/newsroom/testimony/entry.cfm?id=1499

Gonzalez, Maria R. "Edward James Olmos Stands and Delivers at Texas State." *Currents Online News* (October 10, 2006). Available at http://talbot.mrp.txstate.edu/currents/fullstory.jsp?sid=887

Johnson, Greg. "Emmert: Well-being of student athletes the ultimate priority." NCAA.org (July 12, 2010). Accessed May 12, 2011. Available at http://bit.ly/mgjpG8.

Keppler Speakers. "A Real People Profile: Edward James Olmos." Available at http://www.kepplerspeakers.com/speakers/speakers.asp?Edward+James+Olmos

McGee, Jennifer J. "A Pilgrim's Progress: Metaphor in the Rhetoric of Mary Fisher, AIDS Activist." *Women's Studies in Communication*, 26.2 (2003): 191–213.

Rieke, Richard D., Malcolm O. Sillars, and Tarla Rai Peterson. *Argumentation and Critical Decision Making*. 7th ed. Boston: Allyn & Bacon, 2009.

Sen, Amartya. "Democracy as a Universal Value." *Journal of Democracy* 10 (1999): 3–17.

Sheeran, Josette. "The Silent Tsunami: The Globalization of the Hunger Challenge." Speech delivered to the Peter G. Peterson Institute for International Economics. Washington, DC. 6 May 2008. Available at http://documents.wfp.org/stellent/groups/public/documents/newsroom/wfp179183.pdf

Wechsler, Deborah. "Growing with Care, Marketing to Growth." Southern Sustainable Agriculture Working Group, 2004. Available at http://www.ssawg.org/fulks1.html

Winne, Mark. "Leading the Charge, Leading the Change." Speech delivered to the Northwest Harvest Food Bank Annual Meeting. Seattle. 15 May 2008. Available at http://www.markwinne.com/food-bank-speech-may-15-2008-seattle-wa/

Chapter 11

Jaschik, Scott. "Male Impact." *Inside Higher Ed* (July 19, 2005) Available at http://www.insidehighered.com/news/2006/07/19/men

Millen, Jonathan H. "A Model for Delivery Outlines: Empowering Student Speakers." *Communication Teacher* (Winter 2001): 4–6.

Partnership for a Drug-Free America. "Meth Frequently Asked Questions." *Partnership for a Drug-Free America.* Available at http://www.drugfree.org/Portal/DrugIssue/MethResources/meth_affects_community.html

Pew Forum on Religion & Public Life. "U.S. Religious Landscape Survey: Summary of Key Findings." *Pew Forum on Religion & Public Life* (2007). Available at religions.pewforum.org/pdf/report2religious-landscape-study-key-findings.pdf

Powers, Elia. "Anger over Coeducation Plan." *Inside Higher Ed* (August 11, 2006). Available at http://www.insidehighered.com/news/2006/08/11/coed

Chapter 12

Cantu, Martha. "Written Congressional Testimony." U.S. House of Representatives Committee on Education and Labor. 22 March 2007. Available at http://edlabor.house.gov/testimony/032207MarthaCantutestimony.pdf

Cassidy, Sukhinder S. "Information Age: Can the Web Be Free?" India Today Conclave. New Delhi. 13 March 2007. Available at http://conclave.digitaltoday.in/preview.php?name=speechtrans&id=67

Center for Information and Research on Civic Learning and Engagement. "Television Consumption and Civic Engagement among 15 to 25 Year Olds." Available at http://www.civicyouth.org/featured-television-consumption-and-civic-engagement-among-15-to-25-year-olds/?cat_id=9

Center for Information and Research on Civic Learning and Engagement. "Youth Voting." Available at http://www.civicyouth.org/quick-facts/youth-voting/

Cyphert, Dale. "Presentation Technology in the Age of Electronic Eloquence: From Visual Aid to Visual Rhetoric." *Communication Education* 56.2 (2007): 168–92.

Edwards, Janis L., and Carol K. Winkler. "Representative Form and the Visual Ideograph: The Iwo Jima Image in Editorial Cartoons." *Quarterly Journal of Speech* 83 (1997): 289–310.

Hariman, Robert, and John Louis Lucaites. *No Caption Needed: Iconic Photographs, Public Culture and Liberal Democracy*. Chicago: University of Chicago Press, 2007.

Kopp, Wendy. "Commencement Address 2008." Georgetown University. Washington. 17 May 2008. Available at http://college.georgetown.edu/persona/current/commenemcentarchives/51682.html

Mayer, R. E. *Multimedia Learning*. 2nd ed. New York: Cambridge University Press, 2009.

Moyers, Bill. "Prepared Remarks." National Media Reform Conference. 7 June 2008. Available at www.pbs.org/moyers/journal/06062008/Moyers_Media_Reform.pdf

Nunn, Sam. "The Mountaintop." *Vital Speeches of the Day* (April 2008): 146–49.

Obama, Barack. "Renewing American Competitiveness." Flint. 16 June 2008. Available at http://www.barackobama.com/2008/06/16/remarks_of_senator_barack_obam_79.php

Pierce, Charles P. "Just Words." *Boston Globe* 11 January 2009. Available at http://www.boston.com/bostonglobe/magazine/articles/2009/01/11/just_words/?page=full

Saslow, Eli. "Helping to Write History." *Washington Post* 18 December 2008. Available at http://www.washingtonpost.com/wp-dyn/content/article/2008/12/17/AR2008121703903_2.html?sid=ST2008121704047&s_pos=

Twigg, Reginald. "The Performative Dimension of Surveillance: Jacob Riis' *How the Other Half Lives.*" *Text and Performance Quarterly* (1992): 305–28.

Will, George. "Building a Wall against Talent." *Washington Post* 26 June 2008. Accessed August 1, 2008. Available at http://www.washingtonpost.com/wpdyn/content/article/2008/06/25/AR2008062501945.html

Wolffe, Richard. "In His Candidate's Voice." *Newsweek* 6 January 2008. Accessed May 12, 2011. Available at http://www.newsweek.com/2008/01/05/in-his-candidate-s-voice.html.

Chapter 13

Aristotle. *On Rhetoric.* Trans. George A. Kennedy. New York: Oxford UP, 1991.

DeLuca, Kevin Michael, and Jennifer Peeples, "From Public Sphere to Public Screen: Democracy, Activism, and the 'Violence' of Seattle." *Critical Studies in Mass Communication* 19.2 (2002): 125–51.

"Eboo Patel." Ashoka.org. Available at http://www.ashoka.org/node/3151

Hariman, Robert. "In Defense of Jon Stewart." *Critical Studies in Media Communication* 24.3 (2007): 273–77.

Hart, Roderick P., and E. Johanna Hartelius. "The Political Sins of Jon Stewart." *Critical Studies in Media Communication* 24.3 (2007): 263–72.

Inch, Edward S., and Barbara Warnick. *Critical Thinking and Communication: The Use of Reason in Argument.* Boston: Allyn & Bacon, 2010.

Jacobson, Michael F., and Masur, Laurie Ann. 1995 *Marketing Madness: A Survival Guide for a Consumer Society.* Boulder: Westview, 1995.

Patel, Eboo. "Notes for a New American Song." Nobel Peace Forum, St. Olaf College, Northfield, MN. 21 Feb. 2004. Available at http://www.stolaf.edu/news/speeches/patel.html

Roberts, Donald F. "Media and Youth: Access, Exposure, and Privatization." *Journal of Adolescent Health* 27S.2 (2000): 8–14.

Chapter 14

Beaton, Robin. "Testimony to the House Energy and Commerce Committee." 16 June 2009. Available at http://energycommerce.house.gov/press_111/20090616/testimony_beaton.pdf

Brummett, Barry. *Reading Rhetorical Theory.* Fort Worth: Harcourt, 2000.

Damer, T. Edward. *Attacking Faulty Reasoning.* Belmont: Wadsworth, 2009.

Farrell, Thomas. *Norms of Rhetorical Culture.* New Haven: Yale UP, 1993.

Holan, Angie Drobnic. "Politifact's Lie of the Year: 'Death Panels.'" Politifact website. Available at http://www.politifact.com/truth-o-meter/article/2009/dec/18/politifact-lie-year-death-panels

Katula, Richard. "Quintilian on the Art of Emotional Appeal." *Rhetoric Review* 22.1 (2003): 5–15.

Koziak, Barbara. *Retrieving Political Emotion: Thumos, Aristotle, and Gender.* University Park: Penn State UP, 2000.

McCroskey, James, and Jason J. Teven. "Goodwill: A Reexamination of the Construct and Its Measurement." *Communication Monographs* 66 (1999): 90–103.

Neustadt, Richard, and Ernest May. *Thinking in Time: The Uses of History for Decision-Makers.* New York: Free Press, 1986.

Obama, Barack. "A More Perfect Union." Speech in Philadelphia. 18 March 2008. Available at http://my.barackobama.com/page/content/hisownwords

Toulmin, Stephen. *The Uses of Argument.* Cambridge: Cambridge UP, 1958/2003.

Westen, Drew. *The Political Brain: The Role of Emotion in Deciding the Fate of the Nation.* New York: Public Affairs, 2007.

Chapter 15

Agnew, Lois. "'The Day Belongs to the Students': Expanding Epideictic's Civic Function." *Rhetoric Review* 27.2 (2008): 147–64.

Baker, Russell. "10 Ways to Avoid Mucking Up the World Any Worse Than It Already Is." Commencement address, Connecticut College. 27 May 1995. Available at http://www.humanity.org/printview.php?page=baker_at_connecticut&sectionName=voices

Beasley, Vanessa B. *You, the People: American National Identity in Presidential Rhetoric.* College Station: Texas A&M University Press, 2004.

Clinton, William J. "Inaugural Address." January 20, 1993. Available at: http://www.gpoaccess.gov/pubpapers

Condit, Celeste Michelle. "The Functions of Epideictic: The Boston Massacre Orations as Exemplar." *Communication Quarterly* 33.4 (1984): 284–99.

"David Foster Wallace on Life and Work." *Wall Street Journal* 19 September 2008. Available at http://online.wsj.com/article/SB122178211966454607.html

Groff, Anna. "1,145 Students in Five MC USA Schools in Commencement Exercises by May 4." *The Mennonite*. Available at http://www.themennonite.org/issues/11-10/articles/1145_students_in_five_MC_USA_schools_in_commencement_exercises_by_May_4

Hawken, Paul. "Commencement Address." University of Portland, May 3, 2009. Accessed June 30, 2011. Available at: http://www.up.edu/commencement/default.aspx?cid=9456

Jasinski, James. *Sourcebook on Rhetoric: Key Concepts in Contemporary Rhetorical Studies*. Thousand Oaks: Sage, 2001.

Johnson, Lyndon Baines. "Let Us Continue." Address before a Joint Session of U.S. Congress. 27 November 1963. Available at http://www.presidentialrhetoric.com/historicspeeches/johnson_lyndon/letuscontinue.html

Jones, Rev. Dr. Kirk Byron. "Dare to Rest." Baccalaureate address, University of Pennsylvania. 17 May 2009. Available at http://www.upenn.edu/almanac/volumes/v55/n34/bacc-jones.html

McCormick, Blaine. "Benjamin Franklin and the Real 'National Treasure.'" Philadelphia. 17 April 2009. *Vital Speeches of the Day*, August 2009: 362–67.

Poulakos, John, and Takis Poulakos. *Classical Rhetorical Theory*. Boston: Houghton Mifflin, 1999.

Poulakos, Takis. "Isocrates's Use of Narrative in the Evagoras: Epideictic Rhetoric and Moral Action." *Quarterly Journal of Speech* 73.3 (1987): 317–28.

Vivian, Bradford. "Neoliberal Epideictic: Rhetorical Form and Commemorative Politics on September 11, 2002." *Quarterly Journal of Speech* 92.1 (2006): 1–26.

Washington, Booker T. "Address at Opening of Atlanta Exposition," September 18, 1895. Accessed August 4, 2011. Available at http://myloc.gov/Exhibitions/naacp/prelude/ExhibitObjects/BookerTWashingtonSpeech.aspx.

Wiesel, Elie. "Nobel Prize Speech." Oslo. 10 December 1986. Available at http://www.eliewieselfoundation.org/nobelprizespeech.aspx

Appendix

Ball, Jeffrey. "Summit Is Seen as US Versus China." *Wall Street Journal* 14 Dec. 2009. Available at http://online.wsj.com/article/SB126074144005789473.html?mod=loomia&loomia_si=t0:a16:g12:r2:c0.430593:b29345762

Bennett, W. Lance. *News: The Politics of Illusion*. 6th ed. New York: Longman, 2005.

Boxer, Barbara. "House Has Opportunity to Fix Cruel Budget, Protect Families." *San Jose Mercury News* 8 Jan. 2006. Available at http://www.barbaraboxer.com/news/coverage?id=0040

Boykoff, Maxwell T., and Jules M. Boykoff. "Balance as Bias: Global Warming and the U.S. Prestige Press." *Global Environmental Change* 15.2 (2004): 125–36.

Brock, Bernard L., Mark E. Huglen, James F. Klumpp, and Sharon Howell. *Making Sense of Political Ideology: The Power of Language in Democracy*. Lanham: Rowman & Littlefield, 2005.

Chomsky, Noam. "Confronting the Empire." III World Social Forum. 2 Feb. 2003. Available at http://www.chomsky.info/talks/20030201.htm

Dorrity, Ward. "A Fourth of July Tea Party Speech 2009." Available at http://www.starlancs.com/fourth_of_july_tea_party_speech.htm

"Excerpts: 'Developed Countries Have Not Delivered." Speech by Chinese Diplomat He Yafei. *Wall Street Journal* 13 Dec. 2009. Available at http://online.wsj.com/article/SB126073495028689701.html?mod=article-outset-box

Freedom First PAC. "Mission." Available at http://www.timpawlenty.com/node/2

Lakoff, George. *Thinking Points: Communicating Our American Values and Vision*. New York: Farrar, Straus, and Giroux, 2006.

Luntz, Frank. *Words That Work: It's Not What You Say, It's What People Hear*. New York: Hyperion Books, 2007.

U.S. House of Representatives. "The Fiscal Consequences of the Health Care Law." Hearing before the Committee on the Budget, January 26, 2011. Available at http://www.gpo.gov

Credits

Index

Note: Italicized page locators indicate a figure; tables are noted with *t*.